OXFORD STUDIES IN
SOCIAL AND LEGAL HISTORY

OXFORD STUDIES
IN SOCIAL AND LEGAL
HISTORY

EDITED BY

PAUL VINOGRADOFF

M.A., D.C.L., LL.D., Dr. Hist., F.B.A.

CORPUS PROFESSOR OF JURISPRUDENCE IN THE UNIVERSITY OF OXFORD
HONORARY PROFESSOR OF HISTORY IN THE UNIVERSITY OF MOSCOW

VOL. I

ENGLISH MONASTERIES ON THE EVE OF THE
DISSOLUTION

By ALEXANDER SAVINE
PROFESSOR OF HISTORY IN THE UNIVERSITY OF MOSCOW

PATRONAGE IN THE LATER EMPIRE

By F. DE ZULUETA
FELLOW OF NEW COLLEGE, OXFORD

OCTAGON BOOKS

A DIVISION OF FARRAR, STRAUS AND GIROUX

New York   1974

Originally published in 1909 by the Clarendon Press

Reprinted 1974
by special arrangement with Oxford University Press, Inc.

OCTAGON BOOKS
A DIVISION OF FARRAR, STRAUS & GIROUX, INC.
19 Union Square West
New York, N. Y. 10003

Library of Congress Cataloging in Publication Data

Savin, Aleksandr Nikolaevich, 1873-1923.
 English monasteries on the eve of the dissolution.

 Reprint of the 1909 editions published by Clarendon Press, Oxford, which were issued as v. 1, no. 1-2, of Oxford studies in social and legal history; v. 1., no. 1: a translation of Angliiskaia sekuliarizatsiia; original title of v. 1, no. 2: De patrociniis vicorum.

 Includes bibliographical references.
 1. Land tenure—England—History. 2. Monasteries—England. 3. Codex Theodosianus. 4. Corpus juris civilis. Codex. 5. Patron and client. 6. Colonate. I. Zulueta, Francis de, 1878-1958. De patrociniis vicorum. 1974. II. Title. III. Title: Patronage in the later empire. IV. Series: Oxford studies in social and legal history, v. 1, no. 1-2.

HD604.S313 1974   333.3'22   73-22283
ISBN 0-374-96158-1

Printed in USA by
Thomson-Shore, Inc.
Dexter, Michigan

PREFACE

THE nineteenth century has been called the age of historical study, and the twentieth bids fair to follow its predecessor in this respect. At no previous epoch have men felt more keenly that 'the roots of the present lie deep in the past', and England has had its share in the general movement of European thought in this direction. But, as far as the organization of historical research is concerned, we have still a good deal to learn and to do in England. It is not sufficient that there should every now and then arise exceptionally gifted and equipped leaders, like Grote, Stubbs, Maitland; it is not enough that there should be a widespread interest in history as a branch of literature. We ought to try to co-ordinate research and train researchers; thorough and systematic investigation ought not to be left to chance and to the efforts of self-taught pioneers; the scientific side of history should be brought up to the level of its literary side.

How much remains to be done in this respect may be gathered from the fact that there are at present few opportunities for investigators, especially for beginners in research, to publish monographs on their particular subjects. Editions of sources, and commentaries or introductions to them, may find their way to the publications of the Selden, the Royal

Historical or some other learned society; short articles and notes may be accepted by the *English Historical* or the *Law Quarterly Review*. But it is difficult to find a publisher for a special investigation of some length, and even more difficult to make such a monograph fit into a series with other monographs of the same kind. And yet it is clear that without such special investigations general constructive work may result in the raising of houses of cards. Nor can it be doubted that the normal conclusion of research teaching in the Universities should be the production of monographs, the methods and results of which could be tested by learned experts outside the narrow circle of the class-room or of a particular University town.

In Germany and in France the necessity and value of such publications have been realized long ago. The schools of Schmoller and Gierke, of Knapp and Stutz, of the École des hautes études and of the École des Chartes, make a point of acquainting the world at large with the progress of their work. Without attempting to rival such laboratories of historical research in the quantity and excellence of their output, I propose, with the powerful co-operation of the Clarendon Press, to publish a series of 'Studies in Social and Legal History' in which will be collected monographs on these subjects written by my pupils, or by researchers who have done me the honour of consulting me in the course of their investigations. As a rule, a volume of some 300–400 pages will be issued once a year, and it will contain one or two monographs on the social or legal history of England or other countries. The present first volume is devoted to two monographs of this kind, a study of Professor A. Savine, of the

University of Moscow, on the English Monasteries on the eve of the Dissolution, and an essay of F. de Zulueta, Fellow and Law Lecturer of New College, Oxford, on the Patronage of Villages in the later Empire. The work of Professor Savine is connected with my teaching in former years in the University of Moscow, and was originally published as part of a Russian thesis. But it would have been a pity if the more important results of this work, carried out by a scholar already favourably known in the English-speaking world by his studies on the end of bondage and the origins of copyhold tenure, had remained inaccessible to English readers. Professor Savine has made a painstaking and critical investigation of the principal source of our knowledge of property held by the Church before the Dissolution—the so-called Valor Ecclesiasticus. No similar systematic treatment based on a careful comparison with the parallel sources of information extant at the Record Office has been attempted hitherto. The author has not been deterred by any dryness or complexity of detail, and his work will surely not be disregarded by students of the social history of England in the sixteenth century.

The second contribution ranges in an entirely different field; it treats of the formation of private patronage in the course of the fourth and the fifth centuries on Roman soil. The phenomena here described have often been noticed as important institutional roots of feudalism, but the new data afforded by the publication of Egyptian papyri have not been utilized hitherto for the settlement of the problem in question. Mr. de Zulueta started work on the subject in a Seminar on the Codex Theodosianus conducted by me in 1907–8 and has been busy since in developing and strengthening his argument.

I should like, in conclusion, to express the hope that these two monographs may augur well for the progress of the 'Oxford Studies in Social and Legal History'.

P. VINOGRADOFF.

I

ENGLISH MONASTERIES ON THE EVE OF THE DISSOLUTION

BY

A. SAVINE

PROFESSOR OF HISTORY IN THE UNIVERSITY OF MOSCOW

BOOK I

VALOR ECCLESIASTICUS

CHAPTER I

HISTORY OF THE SURVEY

ON the very threshold of the Dissolution we find long returns of the Royal Commissioners who in 1535 were describing the revenues of the English Church. No one has ever made a careful study of this Survey, neither general historians of the Tudor age, nor historians of the English Church, nor authors of the very few monographs on the Dissolution. But as a proper understanding of the Dissolution is impossible without a study of the Valor, I shall attempt to struggle through this labyrinth, however great may be the danger of losing the right way in the wearisome and unattractive maze of names and figures.

In 1532 Convocation had petitioned the King for the repeal of the Annates, representing that these Annates were ruining both the laity and the episcopal sees, and suggesting that the temporalities of the bishoprics ought in any case to be free from taxation. An Act (23 H. VIII, c. 20) was accordingly passed repealing the Annates; and under this Act, which did not distinguish between the temporal and spiritual revenues, the Pope was recognized as entitled to levy a charge of not more than five per cent. on the net income of a see. At the same time Parliament left it open to the King to enter into negotiations with the Pope concerning the Annates, and to give his Royal assent to the Act by means of Letters Patent before the assembling of the next Parliament. Henry was by no means anxious to confirm the measure whilst there remained any hope of agreement with Rome concerning other questions ; and it was not until he had completely broken with the Pope that the Royal assent was given by Letters Patent (July 9, 25 H. VIII). The Annates, however, disappeared in England for a short time only. In the following year (26 H. VIII) it was enacted that newly ordained clergy should pay to the Crown the Firstfruits of 'all dignities, benefices & promocyons spirituall ': and further, that since January 1, 1535, all who held spiritual benefices should give annually the tenth part of their net incomes to the Crown (26 H. VIII, c. 3). In this way the King not only got possession of the Papal Annates, but imposed them upon all spiritual benefices, and added thereto as a fixed tax the Tenth of all the net income of the English Church. The financial emancipation from Rome became for the English Church a worse enthralment to the State.

Act concerning Firstfruits and Tenths.
The Act concerning Firstfruits and Tenths gave rise to many new problems for the Exchequer, though to some extent the method of solution was indicated in the Act itself. Whenever an ecclesiastical vacancy occurred, the new incumbent was not, under pain of a fine, to enjoy the revenues of his new benefice until he had paid or promised to pay to the Crown the Firstfruits thereof; and the Chancellor or the Master of the Rolls was on each vacancy to issue a commission for the purpose of valuing the benefice and making arrangements with the new incumbent concerning the payment of Firstfruits. The Statute also gives detailed instructions as to raising the revenue and accounting for it. The regulations respecting Tenths are even more elaborate. The Chancellor is empowered to send Commissioners in the name of the King and under the Great Seal, into every diocese in order to ascertain the true annual value of each ecclesiastical benefice ; and three Commissioners were to form a quorum. They were required to specify accurately the amount of expenditure to be deducted from the gross income (annual and regular rents, synodals and proxies, regular alms distributed under wills, the fees of stewards, bailiffs, auditors and receivers); and by the 25th section they were permitted to deduct also

from the gross income of monasteries and prelates the regular fees paid to the Chancellor, Master of the Rolls, judges, sheriffs or other officials for the execution of justice in their respective dioceses or jurisdictions. When the Commissioners' returns were completed the Royal Tenth was to be estimated in accordance therewith. Each Archbishop and Bishop was to collect the Tenths in his own diocese and be responsible for the whole quota ; he was, however, entitled to an allowance therefrom if at the proper time he pointed out persons who were in arrears. Each incumbent was to pay his yearly dues by Christmas ; while the Bishops had to pay the whole dues of their respective dioceses by the 1st of April in the following year.

In compliance with the provisions of the Statute, the Chancellor prepared a commission for each shire. All these commissions were dated January 30, 1535. At the summons of the Commissioners, clerks, registrars, receivers, auditors of prelates and clergymen were bound to appear before them and give all necessary information, and the Commissioners were to send in their returns to the Exchequer not later than *in octabis Trinitatis*, 1535.[1]

A detailed instruction was attached to all the commissions,[2] and on the whole seems to have been followed closely. The Commissioners were sent to every diocese, shire, and populous place in England and Wales. First of all, the Commissioners of each diocese in its entirety, following the information given by the Church authorities, are to make a list of all incumbents and ecclesiastical benefices and to classify the latter according to their rural deaneries. Then, the Commissioners are divided into sub-commissions, and several rural deaneries assigned to each sub-commission ; three members making a quorum in a sub-commission. They were to examine under oath all incumbents, and their receivers and auditors ; and they were also bound to inspect the registers, books of account,

Instruction to Commissioners.

---

[1] The text of the Devonshire Commission is printed in Valor Ecclesiasticus, ii. 289 ; the list of all the Commissioners, based on the Patent Rolls, is to be found in Gairdner, viii. 149, nn. 35–82.
[2] A specimen of it is printed in the V. E. before the text of the first volume.

Easter books and other documents which they might think useful, without concealing anything.

Then follow special instructions as to describing the revenues of the separate groups into which the Church benefices were divided :—episcopal sees, cathedrals, archdeaconries, and rural deaneries, colleges, hospitals, monasteries, rectories, vicarages and chapels. I propose, however, to deal only with the instructions which refer to monasteries. The Commissioners are to inquire into and record the names of all the abbeys, priories, monasteries and other religious houses ; the names of all manors, farms, tenements, rents and other temporal revenues ; the names of rectories, vicarages, tithes, oblations and other spiritual revenues ; the name of the shire and village where the said revenues are raised ; and finally the exact annual amount of every separate source of revenue. The Commissioners must deduct from the gross income the regular pensions, rents, alms, and fees which are paid to the receivers, bailiffs, auditors and stewards ; but no other persons are to be taken into consideration by the Commissioners.[1] The Commissioners are to give the names of the officials to whom the regular fees are paid, the names of persons and places to whom the perpetual rents and pensions are paid, and the name of donors for the benefit of whose souls the alms are given. The Commissioners are also to deduct the synodals and proxies but not to make any allowance for other expenses. In the survey the abbot's or prior's name must be given ; and if there should be any offices in the monastery held in perpetuity they must also be specified, together with their revenue.

When all the local returns were completed, all the Sub-commissioners of the diocese were to meet together and com-

---

[1] Here the Instruction clearly went against the Act of 26 H. VIII, c. 3, s. 25, which allowed as deductions from the gross income of prelates and monasteries the annual perpetual fees of the Chancellor, Master of the Rolls, judges and sheriffs. And, as usually happens in political systems tending towards despotism, the subordinate officials ignored the law, which neither rewards nor reproves, and followed the orders of their particular chief. Even when the payments to lawyers were entered in the Survey they were crossed out at the revision (e. g. Winchcombe, Glouc., ii. 459).

pile one general book for that diocese ('a fayer book after the audytours fashyon'). The Instruction also prescribes the plan for the general book: the episcopal see, cathedral, or monastery, with its offices, archdeaconries, rural deaneries and the rest; if a benefice does not belong to any rural deanery it must be entered separately, and its name and position given. The Commissioners were to hand the general book to the Exchequer with their seals *in octabis Trinitatis*, adding to it the local returns of the sub-commissions. The returns made by these Commissioners are known as the 'Valor Ecclesiasticus'.

With all due respect to previous writers, I cannot think that the celebrated Survey has met with the attention it deserves. Its measure of trustworthiness has never been ascertained; while for its external history one must still apply to Dr. Gairdner's Calendar for 1535 and 1536.[1] To the best of my ability I have tried to fill the gap, though I am very far from supposing that I have said the last word on this subject.

The Government had no intention of confining itself to the appointment of Commissioners and the drawing up of instructions for them. The men who in 1535 controlled the machinery of State attached great importance to the work of the Commissioners and therefore wished to direct that work even in matters of detail. The Commissioners of 1535 felt the heavy hand of the Government throughout the whole of their work; they were in constant correspondence with it; soliciting rewards for their real or feigned zeal; apologizing for negligence; relating the difficulties which they encountered; and asking for guidance in their perplexities. *Letters of the Commissioners*

Only one side of this correspondence has come down to us, however; the letters of the Commissioners to the central Government and to Cromwell, and probably only a small part even of these. But in what has been preserved there

---

[1] The chief authorities are: Speed's Hist. (1611), 778; Burnet's Ref. (Pocock), i. 311, 430; Collier's Eccl. Hist. (1714), ii. 95; Nasmith's Preface to Tanner's Notitia, iv; Fuller's Church Hist. (1655), v. 226–9; Hunter's Preface to V. E., Record Commission; Home and Foreign Review, 1864, Jan. 166–7; Blunt's Ref. i. 363; Dixon's Hist. i. 247–50.

is much instructive information concerning the bureaucratic routine of the time and the composition of the Returns of 1535.[1]

Information as to the doings of the Commissioners is sometimes given incidentally, in letters written about other matters. Thus, in April, 1535, it was reported to Cromwell that a certain monk in a 'friendly' examination refused to recognize the supremacy of the King in Church affairs. The denunciation was written on April 18 by three Commissioners whose special duty it was to survey the Church estates and revenues in Nottinghamshire.

The Bishop of Hereford was required as early as February to give information concerning the number and the revenues of the Church benefices vacated since January 1, 1535, in order that the Firstfruits might be collected from them. In a letter to Cromwell on April 16, the Bishop enumerates the vacant benefices but says that he cannot, at that moment, give their exact income; he promises, however, to send the information that was lacking, as soon as the Commissioners, who were then compiling their account of the Church property in his diocese, shall have finished their work ; and he adds that he and the other Commissioners had received the commission and instructions for the survey only a short time ago.[2]

The Norwich Commissioners. Information regarding the initial doings of the Commissioners in the diocese of Norwich is given in minute detail. An importunate flatterer, Reynold Lytylprow, writes many letters to Cromwell. Before the Commissioners had begun their work he begs to be included in the commission and asks that detailed instructions should be sent to him. Lytylprow was put on the commission, and on the Friday before Palm Sunday we find him reporting to Cromwell, among other

---

[1] This correspondence belongs to the State Papers and is therefore summarized in Dr. Gairdner's Calendar (viii, ix, x). The summary is well executed, but in the original documents there are often to be found characteristic and sometimes important details. Four letters (viii. 654, 754, 1082, ix. 1070, n. 3) are printed in extenso by Strype, but with several serious errors. (Strype, Eccl. Mem. I, i. 327–31, I, ii. 219–20.)

[2] Gairdner, viii. 552.

things, that the Commissioners of Norwich had met with some difficulties in their work, and that they were sending to him or Mr. Lumnour for instructions in certain matters.

Another Commissioner, Tho. Godsalve, writes to Cromwell from Norwich 'in haste' on March 20 concerning the journey of this same Mr. Lumnour; among other things, Lumnour will be able to tell Cromwell what the Commissioners of Firstfruits and Tenths have done up to the present time. A third Commissioner, Ric. Southwell, subsequently an eminent official in the Augmentations Court, also writes to Cromwell on March 21, and from this letter we learn that Cromwell had expressed a desire to have continuous and detailed information respecting the progress of the Commissioners' doings, Southwell's letter being written in response.

On Thursday, March 4, the second day of the Assizes at Thetford, a letter came from Lumnour to Sir Th. Lestrange and Jenney, Serjeant-at-Law, ordering the Commissioners for surveying Church property to assemble in Norwich on the Monday after the Assizes (March 8). But the Assizes were not concluded untill Saturday, March 6, so that the Assize Commissioners had not time to get from Thetford to Norwich by Monday; as therefore only nine men assembled on Monday the beginning of the work was postponed until Friday, March 12, on which day they all met together at seven in the morning and worked the whole day. They read and mastered the instructions, made excerpts from them and sent them to the incumbents of the diocese, with a command to return all the necessary information to Norwich by the following Friday, March 19. Southwell concludes his letter with a promise to inform Cromwell from time to time concerning the doings of the Commissioners, but no further letter is extant. One, however, from Lytylprow, dated April 9, is preserved. He is consumed with a desire to see his benefactor, but dares not return to London until the Commissioners of Firstfruits and Tenths have finished their work, which will be in twenty days if the Commissioners are sufficiently zealous. But either Lytylprow under-estimated the amount of the work or the Commissioners did not prove zealous, for the survey of one of

the sub-commissions in the diocese of Norwich is dated
October 4.[1]

Quarrels
about pre-
cedence.   Sometimes Cromwell had to settle quarrels about precedence among the Commissioners.   On April 10 he received
a letter from W. Freurs, the Mayor of Oxford, in which he
relates that on Tuesday last the Justices of the Peace
assembled for the Quarter Sessions, sent for him and for
the Commissary and told them both—the Mayor and the
Commissary—that they had been appointed Commissioners
of Tenths.   In compliance with the Instruction the Commissioners had divided the rural deaneries among the sub-
commissions.   By common consent, Sir W. Barantyne, Sir S.
Harcourt, Sir J. Clerke, the Commissary and the Mayor
were appointed to make the survey of the University and the
rural deanery of Oxford.   But the University found it difficult
to reconcile itself to the interference of the Mayor in academic
routine, and the Commissary declared that he would not
allow the Mayor to take part in the survey of the Colleges.
On this account the Mayor bitterly complains to Cromwell,
assures him of his impartiality, and begs that his offended
dignity may be re-established.   He attributes the Commissary's protest to motives of petty jealousy; it appears that the
Commissary deeply resented the fact that the Mayor and not
he was named first in the commission.   From a later letter
of the five Oxfordshire Commissioners to Cromwell, dated
July 1, we may conclude that the differences among the Commissioners were settled, for the Mayor went to London upon the
business of the Commission.   We have, they say, carefully
' studied the annual revenues of the clergy within the limits
of the shire and University of Oxford. The books of the
colleges and monasteries are however so prolix and tedious
that we shall be unable to finish the summary thereof until
the end of this term.   Wherefore we humbly ask your
grace to grant us an extension of time until the beginning
of next term in order that we may put the whole of our
work into one book.   In the meantime we are sending you

---

[1] Gairdner, viii. 318, 413, 414, 420, 521.   Easter Sunday in 1535 fell on
March 28th, V. E. iii. 369.

some books by the Mayor, the bearer of this letter, that your grace might become acquainted with their form and order, and that, if there is anything of which you do not approve, corrections may yet be made.'[1]

Most of the Commissioners' letters were written by the Bishops—as a rule, the Bishop was the only ecclesiastic on the diocesan commission, but by way of compensation he was usually the chairman, and, as such, it became his duty to inform Cromwell of the progress of the survey. The Bishop was in a delicate position; for it was to the interest of the clergy to minimize, when making the survey, the amount of income, and consequently the Bishop lay open to the suspicion of sympathizing with attempts on their part to escape the Royal taxation, especially as he would have to collect the quota of Tenths and account for arrears; moreover, he was himself one of the chief incumbents and payers of Tenths. It is not surprising, therefore, to find that the Bishops strove to appear zealous servants of their Sovereign, and were eager to assure the all-powerful favourite of their zeal and impartiality.

On April 16 the Bishop of Bath and Wells sent a long letter to Cromwell in which he says that he received, on Palm Sunday, the Royal Commission addressed to himself and to several gentlemen of the shire, and that he immediately informed the Commissioners of their appointment. But being Holy Week and Easter so near and the distances so great, the Commissioners could not assemble at once. They assembled in Wells on Monday after Low Sunday, and the Commission was read. The 'scribys officiallis and mynystres' of the Bishops and Archdeacons have appeared before the Commissioners, and, having taken the oath according to the first article of the Instruction, have made a list of all the spiritual benefices of the diocese. They then, in accordance with the second article of the Instruction, divided themselves into sub-commissions and departed to their respective circuits in order to carry out their remaining duties. The period, however, in

Bishops as Commissioners.

---

[1] Gairdner, x. 647. Dr. Gairdner attributes this letter to 1536, but it was undoubtedly written in 1535. Cf. ibid. viii. 967.

which the work was to be completed must be lengthened, as it
was impossible to finish conscientiously so great a work before
Trinity, especially as many of the Commissioners were at the
same time engaged in other business, such as the Subsidy
Commission, the Musters Commission or the Sewers Commission. On the 17th of September the Bishop sent the
survey of his diocese to Cromwell and assured him of the zeal
of all the Commissioners. The auditors were especially keen,
he wrote ; they rode night and day, incurred great expenses,
and neglected their own private affairs ; they ought, therefore,
to be rewarded. The Commissioners, he added, not only
effectively safeguarded the interests of the King but even
went so far as to strain the Statute with the sole object of
increasing the King's revenue.[1]

On the 11th of May, Sir Thomas Tempest wrote on behalf of
the Commissioners of Durham and Northumberland to Cromwell, assuring him of his own zeal. In these counties also
difficulties were experienced in making the survey. Tempest
asks for instructions how to deal with them, and declares that
when the Commissioners have received these they will continue
their work zealously. On the 21st of July the Bishop also
wrote to Cromwell. When Cromwell received the Yorkshire
returns he expressed his displeasure at the fact that the
Durham Commissioners had not given any information concerning themselves. The Bishop, consequently, is anxious to
exculpate himself, and says that only three auditors were
appointed for the counties of York, Durham and Northumberland, and that for a long time they had been engaged with
the Yorkshire books ; now, however, the Durham books
are ready and the Bishop sends them to London along with
his letter.[1]

The Hamp-
shire Com-
missioners.
On the 2nd of May the Bishop of Winchester, Stephen
Gardiner, writes to Cromwell that the work concerning the
valuation of Church property and revenues is finished ; but,
before sending the survey to the Exchequer, he wishes to
know Cromwell's opinion of the survey, just as, before the
commission began its work, he had asked his advice. The

[1] Gairdner, viii. 551 ; ix. 383.   [2] Gairdner, viii. 700 and 1082.

Commissioners divided their returns into two parts, the valuation of gross incomes, and the allowances thereon. Scarcely any deficiencies will be discovered in the first part, for all the benefices were estimated at their utmost value. But some difficulties arose in dealing with the allowances. The Commissioners followed the Instruction as in duty bound ; but the taxpayers complained that the Commissioners went beyond the Act of Parliament, and, regarding only the interest of the Treasury, wronged them in not making such deductions as were allowed by the Statute. The Commissioners endeavoured to pacify the malcontents by assuring them that the question of allowances was of no importance. If the gross income were exaggerated that would be an almost irreparable injustice ; in this matter, however, the Commissioners had striven to act with great care. As to the allowances, they would be carefully verified by the Exchequer, and then the taxpayers would have an opportunity of explaining their grievances. The disputed points are added to the letter :—

1. Several benefices have attached to them not only the parish church, but also chapels each with its own chaplain ; the Commissioners calculated the revenues of the chapels but made no allowance for the chaplain's stipend.

2. Some chapels have no assured income nor a definite connexion with any benefice ; the complainants think that such chapels ought to be tenth-free ; the Commissioners, however, have taxed these also.

3. The term 'alms' is applied not only to the donations to the poor but also to the expenses of poor scholars : for instance, those at New College, Winchester. The taxpayers think that both these expenses ought to be allowed from the gross income in compliance with the Statute, but the Commissioners, following the Instruction, have deducted only the expenses for the old and poor. Gardiner adds an apology for his zeal. He says that the poor and wretched can live only by means of alms, while a school is not necessary for the children.[1]

[1] Gairdner, viii. 654 ; ix. 1070, n. 3. The points (ix. 1070, n. 3) are printed by Gairdner apart from the letter. The original is in Cott. Cleop. E. iv. 306–7.

Fuller, without giving any proofs, affirmed that the Welsh
returns were made under Edward VI, and Dixon believed this.
The State Papers, however, show that the statement is wrong;
the Welsh returns as well as the English were begun in 1535.
It is true that on April 20 the Bishop of Bangor was absent from
his diocese, but he writes from Hyde, near Winchester, that
the Commissioners are already making a survey of Church
property in his diocese. Sir Rich. Bulkeley, the chief of these
Commissioners, sends to Cromwell a detailed account of the
work of the commission. In Holy Week, the Bishop informed certain gentlemen that they were appointed Commissioners. Bulkeley believes that the local gentlemen are bar-
barous and ignorant, and that the auditors appointed to the
commission have not yet appeared; the work, nevertheless,
has already made great progress. The Commissioners have
examined the incumbents, under oath, concerning the revenues
of their benefices, and required four parishioners from each
parish to verify their testimony; then all who wished to give
evidence were invited to do so. Sometimes protests were
made against the false evidence of the parish priests and the
four parishioners, or offers were made to take the parish on
lease for a larger sum. The Commissioners know not what
to do in such cases, therefore, whilst waiting for Cromwell's
reply, they will go and make a survey of the diocese of
St. Asaph.[1]

In the diocese of Llandaff there was some delay in the
work. On July 20 Cromwell requested the Commissioners
to send him the survey, and a month later Morgan, one of the
Commissioners, writes a letter of apology in which he complains that neither the bishop nor the other Commissioners
give him any help. Nevertheless the spiritual revenues of the
diocese are being ascertained and will evidently exceed the old
valuation. But they could not on the spot make up the books
after the auditors' fashion, for up to the present neither of the
two appointed auditors has appeared. Morgan wonders
whether he should await the arrival of the auditors or send
the books to London in their present rough form.

[1] Gairdner, viii. 564, 599.

The most detailed information comes from the diocese of York. On March 30 the Archbishop informed Cromwell that he had received the Royal commission. He and the Lord Mayor have already summoned the first meeting for the Thursday after Easter, but it is not probable that all will be able to attend, as many of the Commissioners are in the South, and several are ill. The Archbishop fears also that there will not be a sufficient number of auditors, and that it will not be possible to finish the work by the appointed time. When the day fixed in the Instruction came, the Commissioners were obliged to ask for an extension of time, and the Archbishop in his letter dated May 16 justifies this request by reference to the fact that several Commissioners were all the time at Westminster, and that the number of auditors was far too small. A week after, on May 24, the ten Commissioners, with the Archbishop and the Lord Mayor of York as their leaders, officially inform Cromwell to the same effect. The Commissioners had already received the surveys of all the benefices but could not make from them a general book after the auditors' fashion, because some of the auditors appointed by the commission were ill, some had not given any notice whatever of themselves, and some were sent to other dioceses. Moreover, difficulties had arisen concerning which they would like to know Cromwell's opinion. The Commissioners asked for an extension of time and begged the Exchequer not to fine them for this delay. The extension was evidently granted, as the York returns were sent to London on June 30, together with a letter from the Commissioners. The letter itself is lost, but a summary of it, made probably for Cromwell in some London office, is preserved. The fact that a summary was made shows with what attention the work of the Commissioners was controlled from London. Of course the Commissioners proclaim their zeal, explain the gaps in the survey of the town of York and praise their auditors. The Commissioners of York also were accused of making too few allowances. The complainants point out

---

[1] Gairdner, ix. 161.

that some lands are subject to inundations and consequently lose much of their value, but the Commissioners will not take this fact into account ; other properties, such as mills, for example, are constantly in need of repairs, without which they would not bring in even a third part of their real income, but the Commissioners will not make allowance for repairs. Some parsons are forced to hire a chaplain to help them, but the Commissioners will not allow the deduction of the stipends of such chaplains. When the returns were sent in, two of the Commissioners, the Archbishop and Sir G. Lawson, felt it necessary to write to Cromwell apart from the general letter. Lawson greatly praises both the auditors and his colleagues, who did their utmost to carry out the Instruction. He admits that there are still some difficulties and some gaps left. But in so short a time, he confesses, it is impossible to do the work more carefully, and, if Cromwell so wishes, a new Commission might be appointed to make a more thorough investigation. In the Archbishop's letter some interesting personal explanations are found. He did not spare himself when he made the valuation of his see ; the new valuation exceeds not only all the old ones but even the actual income of the see. The Archbishop, however, hopes that the Exchequer will make allowances for places subject to inundations ; by the latter his predecessor lost in one place alone as much as a hundred marks of income. The Archbishop asks that the parsons should not give Tenths on the stipends which they pay to their chaplains ; but he immediately makes a kind of apology for his presumption.[1]

Digest of the diocesan reports.   We have some information as to the way in which the digest was made by the Exchequer out of the diocesan reports. On September 9, Audley, the Chancellor, writing from Colchester, reminds Cromwell that they had commanded the auditors to collect and bring to the Exchequer all the Tenth-books by the 12th of September, on which day he, Audley, hopes to see Cromwell in London ; if, however, it is not convenient for Cromwell to come on that day he will not begin the work, but wait until Cromwell shall inform him

[1] Gairdner, viii. 463, 720, 754, 945, 952, 968.

of his arrival.—On September 10, Polsted, Cromwell's servant, tells his master about certain negotiations with the newly elected Bishops of Rochester and Worcester concerning First-fruits; amongst other things, he says that the report of the Kent Commissioners lies already in Pollard's office in London. On Monday before Michaelmas, Audley complains that up to the present time he has received only twelve or thirteen Tenth-books, and thanks Cromwell for the letter which he enclosed with the books of the dioceses of Winchester and Bath. But it is impossible, he says, to make a digest until all the books are received; therefore he is about to order the negligent Commissioners in his own name and that of Cromwell, to send in the reports at once.—On September 30 Audley informs Cromwell that such an order has already been sent.[1] Unfortunately, soon after this a breach occurred between the two friends, and there are no more letters of the Chancellor to the Secretary among the State Papers of 1535. Still we know, from other sources, that the revision of the reports, though somewhat delayed, was finished shortly afterwards. On March 4, 1536, the Archbishop of York informs Cromwell that he has received the Royal Tenth-book from the Exchequer, and found in it many discrepancies which make the raising of the tax rather difficult. Some benefices are wrongly named, others taxed twice over, some cannot be distinguished from others and some are omitted altogether. It is impossible at present to make a full list of the omissions, especially because the original bills (by this the Archbishop evidently means the diocesan reports of the Commissioners in 1535) are in the hands of the auditors and not in the respective dioceses. The Archbishop thinks that the auditors ought to be present at the drawing-up of the Tenth-books, so that in every detail the latter may agree with the original bills. It is particularly unjust to collect the Tenth twice over from the same person; for instance, the Archdeacon of Nottingham has been taxed both by the Nottingham and the York Commissioners. The letter closes with an entreaty that such misunderstandings may be cleared up.

[1] Gairdner, ix. 31, 372, 450, 487.

On March 7, 1536, T. Tesh, who brought the Tenth-books of the diocese of York from the Exchequer to York, writes about the same deficiencies of these books; but unlike the Archbishop, Tesh considered it possible to make and enclose a list of the discrepancies which he noticed.[1]—Finally, the famous Statute about the dissolution and confiscation of monasteries with incomes below two hundred pounds (27 H. VIII, c. 28) shows that in the beginning of 1536 the books from all the diocesan Commissioners were already in the hands of the Exchequer; article 7 explains that the monasteries with lesser incomes can be discovered from the books of the valuation of all spiritual benefices sent to the Exchequer. The Act was passed during the session which began on February 4, 1536, and ended some time before June 8, 1536, on which date a new Parliament assembled; we may therefore confidently assert that the valuation books were in the hands of the Exchequer at the beginning of 1536.

General character of the correspondence. The above correspondence is so expressive in itself that it hardly needs comment. I shall, therefore, point out only the most important conclusions it suggests; and this as briefly as possible. The idea that in the sixteenth century the English Government wished to complete in two or three months a full and detailed survey of all the Church revenue may seem astounding; and although the work actually took some five or six months, one cannot but view with considerable distrust a work done in so short a time. Here, however, we must remember that the work of the Commissioners of 1535 is not to be regarded as something exceptional. The Valor Ecclesiasticus, however important, is, after all, only one link in the chain of surveys which extends from the great and wonderful Book of the Conqueror to the census of 1901. The drawing up of surveys of large territories in a very short time was to the English Government an old device

---

[1] Gairdner, x. 413, 435. It is possible that the list made by Tesh is that contained in Cott. Cleop. E. iv, and summarized by Gairdner, ix. 1070, n. 4. The list has twenty-eight items, one of which mentions the double taxation of the Archdeacon of Nottingham.

going back to the eleventh, or, according to some investigators, almost to the seventh century. The history of English political liberty has long since passed from the domain of special research into the political creed of the whole civilized world; it accomplished a great mission of liberation; it has surely not ceased to be a great political force. The history of English administration is much less known abroad, although it undoubtedly has a just claim to public attention. A powerful government, which attained great technical perfection, had been developed on the island at a very early date, and, according to the best authorities, was the unconscious nurse, if not the tender mother, of political liberty. The rulers of the State did not grope their way in the dark; they wanted to know the exact amount of their means, and made great use of the methods of statistical inquiry. It is true that the nature of manorial economy made the governmental work considerably easier, the small mobility of the manorial life being attended with great publicity. The monks, barons, stewards and bailiffs between the twelfth and the sixteenth centuries did not attach great importance to commercial secrecy. Access to the court rolls, bailiffs' accounts and manorial surveys was on the whole easy, both for the tenantry and the Government. In its inquiries the latter could and did use the original 'ledger books' of private concerns. The success of the official surveys, however, was also greatly dependent upon the habit of business routine which was so firmly rooted in the minds both of the central bureaucratic *personnel* and of the local agents of the State.

The Survey of 1535 evidently did not make a very great impression upon contemporaries, even upon those who took direct part in it. The central Government did not find any difficulty in the choice of Commissioners; the Commissioners were not at all astonished at the instructions given. The Commissioners of 1535 are the usual agents of the Government: the Bishops, Mayors, Sheriffs, Justices of the Peace, the local gentry and the auditors. They carry out a number of other official orders as well, and the Bishops justly complain in their correspondence of the fact that manifold duties prevent their Fellow Commissioners giving a proper amount of time to the survey. The Government had been long accustomed to hand over part of its work to the best men of the locality. Perhaps the most characteristic feature of the Commissions of 1535 was that the clergy were very insufficiently represented upon them. The Bishops were the only ecclesiastics appointed; seldom and timidly did they raise their voices in defence of the Church interests whilst the survey was in progress. No doubt the laymen who sympathized with the clergy might also have minimized the amount of the Church revenues of which they had to give an account; but there is no reason to accuse the Commissioners of such a tendency. Their chief aims were to get rid as soon as possible of the difficult work thrust upon them, not to bring upon themselves any punishment or reprimand from their respective chiefs, and as far as possible to prove themselves worthy of thanks and reward. They were anxious to do exactly what was required of them by the Government, or at least to persuade their superiors that this was their object. Before and above all things they assert that they follow the 'Instruction' to the letter, that they carry out all its articles, that they take the first clause before the second. But in their correspondence they show some interest also in the pecuniary side of their commission, namely, the augmentation of the King's revenue; if they succeed in raising the valuation of the Church income they gladly point out the fact. This, however, by no means signifies that they described and valued the income of the Church with perfect accuracy. They might be deceived by the taxpayers; they might make omissions and mistakes owing to their great haste. But it is difficult to attribute to them an intention to deceive the Government by purposely undervaluing the Church income.

Results of the Commissioners' work.

The outcome of the Commissioners' work consisted of documents of various kinds. Each individual incumbent gave the valuation or survey of his own benefice—the Sub-commissioners made a separate digest of these for each rural deanery; the Commissioners made a book of them for the whole county or diocese, and finally some kind of digest was prepared by the Exchequer for the whole country. The Instruction ordered the Commissioners to send to the Exchequer the diocesan surveys, and to add thereto the separate surveys of each rural deanery; the Commissioners were not compelled to send the original surveys of each separate benefice, and these surveys are not to be found among the records of the Court of Firstfruits and Tenths into whose possession the documents of 1535 passed. If the Commissioners had carried out the Instruction exactly the surveys of the dioceses and deaneries ought to have been preserved among the records. Some of these surveys, however, were lost before the remaining documents were published by the Government under the name of 'Valor Ecclesiasticus'.

The author of the preface to the official edition not having thought it necessary to describe the manuscripts, I may be allowed to say a few words about them; although I have been able to examine only a few of them.

In the Record Office, under the title of 'Valor Ecclesiasticus', one can find twenty-two volumes and three port-folios. But of these twenty-two volumes eighteen only are taken up with the Commissioners' returns. The eighteenth volume is devoted to the Royal lands in Ireland; Volumes XVII, XIX, and XX are the Exchequer digest of the Commissioners' returns. Some of the first sixteen volumes are the surveys of a diocese or part of a diocese, others are the surveys of counties.[1] The contents of volumes are as follows: I and II, Canterbury diocese; III, Chichester diocese; IV, Exeter diocese; V, Llandaff diocese; VI, Rochester diocese; VII, Winchester diocese; VIII, Bedford county; IX, X, and XI, Lincoln diocese; XII, Oxford county; XIII, Suffolk county; XIV, Somerset county; XV, Surrey county; XVI, Worcester county; XXI, Derby, Stafford, Lancaster, Chester, Salop, St. Davids, Llandaff, Sussex, Surrey; XXII, London and Middlesex, Nottingham, Lincoln, Huntingdonshire.

The three portfolios are called in the Record Office 'Original Returns on Parchment'. Each portfolio contains many surveys; in one of them there are surveys of a diocese (or a part of a diocese?); in the two others are to be found surveys of *counties* (some towns being apparently treated in the same manner as counties). The subject-matter of the contents of the portfolios

MS. of the Valor.

---

[1] The titles that I give are those used in the Record Office in 1904.

is as follows in 1904:—*Portfolio I*: Leicester, Norwich, Bangor, Dorset, Salop, Coventry and Lichfield, Carlisle, Stafford, Winchester, St. Asaph, Southampton, Worcester, Exeter. *Portfolio II*: Northampton, Cornwall, Chester, Hereford, Suffolk, Norfolk, Buckinghamshire. *Portfolio III*: Derby, Durham, Gloucester, Warwick, Westmoreland, Wiltshire, York.

Of all this material I only looked through volumes I, II, XII, XIV–XXI, XXII, and that part of Portfolio I which contains the Dorset returns. The Dorset returns are a roll made of a large number of long narrow membranes sewn together. All the surveys of the separate benefices are drawn up according to one and the same pattern, and evidently form a digest of the original surveys sent in by the incumbents or obtained by means of the inquiry. On the *dorsum* of the last membrane the total net income and tenth of the whole county are given. The surveys of some deaneries are signed by the respective Commissioners.

The return for the diocese of Bath and Wells is a folio volume, made up of ninety-three sheets of paper of very large size. It begins with the Instruction to the Commissioners and ends with the autograph signatures of eleven Commissioners; this leads us to suppose that here we have the original returns of the diocesan commission. In this manuscript the total net income and the Tenth of the whole diocese are given but for some reason scratched out. Together with this volume is bound a later document in a much larger hand : ' Stipend' et salar' divers' capellanorum divina celebrant' in diversis eccliis et capellis intra dioc' Bathon' et Wellen' in com' Soms ac in libro commissionar' ibm *omiss'* ut sequitur.' This is an official supplementary inquiry made not later than 32 H. VIII and signed by the Bishop.—The returns of the diocese of Canterbury take up two folio volumes written on paper of smaller size. In the second volume, after the returns of 1535, there is found a document sent by Cranmer, written in a peculiar handwriting and dated 28 H. VIII. It is a list of all the benefices of the diocese together with their net income.

The Oxfordshire returns form a quarto volume having 264 sheets used and paginated, and many others blank and unpaginated. The surveys of separate benefices and monas-

teries differ from each other in many ways; they are written
in a number of different hands and on paper of different sizes.
For some reason a new unpaginated valuation of the benefice
of Mylton made in 37 H. VIII is bound up together with the
returns of 1535 after f. 23 and the former valuation of 1535 is
crossed out. Some monasteries have two surveys; generally
one of them is detailed and the other short. The first twenty-
three sheets are evidently the work of one of the sub-commissions. The twenty-third sheet ends thus: ' Wa't Stonore,
Thomas Carter, John Williams [possibly these are autograph
signatures] Comyssioners appointed for this behalf. The
some of this boke the deductions alowed 1384. 4. 5, the King
shall have yerely 138. 8. o.' Five rural deaneries and four
monasteries are surveyed in these twenty-three sheets. If we
add together the totals of the Tenths for the five deaneries we
get the sum of £138 17s. 7½d. The monasteries were not
entered along with the rural deaneries, and the total of the
Tenth evidently refers to all the twenty-three sheets and includes
all the district surveyed by the sub-commission. Some of the
surveys of monasteries are undoubtedly the originals sent in
by their administrators. Thus the revenues of the monastery
of Godstow (ff. 60–72) are written in one hand, the allowances
in another, and the petition of the nuns for an allowance for
wine and wax in a third. On the sheets 89–94 a survey
of the monastery of Goryng is written in another different
style, and near the end (f. 93 dorso) there is found yet
another hand which scribbled ' be me dam' Margarete Wodall
pryorese'. In the survey of the monastery of Eynsham
(ff. 95–107) one is struck not so much by the peculiarities
of the contents as by the beautiful writing that has no equal
in all this volume: magnificent capital letters, and an abundance of small artistic characters; but there are several corrections in the figures, badly formed and made at a later time.

The volumes XXI and XXII are called in the Record Office Liber
' Liber Regis'; they are written on vellum in a very careful Regis.
hand. At the beginning of a diocese or county there are
miniatures; three of them represent Henry surrounded by his
courtiers.[1] Volume XXI has the following title: 'In hoc libro

---

[1] A curious piece of information concerning the Liber Regis is given by

continentur veri valores omnium et singulorum episcopatuum monasterior' et aliorum beneficiorum ecclesiasticorum'existen' et jacen' infra comitat' infrascript' qui quidem valores de originalibus recordis dñi regis curie sue decimarū et primic'ar' *de verbo* extract' erāt.' This then is a verbatim copy of the corresponding surveys of the Commissioners. Volume XXII is headed thus: 'Continet hic liber valores episcopatuum monasterior' abbiar' prioratuum collegior' hospitaliū rectoriar' vicariar' cantariar' liber' capellar' ac aliar' promocionum quarumcunque spūalium in et per comitatus subscriptos existen' una cum vero annuo valore epātuum eccliar' que cathedr' et dignitatum ear'dem per dñm H. VIII nuper felicissime memorie Anglie regem anno regni sui 34 pie erect.' This title was evidently written after Henry's death ; but in the titles of the surveys of the separate counties Henry is referred to as now living (nunc regis). It shows that the copyist exactly reproduced the original. All the same, Volume XXII was not copied verbatim. It is possible to make a comparison for the Lincoln diocese because the Commissioners' returns are preserved (vols. ix–xi). The English title of the Survey is translated into Latin in the Liber Regis; the clauses crossed out in the Survey are entirely omitted in the Liber Regis (Rec. Comm. IV. 4, vol. xxii. f. 128) ; the Liber Regis may put 'ballivus' instead of 'bedellus' which is found in the Survey, but I did not notice any more serious points of difference.—The Liber Regis is a document of considerable importance because the original returns of the Commissioners for many of the territories surveyed are lost, and we have only this copy to fall back upon.

The Record Commission edition.   I have compared some parts of the MS. text with the edition of the Record Commission. I have found that the texts agree, and that one is quite safe in making use of the printed edition. In the text of the Record Commission the clauses concerning the allowances are not infrequently printed in italics; these clauses in the MS. are crossed out; against

J. Bacon in the Preface (iii) to the 'Liber Regis seu Thesaurus rerum ecclesiasticarum, 1786': 'The Liber Regis is a beautiful MS. transcribed, as tradition says, by a monk of Westminster, one copy of which was lodged in the King's library, and the other in the Court of First Fruits and Tenths in the Exchequer.'

them on the left margin a cross is made. Not infrequently the sign of a cross is put against expenditure clauses in the text of the Record Commission; in the corresponding passages of the MS. there is also a cross, but the figure itself is also crossed out; this fact is not mentioned in the printed edition. In both these cases the probability is that the officials of the Exchequer, when revising the diocesan reports, reversed the decision of the Commissioners and refused to allow from the gross income such expenses as the Commissioners thought conformable to the Statute and the Instruction. I did not take such clauses into consideration. Probably the same officials, when revising the surveys, made the notes found in the margin—for instance, in the survey of the monastery of St. Augustine, Canterbury, in Kennington an item of expenditure is given as ' pencio vicarii 40 s.'; in the margin is a note of later date 'nota pro valore vicarii ubi oneratur'. It is to be regretted that some of these notes are omitted in the printed edition; for instance, at the very end of the survey of this same monastery two almo are entered amounting to 21s. In the MS. (vol. i. f. 56 *dorso*) they are crossed out, and are therefore printed in italics in the Record Commission edition; but in the margin of the MS. 'stet' is added; this means that the Exchequer finally granted the allowance from the gross income. In the Record Commission edition 'stet' is left out, and the reader is led into error.—It is not always pointed out in the Record Commission edition that some totals are given in the MS. two or three times over; one total is given after making the calculation for the first time, another total is given as the result of a second calculation, and a third one after making the calculation a third time. Thus in the MS. (vol. i. f. 14), three totals are given for the revenues of the see of Canterbury, and the Record Commission edition (i. 7) gives only one.—Misprints in figures are not pointed out in the Record Commission edition; fortunately these seem to be rare.

Neither the Commissioners' surveys nor the copy of them Liber in the Liber Regis cover the whole of England. In the Valorum. Record Office the surveys for six counties (Berkshire, Cambridgeshire, Essex, Hertfordshire, Northumberland and

Rutland), and for parts of two other counties (Middlesex
and Yorkshire), are missing. The gap is partly filled by
the official and private lists of all the English benefices, and
their gross or net incomes calculated from the surveys of
1535. I have seen two of the official lists. In the literary
search-room of the Record Office are found three volumes of
the so-called Liber Valorum which embrace the whole of
England and Wales. In these all the benefices are entered
according to their counties in the same order in which they
are given in the Commissioners' surveys; the net income and
tenth of every benefice are recorded. All the figures are taken
from the Commissioners' returns. The following is the title of
the volume which may be called the first: 'In hoc libro continentur valor' annui diversorum beneficiorum in comitatibus
subscriptis unacum decimis eorundem ex originalibus recordis
dñi regis curie sue primit' et decimar' extracti'.' The excerpts
were evidently made with a practical purpose, as it was necessary that the Court of Firstfruits and Tenths should always
know the income of all the benefices, in order to determine
the amount of the Firstfruits and verify the annual quota of
the Tenths. The reports of the Commissioners being rather
voluminous, it was difficult to find in them at once every figure
that was needed, and excerpts had to be made. Speaking
generally, the quota of Tenths remains unaltered from 1535 down
to our own time. In a small number of cases, however, new
benefices were created by Royal Letters Patent and the decrees
of the Court, and the income of the old benefices was altered,
generally diminished ; the corresponding changes were carried
into the Liber Valorum.—In the Record Commission edition
those parts of the Commissioners' surveys which are lost are
taken from the corresponding portion of the Liber Valorum.—
Three volumes (XVII, XIX, XX) in the Record Office, incor-
porated with the Valor Ecclesiasticus, are uncommonly like the
Liber Valorum. All benefices, with their net incomes and
Tenths, are also registered there according to their counties, and
the later changes in the area and income of certain benefices are
also stated. The title of volume XVII is the same as the first
volume in the Liber Valorum. The order of benefices within
their respective counties is exactly the same, because it is

derived from a common source—the Commissioners' returns.
But the order of the counties is different from that in the
Liber Valorum; the entries of the later changes in taxation
also do not agree in the two lists. It was very probably these
two lists that occupied Audley and Cromwell at the end of
1535 after they had received all the Commissioners' returns.
It is very probable too, that the Book of Tenths mentioned by
the Archbishop of York in March, 1536, is a copy of the
corresponding part of the Liber Valorum.

Such lists were necessary, not only for the Government but
also for private people. Incumbents naturally wished to know
the precise amount of their tenth. Men looking forward to a
benefice were naturally interested in the amount of its income,
and many liked to know the income of the local clergy.

When Queen Anne granted exemption of Tenths to the
poorest incumbents and augmented their income from the
Tenths of other benefices, the practical value of such lists
became still greater. In order to increase the demand for these
lists an enterprising editor used to add some antiquarian and
practical information and then put the book on the market.
There were several such editions in the seventeenth and
eighteenth centuries, the best known being those of Ecton
and Bacon.[1]

The compilation of private lists of the dissolved monasteries Speed's
cannot be explained by practical needs; such compilers were list.
guided almost exclusively by a theoretical, or rather antiquarian interest. The most important lists go back to Cotton,
or to manuscripts of Cotton's collection. In Speed's Chronicle,
after the story of Henry's reign, there is given a list of
monasteries under the title: 'A catalogue of the religious
houses within the realme of England and Wales, with their
orders, founders, benefactors and values, most of them being
suppressed by King H. VIII, together with such other

---

[1] The book of J. Bacon, 'Liber Regis seu Thesaurus rerum ecclesiasticarum' (1786), is to a great extent a reprint of Ecton's 'Thesaurus
rerum Ecclesiasticarum', of the enlarged edition of 1742. The first edition
of Ecton's work was published in 1711, under a very long title beginning
with 'Liber Valorum Decimarum'. Both Bacon and Ecton were receivers
of the Firstfruits and Tenths. Ecton's first edition was not the first
attempt of this kind. It is said in the preface that there are several
books on the same subject which are full of mistakes.

sacred places, as either then were by him left standing, or since
have been erected.'[1]   In a short preface to the list it is explained that the valuations are taken from the 'original book
made by the Commissioners and presented to the King'.   Both
Tanner and Spelman give some information about the origin
of this list.   Speaking of a doubtful council held at the
end of the seventh or the beginning of the eighth century, in
which council the gifts to the newly founded monastery of
Evesham were supposed to have been confirmed, Spelman
casually remarks, ' I cannot find in what year that council was
held.   In the list of monasteries which as I heard was made
by W. Burton and published by Speed, Evesham is said to
have been founded in the year 700.'[2]   Tanner more fully
repeats Spelman's statement.   Under the Letters Patent of
King Henry, Leland, at the time of the Dissolution, studied
the monastic archives and made many notes thereon.   His
papers fell into the hands of a certain Leicestershire gentleman,
Burton by name, who from them made a list of monasteries,
which was printed by Speed.   But later, Tanner inconsistently
says that the compiler used the 'original book' of 1535, as
well as Leland's notes, and Camden's Britannia.[3]   The statements of Spelman and Tanner can hardly be reconciled with
Speed's letters to Cotton, and these are much more trustworthy.   In the Camden Society's Publications are to be
found five undated letters from Speed to Cotton which were
forwarded at the time of the publication of Speed's History.
We gather from these letters that Cotton had read Speed's
proof-sheets, given him coins and made corrections and
additions to Speed's list.   Speed twice remarks in his letters
that he is expecting a list of the monasteries from Cotton.[4]

And I believe I am warranted in thinking that Speed's list
rests upon Cotton's authority.   This list gives the figures of the
revenue of the monasteries.   Tanner had already recognized in
them the figures of the *gross* income, and had inserted them in

---

[1] Speed, 786-802.
[2] Spelman, Concilia (1639), i. 215.
[3] Tanner, p. 13 of the unpaginated preface.
[4] Camden S., xxiii. 108-13.   110, 'If you will send a note of all
monasteryes in the realm, I shalbe much beholding to your worship.'
112, 'I want your worships furtherance for the monasteryes erected in
every Shire.'

his edition along with the figures of the *net* income, which he took from Dugdale.[1]   If these figures were trustworthy they would be an important supplement to the extant documents of 1535. Since the Commissioners' returns for many counties are lost and the Liber Valorum gives only figures of the *net* income, Speed's list is the only source from which we learn figures of the *gross* income of the monasteries.   But are these figures trustworthy?   In order to answer this question we must compare Speed's list with the extant returns of the Commissioners. For Bedfordshire and Cornwall, Speed's figures in every case agree with the figures of the *gross* income given in the Commissioners' returns ; this, however, scarcely indicates a careful choice, as it was very easy to find such figures in these returns. For Buckinghamshire, the figures given by Speed in eight cases correspond to the figures of the *gross* income found in the Commissioners' returns ; in two cases there is a difference in the figures of the pounds (Bittlesden, V.E. 162, Speed, 142 ; Medmenham, V.E. 24, Speed 23).   In the Commissioners' returns for Buckinghamshire the figures of the gross income are given very clearly ; it is not difficult to discover them even in a casual examination.—The figures given by Speed for Cheshire agree with those of the gross income given in the Commissioners' returns, in which they could easily be found. But the amount given by Speed for St. Werburgh's, Chester (£1,073 17s. 7½d.), is neither the net nor the gross income.   It is true that this item stands in the Commissioners' returns in the column where the gross income of other monasteries is given, but the total gross income of St. Werburgh's, Chester, is not given at all in the Commissioners' returns, and the amount, £1,073 17s. 7½d., is the sum which remained after a *part* of the allowances had been deducted.   The compiler's mistake can only be explained by supposing that he was in a great hurry when looking through the returns.   He did not add the separate items of the revenue together, but only copied the totals of the gross income or what seemed to him to be the

---

[1] Nasmith (Tanner,[3] Preface L) is wrong in affirming that Tanner, when making the valuation of monasteries, used not only Speed's and Dugdale's works but also the MSS.   In the edition of 1695 all the valuations of the monasteries are taken from Speed and Dugdale.   In the 1744 edition there are additional valuations, but they are derived from an unknown source.

totals. This is still more evident with regard to Derbyshire and Devonshire. The figures that Speed gives for the three Derbyshire monasteries Beauchief, Gresley and Repingdon agree with the figures of the *gross* income in the Commissioners' returns, but the figures that he gives for the five Derbyshire monasteries Breadsall, Dale, Darley, King's Mead and Yeveley are those which in the Commissioners' returns are given for the *net* income. For Breadsall, Dale and King's Mead the *net* income only is summed up in the Commissioners' returns, but the compiler of the list in his haste naturally took it for the gross income. But for Darley and Yeveley both the gross and the net income are given in the Commissioners' returns, and therefore in these cases the mistake is far less excusable. As to Devonshire, the figures given by Speed for Hartland are the only instance in which there is agreement with the gross income given in the Commissioners' returns. For the four Devonshire monasteries Plympton, Tavistock, Torre and Totnes, Speed's figures are those of the *net* income found in the Commissioners' returns; the mistake arose because the net income only is summed up in those returns. The figures given by Speed for the four Devonshire monasteries Canonleigh, Dunkeswell, St. Nicholas, Exeter, and Polslo are neither the net nor the gross income. This case is similar to that of St. Werburgh's, Chester. The compiler took his figures from the Commissioners' returns, but these figures represent the amount which remained after only a *part* of the allowances had been deducted from the gross income. It is quite clear therefore, that Speed's figures cannot be taken without exception to represent the gross income even in the counties for which the Commissioners' returns are lost, although it is only in the case of these counties that Speed's list has any value at all. In these counties Speed sometimes undoubtedly gives the figures of the net income and not of the gross: Shengay commandry, Camb.; St. Botulph's, Colchester, Ess.; Hedingham, Ess.; Wickham, Yorks.

Stevens's list.

The famous volume of the Cotton MSS. called Cleop. E. iv contains a curious list of monasteries, printed by Stevens word for word.[1] It is fuller than Speed's list because it gives not only

---

[1] Cleop. E. iv. ff. 374–445; Stevens, i. 23–37.

the gross but also the net income of every monastery. But on the other hand Stevens in his list mentions only abbeys, priories and friaries, and even some of these he leaves out (for instance Hedingham and St. Botulph's Colchester, are omitted); whilst Speed also gives us hospitals, colleges, cathedrals, command-ries, preceptories. It is impossible that either of these two lists could be directly derived from the other, yet at the same time there is a close relationship between them. I compared them with regard to the counties of Berkshire, Cambridgeshire, Essex, Hertfordshire, Northumberland and Yorkshire, and I found that the figures of the gross incomes agreed in both lists. I noticed only one point of difference, which, however, is ex-plained by a misprint in Speed's list.[1] Both Speed and Stevens make the same absurd mistake about St. John's, Colchester; each of them gives £8 1s. 8d. as the gross income ; and according to Stevens the net income is £7 7s. 8d. But St. John's, Colchester, was a large Benedictine abbey, and the Liber Valorum gives £523 16s. o¼d. as its *net* income. Both lists omit St. Clement's, York, which is to be found in the Commissioners' survey, although the MS. is partly spoiled. Both lists mention the monastery of Kingswood ; which, though a large one, strangely enough is not given either in the Commissioners' survey or in the Liber Valorum. Kingswood is in Wiltshire, but both lists wrongly locate it in Gloucester-shire. The above-mentioned differences between the lists and the Valor Ecclesiasticus make it difficult to believe that the latter was the common source of both. It is evident that both lists had for their origin some unknown list of monasteries of an earlier date which must have been based upon the surveys of 1535, and gave both the net and gross income. It was into this list that the mistake about St. John's, Colchester, crept ; it was from this list that St. Clement's, York, was omitted ; and into this list it was that Kingswood found its way.—The figures of the net income in Stevens's list have no importance whatever, as the same figures are given in the Liber Valorum,

---

[1] The point of difference is concerning Bolton in Craven, Yorks. Speed gives the gross income as £102 9s. 3d. ; Stevens £302 9s. 3d. The figure £102 is certainly a misprint for £302, for both the Liber Valorum and Stevens give £212 3s. 4d. as the net income.

an official document and more trustworthy.[1]   The figures of the gross income in Stevens's list are only a repetition of those given by Speed, and do not in any way add to the information which we get from his list.

Dods-   In the first edition of the ' Monasticon Anglicanum' Dodsworth   worth and Dugdale placed at the end of the first volume three
and Dug-
dale's list.   lists of monasteries: the first list enumerates the alien priories suppressed in 1414; the second shows the monasteries dissolved by Wolsey; the third, those described in the 1535 survey; it is only this last that has interest for us here.   It gives the figures of *net* income only, and thus adds nothing to the information derived from the Liber Valorum.   The figures of this list agree in almost all cases with the figures of the Liber Valorum, and the few points of difference, as for instance in the case of Anglesey, can be explained by a misprint.   The title of this list is as follows:—' Exactissimus sacrarum aedium apud Anglos et Cambro-Britannos catalogus (in the margin there is a note: Ex vetusto exemplari in bibl. Cotton) qui cum annuo singularum valore, certis ad eam rem explorandam missis, 26 H. VIII, redditus est et postea in libros primitiarum et decimarum relatus.'   Another list of monasteries very similar but not quite equivalent to Dugdale's is to be found in Cleop. E. iv (ff. 446–57).   Possibly both lists have their origin in a common third one based upon the Liber Valorum— Dugdale's list is not dependent upon that of Stevens.[2]

There exist other printed lists of monasteries, but they are of no interest, since they are founded either upon the Liber Valorum or Speed's, Dugdale's or Stevens's lists.[3]

[1] Stevens's figures of the net income of Berkshire, Cambridgeshire, Essex, Hertfordshire, Northumberland and Yorkshire agree in almost every case with the figures in the Liber Valorum; and if there is any difference, as for instance in the case of Reading (Berks.), Denny (Camb.), Old Malton (Yorks.) and Sempringham (Yorks.), it is either unimportant or can be attributed to a misprint.

[2] Mon. Angl., i. 1038–46.   The list in Cleop. E. iv. ff. 446–57 is written in a seventeenth-century handwriting; the title is in English and not Latin. The amount of the net income of all monasteries is somewhat different from that given by Dugdale (£135,522 18s. 10d. and £135,453 14s. 2¾d.). Dugdale mentions in his list hospitals, colleges and preceptories which are not found in Stevens.

[3] When I say all printed lists are almost entirely useless, I speak only of the time after the publication of the Valor Ecclesiasticus.

CHAPTER II

CRITICAL EXAMINATION OF THE SURVEY

IT is hardly likely that the Commissioners of 1535 purposely miscalculated the Church revenue, but there certainly are a great many misrepresentations of the actual state of things in their work. To what extent do these mistakes lessen or destroy the importance of the Survey? To answer this question we must compare the Valor Ecclesiasticus with other valuations made at other times by other people. And here I would again remark that the student of the Dissolution of the monasteries should confine himself to a comparison of the monastic surveys only.

The omission of whole benefices or large parts of benefices Omissions in V. E. cannot but be a most serious blemish. Such omissions do undoubtedly occur in the V. E., but they are not numerous. The Commissioners themselves did not deny the existence of these omissions, and even pointed out the desirability of a new inquiry. One of the York Commissioners tried in 1536 to make a list of the omissions in that diocese.[1] And we know that in the diocese of Bath and Wells another official inquiry was actually set on foot which tried to find out the chaplains' fees omitted in 1535. The list of the latter was bound up together with the Commissioners' returns for 1535. The notes in the margin of the list sometimes quote the date of the decree by which this or that chaplain's fees were exempt from the royal tenth; the dates given are: 37 H. VIII, 3 E. VI, 4 E. VI, 5 E. VI. But the list itself could hardly have been made later than 32 H. VIII, for in it the preceptory of Templecombe, dissolved in this year, is referred to as still existing. The list is no doubt an official one, for it con-

---

[1] Gairdner, x. 435, ix. 1070, n. 4.

cludes with the autograph signature 'Io Eps Bat Wellen'.
The chaplains' fees omitted from the Commissioners' returns
amount to £203 16s. 8d. and the Tenth raised from it is
£20 7s. 8½d.

The large Cistercian abbey of Kingswood is entirely
omitted from the list of monasteries in the Commissioners'
returns for Wiltshire. The large Benedictine abbey of St.
Augustine, Bristol, is also omitted, as well as two monasteries in the city of York, Holy Trinity and St. Andrews.
It is scarcely credible that they were mentioned in the lost
part of the Yorkshire returns, for they are not included in
the Liber Valorum. I did not discover any other omissions
of the same kind : and when it is remembered that some
550 monasteries (not counting hospitals, colleges or friaries)
are surveyed or valued in the V. E., the omission of four
cannot be considered very serious. Moreover, these four
monasteries were not lost to the State ; their lands were included in the Crown administration, and were sold like the
property of the other monasteries.

No doubt in the description of the property of monasteries
in the V. E., individual manors and spiritual benefices
were occasionally omitted ; but I was able to find only
a very few instances. Here are two ; in Somerset there
was an Austin nunnery, Minchin Buckland, whose Crown
bailiff in the survey for 31 H. VIII gives, among other
revenues, the rent of £22 for the preceptory and rectory
of Toller. In March of the same year the manor and
rectory of Toller Fratrum, Dors., were sold by the Crown,
and their combined income was estimated at £22 3s. 6d. The
rectory of Toller Fratrum is mentioned in the Commissioners'
returns for Dorsetshire: 'appropriat' monasterii de Mynchyn
Buckland in com' Soms ideo nichil hic oneratur' ; but in the
survey of the monastery neither the manor nor the rectory
of Toller Fratrum is mentioned. In this case again, the
property omitted from the V. E. was not lost to the Crown.[1]
Then one can refer to a Benedictine nunnery in Leicestershire,

[1] Mon. vi. 672; Grants, March, 31 H. VIII, n. 64 ; V. E. i. 246,
210-11.

Langley. Its survey for 28 H. VIII made by the Crown bailiff might be compared with the survey in the V. E. Many items of the income are found in both surveys—(the figures on the left are from the V. E., those on the right from Comp. Min. 28 H. VIII) :—

	£	s.	d.	£	s.	d.			£	s.	d.	£	s.	d.
Spiritualia	16	13	4	17	6	8	Hukilscote ...		0	7	0	0	12	0
demesnes	4	1	6	7	5	4¾	Tong	...	0	5	0	0	5	0
Diesworth	6	6	8	4	15	5	Charleston	...	0	16	0	0	14	8
Wilston ...	1	3	4	1	16	5	Belton	...	0	10	0	0	10	0
Dalby et Somerby	4	0	0	2	5	8	Redyngton	...	0	3	4	0	4	0

But in the bailiff's survey there are seven places, yielding a good income, which are *not* mentioned in the V. E.: viz. Kettelbe £0 11s. 0d., Prestewolde £0 2s. 0d., Villa Leic' £0 5s. 10d., Barkeby £6 0s. 8d., Belgrave £1 6s. 8d., Atslyffe £1 8s. 0d., Willoughby £1 4s. 4d. It is possible that some of these may have been parts of other possessions described in the V. E., and consequently that some of the figures in the V. E. are greater than those of the corresponding entries in the bailiff's account. There is no doubt that such places as Leic' Villa or Barkeby are simply omitted from the V. E.[1] But in this case, too, the property omitted in the V. E. was not lost to the Crown.

It may be thought that my remarks as to the completeness of the monastic surveys of 1535 are scarcely justified; and my conclusion, that the Commissioners on the whole described the income of the monasteries accurately, may be looked upon with still greater mistrust. With this I cannot agree. I began to study the Commissioners' returns with a strong prejudice, feeling sure I should find in them innumerable cases of concealment, or of too low a valuation of monastic property; but after having made a great many comparisons I was forced to acknowledge myself wrong.

The Valor Ecclesiasticus, in its double returns, furnishes some material for comparison ; and the existence of such double returns can sometimes be explained without difficulty. Many *Double returns.*

---

[1] V. E. iv. 176, and Mon. iv. 225-6.

large monasteries had 'cells', i. e. small monasteries dependent
upon the chief one.   These cells were often in some other
diocese or county, and so might be dealt with under two
different Commissions, one in the diocese of its chief
monastery and the other in its own diocese or county.
I found three instances of this, viz.:—Avecote, Warw.,
cell of Great Malvern, Worcester; Belvoir, Linc., cell of
St. Albans, Herts.; St. Leonard's, Stamford, cell of Durham
Cathedral.[1]

In the two returns for Avecote, the order of the items
and the spelling of proper names are different, but with the
exception of a trifling difference of 1s. in the valuation of the
demesne, the figures coincide.   Both the Commissions made
exactly the same valuation of this small monastery.   As
to Belvoir, the figure of its net income given in the detailed
valuation for Lincolnshire, when compared with the valuation
of the net income for Hertfordshire given in the Liber
Valorum, shows a slight but appreciable difference: £98 19s. 5d.
and £105 0s. 0d.   St. Leonard's, Stamford, is described in
detail in the survey of Durham Cathedral whose cell it is;
only the net income is given in the survey of Lincolnshire, and
the reader is at once referred to the Durham survey.   In spite
of this reference the figures of the net income do not quite
coincide: £25 1s. 2½d. as against £28 6s. 1½d.

The Oxford-shire returns. — All the other double returns are to be found in Oxfordshire.
In the three cases of Dorchester, Studley and Thame it is
possible to explain the presence of two parallel surveys in
one and the same way.[2]   One survey was evidently presented
to the Commissioners by the authorities of the monastery,
the other is a short digest of the first, made by the Commissioners.   In the survey of Dorchester made by the monks
the revenues are fully described; in that made by the Commissioners only the total of the gross income is given, namely
£217 5s. 9½d.: this, for some reason, is a little less than that
given by the monks, which is £219 12s. 0¾d.   But all the
twenty-six items of expenditure in the monks' survey have

---

[1] V. E. iii. 74, 272 ; i. 451 ; iv. 116–17 ; 142 ; v. 305–6.
[2] V. E. ii. 167, 170–71 ; 172, 186–7 ; 169, 213.

been adopted, and the Commissioners' survey of this expenditure is even fuller than that of the monks ; the latter for some
reason either do not mention or do not take into account
the fee of one clergyman, an item given and reckoned in the
Commissioners' survey at £4 6s. 8d.　In the survey of Thame
the numerous items of income given by the monks are
summed up by the Commissioners under five headings.　The
totals of two of these agree, and the totals of the other three
differ but slightly.　The Commissioners' give an item of £2,
derived from the sale of wood, which is omitted from the
monks' return ; and thus the figure of the gross income given
in the Commissioners' survey is increased by £2 6s. 6d., i. e.
from £293 14s. 11½d. to £296 1s. 5½d.　All the items of the
monks' expenditure are left unaltered ; the order and spelling
are varied as well as some verbal expressions, but the figures
remain unchanged.—In the monks' survey of Studley the items
of the income are similarly summed up under five headings ;
the figures of four of these coincide, but the figures of the
'spiritual' income differ ; the monastic survey has the figure
£16 16s. 11d. and the Commissioners £18 1s. 9d.　All the
twenty items of expenditure passed from the monastic survey
into that of the Commissioners, who, when making the digest
thereof, changed only the order and, in some instances, the
formula and the spelling.　The monks' survey is written
almost entirely in English and signed by the auditor of the
monastery ; the whole of the Commissioners' digest is in Latin
and signed by the Commissioners.　There is one curious
point of difference between the two.　The monks' survey mentions the following item of expenditure : 'feodum receptoris
omnium terrarum in comitatibus Bucks Oxon et Warr'
£1 6s. 8d.'　This item in the Commissioners' survey is expressed in the words : 'receptori reddituum in comitatibus
Bucks Oxon et Berks.'　The monastery had lands in
Warwickshire but none whatever in Berkshire.　The auditor
of the monastery, of course, knew perfectly well in what
counties the lands of his monastery were situated ; but it was
easy for the Commissioners to err whilst making the digest
in haste.　And yet they were not entirely dependent upon

the administration of the monastery, they knew how to raise the figure of the 'spiritual' income given to them.—It is certain that in a fourth case (Goring) the detailed survey was likewise made by the monastic authorities, and that the short one is a digest made by the Commissioners. The figures of the expenditure coincide in both surveys. The differences in the figures of income are more numerous than in the cases we have just examined. The gross income of the short survey (£67 9s. 6d.), however, exceeds that of the detailed survey by only £4.[1]

The Bruerne returns.

I do not understand why the monastery of Bruerne was surveyed twice in the Valor Ecclesiasticus.[2] Both surveys are detailed, but not to the same extent ; and there are important points of difference between them, so that neither could be the source of the other. One survey gives £171 9s. 1d. for the gross income and £141 7s. 11d. for the net : the corresponding figures in the other survey are £153 16s. 2d. and £135 10s. 10d. For the sake of convenience I shall call the first survey the 'high' one, and the other the 'low'. The 'low' has fourteen items of expenditure, all of which are found in the 'high' ; in twelve cases the figures coincide, in two the 'high' diminishes the amount of fees by £1. But on the other hand the 'high' has six items of expenditure amounting altogether to £12 1s. 6d., which are not to be found in the 'low'. Some of the items of income suggest that the surveys represent the monastic economy in different years. According to the 'high' survey the monks kept for their own use a meadow at Kyngham, valued at 4s. ; according to the 'low' this land at Kyngham is let for 4s. According to the 'high' only part of the demesne of the manor of Estlatch is let for £4, while the monks kept for themselves

---

[1] V. E. ii. 205-8, 168. For the monastery of St. Swithin, Winchester, we may compare the Commissioners' survey with the source from whence it was derived, namely, the survey made by the monastic authorities. In order to do this, V. E. ii. 2-3 must be compared with V. E. vi. App. vi-x = Exch. K. R. M. b. vol. 166. The figures in both surveys are very similar ; but the Commissioners made a great many corrections in the prior's survey which resulted in an increase of income and a decrease of expenditure. The Commissioners' returns from Hampshire are very short. Comparison points to their having been based upon accurate and painstaking work.

[2] V. E. ii. 201-4, 265-7.

a part of the demesne worth £2. According to the 'low' survey the whole demesne was let for £6 1s. 0d. Moreover, the monastery had holdings and lands in thirty different places let out. The rental figures agree in twenty-nine places and amount to £121 2s. 1d. ; the rental differs only in the case of Estlatch and that by a few pence only, the 'high' valuation being £2 6s. 8½d. and the 'low' £2 6s. 0d. Thus there is a wonderful similarity in the valuation of the holdings, and the fact is an eloquent testimony to the great exactness of the surveys.

Quite another picture is seen in the case of the so-called demesne *in manu*, that is to say, the land which the monks cultivated themselves. In the 'low' survey the income from wood is said to amount to £3 only ; according to the 'high' the wood yields £8 10s. 0d.—It is true that in two cases the demesne valuation is the same. The monks held in their hands the manor of Tangley which is twice valued at £4. The monks kept in their own hands many lands in Sewell which are twice estimated at £8. Only the 'high' survey indicates the area of these lands : viz. 120 acres of arable, 300 of pasture, and 20 of meadow land. But in two other cases there is a great difference between the surveys. In the 'high' one the demesne *in manu* in Bruerne itself is not surveyed, but only valued at £1 18s. 0d. In the 'low' the demesne is described under five headings and estimated at only £1 10s. 8d. The Sandbroke demesne *in manu* is described very briefly in the 'high' survey: 200 acres of arable land, 100 pasture and 20 meadow, the whole is valued at £10 11s. 4d. In the 'low' it is described very fully in sixteen items : 160 acres of arable land are mentioned, 129½ of meadow and pasture. The demesne is estimated at only £7 7s. 6d. Prima facie, the 'low' survey deserves the greater credit, as it describes separately so small an item as half an acre of meadow land attached to the chapel of Treton, and every one of the sixteen allotments is valued separately. The 'high' and short survey, however, is nearer the truth. The demesne of the monastery of Bruerne was surveyed soon after it had passed to

the Crown and the survey was preserved among the so-called
' Paper Surveys '.[1]

The figures given in it—both of the area and the income
—greatly exceed those given in the 'low', and even those
given in the 'high' survey in the V. E. The land area of
Sandbroke grange was fixed at 592 acres; the income of
the grange was estimated at £29 1s. 4d. In the V. E. ii.
201–7, Tangley mede consists of 10 acres, and in the P. S. of
18 acres. Yet we cannot say that the Paper Survey is open
to suspicion, for it is very full of detail ; neither would the
Crown surveyors have greatly exaggerated the area and
income of the land, as it would have been difficult to find
a buyer or a farmer to take land greatly over-estimated.
Nevertheless, a farmer was found to take this land under the
new valuation. In February, 1539, J. Bridges, *miles*, and
Th. Bridges, *armiger*, hired for twenty-one years the demesne
of the manor of Bruerne for £13 17s. 0d. and the grange of
Sandbroke for £35 2s. 8d.[2] We cannot, therefore, avoid the
conclusion that the demesne of Bruerne was estimated in the
V. E. much below its real value. How then can we explain
the striking difference between the inaccurate valuation of the
demesne and the exact valuation of the tenancies? This
arose from the very nature of the case. The monastic income
from the tenancies was a more or less fixed sum and easily
reckoned ; it was difficult, therefore, for the monks and their
servants to conceal its actual amount from the Commissioners.
The rent of freehold, copyhold or leasehold property was not
kept a secret ; the Commissioners could define its amount or
verify it by the cartularies, copies of the court-rolls and the
indentures of leases. No doubt, too, the bailiffs' accounts
furnished the Commissioners with material for checking the
valuation of the demesne *in manu* ; but it was difficult to
master. The bailiffs did not distinguish between the accounts
of the demesne and the accounts of the tenancies ; their aim

---

[1] Augm. O. Misc. b. v. 406, ff. 36–9.
[2] Exch. Augm. O. Part. for gr. 168, m. 1–2. I do not venture to affirm
that the valuation of Sandbroke is higher in the lease than in the Paper
Survey. It may be that the land was simply divided differently between
Sandbroke and Bruerne.

had been to ascertain and fix the balance, and not to show
the gross or net income from the demesne. The amount of the
income from the demesne depended upon many things : upon
the harvest, the repairs, the wood-felling, the selling and buying
of live stock ; and it varied considerably more than did the
receipts from customary rent or even from leaseholds. The
Commissioners naturally shrank from difficult work; it is
constantly pointed out that the demesne is now being valued
for the first time, and that this is being done according to the
oral testimony of the older inhabitants and not according to
the documents of the manorial records. The old inhabitants
would often give only an approximate valuation; or would
not tell the truth if for any reason they sympathized with
the monks.

Two parallel surveys of the Staffordshire monastery, Double
Burton-upon-Trent, occupy a peculiar place in the V. E.[1] returns for
One of them is an ordinary Commissioners' survey in which upon-
the figure £356 16s. 3½d. is given as the gross income, and Trent.
£267 14s. 3d. as the net. The Royal Tenth ought therefore to
be £26 15s. 5d. It is, however, estimated at £41 4s. 6d., and
the following note is entered : 'plus oneratur pro 14. 9. 1
per billam domini cancellarii.' If we add £14 9s. 1d. to
£26 15s. 5d. we get the same sum, £41 4s. 6d. Evidently
the Chancellor was not satisfied with the Commissioners'
survey of the monastery, and therefore procured another, in
which the net income was described as considerably more,
and the Tenth was accordingly increased. It is this additional
Chancellor's survey written on a separate sheet of paper that
is sewn into the roll of the Staffordshire Commission. This
additional survey has the signature ' Thomas Audeley miles
cancellarius '. Only the revenues of the monastery are given,
and concerning the allowances it is said : 'Memorandum to
deducte owte of thys boke the allowaunces according to the
olde boke.' By the 'olde boke' is meant, no doubt, the
Commissioners' survey. The Chancellor either did not verify
the allowances or did not find fault with them. But the

[1] V. E. iii. 144–8.

difference in the income is very great ; the net income in
the Chancellor's survey is increased by more than a half.
The income is divided into 'lay' and 'spiritual'. The chapel
of Caldon is added in the Chancellor's survey and the income
of three parish churches is increased ; the income from eight
spiritual items is left unaltered. In the result, the spiritual
income is increased from £85 5s. 0d. to £99 5s. 0d. The
difference in the lay income is greater. Only nineteen of the
forty-eight items in the Chancellor's survey agree with the
corresponding items in the Commissioners' survey, and these
amount to £123 16s. 8d. The figures of seventeen other
items exceed the corresponding items in the Commissioners'
survey, the total being £219 5s. 9½d., as against £147 14s. 7½d.
The remaining twelve items in the Chancellor's survey (with
a total of £71 11s. 7d.) cannot be traced at all in the Commissioners' survey. The result is that the lay income was
increased from £271 11s. 3½d. to £414 14s. 0½d.

The chief deficiency is the omission of the income attached
to the four monastic offices and of the two chapels called
after two deceased abbots. But besides these, the incomes
from four other places are omitted, and, strangest of all, there
is no mention of the considerable income from the landed
property in Bromley Abbatis. The valuation of the demesne
in manu is also increased, as well as that of the tenancies
and entire manors. Almost as strange is the difference in
the figures of the Anseley rent, £0 13s. 4d. and £13 5s. 4d.
The exact date of the additional survey I cannot give, and
I have not seen the MS. ; but this much is certain, that the
'new book' was compiled when Audley was Chancellor. It
was most likely written before the Dissolution of the larger
monasteries, for the property of the monastery in question
was still untouched. There is some ground to suppose
that the 'new book' was compiled at the end of 1535
or the beginning of 1536, at the time when a digest of
the Commissioners' surveys was being made by the Exchequer, for in the Commissioners' survey they do not
give the amount of the Tenth, but the figure is taken straight
from the Chancellor's survey. If we assign the Chancellor's

survey to 27 H. VIII, then we may regard it as indicating that too much reliance is not to be placed on the figures of the Valor Ecclesiasticus. If an additional survey could have increased by one half the net income of an important monastery, and the original Commissioners' survey could have omitted some estates of the monasteries and greatly decreased the income of others, doubts may reasonably be entertained in other cases; and before we can arrive at any conclusion as to the trustworthiness of the V. E. figures we must compare as large a number of cases as possible.

On July 20, 1536, the King commanded the Archbishop of Canterbury to send to the King's Chancery a list of all the benefices of the diocese, with the names of the incumbents and the amount of the net incomes. On October 31, 1536, Cranmer signed the list that was made in compliance with this order.[1] It is difficult to see for what reason a new valuation of the Canterbury benefices was required one year after the drawing up of the Commissioners' survey. If the Commissioners' valuation excited suspicion, a valuation directed by an ecclesiastic would scarcely have been regarded with greater credit. I do not attach much importance to the figures of Cranmer's survey, but in any case it is worth while to compare them with the Valor Ecclesiasticus. Cranmer's survey describes sixteen monasteries, but the net income of fifteen only is given. The latter survey is evidently quite independent of the earlier. The figures of the net income do not absolutely agree in any single instance. In two cases, however (Boxley and Combewell), the difference is one of a few pence only. In four instances, Cranmer's valuation is greater than that of the Commissioners, but only by some twenty pounds for all four. In the remaining nine Cranmer's valuation is less than the Commissioners' by about £350 for all the nine. On the whole, however, the two surveys are much alike. In the V. E. the net income of the monasteries in the diocese of Canterbury is slightly more than £5,500;

New valuation of Canterbury benefices.

---

[1] Cranmer's survey is printed in the V. E. i. 89–98.

Cranmer's survey reduces this sum by about £300. Difference
of opinion may exist with regard to the credibility of Cranmer's
figures; nevertheless, they certainly do not lessen our confidence in the V. E.

Suppres-
sion
Accounts. Only a few months after the last Commissioners' returns of
1535 had been sent in to the Exchequer, an Act of Parliament
gave to the Crown all the monasteries with an income not
exceeding £200. With a view of taking over the monasteries
for the Crown, special commissioners were sent to each county.
They received very detailed instructions, which, among other
things, ordered them to make a new survey of monastic
income, to compare the new valuation with the old one—that
is to say, with that in the V. E.—and to make a detailed
survey of the demesne of the monasteries. In the years
immediately following, when the larger monasteries began to
be surrendered to the Crown, the commissioners or Augmentations men who received them had also to make new surveys
and valuations. Portions of the accounts and demesne surveys compiled by these receivers are still extant.[1] It
remains to be considered to what extent we are justified
in relying upon them. The instructions to the receivers did
not in so many words direct that the new valuation was to be
higher than the old ; but the Government doubtless wished
and expected it to be so, and the receivers evidently felt ill
at ease when their valuation happened to be lower than that
of 1535. Whenever such a thing did happen, which was
very seldom, the commissioners excused themselves to their
superiors and gave some explanation of the decrease. In

---

[1] Instructions to the suppressors are to be found in Exch. Treas.
Receipt Misc. b. vol. 154, f. 48 ; Gairdner, x. 721 ; xi. app. 15. The
accounts of the commissioners who took over the monasteries are
preserved partly in the original and partly in copies. There are original
surveys for Leicestershire, Warwickshire, Rutland (Exch. Tr. Rec. M.
b. vol. 154, f. 48–65), Sussex (State Pap. Dom. Suppr. Pap., v. 3, n. 128),
Huntingdon (Cleop. E. iv. 336). Some copies evidently belonging to
the seventeenth century are to be found in Cotton MSS., Cleop. E.
iv, for Lancashire (342), and for some monasteries in Nottinghamshire
and Yorkshire (357). Detailed surveys of demesne made when the
monasteries were surrendered to the Crown are found in great numbers
among the so-called Paper Surveys. I shall speak of these more fully
later on.

the V. E. the net income of the monastery of Hastings is said to be £51 9s. 5½d.; the receivers gave it as £47 2s. 1½d. only, and immediately explain the decrease by the fact that some of the land in the Pesemerche is flooded by the sea. The net income for Olveston in 1535 was £161 14s. 2½d.; the commissioners of 1536 fixed it at £158 13s. 7½d., and added 'this is less than the last valuation because our instruction permits of allowances such as the Commissioners of Tenths did not take into account'.[1] When the monastery of Merkyate was taken over by the Crown, the auditor, Cavendish, fixed the income from the demesne at £18 5s. 3½d. only, while the V. E. had the sum of £20 5s. 11½d. A mistake in multiplication when reckoning the income from arable land was made in the V. E., and the income was returned as more than it ought to have been according to the accepted calculations of the time. Cavendish, however, did not consider himself warranted in lowering the 1535 valuation, and left untouched the figure £20 5s. 11½d., knowing it to be wrong.[2] In the survey of the demesne of the monastery of Wroxton, the auditor, Cavendish, and the receiver, Danaster, say that no one will lease a certain rectory at the valuation given in the V. E., but that they do not find it possible to change this valuation.[3] We see then that the tendency of the commissioners who took over the monasteries for the Crown, and of the Exchequer officials who were drawing up new surveys of the monastic demesnes, was to raise the income and so prove their zeal to the Government. They could not have done this very often, because their figures had

---

[1] St. Pap. Dom., Suppr. Pap. v. 3, n. 128 ; Exch. Tr. Receipt, M. b. v. 154, f. 41–55.

[2] Exch. Augm. O. Misc., b. v. 402, f. 11–12 : ' Sum of the demaynes as we have valuyd them is £18 5s. 3½d, and it neverthelesse we have certified the same to be worth as it is valuyd in the boke of the Tenth £20 5s. 11½d.' Compare V. E. iv. 209.

[3] Exch. Augm. O. Misc. b. v. 402, f. 43 : 'the parsonage of Wroxton and Balskett is valuyd at the first survey as it annswerith in the King[es] boke at 13. 16. 4., which he will not ferme (on the other side of this sheet is written the name of the man who wanted the lease : Galter' Reynesford de Wroxton, Oxon, ar(miger)), neverthelesse we have not dymynyssid ne augmentid the same personage on penny by the survey.'

to serve as the basis of the sales and leases of the 'dissolved' lands, and few buyers or tenants would be willing to pay according to an inflated valuation. If, on the other hand, the land remained in the hands of the Crown, the amount of the new valuation fixed the sum demanded by the Crown from the receiver, who, of course, would at once protest against the false and ruinous calculations forced upon him. We are therefore inclined to think that the figures of the Suppression Accounts and the surveys of the demesne are nearer the truth than the corresponding figures in the V. E., and so can be used in order to test the latter.

Suppression Accounts. In the original returns of the commissioners who took over the small monasteries, the old and the new totals of the net income for Leicestershire, Rutland, Warwickshire, and Sussex, are given side by side; it is not known how the new total was received. For Huntingdonshire, the new income and the increment—that is to say, the amount by which the new total exceeds the old—are given. I have deducted this increment in order to find the figure of the old income, and have prepared the following tabulated list of all the totals of the old and new valuation; the figure on the left is that of the V. E., the figure on the right is that of the Suppression Accounts. The monasteries are given according to their respective counties :—

LEICESTERSHIRE.

	£	s.	d.	£	s.	d.
Bradley	20	3	4	20	2	4
Garendon	159	19	10½	218	2	11
Grace Dieu	92	3	9½	97	8	11¼
Kirby Beller	142	10	3¼	143	12	4
Langley	29	7	4½	40	8	11
Olveston	161	14	2½	158	13	7½
Ulverscroft	83	10	6½	85	11	0
	689	9	4¾	764	0	0¾

RUTLAND.

	£	s.	d.	£	s.	d.
Broke	40	0	0	46	18	9½

WARWICKSHIRE.

				£	s.	d.	£	s.	d.
Coventry Charterhouse	...	...		161	6	8	201	7	6
Erdbury	...	...	...	93	6	1	100	5	5½
Henwood	...	...	...	21	2	0½	23	14	3½
Maxstoke	...	...	...	87	13	3½	112	9	4½
Pinley	...	...	...	23	5	10	25	5	5
Pollesworth	...	...	...	87	16	3	110	6	2
Stoneleigh	...	...	...	151	0	3½	208	3	1½
Studley	...	...	...	117	1	5½	141	4	9½
Warwick St. Sepulchre's	...	...		41	10	2	42	7	4½
Wroxall	...	...	...	72	15	6	62	2	0½
				856	17	7	1027	5	6½

SUSSEX.

				£	s.	d.	£	s.	d.
Boxgrove	...	...	...	75	12	3½	82	9	3½
Dureford	...	...	...	98	4	5	98	17	9
Hastings	...	..	...	51	9	5½	47	2	1½
Michelham	...	...	...	160	12	6	163	14	6
Shulbred	...	...	...	72	15	10½	75	17	6½
Tortington	...	...	...	75	12	3½	82	9	3½
				534	6	10	550	10	11

HUNTINGDONSHIRE.

				£	s.	d.	£	s.	d.
Huntingdon	...	...	...	187	13	8¼	217	6	11¼
Sawtre	...	...	...	141	3	8	176	19	2
Stonely	...	...	...	46	0	5½	51	19	6½
				374	17	9¾	446	5	7¾

If we add together the totals for all the five counties we Northern surveys. shall get the sums £2495 11s. 7½d. and £2835 0s. 6½d. The valuation of 1536 exceeds that of 1535 by only 13½ per cent., and when we remember that the figures compared refer to twenty-seven monasteries, and that it was in the interest of the commissioners of 1536 to increase their predecessors' valuation, the result of the comparison must be pronounced favourable to the Valor Ecclesiasticus. It is true that the totals will be considerably altered if we take into consideration the accounts of three northern counties which are preserved only in a copy of a later date. I give below the figures of the two valuations.[1]

[1] The copy gives the two valuations for Lancashire ; for Nottinghamshire and Yorkshire it gives only the new valuation. I give the valuation of 1535 according to the V.E., but the totals as worked out by myself from the items, and not the totals found in the V.E. ; my totals, however, differ but slightly from those given in the MS.

LANCASHIRE.

				£	s.	d.	£	s.	d.
Burscough	...	...	...	80	7	6	122	5	7
Cartmell	...	...	...	91	6	3	212	12	10½
Cockersand	...	...	...	157	14	0½	282	7	7½
Conishead	...	...	...	97	0	2	161	5	9
Holland	...	...	...	53	3	4	78	12	9
				479	11	3½	857	4	7

NOTTINGHAMSHIRE.

				£	s.	d.	£	s.	d.
Worksop	...	...	...	246	8	5	291	9	4

YORKSHIRE.

				£	s.	d.	£	s.	d.
Byland	...	...	...	238	9	4	364	0	3½
Ellerton	...	...	...	62	8	10	74	15	8
Kirkham	...	...	...	269	5	9	421	5	6
Monk-Bretton	...	...	...	239	9	6½	246	16	4
Rievaulx	...	...	...	278	10	2	426	2	11
				1038	3	7½	1533	0	8½

The difference between the two groups of counties is very considerable, and strikingly so between the individual counties. For six monasteries in Sussex the new valuation exceeds the old only by 3 per cent. For five monasteries in Lancashire the new valuation is almost twice as much as the old. To what are we to attribute such a contrast? I can but make suggestions. It may be that not the Commissioners of 1535 only, but also those of 1536, are guilty of inaccuracy. It may be that the receivers of the monasteries in 1536 worked more zealously in the North, and noticed more deficiencies and cases of undervaluation in the V. E. than did their colleagues in the South. It is possible, too, that in the returns for the three northern counties not quite the same thing is understood by 'net income', and that the allowance out of the gross income of such expenses as are taken into consideration in the other counties is not made in the case of the northern. And, unfortunately, the Suppression returns of the three northern counties have come down to us in a later and not very trustworthy copy. Speaking generally, it might be safer to leave them entirely out of consideration; I trust, however, that I have been discreet in the use that

I have made of them. The V. E. is my chief authority,
and I had to be especially careful in forming my judgement
about it. I had to consider all the indications unfavourable to
it, even if they came from an untrustworthy source. Besides,
there are reasons for thinking that the Survey of 1535 was
really much more carelessly made in the northern counties
than in the rest of England. In the North the areas of
counties and dioceses were larger, the population more
scattered, the country less known and more wild than in the
South. If, therefore, the Government wished the northern
surveys to be accurate they ought to have appointed a greater
number of Commissioners for those counties. But we learn
from the complaints of the northern Commissioners that some
of their colleagues were engaged for a long time at work in
other places, and that the number of men on the northern
Commissions was less than elsewhere. It seems that it is just
these northern surveys that were especially late, in spite of
the Commissioners' haste : and it is from a northern diocese
that we hear about the deficiencies in the surveys and get
a list of omissions. If the monastic income in the North was
estimated at too low a figure, there is nothing in this to
wonder at.

It is not only the Suppression Accounts that lead us to
doubt the accuracy of the figures of the Valor Ecclesiasticus
for the northern counties; upon other grounds we are led
to the same conclusion. Let us compare the survey of the
monastery of Whalley in Lancashire as given in the V. E. with
four other surveys of different dates.[1] Two surveys were
made by the monastic authorities before the Dissolution
(1478, 1521), for their own use, and one can scarcely doubt
their accuracy. Two others were compiled for the Crown
after the Dissolution (29 H. VIII, 36 H. VIII). But in
36 H. VIII part of the monastic lands had been already
disposed of by the Crown, and the valuation of that year is
consequently worthless so far as the total income is concerned. The following are the figures of the gross income
of the first four surveys in their chronological order:—

Pre-reformation surveys of northern monasteries.

[1] Whitaker, i. 116–20, 191–1 ; V. E. v. 227–30; Mon. v. 650–1.

£632 4s. 10d., £895 6s. 2d., £551 4s. 6d. (V. E.), £1,113 4s. 10½d. Thus the gross income as given in the V. E. amounts to scarcely half that of the survey made only two years later.

It is still more strange that the gross income of the V. E. is much lower than in 1521, and a little lower even than in the survey of 1478. The total of the gross income in the V. E. is certainly wrong and must be considerably increased. Especially bad is the mistake about the spiritual income, as will be seen if we compare all the five surveys. Thus:—

Ecclesiae	1478			1521			V. E.			29 H. VIII			36 H. VIII		
	£	s.	d.	£	s.	d.	£	s.	d.	£	s.	d.	£	s.	d.
Whalley	129	4	4	228	11	8	91	6	8	318	18	5½	237	13	4
Blackburn	89	16	9	133	1	0	74	6	8	136	18	9	139	2	2
Rochdale	64	0	0	111	0	1	49	13	4	96	6	1	102	0	7
Eccles et Deyne ...	73	17	5½	119	10	4½	57	2	0	116	1	2½	114	18	8
	356	18	6½	592	3	1½	272	8	8	668	4	6	593	14	9

For the gross temporal income the difference in the totals of the first four surveys is somewhat less:—£275 5s. 3½d., £303 3s. 0½d., £278 15s. 10d., £445 0s. 4d. For some localities (Croynton, Mawnton, Standen) the figures of the temporal gross income agree or are similar in all the four surveys; in other localities (Cliderhow, Stanyng) the V. E. figures are less than those of a later survey, but more than the figures of 1478 and 1521; the difference between the figures can then be explained to a great extent, if not entirely, by an increase of the income from the land and is not referable to bad faith or mistake on the part of the surveyors. All the same, the fact remains that the total of the gross temporal income in the V. E. is much too low.

Paper Surveys of northern monasteries.　The detailed Exchequer Surveys of the demesne, the so-called Paper Surveys, point to the same conclusion. In the V. E. the northern counties are surveyed with much less exactness than the others. This will readily be seen if we compare the valuation of the demesne of thirty-two monasteries as given in the V. E. with that in the Paper Surveys. Five of these monasteries were in Yorkshire, the other twenty-seven lie more to the south, most of them in the midland counties. The valuation of the demesne in the V. E. for these twenty-seven monasteries is £620 0s. 1½d., and in the Paper Surveys £656 16s. 8¼d. ; a difference of about 6 per cent. For the five Yorkshire monasteries the valuation of the demesne in the V. E. is £63 0s. 4d., and in the Paper Surveys £98 15s. 10d. ; a difference of about 57 per cent.[1]

The valuations, then, of the net income in the Suppression Accounts for the three northern counties (Notts., Yorks., Lancashire) must be taken into consideration and added to the totals of the five other counties (Leicester, Rutland, Warwickshire, Sussex, Huntingdon) as given above: and the result is that the net income of thirty-eight monasteries in the V. E. is given as £4,309 14s. 11½d., and in the Suppression Accounts as £5,516 18s. 2d. The valuation of 1536 is higher than that of 1535 by a quarter or thereabouts. This is certainly a considerable difference, but it does not render the use of the Valor Ecclesiasticus unjustifiable. And we must not forget that part of the difference can be explained by the growth of the income of the land, while indications from other sources are in favour of the Valor.

Let us proceed to consider these other sources.

The Suppression Accounts utilized above can only serve in a comparison of the surveys of the lesser monasteries in the Valor Ecclesiasticus, for in the year 1536 only such houses as had an income not exceeding £200 were surrendered to the Crown. Let us see whether our conclusion holds good with regard to the valuation of the larger monasteries in the V. E. In order to answer this question we must go further afield, and examine the Suppression surveys of some of the larger monasteries. The famous Glastonbury

Suppression Account for Glastonbury.

---

[1] The tabulated list from which I have taken these figures will be found on p. 60–1. It is curious that for the northern counties—Yorkshire, e. g.—a similar result is arrived at when the V. E. is compared with the Particulars for Grants (vide table, p. 69). It is to be observed, however, that the monastic income is not depreciated in all the northern surveys of the Valor. As seen from the figures given above, the valuation of Ellerton and Monk-Bretton in the Suppression Accounts differs but slightly from that of the V. E. We may also instance the figures of a rich Yorkshire monastery, Fountains, the gross income of which is given in the V. E. as £1,178 19s. 3½d., and the net as £1,004 5s. 4½d. (v. 253–4) ; the Suppressors fixed its gross income at £1,239 6s. 3½d. and the net at £1,115 18s. 2d. (Burton, 143–7).

survey made by two 'Augmentations men', Pollard and Moyle, after the tragic end of the monastery, probably offers the best material for such comparison.[1] Pollard and Moyle themselves compare their figures with the totals in the Valor Ecclesiasticus, and point out with evident satisfaction that they have succeeded in considerably raising the income as compared with the 1535 valuation. Whereas the Commissioners of Tenths fixed the gross income of the monastery at £3,508 13s. 4¾d., Pollard and Moyle, without increasing the rent of the tenants by one penny, raised the gross income to the figure of £4,227 1s. 2⅜d., and thus made it more than the former by £718 7s. 9⅝d. If they were not mistaken, their valuation exceeds that of 1535 by nearly one-fifth. As a matter of fact, however, their reckoning is not accurate. The correct total of the gross income, according to their own survey, must be £4,224 0s. 1¼d. and not £4,227 1s. 2¾d. Again,—and this is more serious—the figure £3,508 13s. 4¾d., given by them, is by no means the gross income of the Valor Ecclesiasticus.   The figure £3,508 13s. 4¾d. in the V. E. was arrived at only after a number of deductions from the gross income had been made.   The actual gross income in the V. E. is £3,642 3s. 0⅜d., and Pollard and Moyle's valuation gives an increase of £581 17s. 0⅞d., that is, less than one-sixth. It is true that the difference between the *net* income as given by the receivers and the Valor Ecclesiasticus appears to be more considerable, and amounts to £770 9s. 5⅝d. (Pollard and Moyle give £773 19s. 4½d. which is an error.) But the difference is increased only because Pollard and Moyle leave out many allowances which were admitted into the Valor Ecclesiasticus ; for instance, so great an expenditure as £145 16s. 8d. for alms. Speaking generally, the figures of the gross income give more trustworthy material for comparison than do the totals of the net income ; it is possible that the Suppression Accounts of the small monasteries would prove more favourable to the V. E. if the figures of the gross and net incomes were given there side by side.   In any case the Glaston-

[1] Pollard and Moyle's survey is printed in Mon. i. 10–21 ; the survey of 1535 in the V. E. i. 142–7.

bury survey does not increase any mistrust of the V. E. which
may have been occasioned by the Suppression Accounts of the
small monasteries; on the contrary it may tend to diminish
it. And the Glastonbury case is very significant. Pollard and
Moyle evidently wished to reveal the mistakes or blunders of
their predecessors; and Glastonbury, in the V. E., was the richest
monastery in the whole kingdom except Westminster Abbey.

Both the surveys of Glastonbury are so detailed that they
enable us to carry the comparison further, and to establish a few
conclusions which, though of a less general character, are perhaps yet more important.[1] I shall not analyse the spiritual
income, which amounts to £352 in the V. E. and in Pollard
and Moyle is raised to £460 (gross income). In both surveys
the temporal income is divided between some sixty places,
mostly manors. In each survey several places are mentioned
that are not found in the other; but such places are not
numerous, and the income attached to them is small (V. E. £24,
P. M. £22). More than fifty places are found in both surveys,
and these can be easily arranged on parallel lines. Pollard
and Moyle could not find any places of importance entirely
omitted by the Commissioners of 1535. The income is
naturally divided into the income from demesne, income from
rent (redditus et firmae tenementorum), income from wood,
income from court (perquisitiones et fines terrarum). But the
P. M. survey is less detailed, and for seventeen places gives only
the totals of the gross income, while the V. E. divides the income into items; consequently these seventeen places have to
be put aside (V. E. £925, P. M. £1078). Again, in six cases
one of the two surveys separates the income from demesne
from that from rent, and the other combines them; in these
cases also these incomes have to be excluded from the general
account (V. E. £314, P. M. £327). With regard to the remaining items the following results present themselves : (*a*) Income
from demesne V. E. £237, P. M. £336. (*b*) Income from wood
V. E. £62, P. M. £136. (*c*) Income from courts V. E. £267,
P. M. £398. (*d*) Income from rent V. E. £1454, P. M. £1468.

Pollard-Moyle survey.

---

[1] As I proceed I shall give the figures of the pounds only, and leave
out the shillings and pence. P. M. = Pollard and Moyle.

Income
from
demesne.

(*a*) The amount given by P. M. is almost twice as much as
that of the V. E. This is partly occasioned by two omissions
in the V. E. The London holdings of the Abbot, omitted
from the V. E., are valued at £3 6s. 8d. in P. M.; perhaps by
these holdings is meant the house in which the Abbot used
to stay during his visits to London. The fishing in the
Mere, not even mentioned in the V. E., is valued in P. M. at
£26 13s. 4d.—presumably the monks did not let the fishing
because they needed the fish themselves. Another cause of
the great difference between the figures of the V. E. and P. M.
is evidently the under - valuation of lands situated around
the monastery itself, which for the most part were not let in
1535. This demesne is valued in the V. E. at £53 and in
P. M. at £94. The rest of the demesne was let in 1535, and
there is very little difference in its valuation. In fourteen
cases out of twenty the figures are identical; in three cases
the difference between the two rents is infinitesimal;
in the three remaining cases the difference in the rental
figures is very great. But there is no reason to believe
that in these cases the Commissioners of 1535 were either
unconsciously or deliberately wrong. It is reasonable to suppose that after 1535 long leases expired, and that the demesne
was let at a higher rent in accordance with the alterations in
land values.

Income
from
wood.

(*b*) The figure given by P. M. is more than twice as much as
that of the V. E., and creates a natural mistrust as to the latter.
In the case of Budleigh the difference is especially great, the
V. E. giving £2 17s. 1d. and P. M. £50 0s. 0d. Unfortunately
the figures of the income from woods in P. M. are not always
trustworthy. Several times Pollard and Moyle themselves point
out that they do not give the actual income from woods of the
last year, nor the average income from woods of the past few
years, but an income which they think might be realized if the
woods were properly managed. Evidently, when calculating the
possible income, they acted in a very arbitrary way. Sometimes the figure they give for the income from woods is considerably lower than that given in the V. E. The wood in Pulton
brings in an income, according to the V. E., of £6 15s. 8½d.,

according to P. M. the income is only 10s., although the woodland area is reckoned to be 146 acres. Again, Pollard and Moyle
in their survey not only pointed out a possible income from
wood, but even tried to estimate the value of all the growing
wood. They say that the wood in Budleigh is worth £898, and
they think that this capital value ought to bring in an income of
£50 ; that is, more than 5½ per cent. They estimate the value
of the woodland area in the manor of Glastonbury at £543:
but for some reason they think that this capital can yield an
income of only £1 10s. 0d., that is a little more than ¼ per cent.
The amount (£8 2s. 2d.) given in the V. E. as the income from
woods for this area seems much more probable. It is difficult
to say why the Budleigh wood seemed to Pollard and Moyle
twenty times as profitable as that of Glastonbury.[1] I do not,
by any means, wish to defend the figures of the income from
wood given in the V. E. ; they seem to me to be too low and
open to suspicion. At the same time it seems clear that all
the calculations of income from wood in the sixteenth century
were exceedingly arbitrary.

(c) The figure given by P. M. is almost twice as much as Income
that in the V. E. Here again the figures of P. M. seem to have from courts.
the semblance of truth. Pollard and Moyle very often say
that they give the actual income from courts of the last year.
It is very probable that the amount given in the V. E. is too
low, though it is most likely not so far from the truth as it
seems to be at first sight. The income from Courts was not an
unvarying sum ; it altered much every year according to the
number and amount of amercements and admission fines.
Moreover, the years immediately following the surrender of
the monastic property to the Crown were not years of
normal manorial life. The Government might proclaim, as
much as it liked, its firm intention to safeguard the interests
of third parties, but the conservative assurances of revolu-
tionaries, and the 'official informations' of despotic govern-
ments on the path of revolution, are seldom regarded with

---

[1] It should, however, be pointed out that it is not only possible but
probable that £1 10s. 0d. does not represent the whole of the income
from woods of this manor.

confidence, and this is not unnatural.   For the tenants of
monastic property, especially for the ignorant country people,
the Dissolution was a dangerous change, if not a catastrophe ;
it caused great anxiety, gave rise to numerous legends, and
evoked an eager desire for legal security.   Before the eyes of the
lower classes the immemorial rights of the rich and influential
landlords had been swept away by a single Act of Parliament
which was very rapidly passed through both Houses ; it is
hardly likely that accounts of the parliamentary discussion
could have reached the remote country places.   The monks,
of course, tried to persuade the local population that their
downfall was but the beginning of a general destruction ; but
not every one believed them.   On the contrary, there were
many who hoped to profit by the partitioning of the monastic
wealth.   But when the Suppressors came and sent away the
monks with their numerous retinue—when they hired locally,
or brought with them workmen to break the walls and to melt
the bells—when all the monastic goods were being sold, and
the cups and images that until now had been objects of pious
worship were placed on the dirty scales of the valuer ; and
especially when the Suppressors required all the copies of
court rolls and all the indentures to be verified, and com-
menced to compile a ‘ new ’ survey, which very often became
an increased one—then a feeling of dismay must have crept
into the souls of the bravest among the copyholders and leaseholders.   The people naturally wished to get rid as soon as
possible of the anxious suspense of a state of transition, and to
secure their rights from the hands of their new landlord or his
representative.   A ‘ copy ’ or a ‘ lease ’ might be as yet far from
expiring, but to a timid tenant it would seem safer to exchange
the old title for a new one, and by means of a new admission
and fine to shelter under the aegis of the new lord.   Another
cause of increase of rental during these early years was the
letting of such lands as hitherto had been managed by the monks
themselves.   It is likely enough that the income from courts during these years may have considerably exceeded the average
amount, and therefore if we want to use the figures in verification of those of the V. E. they must be to some extent modified.

(*d*) The differences between the V. E. and P. M. that I have Rent noted above, have an important bearing on the criticism of the income. Valor Ecclesiasticus, and compel us to regard with some suspicion its figures for the income from demesnes, woods, and courts.   But no less important is the almost entire agreement in the figures of the income from rent, the chief item in the monastic budget.   The sum of £1,454 given in the V. E. is raised to only £1,468 in P. M., and even this trifling increase is fictitious, as the Suppressors themselves confess.   Pollard and Moyle introduced into their deductions from the gross income among other things the sum of £32 0s. 8d., accounted for by the decrease of rents on the decayed tenements and on such lands as were let by the monastery at a lower rent than usual.   If we compare the figures of the income from rent for separate localities, we shall see that P. M.'s figures almost always exceed those of the V. E., but the increase is as a rule very small.   We may well believe that the V. E. takes into consideration the decay of tenements, and shows only that amount of rent which was actually paid by the tenants, while Pollard and Moyle everywhere put down the full estimate of the rent, which had actually decreased in many places, and from which they themselves were forced to make a general allowance of £32.   A detailed comparison of the two Glastonbury surveys brings us to the same conclusion as that at which we arrived in the case of the three Bruerne surveys.   The valuation given in the V. E. of that land which the monks themselves managed may be regarded with justifiable suspicion.   But the figures of the customary and leasehold rents given in the V. E. must be acknowledged to be accurate.   This is a strong argument in favour of a systematic study of the Valor Ecclesiasticus, for the rents constituted a very large part of the monastic revenue.

We have only to look at the V. E. to find the explanation of the fact that the figures of the income from rent are more trustworthy than those of the income from demesne. When the Commissioners were estimating the income from the monastic demesne in hand, they had to consider a complex mass of data and not merely single facts.   They had to ascertain the quantity and quality of the land, the local prices,

the cost of production, the profit of secondary items and many
other things. The Commissioners, through lack of time, were
compelled to rely either upon the word of the monks or on
local testimony. The former naturally sought to minimize the
income, and the statements of the neighbours might also be
biased. The fact that there existed no old valuations on which
the Government could rely, and that everything had to be done
for the first time, increased the difficulties of the situation. All
these considerations are urged by the Commissioners in their
notes ; and it is not to be wondered at if many of the valuations
of the demesne were much below the actual amount.[1] With
rents and leases things were much more simple. In order to
ascertain their amount, or to verify the data given by the monks,
the Commissioners had only to require from the tenants the
original leases and the rentals. In such cases there was no
scope for imagination or estimate, the documents themselves
being sufficient to establish the actual amount of the tenants'
payments. And indeed, there are clear traces in the V. E.
showing that the Commissioners did actually make use of the
original documents to ascertain the rent paid by the tenants.[2]
There is also some indirect information as to this. The
Valor Ecclesiasticus not infrequently speaks of 'the decay
of rents' ; and we find stated not only the usual amount
of the rent but also the sum by which it falls below the
estimate. I can explain the presence of these double
figures only by supposing that the Commissioners extracted
the estimated figures from deeds, and made deductions

---

[1] The figure of the income from the demesne in hand is not infrequently called the *estimate* (appreciatio, estimatio) ; sometimes it is
pointed out in the same sense that the demesne brings in the income
named in average years (communibus annis). In the Northamptonshire
surveys there is usually a reference to the fact that the monastic demesne
had never before been valued ('scitus et terre dominicales nunquam prius
arrentate et modo per visum inquisitionem et scrutationem tam com-
missionariorum quam per homines iuratos valuatae'). The Commissioners
often admit that they have not valued the demesne themselves. Sometimes they rely on information supplied by the monks, as, for instance, at
Waverley, Surrey. In other cases they entrust the valuation to the
inhabitants of the place. This was done, for instance, in the case of
Stoneleigh, Warw.
[2] V. E. ii. 193 ; Tew Magna, ii. 195 ; N. Morton, iv. 212 ; Oborne, iv.
204 ; villa Bedford, iv. 209 ; Markeyat, iv. 209.

if the monks succeeded in proving arrears to be unavoidable.[1]

As to the Wiltshire manors of the abbey of Glastonbury, the figures given in the V. E. can be verified in another way. In the eighth and ninth years of Henry VIII's reign, when there was no question either about the Tenth or the Dissolution, Richard Beer, Abbot of Glastonbury, made a very detailed survey of the monastic property. This work was done for the monks themselves and not for the King's receivers. A proprietor who wishes to know the exact amount of his revenues has no reason for concealing his property or minimizing his revenue from it. There was no Government to hurry the Abbot, and the work could be executed in greater detail than the Crown Survey of 1535. The Glastonbury terrier of 1518 is therefore a very trustworthy source of information. Only a part, however, of this survey is now extant, and this relates to some Wiltshire manors and to one in Berkshire.[2]

The comparison I have just made between the Valor Ecclesiasticus and Pollard's survey will no doubt have more weight if both surveys are compared with Abbot Richard's terrier. We can compare the income from the demesne in eight manors. In the case of four manors the leasehold rent for the demesne is the same in all the surveys (Grutleton, Kyngton, Aishbury,

Margin note: Pre-reformation Glastonbury terrier.

---

[1] The decay of rents is mentioned in many places in the survey of St. Augustine's, Canterbury. For instance, i. 19: 'Hamellis redditus. Redditus ibidem valet in onere ballivi sive receptoris £21 0s. 0d. Inde in decasu redditus ibm £3 19s. 6d.' In the survey of Shene, Surrey, 'decasus redditus' is found four times and 'decasus pensionis' five times. In the survey of Dover, Kent, 'the rents decayed and not paid of long tyme' are put aside into a separate division (i. 54). In the survey of St. Augustine's, Canterbury, rents are mentioned which were never received by the monastery in 1535, e.g. i. 18: 'Plomstede redditus. Redditus ibm olim valebat annuatim in onere ballivi sive receptoris £20 0s. 0d. modo nichil inde recipitur sed respectuatur quia marisci ibidem inundantur aqua maris.'

[2] The MS. is in the British Museum (Harl. MSS. 3961). On the second sheet there is a note: 'Henrici Spelman militis bought in Mr. Rawlinson's sale Oxford.' I do not venture to decide whether it is the original terrier or an early copy. If it is a copy it was made before the Dissolution. In the manor of Kington, among the freeholders, 'Abbas de Malmesbury' is mentioned who pays 10d. (f. 42) of rent. Against the 10d. there is a note in the margin in another writing of later date: 'prius. modo nihil quia dno regi in curia augment.' Cf. f. 65. A part of the MS. is printed by Hoare in his 'Wiltshire'. The letter B. is used in what follows for this terrier.

Badbury). In the case of Cristmalford the figure of the
lease of the demesne is the same in B. and V. E. ; in P. M. the
income from the demesne is combined with that from rent. In
the case of Winterborne the lease is somewhat lower in B. than
in the other two surveys (B. £10 0s. 10d., V. E. £12 0s. 10d.,
P. M. £12 0s. 10d.). In the case of Domerham only the acreage is given in B. and not the rent, but the figures of the V. E.
and P. M. differ widely (£28 9s. 4d., £42 14s. 8d.) ; almost the
whole of the immense demesne was in 1518 still in the hands of
the monks and therefore its income in money was at that time
but small ; the monks, we may suppose, ceased to manage it
only a short time before the Valor Ecclesiasticus was compiled,
and for the first lease of the demesne they very likely took
only a small rent.

The survey of the demesne of Idmiston is very instructive
in the terrier ; the figures given in the V. E. and P. M. in the
case of this demesne differ widely (£2 0s. 0d. and £8 13s. 4d.).
The terrier shows that the V. E. figure (£2 0s. 0d.) is not
arbitrary. The demesne of Idmiston is divided into two parts.
In 1518, 541½ acres of arable land, meadow and enclosed
ground were let to a local villain for the low rent of £2 : in the
V. E. we evidently have the same lease and the same rent.
But besides this there were in Idmiston many mountain
pastures the income from which is entirely omitted from the
V. E. but is found in P. M. ; P. M.'s figure for Idmiston is therefore the more trustworthy. The income from woods can be compared in the case of five manors. In three cases B. and P. M.
show the woodland area in acres, and in each the B. figure is the
larger (36 and 24 ; 400 and 300 ; 275 and 200). The amount
of the income from woods in B. exceeds that given in the V. E.
for all the five manors, and exceeds that given in P. M. for four
manors (£1 13s. 4d., £1 9s. 4d., £1 0s. 0d. ; £10 0s. 0d.,
£1 1s. 0d., £6 0s. 0d. ; £16 13s. 4d., £2 13s. 8d., £5 0s. 0d. ;
£10 16s. 0d., £8 2s. 4d., £6 0s. 0d. ; £20 0s. 0d., £13 2s. 5d.,
£26 0s. 10d.). The terrier, therefore, shows us that the figures
of the income from woods in the V. E. are untrustworthy and
much too low, and that those in Pollard and Moyle are nearer
the actual amount. But we must add that the terrier, like

Pollard and Moyle's survey, does not give the actual receipts from woods for the last year, but such an income as could be realized if the woods were properly managed ('si ista ordinacio bene et diligenter observetur'). I have compared the income from rent for four manors. The figures given in the three surveys for Netylton, Kyngton, and Idmiston, differ very slightly. The difference in the Domerham figures is more considerable: B. £81 4s. 11½d., V. E. £90 12s. 5½d., P. M. £93 15s. 0½d. But if the receipts from rents are lower in the terrier than at the time of the Dissolution, this may perhaps be accounted for not by actual alterations in the rent, but by the supposition that in 1518 not all the *works* of the tenant had been commuted into money rents. On the whole, the terrier, with all the weight of its authority, confirms the conclusions at which we arrived when we compared the Valor Ecclesiasticus with Pollard and Moyle's survey. In the V. E. the figures of the income from woods are low and suspicious; the figures of the leases for demesnes are in most cases accurate; and the figures of the receipts from tenants' rents even more so.

The Paper Surveys enable us to verify only the valuation of Paper monastic demesnes in the V. E. But it was just in making Surveys. and V. E. a valuation of the lands which still remained in the hands of the monks that the Commissioners of 1535 had no trustworthy guide before them, and therefore could and did actually make many mistakes. The Paper Surveys deserve our attention also because they describe the demesnes very fully, point out the division of land into arable, wood, pasture and meadow, and give the area and the valuation of each kind of land. In those cases where the V. E. also gives particulars of the monastic demesne we are able to compare not only the totals but even the separate items of income, and the areas of the different pieces of land. But in using the collection of the Paper Surveys we have to be very careful. Some of these surveys are merely copies of corresponding passages in the Valor Ecclesiasticus; as, for instance, those of Stratford-at-Bow and of Stone.[1] In other cases there is not indeed perfect

[1] Mon. vi. 121-2=V. E. i. 409, Augm. O. M. b. 398, f. 60-1=V. E. iii. 113-14.

agreement between the V. E. and the Paper Surveys, but a great many coincidences that lead us to believe that the V. E. is one of the sources of the later survey; such is the survey of Dureford in the twenty-eighth year of Henry's reign.[1] I leave out of consideration all such cases; if the V. E. is the source of the later demesne survey, then certainly this later survey cannot be used to verify the figures in the V. E. But even in the cases where the Paper Surveys do not depend upon the V. E., I could not always feel certain that I was comparing the same 'parcels', and several times I was obliged to give up the attempt. In the tabulated list given below, the demesne valuations taken from the V. E. and the Paper Surveys are compared in the case of thirty-two monasteries. Many of the Paper Surveys have no date: those that are dated belong mostly to 28 H. VIII; the latest date is 31 H. VIII (Whitby); but the undated surveys were made either at the time of the Suppression or very soon after, for they are of exactly the same type as the dated ones and are signed by the same auditors.[2]

County.	Monastery.	Demesne.			Value.			Reference.	
		V. E.			P. S.			V. E.	P. S.
		£	s.	d.	£	s.	d.		
Beds.	Bushmead	10	0	0	20	1	4	iv. 200	402, 4–6
	Merkyate	18	14	3½	18	2	4	iv. 209	402, 11–12
Bucks.	Burnham	11	0	2	12	2	5	iv. 220	402, 21–2
	Lavenden	14	12	6	14	11	8	iv. 241	402, 17
	Marlow P.	4	1	7	5	16	6	iv. 250	406, 4–5
	Missenden	6	8	0	9	10	6	iv. 246	406, 9–11
	Nutley ...	26	18	4	19	14	8	iv. 232	406, 12–13
Heref.	Aconbury	5	0	0	8	10	0	iii. 17–18	399, 155
	Clifford ...	8	9	0	10	14	2	iii. 30	399, 137–8

[1] V. E. vi. app. xiii–xiv (=R. and S. Portf. $\frac{15}{32}$) is the survey of the monastery of Dureford dated Aug. 15., 28. H. VIII; the corresponding survey of 1535 is found in the V. E. i. 321. The chief difference between the surveys is that the V. E. gives only the total of the income from demesne, and the 1536 survey divides the demesne into eighteen allotments. Further, the V. E. does not say in which counties the monastic property is situated; the 1536 survey indicates the counties, and summarizes the income accordingly. The two surveys, however, are closely connected. Their figures of income and expenditure agree in all cases (four small differences are probably due to misspellings or misprints), and the monastic possessions with the exception of the rectory of Regate are placed in the same order.

[2] The Paper Surveys are collected in one section of the Record Office— Exchequer Augmentations Office Miscellaneous books; my references in the tabulated list indicate the volume of the section and the sheet or page of the volume. P. S.=Paper Surveys.

County.	Monastery.	Demesne. V. E. £ s. d.	Value. P. S. £ s. d.	Reference. V. E.	Reference. P. S.
Leic.	Croxton	55 13 4	57 16 2	iv. 150	399, 175–6
	St. Mary's, Leicester	41 0 0	41 15 4	iv. 146	399, 179
	Olveston	48 10 0	43 0 0	iv. 158	399, 171
Northants.	Canons Ashby	28 0 0	30 2 11	iv. 337	399, 246–7
	Catesby	62 1 8	62 7 4	iv. 339	399, 234–5
	St. James, Northam.	13 10 0	14 0 0	iv. 319	399, 286
	Pipewell	19 13 8	22 14 4	iv. 294	399, 290–1
	Sewardesley ...	5 0 0	5 2 6	iv. 328	399, 236
	Stamford nuns ...	9 14 7	10 7 10	iv. 140	399, 274 = 403, 23
	Sulby	133 6 8	137 9 6	iv. 100	399, 342–3
Oxon.	Wroxton	10 1 4	14 12 9½	ii. 198	402, 43
Salop	Lilleshall ...	16 0 0	20 5 0	iii. 197	400, 1–2
Staff.	Ronton	13 11 8	16 7 0	iii. 114	400, 108–9
Sussex	Shulbrede ...	5 6 8	7 13 4	i. 322	402, 47 = 409, 53
Warw.	Erdbury	13 6 8	14 3 4¾	iii. 56	408, 308–9
	Kenilworth ...	10 0 0	7 6 8	iii. 65	400, 118–19
	Wroxall	22 0 0	22 2 4	iii. 89	398, 70
Worc.	Malvern P. ...	8 0 0	10 6 8	iii. 242	400, 348–9
Yorks.	Coverham ...	12 0 0	13 9 8	v. 243	401, 37–8
	Kirklees	5 6 8	6 10 4	v. 67	401, 195–7
	Nunmonketon ...	4 0 0	19 6 3	v. 255	401, 247, 253, 285
	Swyne	23 0 0	33 16 11	v. 114	401, 381–4
	Whitby	18 13 8	25 2 8	v. 82	401, 301–2

For all the thirty-two monasteries the demesne valuation in the V. E. is £683 0s. 5½d., and in the P. S. £755 2s. 6¼d. The latter valuation exceeds the former by £72 2s. ¾d., or a little more than one-tenth. This excess is much smaller than that in the Suppression Accounts.

When the 1535 figures are verified by means of the Paper Surveys, the cases where not only the totals of the income from demesne can be compared but also the valuations or areas of separate pieces of land, are specially instructive. In the case of a Worcestershire monastery, Westwood, it is not possible to identify all the separate pieces of land in both surveys, and their area is given only in the Paper Survey; but the parallels are curious.[1]

Westwood Paper Survey.

	£ s. d.	£ s. d.		£ s. d.	£ s. d.
Longacre 6 ...	0 14 0	0 14 0	Parsons Hill 3...	0 3 0	0 4 0
Wynnyngefelde 5½	0 5 3	0 5 6	Tappyng 2 ...	0 6 8	0 6 0
Barne close 3 ...	9 6 8	0 7 0	Oxe Medowe 14	2 0 0	1 19 0
Hawles feldes 33	1 0 0	1 2 0	Wodwardes 1 ...	0 3 4	0 3 4
Hadleys crofte 6	0 10 0	0 12 0	Organs 1½ ...	0 3 4	0 3 4
Horessuche 55 ...	1 6 8	1 16 8	Banamyshyll 36	2 0 0	1 16 0
Olde Graunge 15	0 10 0	0 10 0	Braddefeld 44...	2 0 0	2 4 0
Burche hill 9 ...	0 13 4	0 12 0	Boycotefilde 33	1 3 4	1 2 0

[1] V. E. iii. 276 + Augm. O. M. b. 400, 352–3. The Paper Survey was

On the whole, the 267 acres of the demesne bring in an income according to the V. E. of £13 5s. 4d., and according to the P. S. of £13 16s. 10d. The second survey by no means depends upon the V. E. although it is exceedingly similar. Among the possessions of the monastery of Pipewell was 'le Grange Park'. According to the V. E. its area was 10 acres and brought in an income of £0 16s. 8d.; according to the P. S. its area was 10 acres and brought in an income of £1 0s. 0d. According to the V. E. the monastery of Worksop had 200 acres of waste land that brought in an income of £0 15s. 0d.; according to the P. S. also its area was 200 acres but the income is said to have been £1 0s. 0d.[1]

In two cases, namely, Merkyate and Wroxton, we are able to compare the valuations and areas for the whole of the demesne as given in the two surveys.[2]

Merkyate
Paper
Survey.

The Merkyate monks in 1535 let half of the demesne and farmed the other half themselves. Concerning the half of the demesne that was let, both the surveys agree in the figures of the area, the valuation and, apparently, even in the names of the farmers. One tenant took 192 acres of arable land for £2 2s. 8d.; the other took 20 acres of arable land for £0 6s. 8d. and 8 acres of meadow for £2 13s. 4d. In the description of the demesne that remained in the hands of the monks there are characteristic points of difference. According to the V. E. the prioress had 221 acres of arable land and an acre is valued at 9¼d.; according to the P. S. there were only

composed August, 1536. The names of the pieces of land are taken from the P. S.; the figures after the names signify the number of acres, the valuation on the left is taken from the V. E., the valuation on the right from the P. S. It is curious that the last three pieces of land should be numbered in the V. E. among the pasture, and in the P.S. among the arable lands.

[1] V. E. v. 174 + Augm. O. M. b. 399, 339–44. The amount of the remaining demesne land is 190 acres according to the V. E., and 185 acres according to the P. S. The wood is not mentioned at all in the V. E., and the P. S. gives its amount as 178 acres.

[2] We can also point to a third case, that of Blyth, Notts., V. E. v. 176–7 + (Mon. iv. 627 = Paper Survey). According to the V. E. the demesne has 175 acres without Lytle Lanlonde close, and the income from the demesne is £9 15s. 4d. According to the Paper Survey the demesne has 169 acres besides the farm house, and it brings in an income of £7 16s. 9d.

185¼ acres of arable land of which 182 acres are valued at 10*d*. an acre, 3 acres at 16*d*. an acre, and ¼ acre is valued at 8*d*. According to the V. E. the prioress had 9 acres of meadow valued at 6*s*. 8*d*. an acre; according to the P. S. there were 10 acres of meadow valued likewise at 6*s*. 8*d*. an acre. For the pasture the V. E. gives only a general valuation, £1 16*s*. 8*d*.; the P. S. gives a detailed survey but the general valuation is the same, £1 16*s*. 8*d*. No one, of course, would call the difference between the two surveys a considerable one.

The Wroxton surveys are also very much alike. In both, the demesne is divided into eight allotments, and the area indicated in both is identical. May not the 1535 survey have been the source of a later survey made by Auditor Cavendish and Receiver Danaster? Cavendish and Danaster themselves say that they had the 1535 survey before them; but they were far from simply copying it. They give in their survey two new items of income; namely, the income of the land inside the walls of the monastery and the tithe from the demesne. In the case of three out of eight allotments of the demesne ('in land'), the two surveys give a different valuation; in the case of five they coincide. In two of the former instances the difference is small, in the third it is considerable and characteristic.[1] I think that the second survey rests upon an independent study of the demesne. The exact agreement in the figures of the areas which we find in the two surveys, and the similarity in their valuations, point to the trustworthiness of the 1535 survey.[2] Wroxton Paper Survey.

When the monastic lands passed into the administration of the Crown the annual accounts of the separate monasteries and manors came to be collected together at one central institution—the Augmentations Office. The chief receiverships of the possessions of this or that monastery were not Receivers' Accounts.

[1] V. E. ii. 198, 'Innland of verey bareyn grownd 60 a. £1 0*s*. 0*d*.'; Augm. O. Misc. b. 402, 43, 'Innland close 60 a. £4 0*s*. 0*d*.'
[2] It is possible to compare the areas of the home farm of Croxton, Leic. V. E. iv. 150, 'Situs cum clausis ac 600 a. terr. dnic in manu abbatis.' In Augm. O. M. b. 399, 175-6 the demesne is surveyed in detail: 'scite 1 a. +pasture 353 a. +medowe 37½ +arable 320 a.'

continued in every case. In the places where they were abolished, the bailiffs or farmers of the separate manors gave in their accounts and paid the cash direct to the county receiver. But the county receiver distributed his yearly account according to the monasteries, so that in spite of the changes in the administration the accounts of the Crown receivers give as before the gross income of every monastery in their circuits, and it is possible to compare their figures with the figures of the gross income given in the V. E. We cannot, of course, use all the Receivers' Accounts for the verification of the V. E. The dissolved monastic lands quickly passed into other hands, and the receiver was responsible in his account only for those lands which remained in the hands of the Crown. If a part of the monastic possessions, in the year for which the account was made out, had already passed into private hands, then the gross income of the receiver covered only a part of the territory, the gross income of which is given in the Valor Ecclesiasticus ; and the comparison of the two figures in such a case would be to no purpose and unsound. It is necessary, therefore, to select for comparison the Receivers' Accounts of the early years when the monastic lands were yet entirely in the possession of the Crown : and we shall confine ourselves to these in the list below. In order to see whether or no the monastic possessions had yet been touched I was obliged to have recourse to the Royal Letters Patent by which grants of monastic lands were made, and also to the accounts concerning the sale of monastic lands, which were kept by the Treasurer of the Augmentations Court. The annual accounts of the Receivers and the Treasurer run from Michaelmas to Michaelmas ; the exact date of the grant is always given in the Letters Patent. Let us take an instance. I want, say, to know whether I am entitled to use the receiver's account for the monastery of St. Germans, for the year ending on Michaelmas Day, 31 H. VIII. To ascertain this I must look through Dr. Gairdner's Calendar of the Letters Patent and the accounts of the Treasurer after the dissolution of the monastery until Michaelmas, 31 H. VIII. The monastery of St. Germans is not found in either of the collections up to Michaelmas 31 H. VIII. This means that the alienation of the lands of this monastery began at a later date, and I have consequently the right to compare the gross income of the receiver's account with that of the Valor Ecclesiasticus.

Receivers' Accounts.

In the tabulated list below the gross incomes of twenty-two monasteries are compared. The monasteries are divided into two groups, according as the income did or did not exceed two hundred pounds.[1]

County.	*Monastery.*	*Gross total income.* V. E. £	s.	d.	M. A. £	s.	d.	*Reference.* V. E.	Mon.	*Date of* M. A.
Bucks.	Ankerwyke ...	45	14	4	44	12	9	iv. 222	iv. 232	28
	Snetteshall ...	24	0	0	27	6	2	iv. 228	iv. 237	28
Devon	Totnes[2] ...	130	1	9	139	6	3½	ii. 367	iv. 632	28
Leic.	Langley ...	34	6	2	46	12	10½	iv. 176	iv. 225	28
Linc.	Humberstone ...	42	11	3	49	4	0	iv. 68	iv. 431	29
Midd.	Stratford at Bow	121	0	6	143	4	2½	i. 409	iv. 122	28
Northt.	Catesby ...	145	0	6	109	14	0⅛	iv. 339	iv. 640	28
Notts.	Blyth	125	8	2½	123	13	4	v. 176	iv. 628	28
Suff.	Redlingfield ...	81	2	5½	86	8	7½	iii. 478	iv. 118	28
Warw.	Pinley	27	13	7	27	15	11	iii. 90	iv. 118	28
	Pollesworth ...	109	5	0	138	6	2	iii. 77	ii. 369	31
	Wroxall ...	71	16	5	78	10	1½	iii. 89	iv. 95	28
	Malvern P. ...	121	16	5½	122	19	0	iii. 242	iv. 456	28
		1079	16	7½	1137	13	5⅝			
Cornw.	Bodmin ...	289	11	11	340	6	8	ii. 400	ii. 465	32
	St. Germans ...	243	8	0	273	9	0¼	ii. 405	ii. 470	31
Dorset	Abbotsbury ...	483	1	9¾	477	6	8¼	i. 227	iii. 60	32
Hunts.	St. Neots ...	256	3	7¼	256	15	8	iv. 261	iii. 483	32
Linc.	Bardney ...	429	7	0	469	3	3	iv. 81	i. 641	30
Norf.	Wymondham ...	263	18	2¾	258	11	3¾	iii. 322	iii. 340	32
Soms.	Athelney ...	290	19	5¼	430	12	1¼	i. 206	ii. 409	31
Yorks.	Meaux	445	0	9½	602	7	5½	v. 108	v. 397	31
	Whitby... ...	483	1	5	543	10	9	v. 82	i. 421	32
		3184	12	2½	3652	2	11			

Let us add together the totals of the two groups. In the V. E. the gross income of the twenty-two monasteries is valued

[1] A great number of the Receivers' Accounts are printed in the last edition of Dugdale's Monasticon, and I did not think it necessary to turn to the manuscripts. In my list M. A. means Ministers' Accounts, that is to say, Receivers' Accounts. In the column 'Reference' I indicate the volume and page of the Valor Ecclesiasticus and of Dugdale. In the column 'Dates' I give the date of the Receivers' Account; for instance 31 means that the account ends at Michaelmas, 31 H. VIII.

[2] The income of the Rectory of Totton is excluded from the gross income.

at £4,264 8s. 10d. ; according to Ministers' Accounts the same
income amounts to £4,789 16s. 4⅝d.   The second figure
exceeds the first by £525 7s. 6⅝d., a little less than one-
eighth.   Thus the excess of the Receivers' Accounts over the
V. E. figures lies midway between the excess of the Suppression Accounts, which is ¼, and that of the Paper Surveys,
which is ₁/₁₀.   Here again we must remember the growing
increase of the income from land, both nominal and real, in the
years which followed the Dissolution.   If the territory from
which the Crown agents collected £4,789 gross, was valued in
the V. E. at only £4,264, it does not follow that this territory
in the year 1535 yielded a gross income of £4,789, and that
the Commissioners of 1535 omitted the sum of £525.   The
monastery of Wroxall may serve as an example.   The
valuation of the gross income in the V. E. is £71 16s. 5d. ;
the gross income according to the Receivers' Accounts for
the year 28 H. VIII is £78 10s. 1½d.   During the period between these dates, viz. in the spring of 1536, the Suppressors
fixed the gross income of the monastery at £72 9s. 9d.   This
figure is not very much at variance with that of the V. E.
and tends to confirm the accuracy of the latter, so that if the
figure £78 10s. 1½d. is given in the Receivers' Accounts in the
autumn of the same year, it does not mean that the Commissioners of 1535 omitted a part of the monastic revenue, but
that the Crown administration of 1536 raised the income of
the land.[1]

The case of   In the case of several monasteries in the list, separate items of
Athelney.   income may also be compared.   The greatest difference in the
totals of the gross income is found in the Somersetshire
monastery of Athelney: and in this instance we find twenty-
two items of income common to both surveys.   In four items
the figures agree, and in four others they are very similar.   The
most striking difference is in the figures of the income from
courts and from demesne.   In the V. E. the income from courts
of four manors, W. Leng, Sutton, Hame, and Ilton, amounts to
£8 10s. 0d., and in the Receivers' Account of 31 H. VIII the
amount is £44 15s. 4½d.   In 1535 the Sutton demesne was in

[1] Mon. iv. 93-4.

the hands of the monks and was then valued at £1 13s. 0d. ;
in the year 31 H. VIII this demesne was let for £14 0s. 0d. The
difference in the figures of the spiritual income and that from
rent is much less marked, but still inspires mistrust as to the
statements of the Valor Ecclesiasticus. In the V. E. the rectory
of Sutton shows an income of £11 14s. 0d., and in the year
31 H. VIII it was let for £26 13s. 4d. In the case of the manor
of Ilton the Valor Ecclesiasticus gives £62 8s. 1½d. as the figure
of the rent; the Receivers' accounts give the figure as £79 9s. 3d.
If most of the V. E. surveys were like that of Athelney then
we might well abandon the systematic study of this Survey ;
fortunately, such extreme undervaluations are rare : and when
the separate items of income of other monasteries in the list are
compared we find that these great differences are exceptional.
Sometimes it is possible to show that these figures refer to the
valuation of the demesne that remained in the hands of the
monks to the end. In the case of the monastery of Whitby
the second valuation exceeds the first by £60 ; half of this
difference refers to the demesne that was situated round the
monastery, which in 1535 remained in the hands of the monks
and was valued at £17 13s. 8d.; in 1540 it was let for
£49 0s. 8d.

We may also point to the demesne of a Lincolnshire The case
monastery, Louth Park. The somewhat detailed valuation of Louth
Park.
of this demesne given in the Valor Ecclesiasticus can be compared with the annual account of the farmer in the year
28 H. VIII. There is an interval of two years only between
the two documents, but the difference in their figures is very
considerable. As in the case of Athelney, the income from
demesne according to the farmer's account exceeds by almost
half that given in the Commissioners' returns ; from £26 0s. 2d.
it increased to £41 18s. 0d. But the difference in area is even
more remarkable. In the Valor Ecclesiasticus the area of
demesne is said to be 664 acres apart from the wood, which was
reduced yearly by four acres. In the farmer's account the
area of demesne is given as 1689 a. ; but it is not clear whether
the wood is included or not. In any case, the area as given in
the Valor Ecclesiasticus is less than one half of the area given

The case
of Cerne.

in the farmer's account. The difference in the income is not so great as that in the area, because the valuation of the land in the V. E. is higher than in the farmer's account.[1]

If, at the time the Receivers' Account was made, a part of the monastic property had already passed into private hands, then we must compare, not the general totals of the gross income, but the income of the separate manors or benefices. Thus, in the case of the separate manors of the monastery of Wilton in Wiltshire, the figures of the V. E. can be compared with those of the Receivers' Account of the year 32 H. VIII.[2] For Battle Abbey we can use the account of 30 H. VIII.[3] For Cerne Abbey in Dorsetshire the com-

[1] At first sight, the Commissioners' return of 1535 inspires great confidence. Here it is: V. E. iv. 57, 'Predicti abbas et conventus habent terras dominicales infra precinctum monasterii 116 acras pasture spinose et yemali tempore aqua submerse £3 7s. 4d., 58½ acr' consimilis pasture in Somercotts Cockeryngton et Saltfletby £2 18s. 6d., 162½ acr' prati iac' in diversis locis £6 1s. 8d., 123 acr' terre arabilis £3 8s. 8d., ac 104 acr' terre arabilis in Lamcrofte £1 0s. 8d., 120 acr' pasture ibidem pasturat' cum bidentibus £4 0s. 0d. et eciam 4 acr' bosci prostrati annuatim infra precinctum monasterii ad usum abbathie £4 13s. 4d. que valent inter se per estimacionem communibus annis £26 0s. 2.'—The farmer's account for the year 28 H. VIII is found in the State Pap. Dom., Suppr. Pap. vol. 3, f. 41. In this account the demesne is divided into two parts: (1) 'firma terr' dnic' pertin' scitui: 340 a. of arable land 4d. each, 251 a. of meadow 1s. each, 232 acres of pasture' (78 a. £0 1s. 8d. each, 154 a. 1s. each); (2) 'firma aliarum terr' dnic' ibm voc' Lamcrofte; 442 a. 2d. each, 400 a. terre viridis 3d. each, 24 a. pasture 8d. each.' The farmer would not, of course, make out his rent to be greater than it really was.—It may be that the difference in the figures of the demesne area is the result not only of concealment but also of mistake. In 1535 the local inhabitants at the desire of the Commissioners may have estimated the area of demesne as it appeared to them, and after the dissolution the Augmentations' surveyors who described the demesne may, at least in some places, have resorted to a genuine measurement.

[2] V. E. ii. 109 + Mon. ii. 330. The figures on the left are those of the V. E., those on the right are from the Receivers' Accounts :—

	£	s.	d.	£	s.	d.			£	s.	d.	£	s.	d.
Wishford ...	9	3	7	9	17	0	Wyly ...		24	17	11¾	25	6	0
Fougleston ...	23	1	2	28	18	8⅝	South Newton		25	19	10¾	27	16	10¼
Baberstoke ...	8	2	3¾	7	19	2	Uggeford ...		9	4	4	9	6	9

[3] V. E. i. 346 + Mon. iii. 258. The figures on the left are from the V. E., those on the right from the Receivers' Accounts :—

				£	s.	d.	£	s.	d.
Lullyng firma manerii	...	...	...	16	11	8	16	11	8
redd' ass'	...	...	...	19	8	9	19	7	3½
Appultram firma manerii	...	...	...	15	6	8	15	6	8
redd'	...	...	...	14	1	4	14	1	4

parisons are more interesting because the manorial income is separated into items.[1] The manor of Cerne: demesne (1535 in manu, 1540 in firma) £34 9s. 0d., £37 14s. 4d.; redd. ass' £50 18s. 11¾d., £58 11s. 11d.; mercat' et perquis' £13 12s. 3d., £9 3s. 5¼d. The manor of Haukechurche: redd' ass' £8 13s. 4d., £8 13s. 4d.; perquis' £0 9s. 2d., £0 0s. 3d. The manor of Mylton: firma domin' £4 10s. 8d., £4 11s. 6d.; redd' ass' £14 19s. 6d., £15 2s. 7d.; perquis' £5 9s. 3d., nihil. The manor of Symondes-borough: firma domin' £29 6s. 0d., £29 6s. 0d.; redd' ass' £77 19s. 6¾d., £78 3s. 8d.; perquis' £11 1s. 0d., £3 7s. 4d. The manor of Mapercombe and Nettelcombe: firma domin' £4 4s. 0d., £10 9s. 1d.; redd' assis' £9 13s. 6½d., £9 1s. 1½d.; perquis' £3 0s. 2d., £0 0s. 10d. The manor of Maydennewton: redd' ass' £7 10s. 6d., £7 10s. 0½d.; perquis' £0 7s. 6¼d., £0 1s. 10d. The income from rent and from demesne are on the whole very similar in both documents; but the difference in the figures of the income from courts is almost as great as in the case of Athelney. While, however, in the case of Athelney the large increase appears in the survey of later date, in the case of the Cerne manors an excess almost as great is shown in the earlier survey. It follows that either the income from courts varied considerably in different years, or that it was assessed arbitrarily; possibly both these conditions prevailed.

I have compared the V. E. figures with yet another series of documents—the valuations of Royal Grants. Any one who wanted to acquire monastic lands from the Crown, whether as a gift or by purchase, or in exchange, had to send to the Augmentations Court an application accompanied by Particulars. By 'Particulars' was meant a detailed official survey of the land in question; and the valuations of every separate manor (or part of a manor) and of every spiritual benefice had to be included in the survey. If the Council of the Court

Particulars for Grants.

			£	s.	d.	£	s.	d.
Alcyston manerium	...	...	... 61	17	0			
domus tegul'	...	...	... 2	0	0	63	17	0
Clopt' firma manerii	...	...	... 6	13	4	6	13	4
Wye redd' ass'	...	...	... 102	3	2½	94	4	6¼

[1] V. E. i. 253 + Mon. ii. 629. The first figures in each pair are taken from the Receivers' accounts of 32 H. VIII.

granted the petition, it was according to this official valuation that the price, which the petitioner had to pay to the Crown, was calculated, unless he took it as a gift, or in exchange for some of his own land.   When the petitioner had paid this sum he received the Royal Patent for the 'granted' lands.   This Patent enumerates in great detail all the manors and benefices, and in most cases also states the general income from the granted estates.   Numerous 'Particulars for Grants' are preserved among the records of the Augmentations Court, and constitute a very important authority for the history of the Dissolution.   Copies of the Patents were entered in the Patent Rolls, which are calendared in Dr. Gairdner's Letters and Papers: so that the figures of the Valor Ecclesiasticus may be compared with the figures of both collections.   But before we proceed to consider these a few preliminary remarks are necessary.   There is a widely spread idea that the Crown derived very little profit from the alienation of monastic estates.   It is said that even when the monastic lands were sold they were almost invariably purchased very much below their actual value.   If this were correct, then the 'Particulars for Grants' and the Patents would be a very untrustworthy source of information, and absolutely useless for the verification of the Valor Ecclesiasticus.   An examination, however, of the documents negatives the popular view, and leads to the conclusion that on the whole the royal grants were genuine gifts, exchanges and sales, and not a robbery in disguise on the part of the grantees, and that consequently the figures of the 'Particulars' and Patents may be used to check those of the Valor Ecclesiasticus.[1]

'Particulars for Grants.'   In the following table are set out the figures for several monastic manors and benefices as given respectively by the Valor Ecclesiasticus and the 'Particulars for Grants'.   Thirteen monasteries are included in the table; three of these being situated in Yorkshire; and this fact, coupled with the mention of Bruerne, should refute any charge of casual selection,

---

[1] I should be able to prove my statement only in connexion with a general survey of the financial administration of the first Tudors.

or of one deliberately made in support of the Valor Ecclesiasticus.[1]

Monastery and Possessions.	*Gross Income.* V. E.	*Gross Income.* P.	*Reference.* V. E.	*Reference.* P.	*Date of Grant.*
	£ s. d.	£ s. d.			
Markyate : Firma rēorie London	16 13 4	15 6 8	iv. 209	217 m.2	36
Dunkeswell : Hackpen redd' ass' et perquis', Sheldon et St. Hill redd' et perquis' Sheldon grange. Boleham redd' ass' et perquis'	65 13 9	65 5 5¼	ii. 304	102 m.7	37
Torre : Collaton redd' et perquis'	9 10 3½	8 15 4	ii. 361	933	31
Shaftesbury : Luddyngton redd' ass' firma dñic' et perquis'	55 14 3	47 11 3½	i. 377	994	35
Combe redd' ass' firma dñic' et perquis'	17 0 11	15 19 11	i. 279	993	34
anthony : Hempstede redd' lib' redd' cust' et perquis'	28 0 11¾	28 6 6¼	ii. 423	54	37
Bruerne[2] : Bruerne demesne, Sandbroke grange, Caper meade in Shipton, Monkenheyes in Kyngham	10 9 2	51 13 0	ii. 201	168 m.1–2	30
Brewton : Brewton demesnes ; North Bruham redd' ass' firma dñic' et perquis'	47 4 9½	57 4 9	i. 149	83	32
Bury St. Edmunds : Firma de Wistowe	25 13 4	26 16 0	iii. 463	325	31
Battle : Lullyngton firma dñic' et redd' ass'	36 0 5	35 19 0	i. 336	747	31
Ambresbury : Chadelworth redd' liberi, redd' cust' firma dñic' et perquis'	14 4 1	14 7 11	ii. 95	993	34
Fountains : Granges of Morkar, Haddokstanc, Swalbey, Sutton, Bramley, Nutwithcote	52 6 8½	69 2 8	v. 253	259	31
Nunkelyng : Kelyngdñic', Benyngholme redd', Catewyke redd' et Waghen redd'	17 13 0	30 11 4	v. 115	529 m.2	31
Swyne : Swyne dñic', Drypoole grange, Wolburgh grange, Sutton Ynge, Empthorp, Lampthorp grange	32 9 4	47 15 3	v. 114	529 m.1	31
	428 14 4¼	514 15 1			

Taking together all the thirteen monasteries, the second valuation (£514 15s. 1d.) exceeds the first (£428 14s. 4¼d.) by £86 0s. 8¾d. or a little more than one-fifth. It is curious that this difference is entirely referable to the demesne, and specially

[1] In the table P=Particulars for Grants ; in the column headed ' Date of Grant ' the year of Henry VIII's reign is given. The monasteries are placed in alphabetical order according to their counties.

[2] The V. E. has two valuations of the Bruerne demesne and Sandbroke grange (ii. 201–3, and 265). I have taken the lower, *ex abundanti cautela* ; and I give for each monastery only the totals according to my own calculation.

to those portions which remained in the hands of the monks. The figures of the income from rent are almost identical in the V. E. and the Particulars for Grants; the excess of the latter valuation amounting to less than £1 in the whole list: while the court income in the Particulars for Grants is much lower than in the V. E.

Patents.

The valuations of the Royal Patents, like those of the Particulars for Grants, refer generally to the separate monastic manors and benefices, and not to the whole, of each monastery's possessions. When comparing the Patents with the Valor Ecclesiasticus I have used Dr. Gairdner's Calendar of the Letters and Papers for 1540. The figures of the gross income are taken from the V. E. In the Calendar sometimes only the amount of the rent which the grantee had to pay to the Crown is given. According to 27 H. VIII, c. 8, § 27, 8, this rent was a tenth of the income; so that we need only multiply this figure by ten to find the annual amount of the income. The items compared are placed in the chronological order of the Patents for 1540.

Monastery and Possessions.	Gross Income.		Date of Patent.
	V. E.	Pat.	
	£ s. d.	£ s. d.	
Shaftesbury : Chesilbourne manor ...	38 19 3	37 18 4	Febr. n. 14
Battle : Hoton manor	35 17 4¾	34 0 0	n. 40
Selby : Stanford on Aven manor and rectory	58 11 8	67 7 6	n. 98
Bury St. Edmunds : Whepstede manor, Monkeslonds in Hawstede	34 9 0	36 5 0	n. 116
Bury St .Edmunds and Dartford : Manors of Bradfeld monachorum, Stanton, Thorpe Hall	56 3 4	71 8 4	March n. 31
Missenden : Chalfont St. Peter manor et rectory	32 16 0	33 0 0	n. 33
Northampton, St. James: Wakeley manor et rectory	5 6 8	8 13 4	n. 52
Catesby : Lands in Dodford and Stow	6 0 8	4 14 0	n. 53
Bittlesden : Gorall grange	5 13 4	5 13 4	idem
Bury St. Edmunds : Ingham Hall manor	23 17 2	25 5 3	n. 57
Bury St. Edmunds : Culpho manor ...	7 10 0	9 10 0	n. 58
Polslo : Tudheys manor	13 4 8½	13 3 4	n. 60
Nostell : Demesne, Huntewyke grange, Okenshaw and Holewell chief messuages, Bramham manor, Skokirk cell	92 6 10	85 0 0	n. 62
Kirklees : Myrfeld rectory	4 13 4	6 6 8	{ April n. 19 { 32 H. VIII
Bermondsey : Cowykebury manor ...	15 6 8	17 0 0	n. 38
Edingdon : Dulton manor	18 10 11¾	22 10 10	n. 48
Coventry : Farm of Potters Merston manor	13 6 8	13 6 8	May n. 12

Monastery and Possessions.	Gross Income. V. E.			Pat.			Date of Patent.
	£	s.	d.	£	s.	d.	
Ramsey: Barnwell Manor	34	0	10	34	0	10	n. 60
Kirkham: Manors of Kirkham and Whitwell, Kirkham rectory	56	8	9	132	3	4	n. 61
Wigmore: Caynham manor	39	3	11	37	10	0	June n. 5
Christchurch, Cant.: Ebney and Ebney Priory manors	24	13	4	24	13	4[1]	n. 44
Leeds: Comden manor...	6	17	4	4	17	6	idem
Battle: Lullington manor	36	0	5	36	12	3	n. 75
Newburgh: Newburgh manor, Ulthwayte and Skorton granges	43	10	0	52	6	3	n. 84
Whalley: Lands in Maunton and Romesgreve	22	18	0	27	17	1	July n. 4
Lanthony: Redgrave manor	2	19	11	·3	0	0	n. 47
Totnes: Aspryngton manor	25	2	0	30	15	0	n. 53
Cirencester: Latton and Eysy manors	70	12	2½	71	10	10	n. 69
Edingdon: Alvescote manor	28	1	4	28	2	4	idem
Faileigh: Marston manor	7	8	8	7	10	0	idem
Malmesbury: Brymell	69	3	6¾	91	3	4	n. 85
Christchurch, Cant.: Bokkyng manor	59	9	6½	48	13	4	n. 87
Lenton: Kersawe cell	9	6	8	19	10	0	n. 102

The total of the figures of the Valor Ecclesiasticus is £998 10s. 2d., the total of the Patents' figures is £1,139 7s. 9d.; the second sum exceeds the first by £140 17s. 7d. or a little less than one seventh.

Critical examination of evidence is the dullest kind of his- Results. torical research, and the analysis of surveys is the dullest kind of critical work. I fear therefore that only a very incredulous or a very patient reader will have the courage to wade through all the foregoing argument, which, however tedious, is unfortunately necessary. I could not but feel concerned as to the credibility of the V. E.; it is one of my principal authorities, and much of my work would fall to the ground if it should be shown to be untrustworthy. The returns of 1535 have often been characterized as inaccurate, but the assertion is either made without any proof, or is based upon other unproved assertions, and consequently carries very little weight. The Valor Ecclesiasticus, however, raises more serious doubts. A detailed study of the Survey shows us that it is not free from important omissions and undervaluations. Every conscientious writer will distrust the Commissioners' Returns

---

[1] When reckoning the income, the expenditure of £2 13s. 4d. for the repair of the sea wall was taken into account.

of 1535 until they are shown to be at least comparatively trustworthy. This I have attempted in some measure to do. I must leave it to others to say whether I have succeeded ; I would say, however, that this critical examination has finally overcome my scepticism. It has called my attention to other extensive surveys, similar to the Valor Ecclesiasticus, made by the English Government in very short periods of time ; it has shown that Cromwell and Audley carefully supervised the Commissioners of 1535, and that the latter were beyond all things desirous of ingratiating themselves with their principals. There are some important omissions in the Commissioners' Returns, but the number is very small when compared with the number of places surveyed. There are also not a few serious undervaluations. But the extent to which these undervaluations affect the general trustworthiness of the Survey can only be discovered by a comparison of the Valor Ecclesiasticus with surveys made at other times and by other persons. I have compared the Valor Ecclesiasticus with the monastic surveys previous to the Dissolution,[1] with the Suppression Accounts, the official descriptions of monastic demesnes, the Particulars for Grants and Royal Patents. All the totals of later valuations exceed the totals of the Valor Ecclesiasticus, and lead one to think that the figures of 1535 are below the actual income. But the increase found in later valuations is not so great as to justify our abandoning the study of the Valor Ecclesiasticus. The greatest increase is found in the Suppression Accounts, in which it amounts to one fourth. In the other documents the increase is less, and in the demesne accounts is not more than one-tenth. And as a part of the increase can be accounted for by the growth of the income from land, the undervaluation in the V. E. is evidently less than a fourth of the Commissioners' valuation. Moreover, the undervaluation falls almost exclusively on woods, income from courts and from demesne *in manu* ; the rents of freehold, copyhold and leasehold being given with great exactness.

---

[1] This is, of course, the weakest part of my argument. The Whalley and Glastonbury surveys, however important, are not sufficient to enable us to judge of all the monasteries. I must plead lack of time and not lack of material, which is abundant in the archives.

There is no reason, I think, to dwell upon the fact, which my readers will readily understand, that, at most, we can only arrive at probability and not certainty in the matter. It is quite open to any sceptic to take exception to my premisses and to bring forward a different explanation of my instances of coincidence and similarity. It may be that the other extensive surveys are no more to be trusted than the Valor Ecclesiasticus; it may be that the Commissioners of 1535 were able to blind their principals ; it is possible that the later valuers were not more honest than those of 1535. The cases in which the later valuation exceeds that of 1535 might be entirely explained by the growth of the income from land ; and those cases in which the later valuation coincides with that of 1535 may be due to the fact that the later valuers overlooked the errors, both innocent and deliberate, made in 1535, in consideration of bribes from the bailiffs, tenants, buyers or any one to whom the difference between the actual and official income would go.

The supposition that the Valor Ecclesiasticus and the English Dissolution were founded upon a general and systematic fraud may perhaps be held to clear away some difficulties. But when carried to its logical conclusion it would give rise to new difficulties which would prove far more serious and numerous. Upon the whole I consider that an attitude of confidence towards the Great Survey of 1535 is more justifiable than one of scepticism, and therefore I consider myself entitled to pass on to the study of the monastic returns found in the Valor Ecclesiasticus.

BOOK II

MONASTIC ECONOMY ON THE EVE OF THE DISSOLUTION

CHAPTER I

GENERAL OUTLINES OF THE MONASTIC ECONOMY

Literature on the subject. ALL writers on the dissolution of the monasteries are agreed that it produced a great change in the economic system of the country, and have naturally endeavoured to form some idea of the extent of this change. Many writers have not refrained from boldly stating their conclusions. Thus, several authors give in definite figures the area of the monastic lands, and the income of these lands; the proportion of the monastic to the national income; the value of the monastic personalty; the number of monks and nuns; and the population dependent upon them. These calculations vary much in character; some are original, others are borrowed; some are influenced by preconceived ideas, others are impartial; some are fantastic, others more reasonable; some closely follow the official documents, others are entirely free from the dust of records and even from contact with printed authorities. It is to be regretted that the oldest authors are the most independent and trustworthy.

Antiquaries on monastic income. It is only for the totals of the monastic income that the Dissolution surveys give something like exact figures. The antiquaries of the time of Elizabeth and James—Camden, Cotton, Speed, Weever—were the first to make use of these figures for historical purposes, and, unless I am mistaken, our knowledge of the subject has not advanced beyond the point reached by them. The authors of later days have only repeated the figures of Cotton or Speed, or what can be traced back to Cotton or Speed. But even Cotton and Speed did not spend much labour on their calculations. When the 1535 returns were completed, excerpts were made from

them which gave only the names of the benefices, the amount
of their net income, and the tenth extracted from then.. Any
one who was in touch with the Court of Tenths, or the
Exchequer, and consequently had access to these excerpts,
could readily enough copy from them the names of the
monasteries and the corresponding figures of their net income,
and so calculate the general total. It was precisely in this
way that the total of the net income, £135,522 18s. 10d., was
arrived at in the list Cleop. E. iv, f. 446–54 ; and similarly
the total £135,453 14s. 2¾d. in the Dugdale and Dodsworth
list, which goes back to Cotton. It is true that, if an antiquary
wished to find the gross income of the monasteries (the figures
of the gross income are given in Speed's list and in that of
Stevens, which goes back to Cotton) he had a more complicated work to do. The compiler of the list from which Speed
and Stevens derived their information worked from the Commissioners' returns, but he must have worked hastily and carelessly; he did not, for instance, add together the separate items
of income, but adopted the figures of the totals ready at hand,
when he could find them, which was not always the case ; and
the amounts that he gives as the gross income are not infrequently in the Commissioners' returns those of the net income,
or indicate something between the net and the gross income.
The total of Speed's list (I do not give Stevens's list, as it is incomplete) is £171,300, the shillings and pence being omitted.[1]

It is curious that these same antiquaries made an attempt to
ascertain the total of the net income of the monasteries in quite
a different way.[2] In this more complicated calculation, the

[1] In neither list did I verify the addition. When comparing the two
totals one must remember that the lists do not quite agree in the number
of monasteries given ; thus, in Dugdale's list only a few of the friaries are
mentioned.

[2] This calculation is found in Cleop. E. iv, 458–74. The Church income
before the Dissolution is said to be £320,180 10s. 0d. 'according to the
taxation of the firstfruits and tenths.' As to the tenths after the Dissolution, a long table, of unknown date, is given, arranged according to
dioceses. Its total is £15,041 1s. 2¾d. and corresponds to the income of
£150,410 12s. 0d. (sic). This figure, however, includes some income that
did not belong to the Church before the Dissolution, that of five new
dioceses created by Henry VIII, and amounting to £1,888 13s. 4d. This
sum of course ought not to be taken into consideration when we compare
the Church's income after the Dissolution with its income before that

net income of the whole English Church before the Dissolution is first given; then the net income of the English Church
after the Dissolution is calculated, though the exact date of
assessment is not given; lastly, the difference between the two
totals is stated, indicating, of course, the amount of the secu-
larized income, which is estimated at £161,100. I am not by
any means concerned to defend all the figures of this valuation,
but on the whole they seem to me to be fairly trustworthy.

Later
authors.

These three calculations are all that has been hitherto done
in the direction of an estimate of the monastic income. The
other calculations known to me either go back to those just

event; £150,410 12s. 0d. minus £1,888 13s. 4d.=£148,511 12s. 0¼d. (sic).
On the other hand, we ought to take into consideration that part of the
Church's income after the Dissolution which was not subject to the taxation of tenths. After the Dissolution, both Universities and several colleges
were by statute freed from the payment of the tenth; their income, which
amounted to £10,568 8s. 0½d., should therefore be added to the income
subject to the taxation of tenths; thus £148,511 12s. 0¼d. + £10,568 8s. 4½d.
=£159,080 0s. 4¾d. Therefore, in consequence of the Dissolution, the
Church's income fell from £320,180 10s. 0d. to £159,080 0s. 4¾d.; which
means that the State took from the Church the net income of £161,000
9s. 7¼d. What are the authorities for this curious calculation? The figure
£320,180 10s. 0d. is evidently derived from a trustworthy source. Six years
elapsed from the time the royal tenth was established (26 H. VIII, c. 3)
until the Court of Firstfruits and Tenths was founded (32 H. VIII, c. 45).
During this time the Treasurer and General Receiver, John Gostwyke, was
responsible for the collection of the tenths. When he handed the records
over to the new authority he delivered also an account for all the six
years of his administration. In 1535, the first year, the estimates amount
to £32,018 1s. 0d. and correspond to the income of £320,180 10s. 0d., that
is to say, the figure on which all the above calculations are founded.
I have no doubt that this figure is borrowed from Gostwyke's account.
A copy only of this account is preserved (Lansd. 156, f. 146=Gairdner,
xvi. 352) which, according to the editors of the Calendar, is in a handwriting of the time of James I. It is possible that we are indebted for
this copy to Cotton's antiquarian friends, by whom the whole of this
calculation in Cleop. E. iv. 458–74 had been made, and it may have been
prepared solely for the purpose of this calculation. I do not know the
source of the tabulated list of tenths made after the dissolution, giving
a total of £15,041 1s. 2¾d.; as it is a very detailed list it may have been
copied from an official document. It was certainly composed after the
establishment of the five new dioceses. The final figure of the estimates
(£161,400) was widely quoted in the literature of later times. The text
of Cleop. E. iv. 458–74 is printed word for word by Weever, 185–96.
Weever's book, however, was not much read. But Speed was very
popular, and he used the same MS. estimates (801–2), quite independently
of Weever. Speed says that out of the £320,180 10s. 0d. Henry VIII
used £161,100 9s. 7¼d. for lay purposes. Later authors generally quote
Speed.

mentioned, or else have no trustworthy foundation whatever. The list of monasteries and the amount of the total net income (£140,000) in Tanner's third edition rests upon the authority of Speed and Dugdale. Nasmith, the editor of Tanner's 'Notitia', attempted to fix the extent to which the Commissioners of 1535 diminished the actual income of the monasteries, and he came to the conclusion that the figure £140,000 must be raised to the sum of about £200,000.[1]

Both figures are given, and not infrequently, in the writings of many later authors, generally on the authority of Tanner. Hume, the nameless author of the anti-Jacobite pamphlet of 1717, Blunt, the author of an article in The Home and Foreign Review, Dixon, Dr. Gasquet, Mr. Archbold, Prof. Kovalevsky, all take their totals of the Church and monastic income from Speed, Dugdale, and Tanner.[2] Collier took his total, £135,522 18s. 10d., straight from the manuscript; but this manuscript is the list of Cleop. E. iv. 446–54 already mentioned, which agrees almost entirely with Dugdale's list. Burnet's figure, £131,607 6s. 4d., is almost identical with Dugdale's figure, but Burnet does not indicate the authority of which he made use; neither did Lingard think it necessary to give the authority for his figure, £142,914 12s. 9¾d., which is nearly equivalent to Tanner's total. Figures for which the authority is unknown do not inspire one with much confidence.[3]

Important as it is to ascertain the general amount of the monastic income, it is still more important to ascertain the approximate area of the monastic lands; and it was but natural that writers should attempt to determine this, or at least express their opinions on the subject. Unfortunately, *all* the

Area of monastic lands.

---

[1] Tanner's Preface, iv.

[2] Summary of all religious houses and a calculation of what they might be worth at this day 1717 (British Museum, England, Religious Houses), Hume's History, iii. 245–6 (1854), Home and Foreign Review, 1864, Jan. 166–7; Blunt, History, i. 369; Dixon, History, i. 247–50; Gasquet, Henry VIII and the monasteries, ii. 387 (1902); Archbold, Somerset Religious Houses, 12; Kovalevsky, Economic growth of Europe, ii. 745 (Russian).

[3] Collier, ii. 165; Burnet, i. 430; Lingard,[5] v. 97. It is strange that Bishop Stubbs (17 Lectures,[3] 288) did not think it possible to define the monastic income with any kind of certainty.

calculations and suppositions carry but little conviction, and some of the figures given are entirely without foundation. We can reconcile ourselves to the fact that the author of an anti-clerical pamphlet of a very early date does not indicate how he arrived at the conclusion that the monks and ecclesiastics possessed more than a third of the kingdom ;[1] but it is more' serious when authors who have written much later and are much better authorities on the subject do not give any explanation of their figures. The reader does not know why Green estimates the whole area of monastic lands as one-fifth of all the English territory ; why Abbot Gasquet says that it amounted to two millions of acres, or why Dr. Gairdner states that it occupied about one-third of all the territory.[2]

A pamphlet of 1717.   In the above-mentioned anti-Jacobite pamphlet of 1717[3] I found an amusing argument respecting the area of monastic lands. The chief object of this pamphlet being to rouse public opinion against the Pretender, the author vehemently attacks the three chief points of the Jacobean creed: the Church's independence of the Crown, Divine Right and Passive Obedience. But at the same time, realizing that such arguments would be without effect when addressed to the Jacobites themselves, and yet wishing to win them over to his side, he points out that the Restoration of the Stuarts would be very unprofitable even to the squires. He says that the first consequence of the Restoration would be the establishment of the Roman Catholic religion as the religion of the State ; and that the lands of the Roman Catholic Church confiscated at the Reformation would be given back to their original owners. But more than a century and a half has elapsed since the Dissolution, and the remembrance of the monasteries has faded in the mind of society, wherefore the author proceeds to calculate for the country gentlemen the great loss that would threaten them if Roman Catholicism were reinstated. He naïvely confesses that he has not taken

[1] *Suppl. for beggars*, 1–4 (*Suppl. for commons*, 78–9, has a reference to this very passage).
[2] Green, ii. 201 (Archbold, 170, evidently quotes this passage from Green); Gasquet, Preface to Cobbett, xii–xiii ; Cambr. Mod. H., ii. 467–9.
[3] Summary of all Religious Houses, &c., xiii–xvii.

the trouble to look up the manuscripts, and that his calculation is founded upon Speed's list of monasteries. Speed gives £171,314 18s. 1d. as the total of the monastic income; but this is the income of only 653 monasteries out of the 1,041 mentioned by him; the whole monastic revenue according to the rule of three ought to make £273,106 18s. 3½d. And as the author affirms that a penny of the Dissolution epoch corresponds to a shilling of 1717, the income of £273,106 18s. 3½d. must be multiplied by 12 in order to determine its real value in 1717, and this would produce the sum of £3,277,282 19s. 6d. But it is only with regard to the demesne that the monastic income coincided with the income from land, and the demesne was not more than one-sixth of the monastic property. From the remaining five-sixths the monks received a rent, which on an average amounted to one-fifth of the income from land. In order to find the income of monastic lands, the monastic rent must be multiplied by five and added to the income from demesne, viz.

$$\frac{£3,277,282 \ 19s. \ 6d.}{6} + \left(\frac{£3,277,282 \ 19s. \ 6d.}{6} \times 5 \times 5\right)$$

$$= £14,201,559 \ 11s. \ 2d.$$

The author then proceeds to calculate from what proportion of the English territory this income of fourteen millions is received, and, to that end, makes use of the figures of the land tax of his own time. This land tax, he says, brings in on an average two millions a year, and amounts to four shillings in the pound; but, land valuation being low, the tax on an average does not represent more than 10 per cent. of the income from land, which can therefore be taken as amounting to twenty millions. The national income from land being twenty millions and the income of monastic lands fourteen millions, it follows that the monks had in their hands seven-tenths of the whole kingdom, which, if the Pretender should triumph, would be taken from their present owners and given back to the Church. The author admits that his conclusions may seem utterly improbable and monstrous, but believes that anything is possible in a Roman

Catholic country. Not long ago the Grand Duke of Tuscany ordered a land survey of his country to be made, and it was found that the Church held possession of $\frac{17}{20}$ of the whole territory.—There is not the slightest need seriously to refute this 'political arithmetic'. It is manifestly wrong, because in the ingenious train of arguments there is hardly one sound premiss; and the ultimate conclusion is even absurd. The statistical juggler in the vehemence of accusation overreached himself in so far as he quite overlooked the clergy, whose income was about the same as that of the monasteries, and from the national point of view was also chiefly an income from land. If the monasteries possessed seven-tenths of all the territory, then almost the same area must be assigned to the clergy; and then the entire kingdom would not be large enough for this statistical fairy tale.

Nasmith.   The attempt to determine the area of the monastic lands, made by Nasmith in his preface to the third edition of Tanner, is much nearer the reality.[1] Nasmith does not mention among his authorities the pamphlet of 1717, but I have hardly any doubt that he refers to it both in his polemics and otherwise. Nasmith defines the monastic income in the sixteenth century as approximately £200,000. He objects to the statement that the figure of the monastic income must be multiplied in order to arrive at the amount of the income from land. He thinks that the monks kept in their own hands no small part of the monastic estates; and in such cases the monastic income would coincide with the income from land. The pamphlet, however, does not deny this fact, and it disagrees with Nasmith only in regard to the area of the demesne. Nasmith regards as groundless the statement that the monastic rents constituted ' so small ' a part of the income from land, i.e. that the quit-rents were very low. Finally he affirms that even in his day (his edition of Tanner appeared in 1787) the income from land had increased only tenfold, and that the land area which under Henry VIII brought in an income of £200,000 ought at the end of the eighteenth century to bring in two millions. But with reference to the national income from land

[1] Tanner,[3] Preface, p. iv.

he repeats in 1787 the argument of the pamphlet of 1717, and accepts the same figure of twenty millions. If the monastic income from land were two millions and the national twenty millions, the monasteries obviously possessed about one-tenth of the whole territory.

Some investigators of our day would like to decide the question in another way which seems both simpler and more reliable. The process of estimating the sixteenth-century income from land on the pattern of the income from land of a much later time is a very difficult task. Not only must the changes in the value of money be taken into consideration, but also the changes in the relation between ground rent and land value, and both these elements are very difficult to ascertain even approximately. It seems possible, however, to define the area of monastic lands without going outside the sixteenth century. If we collect all possible data respecting the income of some particular unit of land—an acre for instance, we can calculate the average income from an acre ; and if we know the total of the monastic income and divide it by the average income of an acre we shall have the area of the monastic lands. Professor Kovalevsky who uses this simple method,[1] takes from Speed the total of the Church income and from Thorold Rogers the average income of an acre under cultivation ; and having divided £320,000 by 6d. he discovers that the number of acres of Church land is 12,800,000. Now the monastic income, according to Speed, Stow, and Tanner, amounted to about a half of the whole income of the Church ; consequently the area of monastic lands was, at least, one-sixth of the whole of England.

At first sight, the conclusion thus arrived at, that the monasteries possessed several millions of acres, seems very definite, but in truth it is very vague and indefinite. The monasteries had a variety of titles under which they held the lands said to belong to them.[2] Under the term ' title ' are included military tenure and frankalmoign, socage and burgage, copyhold and leases of various duration, tenure at the will of the lord ; on a good many estates the monasteries had

Professor Kovalevsky.

---

[1] Kovalevsky, ii. 745–8.   [2] Pollock and Maitland,[2] i. 144–5.

only rights in regard to the tithe. The amount of monastic income varied considerably even on account of the various titles to the land. In some cases the monastery paid a rent because it was a tenant, in other cases it received a rent because it was the landlord ; for the land which the monastery itself managed it usually neither received nor paid any rent, but took for itself all the produce of the land. The amount of the rents, both of those paid and those received by the monastery, varied considerably according to the nature thereof, whether the tenure was copyhold, freehold, lease-hold, or at the will of the lord, and according to the existence or not of admission fines, and the amount thereof. Thus people outside the monastery could also have titles to some of the land included in the monastic surveys given in the Valor Ecclesiasticus; and it is possible that such tenures may have sometimes entitled their holders to a greater share of the income from land than that which fell to the lot of the monasteries. The land that was yielding an income to a monastery might at the same time yield an income to another person, and sometimes even to several persons, and the income of these others might even exceed that of the monastery. Can we say that the land ' belongs ' to a monastery in those cases where the monastery has only some kind of right to it and receives from it only a fraction of the income ? If we say ' yes ', then for a very considerable part of 'its' estates the monastery must acknowledge co-owners or co-possessors, and the term ' belongs ' must be used in a very limited sense. If we answer ' no ', what is the legal or economic division that we are to draw between that which the monastery possesses and that which it does not possess ? What kind of title, and what share of the income are sufficient to make the land ' belong ' to the monastery ?

Every attempt to express in acres the area of monastic lands must also take into consideration the fact that the whole of the monastic income was not income from land, and that the whole of the monastic income from land was not income from agri-culture only. In the Commissioners' returns for 1535 the funda-mental basis of the division of monastic income is that of temporal

and spiritual. In the spiritual income are included freewill offerings, which without doubt do not belong to the income from
land. The chief item of the spiritual income is the tithe, but
is tithe an income from land ? A lawyer will not admit that the
lands, of which a monastery has only a right to the tithe, belong
to that monastery ; neither will an economist pronounce tithe
to be an income from land, except from the point of view of
national production ; in this case only will he consider tithe a
constituent part of the national income from land. In the
temporal income of monasteries there are also items that are not
income from land, such, for instance, as the perquisites of Courts.
How can such items be expressed in terms of acres ?—Well,
let us suppose that we are limiting ourselves to that part of the
monastic income which can be regarded as income from land,
and can be made to correspond to a fixed area of land. If our
authorities do not enable us to calculate exactly the number of
acres belonging to the monasteries, one would think that we
might rely upon ' averages ' and the division. But how shall we
determine the average income of an acre for all the monastic
territory? Monasteries possessed salt-works, mines, fisheries,
and the income of these cannot easily be expressed in acres.
Monasteries had considerable estates in towns, where the
income from a given unit of area was much greater than in the
country ; this can, however, be translated into acres, though
not without difficulty. To what extent does the income from
town property increase the average income of monastic land ?
We can avoid the difficulty, of course, by eliminating the income
from fisheries, mines, and town lands, and by expressing in acres
the agricultural income only ; but how shall we calculate the
average agricultural income ? Professor Kovalevsky seeks to
evade the difficulty by taking from Rogers the income of 'an
acre of land under cultivation '. But in the country the monks
had not arable land only ; there were meadow lands, pastures,
woods and waste, and the various kinds of land differed considerably from each other in the income which they yielded.
If we divide the country income of the monasteries in order to
find the average income from an acre of arable land, we shall
obtain not the actual area of monastic lands but only what

would have been the area of monastic lands if they had all been arable. Is it possible to calculate the average income of country land in general? We can ascertain the average income of arable land, meadow, wood, garden and pasture in the sixteenth century. But to pass from these to the average income of land in general further information is necessary, —we must know the average relation between the areas of the different kinds of land. Let us imagine several monasteries with the same land area but with a different distribution of the land into arable, pasture, &c. Let us suppose that every acre of arable land yields to all these monasteries the same amount of income. Let us suppose that every acre of meadow brings in an income the same for all the monasteries, but different from the income of the arable land, let us make the same supposition with regard to the income of wood and pasture. It is quite obvious that the average income of the land will differ in each monastery in spite of the fact that the income of each separate kind of land is supposed to be the same for all the monasteries. The average income of the land will be highest in those cases where the amount of unprofitable land is least, and it will be lowest where there is the highest percentage of unprofitable land. Thus an inquirer must find out the average distribution of monastic land into the different kinds ; and here he will meet with an insurmountable difficulty arising from the authorities. The Valor Ecclesiasticus gives hardly any material for deciding the question of the division of land into the different kinds, and I am afraid that the information derived from all the other sources will also prove inadequate. If the investigator be particular and strict, difficulties must arise with regard to the authorities even in deciding simpler questions, such as the average income of the different kinds of land. It seems to me that even an approximate translation of a large income from land into acres is an almost hopeless task when dealing with the sixteenth century ; and I would add that, as the monastic titles to the land were extremely variable and fractional, the definition of the land area of monastic lands appears to be not only very difficult but also very unimportant.

English authors have for the most part understood that Relation of
monastic
income to
national
income. estimates of monastic estates in acres meant very little to the English reader, and therefore they try to convey an idea of the area of monastic lands by stating that it amounted to this or that fraction of English territory. All the fractions given by them, all these tenths, thirds and fourths, do not really represent the area, but only the relation of monastic income from land to the national income from land. The anonymous author of the Jacobite pamphlet believes that the monks were seised of seven-tenths of England, but this is only another way of saying that of the twenty millions of the national income the monks have fourteen millions. All his argument rests upon the calculation of the national income from land. And, daring though he is, he does not venture to give what may be regarded as a trustworthy figure for the national income from land in the sixteenth century; and it is just because of this that he translates the monastic income in the Valor Ecclesiasticus into the economic language of his own day. Nasmith pursues the same course. Other English authors have compared the monastic income, not with the income from land, but with the whole of the national income. Lord Herbert had given utterance to his view that the monastic income amounted to one-fourth or one-third of the national income. Collier believes that even the estimate of one-fifth is much too high; he speaks of it as a tenth.[1] Hume's supposition concerning the amount of the national income at the beginning of the sixteenth century, although utterly without foundation, was, for some reason, largely accepted. Lingard, although he dislikes Hume, quotes this from him, and the same is done by Cobbett and even Dixon.[2] If it were at

[1] Herbert, Henry VIII, 1649, pp. 375-7 (in this book pages 369-404 are numbered twice, this is the second pagination); Collier, ii. 108.

[2] In the first edition of Hume's History (England under the house of the Tudors, 1759, p. 222) *three* millions are mentioned; he says, 'the whole lands and possessions of England had, a little before this period, been rated at three millions a year; so that the revenues of the monasteries (Hume took from Speed the figure £161,100) did not really much exceed the twentieth part of the national income, a sum vastly inferior to what is commonly apprehended.' But in the first posthumous edition of the 'History' (1778, iv. 182) *four* millions are given; *four* millions are given

all possible to define the amount of the national income, this method would be the more correct, as the monastic income was not derived from land only.   But we are utterly unable to discover what, in 1535, was the total national income, and all the above calculations are entirely without foundation. We must confine ourselves to the less pretentious task of propounding only those questions which can be answered from the authorities.   When we are dealing with the monastic economy previous to the Dissolution our chief authority must be the Valor Ecclesiasticus ; it does not give us the exact figures for the whole country, but it enables us to depict with considerable certainty many sides of monastic economy. Unfortunately, however, this rich treasury remains almost unexplored, and, of all the authors mentioned, only the old antiquaries systematically used the returns of 1535.   But even they only took from the returns the totals of the monastic incomes, and did not do anything in the way of analysing the returns for the separate monasteries, or dividing the revenue into temporal and spiritual.   Only in Mr. Archbold's book [1] do we find any attempt to make use of this authority, which seems to cry aloud for analysis, and which yields the readiest and most straightforward answer to the question, What exactly did the Crown and the laity gain from the monasteries ?   Mr. Archbold wrote about the monasteries of one county only ; but the Somerset religious houses were very similar to the monasteries of other counties, so that his local study may well have a general application.

The V.E. a geld book.   The Valor Ecclesiasticus is a 'geld book'.   No mandate was given to the Commissioners of 1535 to describe the

also in the 1854 edition (iii. 245–6).   The authors who repeat Hume's statement adhere for some unknown reason to *three* millions.   Cobbett, Letter xvi. p. 452.   Lingard repeats Hume's figure but makes a sceptical remark (ii. 98–100) ;   Dixon, i. 247–50, 322.   I do not understand Dr. Cunningham's approval of Dixon's figures (Growth,[4] i. 531).   For the year 1535 Dixon simply took from Speed the figure £320,000, and from Hume £3,000,000, and divided the second by the first ; in one passage he says that the monastic wealth is a half, and in another a third of the wealth of the whole Church.   Th. Rogers (A. and P. iv. 113) supposes that the monks possessed one third of the national wealth.

[1] Somerset Religious Houses, 1892.

monastic economy; they were instructed to calculate the amount of the tax payable by every benefice and to raise it to the amount of one-tenth of the net income. To ascertain the amount of the net income it was necessary to look into some parts of the monastic household, but the Commissioners naturally sought to confine their work to the calculation of the net income only. The chief object of their investigation was the monastery budget : in other words, the pecuniary statement of the household income and expenditure. If this is a detailed one, it furnishes some idea of the household management; and so it comes that the Valor Ecclesiasticus gives much valuable information concerning the economic structure of the monastic world. But a budget, however detailed, leaves us in the dark respecting many things in the household, and the Valor Ecclesiasticus cannot by any means be regarded as a collection of very detailed budgets. The Commissioners of 1535 were bound by their official Instructions, which they studiously followed, being closely watched by the Government. The latter was, however, not equally interested in all the items of the monastic budget; and thus the inquiry of 1535 was confined to ascertaining the amount of net income. The Commissioners could not omit one single item of monastic revenue ; but their Instruction jealously abridged the tenth-free expenditure. They could deduct from the gross income only (a) the regular fees of stewards, bailiffs, receivers and auditors, (β) the regular rents and pensions, (γ) the regular alms distributed under the will of the donors, (δ) the regular diocesan payments. Whatever remained over after these deductions was considered the net income. Of course, this net income also was spent by the monks, but, as expenditure, it did not interest the Commissioners and did not appear in their accounts. Thus the income-budget alone entered in its entirety into the Valor Ecclesiasticus.

Entirety is not minuteness. The Instruction required the primary surveys of the individual budgets to be very detailed. The Commissioners had to register the amount of every item of income and the place whence it was derived ; and for every separate item of tenth-free expenditure they had to give the amount and the name of the receiver. The Instruction does not require the same details in the survey of a diocese or a county ; and only points out the exact order in which the benefices are to be placed and the necessary outward form: 'after the auditors' fashion.' The differences between counties and even separate monasteries in one and the same county, so noticeable in the Valor Ecclesiasticus, can probably be explained by the want of definiteness in the Instruction ; some Commissioners may have thought that too much detail would be out of place in the returns of a county or diocese, and that the justifications of their few totals would be furnished by the detailed returns of the sub-commissions, which according to the Instruction were to be added to the returns of a county or diocese. The shortest returns were made by the Hants Commissioners. The surveys of all the monasteries in this county give only the figures of the gross income and of the allowances. To this there are two exceptions (Hyde Abbey and St. Swithin's, Winchester); but even these can be said to be surveyed with more detail only because the totals of the gross income and allowances are reckoned separately for every monastic office. But in the neighbouring county of Surrey all the monastic budgets are given in detail, for the Commissioners of this county when making the allowances retained a considerable part of the particulars given in the primary returns.

In other counties, for instance in Oxfordshire, even more detailed surveys are found ; in some cases the surveys given to the Commissioners by the monastic authorities have evidently been put in their entirety into the county returns. On the other hand, for the six counties—Berks., Camb., Essex, Herts., Northumb., Rutland—and for a part of the seventh, Yorks., we have no Commissioners' returns at all.[1] We

---

[1] The Commissioners' returns for Middlesex are not now extant in their entirety. The surveys that are lost are those of chantries and parish churches ; the monastic surveys are all preserved. Those of three Northumberland monasteries (Bamburgh, Farne Island (Insula Sacra), Neseham : V. E. v. 64, 304–5, 310) are for various reasons entered in the surveys of other counties.

possess instead only the official figures of the net, and the private figures of the gross income.

Thus the Instruction, which considerably lightened the work of the V. E. Commissioners, proves a source of great difficulties to the investigator of our own day. At almost every step he meets with obstacles and prohibitions, and no matter how great his unwillingness may be, he is bound by the Instruction and compelled to obey it, almost as obediently as did his predecessors the Commissioners. Like them, he has, to some extent, to make ' a fair book after the auditors' fashion '.

The monastic surveys of the Valor Ecclesiasticus are divided on one side into receipts and allowances (*reprisiones, allocationes*), and on the other side into the spiritual and temporal budget (*temporalia, spiritualia*). Only the first division, which enables us to distinguish the net income from the gross, has been utilized by historians—the antiquaries' lists give the figures of both. But the division of the income into temporal and spiritual remains unexplored: even the old antiquaries were not interested in it. This fact may probably be accounted for in two ways : in the first place, the spiritual budget was not separately given in all the monastic surveys, and therefore Cotton, Speed, and Dugdale could not always note this distinction in their lists ; and the idea of compiling very imperfect lists, which could not give a total for the whole country, did not commend itself to them. Moreover, the spiritual income and expenditure, especially the spiritual income, is not infrequently involved in the temporal one (for instance, Christchurch, Canterbury; Lacock, Wilts.), and in order to disentangle it, an attentive study of the whole survey and long calculations were necessary, whereas the old antiquaries always sought in the Valor Ecclesiasticus for totals ready at hand. But any student who would make an analysis of the monastic returns must from the very first separate the spiritual from the temporal income wherever possible, for such a division alone will give him the two different sides of the monastic struggle for life. The spiritual revenues of the monasteries are mostly the revenues of such

Rubrics of monastic surveys.

parish churches as had passed into the hands of the monks ; the technical term is 'appropriation'. As in the case of other parish revenues, so in these we can distinguish the income from lands attached to the church ('*gleba*'), the tithe of different kinds, voluntary offerings, pensions paid by other churches—a kind of partial appropriation. The spiritual expenses, with a few exceptions, are met by the spiritual income, and are divided into synodals and proxies, or visitation money, pensions to other churches and alms.[1] The spiritual budget shows the territory acquired by the monks not from the laity but from the clerics, that is, the parochial clergy. A lay historian is naturally much more interested in the other side, viz. the lands obtained from the laity and valued in the temporal budget of the monasteries, and when I had to choose between the totals of the temporal and the spiritual budget I naturally chose the former. In my list I am thus giving the gross and the net income of the whole budget, and then the gross and the net income of the temporal budget.

Mistakes in the totals of income. In the first two columns of figures my table seems to agree with the lists of the old antiquaries, but I arrived at my general totals of the gross and net income in a different way from theirs. They copied from an official excerpt (Liber Valorum) the totals of the net incomes given therein, and from the Valor Ecclesiasticus they took the calculated totals of the gross incomes, or what they in their examination thought were the totals of the gross incomes. I used the official excerpt only for those counties the surveys of which are lost ; in the Valor Ecclesiasticus, I read and calculated for every monastery all the items of income and expenditure ; and in this way I arrived at my totals by a systematic process of additions and deductions. My totals very often do not agree with those of the Valor Ecclesiasticus which found their way into the old lists, but I do not desire, nor have I any reason, to find fault with the old totals. The difference between these and my totals is generally small as regards the individual monasteries, and I believe that for the whole country it would

[1] I include the 'corrodia' along with the spiritual expenditure.

only amount to a very small percentage of the grand total, all
the more so because the differences between the totals for the
separate monasteries tend to counterbalance each other. Some
of the differences between my totals and those of the Valor
Ecclesiasticus may arise from the fact that we—i. e. the calculator of 1535 and myself—do not interpret a vague or incomplete survey in the same way; this explanation, however, is
applicable only in a minority of cases. In order to arrive at
the totals in the surveys of large monasteries, one must add
and deduct scores, and sometimes hundreds of figures. Every
accountant knows by experience how easily mistakes creep
into a long chain of additions and deductions notwithstanding
all his care, and so will not be too severe as to the mistakes
of others, made so long ago as the sixteenth century. And
the difference between my figures and those of the Valor
Ecclesiasticus may generally be accounted for by simple
mistakes in reckoning. Sometimes it is I who make the
mistake, sometimes the auditor of 1535, and sometimes
both of us. I confess that sometimes I had to reckon over
and over again the income and expenditure of the large
monasteries before I could arrive at the old figures and not
make an altogether different total. I permit myself to express
the hope that the sixteenth-century calculator did not make
mistakes less often than I did. But I know well that there
are very many mistakes in my totals. In any case, they are
not a copy but a verification of the Valor Ecclesiasticus, and
it is for this reason that I publish them.[1]

I am aware, of course, that the difference between the sum of
separate items and totals might be explained otherwise than by
mistakes in reckoning. A copyist, for instance, might omit or
add an item or put in a wrong figure. In such a case the total
of the Valor Ecclesiasticus would be right, and the ' right ' total
found by adding together all the separate items would be
wrong. But when we find a difference it is impossible to say
whether the mistake is in the total or in the items. Especially
puzzling are the cases where the number of items is so small
that it would be difficult for an accountant to make a mistake

---

[1] The list of monasteries and their income is printed in the Appendix.

in reckoning. Here is an instance: Cartmell, Lanc., V. E. v. 272, 'In redd' et firmis in diversis villis et villatis subscriptis, viz. villa de Cartmell £61 4s. od., Sylverdall Bolton et Hest £3 17s. od., libera firma liberorum tenentium in Cartmell £1 12s. 7d., firma molendini aquatici ad bladum £6 os. od. In toto £78 19s. 7d.' Here there are only four items, but the total is not the correct outcome of them either in the pounds or in the shillings; the correct total would be £72 13s. 7d. Where is the mistake here, in the items or in the totals? I do not know. When analysing the monastic surveys I had, however, to act in a uniform manner; I therefore assumed as a basis that the items were right and that the difference between them and the total arose from mistakes in calculation. In a very few cases and only for special reasons did I give a preference to the totals. I did so in the case of St. Mary's, York. This survey is sufficiently detailed, the revenues are classified according to offices and do not *prima facie* excite mistrust. If we add up the items we get the gross income of £1,053 18s. 1¾d., and the net £650 7s. 9¼d., the gross temporal income £578 15s. 2¼d. and the net temporal £391 13s. 11¾d. But at the end of the survey (v. 9 *in fine*) quite different totals are given; the gross income is £2,091 4s. 7⅛d., the allowances £440 17s. 7d., the net income £1,650 7s. 0⅛d., and the amount of the tenth £165 os. 8½d. is calculated on the total £1,650 7s. 0⅛d. At the end of page 11, where the budget of the monastic 'cells' is added to the monastery budget, all the three totals are repeated. We can check the survey by the 'Computus ministrorum dni regis 32 H. VIII super monasterium B. Marie in suburbiis civitatis Eboraci': this Computus is summarized in the Monasticon, iii. 570–3. It is evident that not all the monastic estates were entered in the account of 32 H. VIII, but the total net income (£1,582 19s. 4½d.) is so much nearer to £1,650 than to £650 that we are bound to adopt the larger figure. If, in the case of separate manors, we compare the Valor Ecclesiasticus with the account of 32 H. VIII, we shall see that in the Valor Ecclesiasticus the revenues of many manors are very much diminished and sometimes even altogether omitted.

Here are some instances : (*a*) According to the V. E. the manor of Clifton yields an income of £24 2*s.* 9*d.*, according to the Computus £61 2*s.* 0*d.* There was a mill at Clifton which according to the V. E. brings in £0 13*s.* 4*d.*, and according to the Computus £7 0*s.* 0*d.* (*b*) According to the V. E. the manor of Harton and Barton brings in an income of £5 14*s.* 0*d.*, and according to the Computus £24 13*s.* 6*d.* (*c*) In the V. E. the manor of Hornesey is mentioned only once in the income budget, thus :—' Sacrista ' receives at Hornesey a free farm worth two shillings. It is clear from the Valor Ecclesiasticus itself that there was misunderstanding about the Hornesey revenues, and that it was a large estate. Among the ' reprisiones granatarii ' (page 6) the following items are mentioned : W. Constable militi senescallo dominii de Hornesey pro feodo suo per annum £2 0*s.* 0*d.* Iohanni Roger receptori denariorum et decimarum in Hornesey pro feodo suo per annum £7 0*s.* 0*d.* ; moreover, under the will of a bishop of Rochester the sum of £3 6*s.* 8*d.* was annually paid out of the revenues of the parish church in Hornesey to a certain ecclesiastic, but for some reason this item of expenditure was not taken into account by the exchequer. The account of 32 H. VIII confirms the statement that Hornesey was a large and profitable estate; ' redditus et firmae in Hornesey £67 16*s.* 6*d.*, redditus et firmae in Hornesey Beck £7 3*s.* 9*d.*, rectoria Hornesey cum manerio et piscaria £44 6*s.* 8*d.*' In the sixteenth century the monastery was considered very rich ; its abbot wore a mitre, sat in the House of Lords, and rivalled the Archbishop of York in his style of living. The survey of a small monastery—Heringfleet—in Suffolk also gives rise to many misunderstandings. The net temporal income was said to be £13 3*s.* 11*d.* (it should be £13 10*s.* 11*d.*), the net spiritual income is £5 2*s.* 7½*d.* ; but for the total of the net income, instead of £18 13*s.* 6½*d.*, we have the incomprehensible figure £49 11*s.* 7*d.*, and the tenth is reckoned according to this amount. In the case of Heringfleet I give the preference to the separate items ; though perhaps it might be more correct in this instance also to make use of the ' wrong ' total, but I had no opportunity of verifying it. Fortunately,

I have not found any other glaring inconsistencies between the items and the sum of them. There is one other instance where I have adopted the total rather than the items; but here the contradiction is less striking; I refer to the survey of Bromfield, Somerset. The sum of the items of income is £68 1s. 0d., but the survey has the total £78 19s. 4d. But whoever made the survey noticed the discrepancy between the total and the items, and made a note in the margin 'N.B. magis pro £10 13s. 4d.' If this figure be added to the sum of the items, the amount obtained agrees sufficiently with the total of the survey to justify us in considering the latter to be trustworthy.

Limits of inquiry.

And here I would say a few words as to the limits within which I have confined my inquiries, and which will appear from the following lists. I have studied the monasteries of England only.[1] All the nunneries but not all the monasteries mentioned in the Valor Ecclesiasticus have found a place in my list. I have not touched the friaries, and this doubtless renders my work incomplete. I would, however, point out in extenuation, that, in the first place, friaries were poor monasteries, and their general income only a small part of the general monastic income: secondly, that friaries are town monasteries founded in cities for the use of citizens and that they never lost their city character; their estates were exclusively town property; therefore to one interested chiefly in the agrarian side of the Dissolution friaries have no great importance. Colleges, again, do not enter into my list at all. It is true that some of them shared the fate of the monasteries; nevertheless, colleges are not monasteries. As a rule, too, I have not included hospitals in my list, although there would seem to be no definite distinction between a hospital and a monastery. One and the same corporation is sometimes called a monastery, sometimes a hospital and sometimes by both names indifferently. One London survey in the Valor Ecclesiasticus is called 'prioratus novi hospitalis B. Marie extra

---

[1] The surveys of the English monasteries contain some entries relating to their possessions in Wales. I have attempted to exclude them, but I question whether I have been altogether successful in doing so.

Busshopesgate '. I have included in my list such hospitals as are called monasteries in the Valor Ecclesiasticus.

The number of monasteries in my list is 553. As a rule, I have considered the cells as separate monasteries, and only in a few instances have I departed from this rule. Out of the Preceptories that are entered in the survey of St. John of Jerusalem, London, I have dealt separately with Balsall only. A certain cell, Ebbenay by name, belonging to Christ Church, Canterbury, I have not treated as a separate monastery, although in the Valor Ecclesiasticus it is referred to as a priory. In the survey, the manor of Ebbenay is distinguished from the priory of Ebbenay, and, what is more important, the priory of Ebbenay is said to be let. From this statement I conclude that monastic life at Ebbenay had ceased and that the former 'cell' had become a simple tenement of the larger monastery. It is also necessary to mention the monasteries which had been dissolved under Henry VIII before 1535. Many of them had returned into the hands of the Church, mostly to various colleges. In such cases, the former monastic revenues are described in the Valor Ecclesiasticus along with the other revenues of the spiritual corporations to which they had been granted. It is curious that in the Valor Ecclesiasticus the old monastic revenues seem sometimes to preserve their unity in the hands of the new proprietor. The revenues of four dissolved monasteries (Selborn, Hants ; Daventry, Ntht. ; Littlemore, Oxon. ; Sele, Sussex) are included in the survey of two Oxford Colleges (Magdalen and Christ Church); these revenues are described separately from the other property of the colleges, as though they were independent economic units ; and the survey also points out to what monasteries these revenues previously belonged. I have not included in my list any such 'late' monasteries. I must also remind the reader that the monasteries of Kingswood, St. Augustine's (Bristol), St. Andrew's (York) and Holy Trinity (York) are entirely omitted from the Valor Ecclesiasticus.

For all the monasteries in the list [1] only the sum of the net County totals.

---

[1] Or rather for 552 monasteries. The net income of St. Clement's, York, is not given in the V. E.

income can be given. It amounts to £136,361 12s. 8$\frac{17}{24}$d., and is thus distributed according to the counties :—

	£	s.	d.		£	s.	d.
Beds.	2252	15	10	Lincoln	7498	5	7½
Berks.	4309	18	8¼	Middlesex	11533	18	6
Bucks.	1061	16	4	Norfolk	5180	5	6
Cambr.	2491	3	3¾	Northants	3270	4	8⅛
Cheshire	2113	3	7	Northumb.	1177	9	1
Cornwall	998	7	1¼	Notts.	2042	1	2¾
Cumbld.	1311	7	0½	Oxon.	2538	13	10¼
Derby	802	0	10	Rutland	40	0	0
Devon	5131	13	2⅞	Salop	1966	12	8¾
Dorset	3747	9	10¼	Soms.	7579	5	5⅝
Durham	1515	13	9	Stafford	1613	1	9¼[11]
Essex	5417	15	10⅝	Suffolk	3401	12	3⅜
Gloucester	6072	9	1½	Surrey	4068	16	2¼
Hants	5187	11	3½	Sussex	2635	7	4¾
Hereford	732	1	0⅜	Warwick	3044	9	1½
Herts.	2402	12	8¼	Westmor.	154	17	7½
Hunts.	2275	18	11	Wilts.	3555	18	7⅞
Kent	6897	8	2⅝	Worcester	4049	1	1¼
Lancaster	1698	15	9½	Yorks.	11934	8	8⅛
Leicester	2657	0	7¾	Total ...	136,361	12	8$\frac{17}{24}$

In twenty-three counties the Valor Ecclesiasticus enables us to define the gross income for all the monasteries, and the amount is £91,303 15s. 5¼d., which is thus distributed according to counties :—

	£	s.	d.		£	s.	d.
Beds.	2596	1	4¾	Lancaster	2345	18	6
Bucks.	1280	14	7½	Leicester	3095	16	1½
Cheshire	2364	12	6	Lincoln	9110	9	5¼
Cornwall	1102	15	4¾	Middlesex	13025	10	5½
Cumbld.	1472	10	8¾	Notts.	2594	13	0
Devon	5511	17	5⅛	Salop	2347	9	3¾
Dorset	4431	2	4⅜	Soms.	8993	3	10⅜
Durham	1786	19	2¼	Surrey	4596	1	4½
Gloucester	7171	19	6½	Sussex	3088	6	9¼
Hants	6506	7	6	Westmor.	166	10	6½
Hereford	849	15	9½	Wilts.	4177	15	9⅝
Hunts.	2687	3	9½	Total ...	91,303	15	5¼

If we add together the net incomes of the same counties we get the sum of £77,791 6s. 11$\frac{13}{24}$d., which represents about 85⅕ per cent. of the gross income.

In the case of twelve counties it is possible to compare the four totals of all the monasteries, i.e. the gross and net total incomes and the gross and net temporal incomes. In twenty other counties the same comparison is possible to a very large extent, and so generally for the great majority of the monasteries. I give the totals according to the counties, indicating such monasteries as are omitted :—

County.	*Gross total.*			*Net total.*			*Gross temporal.*			*Net temporal.*		
	£	*s.*	*d.*	£	*s.*	*d.*	£	*s.*	*d.*	£	*s.*	*d.*
Beds. without n. 4	2193	7	7¼	1908	3	4½	1515	14	5½	1380	16	9¼
Bucks.	1280	14	7½	1061	16	4	770	16	11½	650	6	4¼
Cheshire	2364	12	6	2113	3	7	1379	2	9½	1247	11	0½
Cornwall without n. 2	1091	14	4¾	987	12	1¼	636	9	2¾	579	10	8¼
Cumberland ...	1472	10	8¾	1311	7	0½	756	8	8¾	712	12	4¼
Derby without nn. 4, 8	582	6	5½	450	7	7½	334	12	5½	292	13	0½
Devon without n. 5	5483	1	1⅛	5105	14	1⅞	3853	4	11⅜	3643	12	1⅞
Dorset without n. 5	4414	13	0⅜	3733	6	2⅛	3828	2	7⅜	3527	9	5⅜
Durham	1786	19	2½	1515	13	9	1222	1	4½	1108	6	4
Gloucester without nn. 1–3, 6 ...	5150	19	0¼	4419	15	10½	3922	1	2¾	3610	6	2¾
Hereford	849	15	9½	732	1	0⅙	534	7	11½	460	0	0½
Hunts.	2687	3	9½	2275	18	11	2361	6	8½	2063	12	9¼
Kent without nn. 3, 5, 14, 18, 20–21	5730	18	10¼	4651	12	8⅛	4616	19	6⅛	4079	1	7⅝
Lancaster ...	2345	18	6	1698	15	9½	1529	10	11	1292	2	2½
Leicester without n. 4	2821	4	11½	2425	12	9¾	1985	11	1½	1807	2	6½
Linc. without n. 11	8981	0	9¼	7374	3	7½	6701	13	3¼	5963	8	5¼
Middlesex ...	13025	10	5½	11533	18	6	11281	19	3	10446	6	4¼
Norfolk without nn. 2, 5, 20, 25...	5520	13	2	4616	13	3⅛	3736	3	4½	3203	10	8¼
Northants without n. 5	3772	15	3⅜	3225	4	8⅛	3017	8	2⅜	2753	12	1⅜
Notts.	2594	13	0	2042	1	2¾	1457	5	4	1303	0	7¼
Oxon. without nn. 2–3, 9, 12 ...	1756	19	5¼	1466	17	3¼	1298	1	3	1136	12	3
Salop	2347	9	3¾	1966	12	8¾	1788	14	3¾	1610	2	10¾
Somerset	8993	3	10⅜	7579	5	5⅞	7394	0	5⅞	6900	2	8⅜
Staff. without n. 1	1875	14	5½	1602	0	3 11/16	1328	7	9½	1209	7	8¾
Suff. without n. 16	4459	18	9½	3391	12	3¾	3760	6	1	3264	3	11¼
Surrey without n. 6	3634	17	10½	3291	4	1¾	2756	11	2¾	2542	6	3
Sussex without n. 9	3036	4	5¼	2607	15	1¾	2182	14	5¼	1966	3	4⅜
Warwick without n. 3	3646	5	11	2844	9	1½	2501	12	0	2194	19	1
Westmoreland ...	166	10	6½	154	17	7½	103	7	2½	97	12	1½
Wilts. without nn. 2, 13	4065	18	9⅞	3454	6	4⅜	3432	8	11⅞	3021	14	7⅛
Worcester without nn. 2–3 ...	4617	10	7¼	4006	11	10¼	3553	0	6½	3253	14	8½
Yorks without nn. 5, 6, 8, 23, 25, 26, 34, 40, 44, 48, 50, 51, 53, 58, 59, 61, 63, 64...	9630	7	6½	7584	1	6	6428	19	2¾	5762	8	11
Totals	122,381	14	4⅛	103,132	16	5⅙	91,969	4	0	83,084	10	4⅜

If we express the total of the gross income—£122,381 14*s.* 4⅛*d.*—by the number 100, then the total of the net would be expressed approximately by 84¼ (we must remember that for 23 counties the total of the net income amounted to 85⅕ per cent. of the gross); the total of the gross temporal income approximately by the number $75\frac{1}{6}$ and that of the net temporal approximately by the number $67\frac{4}{5}$. The net income then amounts to a little more than five-sixths of the gross income; the gross temporal income to about three-fourths of the gross income; and the net temporal income to a little more than two-thirds of the gross income. I have arrived at these proportions by calculation from the monasteries with a net income of £103,132 16*s.* $5\frac{1}{6}$*d.* And the net income of all the monasteries that I have studied is estimated (see above) at £136,361 12*s.* $8\frac{17}{24}$*d.* The number 103,132 is a little more than three-fourths of the number 136,361. Thus the proportion 100, $84\frac{1}{4}$, $75\frac{1}{6}$, $67\frac{4}{5}$ is based upon observation of three-fourths of the whole monastic income. I assume that the same proportion (100, $84\frac{1}{4}$, $75\frac{1}{6}$, $67\frac{4}{5}$) holds good with regard to the remaining fourth. Having, then, ascertained the amount of the whole monastic net income, we can readily guess at that of the other three: viz. the whole monastic gross income, the whole monastic gross temporal income, the whole monastic net temporal income. These respective items, taking the whole monastic net income to be £136,361, work out as follows: £161,853, £121,659, £109,736. Thus we may say that, in round figures, the monasteries named in my list have, according to the Valor Ecclesiasticus, a gross income of a hundred and sixty thousand pounds and a net income of a hundred and thirty-five, and that the temporal gross income included in these figures amounts to a hundred and twenty thousand pounds and the temporal net income to a hundred and ten thousand. But we must not forget that no colleges or friaries, and but few hospitals, have been taken into account.

CHAPTER II

THE NON-AGRICULTURAL INCOME OF THE MONASTERIES

IN order to give the four sums worked out at the end of Spiritual
the previous chapter a more definite meaning they must be Income.
analysed—a rather lengthy process, I am afraid.

The gross spiritual income—about forty thousand pounds
—is nearly a fourth of the whole monastic gross income.
This spiritual income is almost entirely derived from cathedrals and parish churches which have passed into the hands
of the monks, the only items of a non-parochial character
being the offerings at shrines which were the object of
especial reverence ; everything else is parochial income.
A very large number of benefices (rectories, vicarages,
chapels) belonged entirely to the monasteries, and from
them the monasteries received all the parochial revenues :
the income from the glebe, tithes of different kinds, receipts
from other benefices, voluntary offerings and other small
revenues. But it was not infrequently the case that a
monastery had a right to a part only of the parochial income, or to some fixed portion of the gross income, or to
a definite part of the tithes, or to a definite sum of money.
I give a few instances. The monastery of Horton, in Kent,[1]
with a gross income of £111 16s. 7d., had a spiritual income amounting to £25 15s. 0d. Included in this is a
certain rectory (the parsonage of Braborne) which belonged
entirely to the monastery and yielded an income of
£16. The monastery owned part of the tithe in two
places (Atterdondane, Honychild) valued at £0 15s. 0d.
+ £0 15s. 0d. From two rectories (Purley in Essex and
Horton) the monastery received fixed money payments and

---

[1] I shall give the reference to the V. E. only where the survey of a
monastery takes up several pages and some particular passage has to
be pointed out. But if the survey is short, or if I am referring to the
whole of it, the reader will easily find it in my list of monasteries.

pensions amounting to £8 0s. 0d. + £0 5s. 0d. The Dorset monastery of Tarrent, with a gross income of £239 10s. 10d., had a spiritual gross income of £21 17s. 4d. The three rectories, Crafforde Parva, Wodeyats and Hamford, belonged entirely to the monastery. The income of two of the rectories is divided into 'tithes of different kinds', and 'offerings and other revenues' (£6 0s. 0d., £0 4s. 0d.; £5 16s. 8d., £0 3s. 4d.). The third rectory, Crafforde Parva, had from the parishioners £3 0s. 0d. and from the tithe of demesne in the hands of the abbess £3 6s. 8d. Besides this, the monastery owned part of the tithe at Kayneston, valued at £3 6s. 8d. Bindon, a monastery in Dorsetshire with a gross income of £236 8s. 9¾d., had a spiritual income amounting to £51 0s. 0d. This monastery owned the whole of the rectory of Chaldon, whose lands and tenancies produced the rent of £1 0s. 0d. ('terre et tenementa glebe eiusdem personatus'); its tithes were valued at £7, and the offerings and other revenues at £3 6s. 8d. In the parish of Winfrith a part only of the Church land ('terre et tenementa glebe eiusdem porcionis' belonged to the monastery, but both brought in a good income (£4 13s. 4d. + £26 13s. 4d.) and the rector paid to the monastery a pension of £2 0s. 0d. The remainder of the income was derived from parts of the tithes in other parishes. It is very seldom that we come across more detailed descriptions in the surveys. The most detailed seems to be that made of the rectory of the Holy Cross, preserved in the survey of Pershore, an abbey in Worcestershire. Here the income of £43 8s. 1d. is divided into thirty-two items. The principal item is the tithe: the corn and hay tithe yields £32 6s. 5d.; the tithe of increase, of wool, flax, hemp, and fish yields £2 5s. 6d.; the 'private' (probably personal) tithe and other receipts amount to £6 6s. 8d. The offerings amount to £0 19s. 1d.; payments received from other benefices, £0 6s. 8d. Smaller kinds of revenue are also enumerated in detail: mortuaries, chrismaries, weddings, burials, Sunday payments and churchings. Nothing is said about the income from the Church land.[1]

---

[1] The description of the revenues of Tewkesbury, Glouc., a monastic rectory, is also very detailed (V. E. ii. 471 in fine, 482).

Some of these incomes were closely connected with Oblations. Roman Catholicism, and after the breach with Rome they either diminish very considerably, or disappear altogether. The religious policy of the Tudors proved a source of much disturbance among the people ; those who would not abandon their former faith or who actively resisted the Government, naturally caused a falling off of the voluntary contributions ; while the religious zeal even of the passive multitude which obediently followed its superiors, was greatly abated. Fuller complains, half seriously, half ironically, that with the downfall of Romish superstition the hand of the giver grew poor ; and that the amounts of voluntary gifts returned in 1535 very soon ceased to correspond with those actually received. These lamentations may suggest that a considerable part of spiritual income entered in the V. E. disappeared simultaneously with the monasteries. But a study of the surveys in the Valor Ecclesiasticus does not corroborate this inference. If the monasteries did receive a large income from the voluntary gifts of parishioners and pilgrims, it did not appear in the pages of the Commissioners' returns. Oblations and the income from the Church services constitute there a very small part only of the monastic spiritual budget. Oblations were very considerable in one case only, that of St. Mary's, Walsingham, an Augustinian house which comprised the famous chapel wherein the milk of Our Lady was preserved. It seems that in the last year before the survey was made these oblations amounted to £260 12s. 4d. So that either the popularity of Our Lady of Walsingham was quite exceptional, or the monks at other pilgrim centres concealed their revenues. Oblations at the shrine of Thomas Beckett were valued at £36 2s. 7d. only. We very seldom come across even so modest a sum as £10 (the amount of the oblations to the Blood of Our Lord in Hayles), or £6 13s. 4d. (the amount of the oblations to the image of St. Brigitt).[1] It is true that oblations flowed not only to the shrines which were great centres of pilgrimage ; for corresponding items are also found in the budget of obscure parish churches. Unfortunately in their case the oblations are joined with other

[1] V. E. i. 8; ii. 456; i. 425.

small revenues of the parish, and are contrasted on the one hand with the tithe and on the other with the income from the Church land.[1] Even when the oblations are thus united they do not amount to much. The Dorset monastery of Abbotsbury had a gross spiritual income of £90 18s. 8d., but oblations and other receipts amounted to only £9 17s. 0d. In the case of Bindon the corresponding figures are £51, and £3 6s. 8d. Often the difference between the two figures is even more striking. For the rectory of Hartland, belonging to a Devonshire monastery of the same name, the corresponding figures are £58 5s. 0d. and £2 5s. 0d. ; for the rectories of Wodeyats and Hamford belonging to the monastery of Tarrent in Dorsetshire the figures are £12 4s. 0d. and £0 7s. 4d. In the surveys of parish churches, oblations are occasionally separated from the other small revenues and then, of course, they appear even more insignificant when compared with the general income. The abbey of Wilton received within its county the spiritual income of £40 18s. 2d. and the oblations amounted only to £0 12s. 2d. The rectory of Cowland brought to the Devonshire abbey of Canonleigh an income of £8 1s. 0d., the oblations amounted to 5s. only. The oblations are more considerable in the rectory of Haitfield which belonged to the monastery of Roche in Yorkshire (£41 14s. 8d. and £2), but this is quite exceptional. In studying the Dissolution one must take into account the decrease of the parish income caused by the Reformation. With the establishment of the Anglican Church the spiritual income of the monastic estates was certainly diminished in some directions, but the decrease was small in comparison with the whole spiritual revenue of the monasteries.

Glebe.   The income of parish churches from land is a more important element. From an agrarian point of view the historian naturally looks upon it as the most interesting side of the spiritual revenue, and is anxious to form accurate ideas concerning it. Here, however, the summarizing method of the Valor Ecclesiasticus makes itself felt with peculiar force. Even

[1] I believe, however, that in the column 'oblations and other profits' (alia proficua) one kind of tithe, the *personal*, called the 'private', or tithe of the parishioners, is added to other profits.

in the surveys of non-monastic churches the income from Church land is by no means always distinguished from the whole budget of a parish church ; while in monastic surveys such distinction is found only in a small minority of cases, and therefore, instead of a long list of figures, we must content ourselves with a limited number of instances. Even within the limits of one monastic survey all the rectories are not similarly described. Nothing would be more interesting than to discover what proportion the income from land of appropriated churches bears to the whole spiritual revenue of a monastery. From the Valor Ecclesiasticus it is possible to determine the income from glebe in the case of separate parish churches more often than in that of monasteries. I subjoin a few instances ; the smaller amount indicates the income from the glebe, the larger that of the rectory ; the first name after that of the county signifies the monastery, the second, the rectory :—

				£	s.	d.	£	s.	d.
Devon	Hartland	Crowland	...	8	1	0	1	3	0
		Launcell...	...	22	12	0	2	5	0
Dorset	Middleton	Stocklond	...	16	9	4	2	8	4
Suffolk	Sibton	Rendham + Sibton ⎱ ⎰ Tunstall ...	38	18	11½	2	5	0
Worcester	M. Malvern	Powik ...	...	8	0	0	0	13	4
	Pershore	Choynhyll	...	15	1	0	2	0	0
		Mathor ...	...	13	0	0	0	14	0
Yorks.	Roche	Haitfield	...	41	14	8	2	17	0

In certain exceptional cases it is possible to calculate what proportion the amount of the glebe income bears to the whole spiritual budget of a monastery.

In the monastery of Abbotsbury in Dorsetshire the spiritual gross income of £90 18s. 8d. corresponds to a land income of £8 17s. 8d. ; at Bindon in Dorset the corresponding figures are £51 0s. 0d. and £5 13s. 4d. ; at Shaftesbury, Dorset, £88 10s. 2d. and £7 8s. 0d.; at St. Thomas, Stafford, £50 2s. 4d. and £6 6s. 4d. ; at Knaresborough, Yorks., £62 4s. 8d. and £6 7s. 4d. Sometimes monastic rectories held lands other than the ' glebe '. The Yorkshire monastery of Hampole had two rectories, Athewik cum Marre and Melton. Athewik brought in a gross income of £26 14s. 0d., of which £2 13s. 4d. was derived from ' Gleba ', besides this a rent of £1 18s. 0d.

was received from an enclosed piece of ground and two freehold tenements. Melton brought in a gross income of £21 17s. 4d. of which £2 13s. 4d. was received from the parsonage and 'Gleba'; moreover the church had a mill which brought in an income of £2 6s. 8d., and several holdings brought in a rent of £2 1s. od. These are some rectories which seem to have lost the character of Church estates, and to have become as it were temporal granges or even manors ; sometimes they were entirely merged into a manor. In the survey of the abbey of St. Augustine, Canterbury, four places are mentioned to which the name 'rectoria sive grangia' is given (Allonde, Newlande, Sholldon, Asheleye [1]). In the neighbouring survey of Christchurch, Canterbury, the name 'manerium sive rectoria' is applied to Godmersham.[2] In the survey of a Worcester priory, Parva Malvern, the rectory of Elsefylde is even placed in the temporal budget ; it does not in any way differ from the manor, or, at least, is completely amalgamated with it. Several monastic rectories include in their income an item 'perquisita curiae'; this name is generally applied to the receipts from the manorial court. The Shaftesbury nuns (Dorset) owned the rectory of Bradford ; its tithes, oblations, and other parish revenues were let for £47 ; the glebe was let for £3 18s. 2d. ; besides this the 'perquisita curiae' bring in to the rectory an income of £1 5s. 6d. The Somersetshire priory of St. John, Wells, had the rectory of Westdowne ; its demesne yielded an income of £3 ; the tithes £5 ; 'perquisita curiae et aliae casualitates' £0 2s. od. I would not by any means be understood to affirm that these rectories had manorial courts of their own ; they could receive the amount of income due to them from some other court. But the survey of the rectory of Evercryche is not unlike the survey of a small manor. This rectory belonged to the same priory of St. John, Wells. The perpetual customary rents of the tenants yield £4 17s. 4d., the tithes £6 1s. 8d. 'perquis' cur' et' al' cas'' £0 1s. 6d. In any case it is quite clear that in the spiritual revenue of the monasteries there is found an income which is classed in the survey with the spiritual revenue only for technical reasons, since, economically

[1] V. E. i. 20–21.   [2] V. E. i. 10.

speaking, it is identical with the income from manorial demesne and the temporal rents. The number of examples being so small we cannot well draw definite conclusions; but the ideas which suggest themselves would lead us to believe that about one tenth of the gross spiritual income of the monasteries was derived from the Church land, and consequently would fall under the purview of an agrarian historian; and we have fortunately a means whereby to verify this idea. The monastic rectories closely resembled the benefices which remained in the hands of the parochial clergy, and the non-monastic rectories are on the whole described more fully than the others.

In the deaneries of some counties the income from Church land is distinguished from the general parochial income; in some of the Kent deaneries even the number of acres of the parish land is given. In the deanery of Sutton in Kent twenty benefices are valued at £256 13s. 6d., of which £16 16s. 7d. is derived from land.[1] In the Kent deanery of Lymme thirty-five benefices are valued at £575 15s. 7½d., of which £44 0s. 7½d. is derived from land.[2] In the Dorset deanery of Whytechurch fifty-seven benefices yield an income of £722 16s. 8d., of which £60 8s. 0d. is derived from land.[3] These figures compel us to modify somewhat the idea just formed as to the proportion of the income from land in the spiritual budget of monasteries. It would be safer to assume that the income from land constituted about one-twelfth of the gross spiritual income.

The bulk of the spiritual income of the monasteries consisted of tithes of different kinds, which evidently amounted to no less than five-sixths of the whole. The vaguest part of the tithe revenue is the tithe of the monastic demesne. As

Tithes of monastic demesne.

---

[1] V. E. i. 49–52. I did not take into account the chantry of Newestede et Bokenfeld, because in the survey its revenue from land is not given as a separate item. I also omitted the Vicarage of Ashetisford because its survey was made only under E. VI.

[2] V. E. i. 46–51, I omitted the rectory of Snergate (i. 49) because its income is not divided into items. Of course I likewise left out the priory of Bilsington.

[3] V. E. i. 257–60, I did not take into consideration the manor of Chelsey bequeathed by one of the rectors of the deanery (Lychet Mawtravers, i. 260). The income of the manor was spent for the benefit of the grantee's soul.

a rule, monastic lands, according to the Roman Catholic
canon law, paid tithe just like any other lands, but from very
early times the monks strove to evade the payment; exemption
bulls, however, were so disastrous to the parochial clergy that
they, together with the Government and the representatives
of the laity, naturally opposed all the privileges that the
monks tried to obtain.   The Roman Curia was bound to play
a complicated diplomatic game.   The monks were regarded
by Rome with not less sympathy than the parochial clergy,
and the Pope was ready to meet the monastic wishes half way.
But at the same time he would not damage his good relations with the laity, the Government and the secular clergy,
nor imperil the economic foundations of the parochial system.
Therefore the papal policy on this question was very equivocal
and brought about a variety of somewhat uncertain situations;
all the more so because at times the papal bulls clashed with
the statutes of Parliament.   A good account of this is given
by Selden.[1]   General principles had been laid down by the
Lateran Council of 1215, confirming the arrangement that
monks must pay to the parish churches the tithe on their
lands, but making exemption in favour of three orders, viz.
Hospitallers, Templars and Cistercians, who were excused
payment of tithe on the demesne in hand; therefore in the
sixteenth century the Hospitallers and Cistercians did not pay
tithe on the lands which they managed themselves.   But by
a series of special bulls the popes had extended this privilege
to others, sometimes to whole orders, sometimes to separate
houses.   Selden does not venture to give a definite opinion
respecting the validity of such bulls at common law.   One
Act of Parliament (2 H. VIII, c. 4) had, indeed, expressly set
aside every Papal bull that exempted from payment of tithe
land which had not been exempted by the Lateran Council
of 1215.   But the ecclesiastical courts acknowledged many
such bulls, and by the time of the Dissolution the number
of monasteries that did not pay tithe on their demesne land
was very considerable.   Besides, monasteries which had

---

[1] Selden, Tithes, ch. 13, ii.   Later authors on the whole only repeat
Selden.   Jones, 80-1; Cripps, 290; Phillimore, ii. 1152-4; Grove,
Alienated tithes, 598-605.

received no special bull could all the same evade payment of tithe. Not infrequently it was the case that the parish church to which the tithe had to be paid belonged to the monastery itself. In such a case the monastery having to pay tithe to itself could drop the payment without prejudice to any outside interests. Where such conditions had existed for a long time, we may well believe that the monastic demesne in question would become altogether tithe-free, or at least would not have paid it from time immemorial; and consequently that the monks could, without arousing any questions, make no mention of the tithe in the return which they presented to the Commissioners of 1535. They did not, however, always act thus. There are not many entries in the Valor Ecclesiasticus respecting demesnes in hand, but we do find some cases in which tithe was paid by a monastery to a parish church belonging to itself, and in such cases the tithe is entered in the survey of the parish church. Thus, in the survey of the Dorsetshire monastery of Middleton the demesne tithe is stated to bring in £20; and this sum is entered in the budget of Middleton rectory, which belonged to the monastery. The demesne tithe of another Dorset monastery (Cerne) is also entered in the survey of Cerne rectory which belonged to the monastery. The demesne tithe is likewise entered in the survey of the monastery of Missenden, Bucks., although both the rectory and the vicarage of Missenden belonged to the monastery.[1] In these cases the fact of the title to the tithe and the title to the church being in the same owner did not efface all traces of the tithe. Nevertheless, the rarity of demesne-tithes in the V. E. cannot but arouse suspicions. No doubt in many cases the tithe is not mentioned because the monastery was exempt, but it is a question whether such an explanation is applicable to all cases. I believe that not infrequently the lack of information concerning the demesne tithe arises from the fact of the merger of the titles to the tithe and the church; either the tithe was added to the demesne revenue and was entered in the monastic temporal budget, or the monks succeeded in completely suppressing it

[1] The demesne tithe is also given in the survey of Tewkesbury, Glouc., ii. 479.

in their returns to the Commissioners. Therefore the total amount of the tithe collected by the monasteries must probably be somewhat increased at the expense of the monastic temporal budget.

Parochial tithes.

But even if we stand by the amount given in the 1535 returns, the tithe gathered by the monks constituted a very considerable portion both of the whole monastic budget and of the general total of English tithe-income in the sixteenth century. After the Dissolution, the tithe, along with other monastic possessions, passed to the Crown. A small part of it was returned to the Church, but the bulk of it, as well as of the other monastic property, was thrown into the market and passed into the hands of the laity. The consequences of this were very important and are felt strongly in English life even to the present day.

If the laity had always been entirely unconnected with the use and management of the spiritual income of the monasteries it might have been difficult to transfer the tithes into lay hands. Even the pliant clergy of the young Church of England would in that case have spoken about sacrilege, and have roused the sympathy of their flock; the Government would not have found it easy to throw the monastic tithes on the market in the same way that they had disposed of the manors and town houses. But as a matter of fact, the laity, long before the Dissolution, had succeeded in getting access to the spiritual income of the monasteries without being helped in any way by the Government. The raising of the chief spiritual income, the tithe, was a complicated business and unsuitable for a monk, for as a gatherer of tithe he would often have to leave the monastery and enter into discussions of a delicate character with the parishioners. The monastery trusted but little the vicars of its churches, because their interests were opposed to those of the monastery. The vicars whom the monastery appointed to its own parishes either received a salary or a part of the parish revenues; they must have looked with envy upon the greater part of the receipts which went into the hands of the monks, who often did nothing for the parish. The monks, therefore, did not entrust the collection of tithe to the vicar, fearing that a considerable part of the tithe might either be appropriated by him or not collected at all from the parishioners; but they had recourse to the intervention of the laity, and either charged the bailiff of the nearest manor with the tithe gathering, or appointed special receivers or actually leased it to laymen.   Thus, the very fact of the tithe being centred in monastic hands weakened its 'spiritual' character and assimilated it to a temporal rent. When all the tithe was paid into the hands of the local clergy-man the parishioners knew very well how and upon what it was spent.   They might dislike the payment and consider that the clergyman received too much, but it was clear to all that the tithe was inevitable and that the payers received in exchange for it certain spiritual boons.   The tithe went to their *own* church and to their *own* clergyman, neither of which could exist without the tithe and both of which were necessary to the parish.   But in monastic parishes a part only of the revenue was spent on the spot; a greater part went elsewhere, to people who were strangers and for wants entirely unknown to the parish.   The parishioners paid because they were compelled to pay, just as they were forced to pay rent to the lord of the manor, but the idea that they were parting with a portion of their crops to satisfy their own spiritual needs was gradually effaced from their minds   The assimilation of tithe to temporal revenue increased still more where it was collected by the same individual who received the seigniorial rent, and thus the people grew accustomed to the lay control of the 'spiritual' revenue.

But the secularization of tithe was carried still further in the monastic economy.   Whilst the monastery still meant Leases of
Benefices. a large household and comprised a numerous administrative personnel, it was convenient enough to collect the tithe by means of its own servants.   But long before the Dissolution, the monks, like the temporal lords, had begun to curtail their households on the demesne.   They let out the demesnes and often entrusted the farmers with the collection of the tenants' rents.   The hitherto numerous staff of servants became un-necessary and was accordingly reduced.   This made it difficult for the monks themselves to collect their spiritual income, and they began to hand over their benefices to the laity to farm

for them.   In the sixteenth century the farming of rectories
had become fairly common.

In the Valor Ecclesiasticus we find the words 'valet ad
firmam' added to a great many benefices.   I do not venture
to assert that all such benefices were leased; the word 'firma'
is sometimes applied in the survey to the lands kept by the
monks in their own hands: but for the most part the
words 'valet ad firmam' of course indicate a lease.   In the
survey of the monasteries of Missenden and Nutley in
Buckinghamshire the benefices are divided into two kinds—
of some of them it is said 'in manu abbatis valet communibus
annis'; of others 'valet ad firmam'.   Now this distinction is
sufficient to justify us in considering the latter as leased.
Moreover, in the Missenden survey there is a direct reference
to the leasing of rectories: among the revenue items are
given the admission fines paid by the farmers of the rectories.[1]
Nor can there be any doubt about the farming of rectories
when the word 'rectoriae' is accompanied by the words
'dimissae per indenturam,' 'dimissae pro termino annorum,'
or even 'dimissae' standing by itself.   To give a few such
instances: The monastery of Markby, Lincolnshire, had five
and a half rectories, two of which were farmed.   The monastery
of Peterborough is mentioned as having six whole churches,
five of which were farmed, but nothing is said of the sixth.
In the survey of the Abbey of Shaftesbury in Dorset two
rectories are mentioned, and both were farmed.   The monastery of Hartland in Devonshire had seven rectories, only two
of which remained in the hands of the monks; two were
farmed 'at the will of the monastery', that is to say, without
terms; three were farmed for years, and the names of the
farmers are given.   The abbey of Cirencester in Gloucestershire had eleven rectories, all of which were farmed.   Another
still richer abbey in Gloucestershire, Tewkesbury, had sixteen
rectories; fifteen of them were farmed, and only the rectory
of Tewkesbury itself was left in the hands of the monks.
The monks had recourse to the services of the farmers when

[1] V. E. iv. 247, 'in finibus pro dimissione rectoriarum predictarum pro
termino annorum diversis personis per indenturam dimissarum £1 6s. 8d.'

they had only a part of the revenue or some special kind of tithe of a benefice. The monastery of Cirencester possessed the manor of Shrivenham in Berkshire, and in the survey is entered the grain-tithe of four places, which was let out to four different persons.[1] If I am right in my interpretation of the survey of Jervaulx, a monastery in Yorkshire, it would seem that of the two rectories, Estwhitton and Westwhitton, one part of the parochial income was let out, and the other remained in the hands of the monks.

If a rectory was farmed to a layman, it soon became assimilated to lay property. The monks had broken their personal connexion with the parish ; the farmer alone entered into immediate contact with the parishioners. The difference between the rectories that belonged entirely to the monks and those from which they had only the right to a fixed payment (*pensio*) thus became very slight, for even with regard to their own rectories the monks were merely receivers of rent. The farmer stood between the monks and the parish ; he collected the parochial receipts for himself, and naturally tried to collect more than he had to pay to the monks. He became accustomed to look upon the rectory as a source of income for himself, and he acquired a definite interest therein. After the Dissolution he would petition the Augmentations Court to renew the lease, or, if he had sufficient money, even to sell the rectory to him, and the Government would readily agree to such proposals, seeing in them only a confirmation of the situation. Thus the clerical property dropped by the monks could never return to the parochial clergy, but passed for ever into the hands of the laity, and England, to the great grief of irreconcilable churchmen, became a country of alienated tithes.[2]

[1] V. E. ii. 466.

[2] The author of ' The Alienated Tithes' clearly saw the connexion between the pre-Reformation farming of tithes and their later transference into the hands of the laity : Grove, part iii, pp. clxi, clxii.   But Grove exaggerates the number of tithe leases.   The monks in 1535 often let out the tithe ; but it does not follow from the Valor Ecclesiasticus that they let it more often than they kept it in their own hands. 'Rome,' of course, is much less guilty in regard to these leases than she seems to Grove. Grove ought to have thought of the owned church, the ' Eigenkirche ' (cf. Pollock and Maitland,[2] i. 497–9), but this is too dangerous a remembrance for a churchman.

Classifica-
tion of
monas-
teries
according
to the
amount of
their
income.

The famous statute of 27 H. VIII, concerning the dissolution of small monasteries, classifies all monasteries into two
sections, and the net income was made the basis of division.
The monasteries with an income of less than two hundred
pounds were suppressed; such a division, though very convenient for the purpose of suppression, is not of much value
in studying the monastic household. One must judge of the
dimensions of the household by the gross and not by the
utterly artificial 'net' income of the Survey. The division of
all monasteries into two classes is also much too rough to
afford any sort of concrete idea of the relative importance of
the large and small households. I will confine myself to
the temporal gross income, and divide the monasteries into
five groups: those with a gross temporal income of less
than twenty pounds, those with from twenty to a hundred
pounds, then from a hundred to three hundred, next from
three hundred to a thousand pounds and lastly all those
having more than a thousand pounds of gross temporal
income. Of course such a classification is arbitrary, but it
seems a convenient one in that it distinguishes the very small,
the small, the medium, the large, the very large monasteries.
The Valor Ecclesiasticus enables us to distinguish the temporal income from the spiritual in the case of 428 monasteries
out of the 553 given in my list. These 428 monasteries,
ranged under the above five headings and taking them in the
order given above, give the following figures: 47, 170, 131,
65, 15. The most numerous, therefore, are the monasteries
with a gross temporal income of between twenty and one
hundred pounds. There are also a great many monasteries
in the group with an income between a hundred and three
hundred pounds: and if we count the monasteries with an
income between twenty and three hundred pounds we find
that their number is almost two and a half times the number
of all the rest. Into what classes can the remaining monasteries of my list be divided? Unfortunately, even their whole
gross income is not always known. If I wish to divide into
groups all the monasteries of my list, I must make the basis
of the division the net and not the gross income. If the same

classification as was used above for the gross income be also taken for the net—viz. up to £20, £20–£100, £100–£300, £300–£1,000, over £1,000—then the corresponding figures for the 553 monasteries of my list will be as follows, beginning with those of the lowest income : 53, 188, 199, 89, 24. The most numerous are the monasteries with a net income of £100 to £300 ; but the number of monasteries with a net income of £20 to £100 is only a little less. On the whole, the result of grouping according to the total net income is very similar to that obtained by grouping according to the gross temporal income, and there is this common characteristic in both groupings, viz. that the number of monasteries with an income of £20 to £300 is almost two and a half times the number of all the rest.

The Government 'Instruction' merely pointed out the order of the benefices and required the returns to be made 'after the auditors' fashion', consequently the Commissioners of 1535 were left with an almost free hand. Their returns vary greatly in character, and a statistical digest of them is therefore very much limited by this fact. Some of the surveys are made in a very summary way that hardly differs from the Liber Valorum ; others are so detailed that they remind us of bailiffs' accounts. In the Hampshire returns only the gross and net incomes of the monasteries are given, and the investigator gains but little from the fact that the income of the large monasteries is apportioned under their respective offices ; but in the Oxfordshire returns not unfrequently very detailed descriptions of the monastic households, especially of the demesne, are found, and the area and income of even small pieces of land are given in figures. When the monastic income is set out according to the manors, the whole is sometimes summarized in one entry, and sometimes distributed over several. The income from demesne is sometimes distinguished from the income of tenancies and sometimes not. In some cases the freehold rents are united with the customary rents ; in others 'perquisita curiae' sometimes signifies only the income from Courts, sometimes the admission fines are included in it. Separate special entries are or are

Exact totals impossible.

not made of the income from woods, markets, fisheries and mines, in the same arbitrary fashion. And when this or that source of income is not to be found in the survey we often are at a loss to say for certain whether the reason lies in the non-existence of such income or in the fact that the surveyors did not make a separate entry of it. The investigator derives but little satisfaction from the answers which the Valor Ecclesiasticus gives to his questions. He is unable to give well-authenticated totals for the whole of the country; he is obliged to content himself with partial totals, and by their means arrive at more or less probable suggestions respecting the general situation.

The urban income. In studying the economic consequences of the Dissolution it is necessary to make a distinction between the urban and the rural income of the monasteries. Some monasteries were themselves situated in towns, and many country monasteries owned lands and rents in towns. But even a very large monastery situated in a town of any importance did not occupy the same position in regard to its neighbours as a moderate-sized monastery did in the country. The dissolution of a large town monastery did not represent anything like so serious a loss as did the downfall of any considerable and revered monastery in the country, especially in more remote districts. In attempting an estimate of the area of monastic lands we have no right to apply to the urban income the same procedure as we have used in the case of the rural income: and in any endeavour to ascertain, in connexion with the Dissolution, how the town people and urban capital were transferred to the country, it must not be forgotten that a certain proportion of this capital was used for the acquisition of the town possessions of the monks, and that a certain proportion of thriving citizens remained within the city boundaries in spite of the acquisition of monastic lands.

I have attempted to estimate the proportion that the urban income bears to the whole of the temporal income of a monastery. An exact calculation in the case of all the monasteries in the Valor Ecclesiasticus is, as I have said,

impossible. The urban income is not mentioned in a great
many of the surveys; but it is only in the case of its absence
in very detailed surveys that we have a right to conclude
that such an income did not exist at all, for the absence of
entries respecting town estates can often be explained by the
summary nature of the surveys, which include in one total both
the urban and the rural revenues. I have not, therefore,
sought to establish the exact relation of the urban to the
rural income, but rather to determine the extreme limit
of probable suggestions on the matter—that is, I have sought
to ascertain the maximum of the known amount of the urban
monastic income. It is but natural that the urban income
should be the greatest in the Middlesex monasteries. The
London monasteries with a gross temporal income of £200
to £700 have most of their property, in some cases the whole
of it, in London. I give the figures of their total and of
their urban revenue; I have placed them in the order of
the percentages of urban revenue beginning with the lowest.

	£	s.	d.	£	s.	d.
St. Mary Graces	580	4	8½	291	0	4
St. Mary, Bishopsgate	549	14	9½	277	13	4
St. Bartholomew	701	10	1¾	451	3	7
Minories	304	19	2½	201	15	10½
Haliwell	318	11	8	222	0	4
Charterhouse	613	15	11	427	11	4
St. Mary, Clerkenwell	243	13	9	172	19	4
St. Thomas of Acres	307	17	8	249	5	8
St. Helen	365	6	0	312	6	8
Elsyng Spittal	223	13	11½	190	18	2

In the other Middlesex monasteries the percentage of the
urban income is lower. If we reckon the London income
of all the sixteen monasteries in Middlesex which are entered
in my list, we shall get a sum slightly exceeding four thousand
pounds (£4,059 2s. 4¼d.); the gross temporal income of the
same monasteries amounts to £11,281 19s. 3d. The London
property therefore brings in more than a third of the income.
But the Middlesex monasteries were in a quite exceptional
position, and we cannot make inferences from them as to the
whole of the country. Even if we take the monasteries in the
principal towns of counties or dioceses, i.e. in important town
centres, the percentage of their urban income will be much

lower than in Middlesex. I give some instances of this, in the order of the absolute amounts of their gross temporal incomes ; the larger numbers will again indicate the gross temporal income, the smaller the urban income :—

	£	s.	d.	£	s.	d.
St. Oswald, Gloucester	60	9	1	22	0	0
Delapré, Northampton	83	15	6½	3	19	0
Huntingdon [1]	126	11	4½	26	0	11
St. Thomas, Stafford	130	19	5½	14	6	0
St. James, Northampton	146	17	2½	40	1	5
St. Gregory, Canterbury	166	4	5½	11	17	2¾
St. Andrew, Northampton	212	16	1	44	17	2
Bath	545	15	7	62	13	9½
Lantony, near Gloucester	577	9	2	72	14	8½
Coventry cathedral	653	19	10	160	18	4½
Norwich cathedral	675	6	1½	39	0	0¼
St. Mary, Leicester	732	12	0¾	47	2	0½
St. Werburgh, Chester	751	9	1½	71	10	5½
Oseney, Oxford	755	17	6½	82	10	0
Worcester cathedral	1095	16	8¼	98	17	4
St. Peter, Gloucester	1473	13	2	163	17	2½
Christchurch, Canterbury	2608	0	9⅞	247	6	10

In these seventeen monasteries, with a gross temporal income of £10,797 13s. 3⅞d., only £1,209 12s. 6d.—i.e. a little less than one-ninth—is urban income. But in judging of the whole country we must not, of course, confine ourselves to the monasteries in large towns; those situated in small towns, or altogether in the country, must also be taken into account. I put them into a third list in the same order [2] :—

			£	s.	d.	£	s.	d.
Ankerwyke ...	...	Bucks. ...	45	5	0	9	6	8
Burneham ...	...	Bucks. ...	72	3	11½	2	0	0
Garendon ...	...	Leicester ...	172	15	2¼	15	14	6
Nutley ...	...	Bucks. ...	177	9	1½	20	18	0
Newark ...	...	Surrey ...	219	2	0½	66	17	4
Vale Royal ...	...	Cheshire ...	239	6	2	28	0	4
Combe ...	...	Warwick ...	327	4	11	10	15	0
Wardon ...	...	Beds. ...	410	13	4¼	10	0	0
Bermondsey	...	Surrey ...	412	6	0	17	6	1

---

[1] In this case it is especially clear that the urban income is to a certain extent an agricultural income. The priory has lands 'in burgo de Huntingdon', consisting of arable land, meadow, pasture and wood worth £10 7s. 4d. Vide also Tewkesbury, Glouc., ii. 472, Tewkesbury burgus.

[2] I have not considered as urban income the rents of the manors of Glastonbury (£260 13s. 6d.) and Ramsey (£112 15s. 7d.), but in spite of this I do not think that my instances are artificially chosen; among them is given the monastery of St. Mary, Southwark, whose income is almost entirely urban. The urban income of many monasteries is not given at all. Speaking generally, my estimates exaggerate rather than minimize the urban revenues of the monasteries.

			£	s.	d.	£	s.	d.
St. Mary Southwark	Surrey	...	456	8	8½	398	13	7½
Dartford	... ...	Kent ...	471	11	7	50	11	10
Pershore	... ...	Worcester	549	13	11	3	11	0
Chertsey	... ...	Surrey ...	591	9	8¾	12	11	10
Merton	... ...	Surrey ...	758	10	3½	59	0	2
Ramsey	... ...	Hunts. ...	1786	9	8¼	15	1	0
Glastonbury	...	Somerset ...	3289	13	8⅞	37	5	11

In the sixteen monasteries of the third list, with a gross temporal income of £9,980 3s. 5⅛d., only £757 13s. 3½d. is urban income ; that is to say about one-thirteenth. If we add together the totals of all the three groups we shall get the sums £32,059 16s. 0d. and £6,026 8s. 1¾d. ; this means that in the combined temporal budget of all the forty-nine monasteries given by me, the urban income amounts to about 18¾ per cent. of the gross temporal income. It is clear, I think, that this is a maximum figure for the urban monastic budget ; in reality the percentage of the urban income must have been lower. The sixteen London monasteries, with their high percentage of urban income, are entered in the first group in their entirety ; and the other monasteries, whose percentage of urban income is much lower, are represented by about one-fifth of their budget.[1] We shall, I think, get approximately at the actual percentage of urban income by adopting the following mode of procedure : viz. by calculating one-fifth of the totals of the sixteen Middlesex monasteries and adding it to the totals of the second and third lists. If in our calculation we leave out the shillings and pence we get the following sums : £23,033 and £2,778.[2] For the whole of the country, on this hypothesis, the urban income of the monasteries would amount to about 12 per cent. of their gross temporal income. This figure is, of course, conjectural, but it seems to be probable. The urban income of the monasteries, then, was probably about £14,000.[3]

[1] The gross temporal income of the monasteries of the second and third lists approaches £21,000. On p. 100 the gross temporal income of all the monasteries was shown to be £120,000. But more than £11,000 out of this amount refers to the Middlesex monasteries. When we deduct these we get £109,000, and £21,000 is a little less than one-fifth of this remainder.

[2] $10,797 + 9,980 + \frac{11281}{5} = 23,033$; $1,209 + 757 + \frac{4059}{5} = 2,778$.

[3] The gross temporal income of all monasteries being about £120,000, the urban income is $£\frac{120000 \times 12}{100} = £14,400$.

The fact that the monasteries possessed a considerable urban income should warn us against exaggerated ideas about the influence of the Dissolution on the agrarian history of England. At the same time it is true that the bulk of the monastic income was derived from the country, and this to an extent sufficient to repay a careful study.

The non-agricultural income.

The most important items in the temporal budget of the monasteries are the receipts from demesnes in hand and from the payments of the tenants. Here we have purely a landed revenue, and to it we must look for the basis of any conclusions or theories as to the dimensions and character of monastic economy. The monasteries had, of course, other sources of revenue, much less important and less interesting, but which must not be overlooked in considering the general budget, and determining the relative proportion of the landed income.

Statutory prohibition of profit-making.

One of the most remarkable features of the monastic budget is the utter insignificance of the income from non-agricultural trades. There is nothing astonishing in the fact that the monasteries of the sixteenth century did not work for markets, and do not appear in the Valor Ecclesiasticus as employers or organizers of domestic industries, for if the very existence of a corporation is threatened it cannot well be a pioneer of industry, even though there be no statutory checks to its activity. Such checks, however, were not wanting. The Parliament of 21 H. VIII attempted to confine the agricultural activity of the monasteries within narrow limits (21 H. VIII, c. 13). The preamble of this Statute lays stress on the need of religious reform, of more dignified Divine service, of better preaching of God's Word by active example, and expresses a desire to help the needy and keep up the ancient 'hospitality', and to improve the position of the poorer curates. Many enactments against pluralities and non-residence had their origin undoubtedly in purely moral and religious motives, for the laity did not receive any appreciable material gain from a more just division of the Church revenues among the clergy. The enactments against the profit-making by the Church were also aimed, in the first place, at religious reform, but here it was more difficult to assume an attitude of absolute integrity, seeing that it was to the direct interest of the lay legislators to remove inconvenient competition and to concentrate commerce and industry in the hands of the laity; the Statute itself admits as much. Ecclesiastics are forbidden to embark in business in order to maintain the 'good oppynyon of the lay fee toward the spirituall persons'—in other words, to pacify the irritation caused by the rivalry of the clergy. The clergy are not allowed to carry on business, they are forbidden to buy anything with the purpose of selling it for a profit; and any one doing so is to pay threefold the amount of the purchase, to be divided between the Crown and the informer. They are only allowed to make purchases for their own consumption, and only in the event of the goods bought proving unsuitable are they allowed to sell them again. Similarly, all business undertakings that aim at profit-making, and are not confined to production for their own consumption, are forbidden. In this connexion the Statute, however, specifies only breweries and tanneries, and expressly denounces the carrying on of such businesses by fraudulent means, and imposes for any infringement a monthly payment of £10.

The prohibitions extend also to agriculture. The clergy were not allowed to work for the market or for profit in any way. The only motive of their agricultural activity was to be production for the consumption of themselves or their guests. They were not to take land on lease for cultivation, and if they already held a lease they had to transfer it into lay hands as soon as possible. They could not at their own pleasure increase the cultivation of their own land. In this the Statute had specially in view the monasteries (ss. 7, 23). They were divided into two classes: those with an income of not more than 800 marks and those whose income exceeded this sum. The monasteries with an income of not more than 800 marks were allowed to keep in their own hands that part of the demesne which they had cultivated during the last hundred years. Here evidently an immunity was granted, for those years of the century were allowed to be taken into account in which the demesne in hand was at its *maximum* ('in as ample and as large manér as they or their predecessors at any tyme by the space of 100 yeres last have done used and occupyed'). With regard to the poorer churches and monasteries, provision was made for cases where the income from demesne would not be sufficient for the use of the church or monastery itself. An exemption from the general rule was allowed in such cases and permission was given to take land on lease ; but it was made a necessary condition that the profit of the farm should be used to cover the deficit of the clerical household and should not exceed it.[1] No exemption was allowed for the monasteries and clergy having an income of more than 800 marks; they must sow only so much corn and feed only so many cattle as were required for their own consumption and for hospitality. The richest monasteries and churches had so much demesne that, from the legislator's point of view, it was always sufficient for their own consumption, and therefore production for the market could be absolutely forbidden.

The industrial income.

But are we to believe that in the sixteenth century the monasteries had entirely ceased to keep artisans for home use, and that they bought all non-agricultural products in neighbouring towns? And even if it were so, were not the workshops, saltworks, tanneries, fulling mills, corn mills and artisans' tenements of the period of self-sufficient economy still existing? And these, one would suppose, must have been let. We are almost warranted, then, in expecting some indications concerning this special income, at all events in the detailed surveys. Some information concerning the leasing of trade establishments is found in the returns of 1535, but except in the case of corn mills such information is very rare, and figures concerning the independent industrial enter-

---

[1] Until this Statute, the monks often appear under Henry VIII as farmers even upon Crown lands: Brewer, ii. 1007 ; iii. 2993, 3062–13 ; iv. 464, 2939. The Statute did not remain a dead letter. Informers referred to it when they accused the clergy and the monasteries which still held land on lease (Gairdner, v. 1133 ; ix. 1104). In order to evade the Statute the monks had to obtain special licences from the Crown for the lease of lands (Gairdner, ix. app. 2 = Pat. Rolls, 27 H. VIII, p. 2, m. 11).

prises of the monasteries are still rarer.   Of course, the silence
of the surveys may be explained to a certain extent by their
summary nature, or as a successful attempt of the monks to
evade the royal tenth.   When in metalliferous Cornwall we
do not find a single entry concerning the mining revenues of
the monasteries we may reasonably doubt the fullness or the
accuracy of the survey.   The detailed surveys of urban possessions of the monasteries made at a later time for the royal
grants show that among the 'tenementa et burgagia' in the
Valor Ecclesiasticus, artisans' tenements are sometimes found.
But a reference to the shortcomings of the returns does not, of
course, do away with the difficulty.   No information concerning the industrial income is to be found in the detailed surveys, which sometimes take note of very small agricultural
revenues.   Mills are very often mentioned in the Valor
Ecclesiasticus, and with the mills are ranked other buildings
which never held corn within their walls.   However, most of
the mills in the Valor Ecclesiasticus were evidently corn
mills; 'molendina fullonica' are seldom found.   In this regard
we cannot hope to explain everything by the summary nature
of the surveys; and we may reasonably believe that fulling
mills which are so seldom found in the surveys were also
seldom found in reality.

The entries of saltworks, quarries and mines are very rare. Minerals.
True, I have not collected all such entries, but I believe that
the cases given include most of the evidence, although there
are only about ten of them, and their revenue forms a quite
infinitesimal part of the whole monastic income.   I found
five instances of quarries, two of which the monks undoubtedly
worked themselves.   Of ironworks there is only one certain
instance, and evidently the monks worked this themselves
There are three instances of saltworks; in one case the
monks managed the business themselves, and even the cost
of production is indicated.   There are two entries of sea-
coal, evidently in both cases worked by the monks themselves.[1]   It is, I think, worth while to note the paucity of entries

---

[1] Quarries: Revesby, Linc., iv. 42: ' Holbek in precio petrarum ibidem
lucrat' communibus annis £6 11s. 6d.'   Pershore, Worc., iii. 260: 'Hawkys-

of sea-coal. Not infrequently the Commissioners paid great attention to the matter of fuel, and included in the income from woods the value of the wood burnt in the monastic buildings. It would, therefore, be natural to expect many more entries of sea-coal if the monasteries had really worked the coal mines. What, then, is the meaning of the exceptionally few entries of the working of sea-coal and salt? Do they indicate the modest dimensions of English industry at that time, or the small part that the monasteries took in the national production? Probably both things are indicated, but not to an equal extent. The historian of English industry cannot be indifferent to the eloquent silence of the Valor Ecclesiasticus —to the almost entire absence from the temporal budget of the monasteries of entries of mineral revenue. He would prob-

<hr/>

bury et in proficuis petrarum quarre ibidem communibus annis £0 1s. 8d.' Lantony, Glouc., ii. 423: 'M. Baryngton firma unius quarrure £0 6s. 8d.' Winchelcombe, Glouc., ii. 457: 'Enworthe firma unius quarrure lapidum per annum £0 10s. 0d.' Gloucester, St. Peter, ii. 416: 'Upton firma unnius quarrii lapidei £0 1s. 0d.'—Iron: In my only instance, the income from an iron mine is strangely united with the income from oblations. Monkbretton, Yorks., v. 42: 'exitus miner' ferri cum oblacionibus infra monasterium £3 6s. 8d.' It may be that the following refers to an iron foundry in the survey of Wombridge, Salop, iii. 194: 'Redditus assise unius molendini ferrar' in Woborne per annum £0 13s. 4d.' But it may be that a fulling mill is meant, the same 'ferina pannorum' as in Holme Cultram, v. 282? — Saltworks: Holme Cultram, Cumb., v. 282: 'ferina salis infra dominium de Holme £7 13s. 4d.' Bordesley, Worc., iii. 273: 'Droyte Wyche valet in proficuis salis provenientibus in eadem villa per estimacionem communibus annis £4 8s. 0d. inde allocatur pro focale et lignis emptis ad faciendum salem predictum £1 8s. 0d.' Westwood, Worc., iii. 276: 'in quatuor bullariis aque salse in Wyche ad firmam dimissis £3 6s. 8d., in quatuor quarteriis salis precio communibus annis £0 16s. 0d., et unius sele ibm ad firmam dimisse £0 3s. 4d.'—Seacoal: Nostell, Yorks., v. 62. In the survey of the demesne in hand an entry is made: 'mineria carbonum £0 13s. 4d.' Wombridge, Salop: 'exitus mine carbonum £5 0s. 0d.'; this evidently is also a home farm in hand. In the survey of Furness, Lanc., among the Lincolnshire possessions, under the heading 'casualia', a sale of lead is mentioned ('vendicio plumbi £10 0s. 0d.'). The scarcity of information respecting the mineral income may be accounted for to a considerable extent by the summary character of the survey. The Valor Ecclesiasticus does not say anything about income from salt mines among the briefly described revenues of the monastery of Vale Royal, Chesh., but we know from other sources that the monastery possessed some saltworks. In 9 H. VIII, the monastery let on a 40 years' lease three saltworks in Northwicke at the yearly payment of £3 6s. 8d.; the monks lent lead to the farmer for 40 years, and accurately divided the expenses of repairs between the farmer and themselves (Part. for grants, n. 994, m. 7, 35 Hen. VIII).

ably come to the conclusion that the working of minerals was much more developed outside the monastic world than within it, and could very reasonably suggest that the monks in the sixteenth century occupied but a modest place in the national industry, and were rather *rentiers* living on their revenues.

The entries found in the Valor Ecclesiasticus respecting Mills. trade enterprises suggest the same ideas.   In the Commissioners' returns only tanneries, bakeries, tileries and mills are mentioned.   Tanneries are mentioned in one Oxfordshire, two Yorkshire and one Lancashire monasteries; and it may be that one of these had already ceased to exist in 1535.[1] A bakery is mentioned in the monastery of St. Neots, Hunts.; it is called a 'general' bakery, and it is possible that it was an ancient seigniorial oven.[2]   Tileries were owned by the monasteries of St. Augustine, Canterbury; Christchurch, Canterbury; and Battle.[3]   The entries of mills are very numerous.   Very often it is not said what kind of mill is meant, but sometimes particulars are given.   These are of two kinds : either the motive power is indicated, as : ' molendinum aquaticum, ventriticum, equinum '; or the material worked upon is stated, as : ' molendinum granaticum, bladiferum, fullonicum.'   The two descriptive characteristics are seldom found

---

[1] Osney, ii. 215 : 'Firma unius tenti voc' les Taulhous in dco monasterio dim' Wllmo Toby £2 0s. 0d.'   Bruerne, Oxon., ii. 265, 201 : 'tentum in Bruerne voc' le tanhouse locatur per indenturam £3 1s. 0d.'   Jervaulx, Yorks., v. 241 : 'in reddit' et firmis domus tannarie prout dimittitur ad firmam £7 0s. 0d.'   Furness, Lanc., v. 269 : 'tannaria in Hawcotte et Newbarns £1 10s. 0d.'   Newburgh, Yorks., v. 92 : 'scitus prioratus unacum . . . uno tento que nuper fuit tannaria monasterii in manibus suis occupata.'

[2] Comp. Evesham, Worc., iii. 250 : 'Salford Abbatis in redditu unius furni £0 1s. 0d.'   St. Neots, Hunts., iv. 261 : 'villa S. Neoti firma communis pistrine £1 6s. 8d.'

[3] Battle, Sussex, i. 346 : ' Alcyston firma domus tegulatae ibm et dimisse per indenturam pro termino annorum Ricardo Amilton reddendo per annum £3 13s. 4d.'   St. Augustine, Canterbury, i. 20 : 'furnus tegularis valet annuatim ad firmam in denariis £1 0s. 0d.'   Christchurch, Canterbury, i. 12 : 'de firma de le Tylehost in Holyngborne per annum £3 8s. 6d., de vendicione bosci ibm nichill quia pro comburacione tegularum ibm.' i. 10 : 'de firma de le Amery Court in le Bleane per annum £5 13s. 4d., et de vendicione boscorum ibm nichill quia reservantur pro comburacione tegularum.'

together. I am inclined to think, speaking generally, that we have before us a fulling mill only when it is directly so stated, and that in all other cases corn mills are meant, although I know of one instance where the V. E. merely mentions a mill, which in the later survey appears to be a fulling mill (V. E. iii. 463; Part. f. gr. 325). Direct indications of fulling mills are rare in the V. E. and I can give only thirteen instances.[1] But even admitting that among the other mills some were fulling mills, yet the artisans' shops mentioned in the Valor Ecclesiasticus are very few; they represent only a small number of trades and these were partly let by the monasteries. So that, in the sixteenth century the part taken by the monasteries in English industry appears to be very small. The income from trade, even if we include rents paid for artisans' shops, occupies a quite unimportant place in the monastic budget.

Corn mills.

The monasteries had, on the other hand, a great many corn mills. In order to define the place in the monastic budget of the income from corn mills, I have taken my instances only from those surveys in which this revenue is given and distinguished from other revenues. The sixty monasteries selected are of various sizes and in different counties. I confine myself to this list as I consider it sufficient, but it might easily be extended. Beds., Wardon, £37 13s. 4d.; Bucks., Burnham, £0 13s. 4d.; Cumb., Holme, Cultram, £15 13s. 4d.; Devon,

---

[1] Maidenbradley,Wilts., ii. 98: 'Maidenbradley redditus firme molendini fullonici ibidem per annum £0 12s. od.' St. Augustine's, Canterbury, i. 17: 'Sturrey manor molendinum fullonicum valet annuatim ad firmam in denariis £5 6s. 8d.' Boxley, Kent, i. 79: 'Boxley £3 os. od.' Malling, Kent, i. 106: 'Est Mallyng de proficuis molendini fullonici ibidem per annum £3 6s. 8d.' Westminster, St. Peter, i. 416: 'Batricksey manor firma molendini fullonici ibidem ad firmam dimissi per annum £6 os. od.' Westacre, Norfolk, iii. 392: 'manerium de Narford in firma molendini fullonici £3 os. od.' Jervaulx, Yorks., v. 241: 'molendinum fullaticum de Estwhitton £0 10s. od.' Holme Cultram, v. 282: 'in (firma) panne ferine infra dominium de Holme £3 12s. od.' Whitby, Yorks., v. 82: 'molend' fullonic' £1 os. od.' Cirencester, Glouc., ii. 463: 'firma unius molendini fullonici in Cirencester Ricardo Fowler dimissi per annum £7 13s. 4d.' Pentney, Norf., iii. 399: 'manerium de Narford valet in firma molendini fullonici £2 os. od.' Winchelcombe, Glouc. ii. 460: 'firma 2 molend' fullonicorum in Coots £2 1s. od.' Cf. Lantony, Glouc., ii. 425, Ailberton.

Buckfastleigh, £21 6s. 8d.; Buckland, £4 6s. 8d.; Canonleigh,
£3 3s. 8d.; Totnes, £0 10s. 8d.; Dorset, Tarrent, £3 0s. 0d.;
Glouc., Lantony, £9 2s. 0d.; Tewkesbury, £18 10s. 0d.;
Winchelcombe, £6 19s. 4d.; Heref., Wigmore, £3 3s. 4d.;
Hunts., Huntingdon, £1 13s. 4d.; St. Neots, £24 3s. 8d.;
Kent, Sheppey, £2 16s. 8d.; Malling, £19 17s. 4d.; Linc.,
Bollington, £4 13s. 4d.; Revesby, £11 0s. 0d.; Swineshead,
£2 0s. 0d.; Stamford St. Michael, £2 0s. 0d.; Willoughton,
£0 13s. 4d.; Middl., Westminster, St. Peter, £46 5s. 6d.;
Northants., Pipewell, £1 6s. 8d.; Notts., Lenton, £12 13s. 4d.;
Newstead, £2 0s. 0d.; Rufford, £31 6s. 8d.; Welbeck,
£2 0s. 0d.; Worksop, £8 13s. 4d.; Oxon., Rewley, £3 6s. 8d.;
Studley, £0 6s. 8d.; Wroxton, £6 6s. 8d.; Soms., Glastonbury,
£18 6s. 8d.; Henton, £3 10s. 0d.; Keynsham, £17 13s. 4d.;
Wells, St. John, £1 18s. 0d.; Staff., Hulton, £0 11s. 8d.;
Ronton, £0 18s. 4d.; Stone, £4 0s. 0d.; Suff., Leiston,
£2 6s. 8d., Woodbridge, £3 0s. 0d.; Surr., Bermondsey,
£8 0s. 0d.; Chertsey, £17 6s. 8d.; Merton, £22 19s. 0d.;
Newark, £2 13s. 8d.; Waverley, £10 10s. 0d.; Suss., Battle,
£10 13s. 4d.; Lewes, £3 6s. 8d.; Robertsbridge, £2 0s. 0d.;
Michelham, £3 13s. 4d.; Warw., Pollesworth, £10 6s. 8d.;
Wilts., Maidenbradley, £4 12s. 0d.; Malmesbury, £8 19s. 8d.;
Wilton, £4 0s. 0d.; Worc., Bordesley, £10 1s. 4d.; Evesham,
£10 11s. 8d.; M. Malvern, £6 14s. 8d.; Westwood, £4 11s. 0d.;
Yorks., Nostell, £10 0s. 0d.; Pontefract, £5 0s. 0d.; Roche,
£3 12s. 4d.

The total revenue from the mills of these sixty monasteries
amounts to £519 2s. 0d. The gross temporal income of these
monasteries slightly exceeds twenty-three thousand pounds.
The revenue from the mills therefore amounts to about 2¼ per
cent. of the gross temporal income. The mills occupy a very
considerable place in the temporal budget of some monasteries.
Wardon has a gross temporal income of £410 13s. 4¼d. and
an income from mills of £37 13s. 4d. The corresponding figures
for Malling in Kent are £196 0s. 10½d. and £19 17s. 4d.; for
St. Neots, Hunts., £192 13s. 11½d. and £24 3s. 8d.; for
Rufford, Notts., £186 13s. 4d., and £31 6s. 8d.; for Pollesworth,
Warw., £60 0s. 0d. and £10 6s. 8d. The temporal income

of the above sixty monasteries amounts to about one-fifth of
the income of all monasteries which I here consider. If in
the remaining monasteries the income from mills was in a similar proportion to the gross temporal income, then the whole
would amount to about £2,500. I believe, however, that the
income from mills was somewhat less than this, and that it would
be more prudent to estimate it at about two thousand pounds.
My list includes only such monasteries as had mills, and some
monasteries had no mills at all. On the other hand it is possibly
the case that all the mills possessed by the monasteries in this
list have not been taken into account. Only the mills situated
in Glastonbury itself are entered in the Glastonbury survey.
In the Tewkesbury survey the mills in Teynton are mentioned
but not separated from the demesne income (ii. 472). The
revenue of the mills came from different sources, and a part
of it ought to be considered as pure income from land, for plots
of land were often attached to the mills. Then the mills also
produced a profit, like any other industrial business. Finally,
in those places where the monastery was lord of the manor
the mills yielded a profit as being monopolies; and the
reason why the monasteries kept so many mills in their
own hands until the sixteenth century will undoubtedly be
found in this monopoly. It is difficult to distinguish between
these three sources, but there can be no doubt that the
greatest part of the revenue from mills was not a landed
revenue.

Revenue
from
markets.

The market revenue of the monasteries was also not
principally a landed revenue, for it consisted of the rents paid
for stalls and booths in the market and of market tolls.
Sometimes the surveys distinguish between the profits derived
from a Sunday market and a fair.[1] The revenue from markets
is very much less than that from mills, but it must of course
be taken into consideration in an attempt to establish even

---

[1] Cirencester, Glouc., ii. 464 : 'ballivatus ville Cirencestre, Exitus duarum
nundinarum apud Cirencestr' quolibet anno tentarum £3 0s. 6d. Exitus
stallagii in mercato ville ibidem cum redditu duarum shoparum subtus
le Bothehall £2 0s. 0d. Exitus tolneti pro Ponder Lane et pens' in mercatu
sic ad firmam dimissi £1 0s. 0d. Exitus tolneti animalium venditorum
in mercatu ibidem sic ad firmam dimissi £1 0s. 0d.'

the approximate dimensions of the monastic income. Sometimes the monks let out their market revenues, sometimes they
kept them in their own hands and employed a special officer to
collect them, or else they entrusted the collection to their local
bailiff.[1] Market entries are much rarer in the Valor Ecclesiasticus than the registration of mills, and the thirty examples
that I have collected constitute the majority of the entries to
be found in the survey.   The market revenue yields in Devon :
Buckfastleigh, £5 0s. 0d.; Tavistock, £16s. 8d.; Dorset, Shaftesbury, £2 4s. 6d. ; Sherborne, £0 13s. 1½d. ; Tarrent, £2 0s. 0d. ;
Gloucester, Cirencester, £7 0s. 0d. ; Winchelcombe, £0 3s. 0d. ;
Hunts., St. Neots, £9 6s. 8d. ; Kent, Christchurch, Canterbury,
£1 1s. 2d.; Malling, £3 6s. 8d.; Norfolk, Blackborough,
£1 0s. 0d.; Bromholme, £1 4s. 0½d.; Hempton, £1 0s. 0d. ;
Horsham, £11 6s. 9d. ; Hulme, £2 6s. 5d. ; M. Walsingham,
£0 12s. 0½d. ; Westacre, £2 9s. 6½d. ; Northnts., Peterborough,
£5 19s. 0d. ; Notts., Lenton, £12 0s. 0d.; Soms., Henton,
£3 0s. 0d. ; Suffolk, Leiston, £0 3s. 0d.; Surrey, Chertsey,
£0 18s. 1d.; Waverley, £0 6s. 8d. ; Newark, £0 2s. 8d.;
Wilts., Malmesbury, £2 0s. 2½d.; Worcester, Evesham,
£17 6s. 8d.; Pershore, £0 10s. 0d.; Worcester Cathedral,
£4 10s. 0d. ; Yorks., Pontefract, £15 0s. 0d. ; Widkirk,
£13 6s. 8d. The revenue from markets for all the thirty monasteries amounts, according to the Valor Ecclesiasticus, to
£127 3s. 6½d.   Of course, many surveys only omit the
revenues from markets because of their brevity.   But as the
entries of revenue from markets are very few I do not think
that the total calculated above need be multiplied many times
to arrive at the total for the whole country ; it would probably
be sufficient to double it.   In the income from markets I have
not included the rent paid for shops, but I have included the
rent paid for stalls (*stallagium*).[2]   Entries of ferry and river

---

[1] A part of the income from markets was let out at Cirencester, Glouc. ;
the corresponding passage of the survey is given in the note above.   The
following is an instance of the monks having a market bailiff : St. Neots,
Hunts. : 'Villa Sci Neoti firma tolneti mercati et nundinarum £9 6s. 8d.
Reprisiones in feodo Thome Tony ballivi mercati ville Sci Neoti
£0 6s. 8d.'
[2] Here is an instance.   Widkirk, Yorks., v. 64 : 'exitus et proficua

tolls are very rare in the Valor Ecclesiasticus and affect very little the amount of the revenue that is *not* derived from the land.[1]

Very curious are the cases where a monastery gets an income from some trade. It is true the information about such cases is very meagre. Twice, payments from brewers are mentioned, and quite exceptional is an entry about a monastery in Somersetshire which by Royal Grant received a rather considerable toll ($\pounds 31$ 6s. 8d.) from cloth made in Wiltshire.[2]

Fisheries.   If the Commissioners' returns rightly represent the actual state of affairs, the revenues from fisheries were very small, although one would naturally expect the reverse, for the monks fasted more than the laity and needed much fish; one would think that they would have kept the fisheries firmly in their own hands. But either the monks succeeded in concealing their income from fisheries, or else they bought their fish; indeed, in later enumerations of monastic debts the fishmongers of the neighbouring town are not infrequently found among the creditors. In the Valor Ecclesiasticus, too, the fisheries are mentioned much more seldom than even the market dues. I have discovered eighteen

---

tolneti et stallagii nundinarum ibm communibus annis $\pounds 13$ 6s. 8d.' A curious piece of information about a fair is found in the survey of St. James, Northampton, iv. 319: 'Nundinae Sci Jacobi. De aliquo proficuo proveniente de nundinis tentis in die Sci Jacobi annuatim non respondetur pro eo quod nullum proficuum inde provenit ultra custa et expensa in et circa easdem eodem die facta super sacramentum dicti abbatis.'

[1] Here are four entries noted by me. Whitby, Yorks., v. 82: 'firma aque de Eske $\pounds 2$ 13s. 4d., tolleria aque et vill' ibm $\pounds 2$ 13s. 4d.' Thurgarton, Notts., v. 151: 'Gunthorpe valet in quodam passagio ibidem vocato Gunthorp Ferries per annum $\pounds 1$ 13s. 4d.' Selby, Yorks., v. 12: 'officium pietenciarii passagium de Selby $\pounds 10$ 0s. 0d.' Tewkesbury, ii. 483: 'passage de Overlode iuxta Tewkesbury $\pounds 3$ 0s. 0d.'

[2] Malmesbury, Wilts., ii. 119: 'Malmesbury burgus amerciamenta sive fines brasiatorum in burgo voc' alewights communibus annis $\pounds 2$ 0s. 0d.' Cirencester, Glouc., ii. 464: 'ballivatus ville Cirencester de finibus pro cervisia brasianda unacum amerciamentis eiusdem per annum $\pounds 2$ 0s. 0d.' Hinton, Soms., i. 156: 'Com' Wiltes' redditus de ulnage pannorum lane valet in annuali redditu exeunte et accidente de ulnag' pann' lan' ex dono sive concessu domini regis in comitatu predicto ultra $\pounds 2$ 0s. 0d. deduct' pro feodo Ambrossii Dancy ballivi sive collectoris redditus eiusdem sic remanet clare $\pounds 31$ 6s. 8d.'

instances only in which the amount of the revenue from fisheries is given separately from the other revenues :—Burneham, Bucks., £2 0s. 0d. ; Holme Cultram, Cumb., £5 9s. 0d. ; Buckfastleigh, Devon, £1 3s. 4d. ; Canonleigh, Devon, 6d. ; Tavistock, Devon, £15 0s. 0d. ; Cerne, Dorset, £0 3s. 0d. ; Winchcombe, Glouc., £4 0s. 0d. ; St. Neots, Hunts., £1 6s. 8d. ; Ramsey, Hunts., £28 17s. 6d. ; Faversham, Kent, £1 13s. 4d. ; Furness, Lanc., piscaria de Lanc' £2 0s. 0d. ; Hickling, Norfolk, £0 10s. 0d. ; Peterborough, Northants, £1 6s. 8d. ; Campsey, Suff., £0 3s. 4d. ; Evesham, Worc., £1 6s. 8d. ; Amesbury, Wilts., £0 2s. 0d. ; Hulme, Norf. £7 0s. 0d. ; Buckenham, Norf., £0 2s. 0d. In addition to these there are instances where fisheries are mentioned in the Valor Ecclesiasticus but are not distinguished from other sources of income. Examples of this are to be found in the surveys of Burneham (Bucks.), Sawtre (Hunts.), Furness (Lanc.), Crowland (Linc.), Stainfield (Linc.), W. Dereham (Norf.), Godstow (Oxon.), Pershore (Worc.).[1]

Monastic surveys also comprise certain revenues which we may call curial ; varied in character, and sometimes divided into classes, sometimes brought together in one entry under various names. A curial income might be looked for wherever a Court was convened ; and, speaking generally, every monastery possessing a manor ought to have had a curial income. But as a matter of fact the curial income is not mentioned in all manors nor is it said to have been raised by all monasteries. Of course the absence of curial income items by no means proves the non-existence of such income, and can generally be attributed to the summary nature of the surveys. One cannot expect the curial income to be given as a special item in the returns for Hampshire, for they give nothing but the gross and net income of the various monasteries ; but many surveys of other counties also do not mention the curial income at all. Here are some instances : Derb.—Beauchief, Dale, Darley, Repingdon ; Kent

The curial income.

---

[1] As an instance, I give the entry for Stainfield, Linc., iv. 82 : ' Grangia vocata Barleymowthe cum piscaria pratis et pastur' adiacen' dimissa Roberto Trusse per annum £5 0s. 0d.'

—Dartford ; Lanc.—Burscough, Cockersand, Conishead, Fur-
ness, Whalley ; Linc.—Barlings, Crowland, Kirkstead, Spalding, Stixwold, Swineshead ; Norf.—W. Dereham ; Notts.—
Worksop ; Oxon.—Eynsham, Godstow ; Salop—Lilleshall ;
Sussex—Battle, Boxgrove, Robertsbridge ; Yorks.—Bridlington, Fountains, Gisburn, Marton, Meaux, Newburgh, Whitby.
In those surveys in which the curial income is mentioned, it is
not always given for all the manors of the monastery. In the
Record Commission edition of the V. E., the monastery of
Christchurch, Canterbury, stands before all others ; the curial
income of its first manor (Monketon) is given as a separate
item, but in the case of the second manor (Brokesend) all the
income from demesne is included in one entry and not a word
is said about the curial income.[1] Sometimes the curial income
is mentioned in the survey of a manor, but is not distinguished
from the general manorial income. To several manors of the
monastery of St. Augustine, Canterbury, the following formula
is applied : ' redditus et firme ibidem cum perquisitis curie in
onere ballivi sive receptoris ibidem valent ' (Northborne,
Chystlett, Sturrey, Stodemershe, Litylborne, Langeporte and
Rede, Kennyngton, &c.). Almost the same formula is found
several times in the survey of Sempringham, a monastery
in Lincolnshire. Sometimes the curial income is not given
because the farmer owns it and it is included in the farm.
In the survey of the monastery of Christchurch, Canterbury,
we read concerning four manors, Bockyng, Stysted, Meopham
and Chartham : ' de proficuis curie ibidem nihil quia firmarius
habet ex convencione.' In the survey of Swineshead, Linc.,
we find : ' manerium de Hole Hekyngton, &c., cum perquisitis
curie ibidem ut modo dimittitur Iohanni Bothe pro termino
annorum.' Sometimes the curial income is separated from
the whole manorial income and joined to the income from the
woods. This occurs in almost all the Warwickshire and in
some of the Devonshire surveys, for example, Buckland,
Canonleigh and Nuneaton ; Tavistock, bertonia de Morvall
cum Morelham. In some cases, however, the absence of

---

[1] In the survey of Rufford, Notts., the curial income of the Yorkshire
estates is given, but not that for the Nottinghamshire estates.

entries of the curial income in a manor may be explained by
the non-existence of the curial income itself. Instances are to
be found in the Valor Ecclesiasticus, though certainly they
are rare, in which it is definitely stated that the manor in
question does not yield a curial income.[1] Sometimes we have
it explained why a manor yields no curial income. In the
last year for which accounts had been kept in the three
manors of Gedgrave, Stratford and Benehall, belonging to the
Suffolk monastery of Butley, no curial income is shown because
the court had not been convened that year. In regard to
a manor in Wiltshire it is said that the court is convened only
once in three or four years.[2] Some manors having no court
of their own were attached to another manor.[3]

The curial income is often described by the two words Names for
'perquisita curie', and then it is impossible to say of what it the curial
consists. Here are some instances: Linc., Bardney, Bolling- income.
ton, Thornton; Salop, Wenlock, Buildwas, Haghmond;
Staffs., Tutbury; Suff., Campsey; Surrey, Lewes, Merton;
Wilts., Edindon; Yorks., Jervaulx, Roche. The meaning of
these words is not rendered less obscure when to 'perquisita
curie' the term 'casualitates', almost equally vague, is
added. An instance of this is Warw., Wroxall. 'Amerciamenta'—fines imposed by the manorial court—has a more
definite meaning. 'Amerciamenta' is joined to 'perquisita'
in many of the Leicestershire surveys, for instance, Garendon,
Kirby Beller, Launde, St. Mary's Leicester, Croxton, and in
some Middlesex surveys—as Syon, St. Peter's, Westminster;
also in the survey of Chertsey, Surrey. Among the items of
the curial revenues are sometimes included, in various com-

[1] Christchurch, Canterbury, i. 13: 'Chayham manerium de perquisitis
curie ibidem nichill'; ibm. i. 14: 'Bockyng in Mersey manerium.' Farleigh, Wilts., ii. 143: 'Corton manerium, Wraxhall manerium.'
[2] Amesbury, Wilts., ii. 95 : 'Chawlo et Petywyke in amerciamentis curie
cum acciderit quolibet tercio vel quarto anno ibidem tente cum finibus
terrarum heriettis et aliis proficuis.'
[3] Edington, Wilts. The manor of Edington had both a court and
a curial income, but the manors of Tynhyde and Beynton had no curial
income because their court was at Edington, 'quia (curia) in Edington.'
The manor of Lavington had no curial income because its court was
joined to the manor of Escott. The manor of Buckland had no curial
income because its court was joined to the manor of Coleshull.

binations, the 'herietta, relevia, fines, extrahurae'.[1] The reliefs
and heriots may be said to be curial income only in the sense
that their amount is established by local custom, and that the
local court is recognized as the guardian and interpreter of the
custom. Thus revenues, more or less akin to death duties,
may be included in the same column as the 'perquisita curie'.
In one of the Wiltshire surveys a curious though not quite
clear attempt is made to divide the 'casual' profits into two
classes ; pure income from courts, to which apparently the
term 'certum' is applied, and receipts of a mixed character.[2]
Among the latter we come across 'fines', but sometimes the
expression 'fines terrarum' is used. Both these expressions
are very often found in the Valor Ecclesiasticus, and evidently
in most cases signify admission fines, which to a great extent
are landed revenue ; but in some passages the sense of the word
'fines' either remains vague or certainly does not bear the
character of landed revenue.[3] The curial income of the monasteries was not confined to the income of manorial courts only.

---

[1] In the survey of Magna Malvern, Worc., the most frequent formula
used is 'in finibus heriettis et amerciamentis'. The same formula is
expressed more fully in the survey of Wilton, Wilts. : 'in perquis' curie
scilicet de amerciamentis finibus heriettis et aliis proficuis.' 'Relevia'
appears in the survey of Pershore, Worc. : 'in finibus heriettis releviis et
aliis amerciamentis.' An instance of 'extrahurae' can be found in the
survey of Worcester Cathedral, 'in finibus heriettis releviis extrahuris et
aliis perquisitis curie.'

[2] This is the survey of Amesbury, Wilts. The descriptions of the
curial income vary according to the manors. Here are four different
formulae : (a) Ambresbury Villa : 'In perquisitis 2 turnorum cum 2 curiis
communibus annis ut in certo £0 2s. 2d. ; amerciamentis et aliis ad idem
pertinentibus £0 13s. 6d.' (b) Melkysham : 'In perquisitis 2 curiarum
legalium cum 18 hundredis cum certo eorundem finibus terrarum heriettis
et aliis casualitatibus.' (c) Wallope : 'In perquisitis 2 curiarum legalium
cum 2 curiis baronum ut in certo finibus heriettis.' (d) Wygley : 'In
perquisitis 2 turnorum et 2 curiarum baronum ut in certo finibus terrarum
heriettis et aliis pertinentibus.' It seems that the receipts are everywhere
divided into two parts : one part is the income from the leet and court
baron, to which the words 'in certo' are applied : the other part consists
of mixed receipts. But the terms 'certus redditus', 'certitudo,' are found
in other combinations. Bradenstoke, Wilts., ii. 123 : 'Lyneham de certo
redditu et perquisitis curie ibm tente communibus annis.' The monastery
of Cirencester had seven hundred courts (ii. 464) ; their income is composed of 'visus franci plegii', and 'communis finis ex certitudine'; the
monastery of Buckland held the hundred of Roughburgh, from which it
received the 'certus redditus' (ii. 378).

[3] 'Finis' does not signify a revenue from land in such an entry as

Large monasteries sometimes received the revenues of the courts of the hundred. The monastery of Cirencester (Glouc.) had seven hundred courts, Glastonbury (Soms.) had five, Peterborough (Northants) had three. And in the survey of the monastery of Wilton there is an interesting enumeration of the revenues of the hundred.[1] There is one case in which the curial revenues of the Quarter Sessions are entered in the survey.[2]

Thus we see that the revenues called in the Valor Ecclesia- The ad-
sticus by the general name of 'perquisita curie' or 'casuali- mission
fines.
tates' were very varied in character. Unfortunately we cannot classify them according to their source of origin, because as a rule only their general total is given. The revenues of the court of the hundred are sometimes given in a separate entry, but rarely. In other surveys the admission payments, 'fines terrarum,' are distinguished from the general mass of curial revenues. These admission fines stand by themselves as a special kind of revenue from land, and are entirely distinct from curial fees and fines, from death duties collected from the tenants, and payments of different kinds embraced in the term perquisites of court, or 'casualitates'. And as the landed revenues of monasteries are of the greatest interest to the economic his-

---

Halesowen, Salop: 'manerium de Hales, iii. 206.' The usual entry 'in finibus heriettis et amerciamentis curie £3 0s. 0d.' stands first; then follows an unexpected item, 'in finibus custumariorum sectatorum £1 5s. 0d.' It is possible that 'fines custumariorum sectatorum' means here the same thing as 'communis finis ex certitudine' in the survey of Cirencester, ii. 464. 'Communis finis' used not in the sense of revenue from land is also found in the survey of Bury St. Edmund, iii. 459 : 'Exitus de communibus finibus tenencium infra dicta dominia cum perquisitis curie et aliis amerciamentis £4 6s. 8d.' 'Communis finis' is found in the Glastonbury Terrier of 1518 (Harl., 396, manor of Netylton, ff. 15 38), to the amount of one pound, and is joined with 'turnus vicecomitis'. 'Communis finis ex certitudine' is mentioned in the column 'fines her' etc.' in the Part. for grants for the manor of Leigh, Wilts., which belonged to Tewkesbury Abbey (Part. for grants, n. 995, 38 H. VIII, mm. 6–7).

[1] V. E. ii. 110, Chalke Hundred: 'In auxilio vicecomitis finibus generosorum amerciamentis placitorum catallis felonum extrahuris finibus decennarum et rewmannorum et aliis casualitatibus ad eundem hundredum pertinentibus £17 0s. 0d.'

[2] Peterborough, Northants, iv. 280: 'In finibus coram justiciariis dni regis ad pacem cum le pype silver et virida cera communibus annis £7 2s. 7¾d.' 'Virida cera' (green wax) is also mentioned in the survey of Bury St. Edmunds, ii. 459, among the 'recepta forinseca'.

torian, the entries of admission fines deserve careful study. Admission fines are mentioned in almost all the Somersetshire monasteries, in three in Buckinghamshire and three in Devonshire.[1] I give below both their admission fines and their curial income. The first thirteen monasteries are in Somerset, the following three in Devon, and the last three in Bucks. On the right are the figures of the admission fines, on the left those of the curial income ; n.m. = not mentioned.

	£	s.	d.	£	s.	d.
Athelney	5	6	8	3	16	8
Bath	18	2	0	18	5	8
Bruton	17	0	4	21	3	4
Glastonbury	132	2	8¼	257	3	3
Hinton	6	13	4	3	9	4
Keynsham	13	2	0	10	0	8
Minchin Bockland	0	10	8	4	6	8
Montacute	10	6	4½	23	5	2
Muchelney	14	8	10½	36	7	0
Taunton	10	1	0	18	14	0
Templecombe		n. m.		6	9	4
St. John's, Wells	1	4	8		n. m.	
Worspring	1	5	0¼	5	13	4
Ford	5	9	7	14	18	5
Frethylstoke	1	16	7¼	4	5	7
Newenham	9	18	6	8	10	0
Burnham	1	10	6	0	10	0
Missenden	5	0	0	2	0	0
Nutley	0	18	8	3	6	8

Taking these nineteen monasteries as a whole, we get a curial income of £254 17s. 5¾d., corresponding to admission fines of £442 5s. 1d. If we could assume that in the case of other monasteries the curial income was made up in the same way, then the greater part of the court receipts would have to be ranked with the revenue from land. But the curial income of these nineteen monasteries occupies a place in the Valor Ecclesiasticus, if only on account of its large sum. The gross temporal income of the monasteries slightly exceeds seven thousand five hundred pounds, of which the *perquisita curie* with *fines terrarum* amount to £697 2s. 6¾d., that is to say to about 9 per cent. So high a percentage of the curial income is not found outside Somersetshire. I give below

---

[1] The admission fines mentioned in the survey of Nutley and Missenden are raised from the lands which are let out for years 'per indenturam'. Nothing is said in the survey about admission fines from customary tenements.

a long list of monasteries, together with the figures of their curial income.

		£	s.	d.
Beds.	Bushmead	1	0	0
	Caldwell	1	0	0
	Harwold	0	13	4
	Merkyate	1	6	8
	Newnham	2	0	0
	Woburn	2	0	0
Bucks.	Ankerwyke	0	16	2
	Lavenden	2	0	0
Cornwall	Bodmin	12	8	2
	St. Germans	7	10	0
	Launceston	11	13	0
Cumb.	Holme Cultram	2	0	0
Devon	Buckfastleigh	40	2	8
	Plympton	32	4	7⅞
	Totnes	1	1	8
Dorset	Cerne	47	18	1¼
	Middleton	55	19	3½
	Shaftesbury	154	3	7
	Sherborne	104	2	8½
	Tarrent	2	7	4
Glouc.	St. Peter's, Gloucester	36	3	1
	Lantony	2	10	2
	Tewkesbury	28	18	3¾
	Winchelcombe	4	4	0
Hereford	Aconbury	0	10	0
	Dore	0	6	8
	Wigmore	3	6	8
	Wormesley	0	7	0
Hunts.	Huntingdon	0	16	8
	Ramsey	32	15	6
	St. Neots	2	13	4
	Sawtre	0	10	2
Kent	Horton	1	10	1
	Malling	4	16	2
	Sheppey	1	0	9
Lanc.	Cartmell	1	0	0
Leic.	Croxton	1	17	0
	Garendon	0	6	8
	Kirby Beller	2	6	8
	Launde	0	10	4
	St. Mary's, Leicester	4	8	8
	Olveston	2	0	0
Linc.	Bardney	1	0	0
	Bollington	0	6	8
	Hagnaby	0	1	0
	Kyme	0	1	8
	Markby	0	4	8
	Newsome	0	10	0
	Thornton	6	0	0
Middl.	St. Barthol. London	2	16	4½

		£	s.	d.
	Stratford at Bow	0	10	0
	Syon	135	7	0
	Westminster	66	1	7½
Norfolk	Hickling	9	16	11
	Hulme	79	1	5
	Langley	0	8	0
	Norwich Cath.	17	9	8½
	Pentney	0	7	4
	Shouldham	0	11	8
	Walsingham	4	3	11½
	Wendling	0	19	8
	Westacre	0	18	10
	Wymondham	13	7	6
Northants	Peterborough	31	2	7⅞
	Pipewell	1	5	0
	Fineshade	0	2	0
	Sulby	0	9	8
Notts.	Lenton	1	10	0
	Newstead	0	18	10
	Rufford	1	12	3
	Thurgarton	0	11	10
Oxon.	Studley	1	0	0
	Thame	1	0	0
Salop	Buildwas	0	5	0
	Halesowen	5	12	0
	Haghmond	0	6	8
	Shrewsbury	1	0	0
	Wenlock	10	0	0
	Wombridge	0	5	0
Somerset	Barlynch	3	10	0
Staff.	Hulton	0	12	0
	St. Thomas's, Stafford	0	3	2
	Stone	0	13	4
	Trentham	0	12	0
	Tutbury	0	16	3
Suffolk	Bury St.Edmunds[1]	21	15	0
	Campsey	4	16	11
	Ixworth	0	7	8
	Leiston	3	6	8
	Redlingfield	1	12	1
	Woodbridge	0	6	4
Surrey	Bermondsey	4	10	0
	Chertsey	30	3	3
	Merton	11	17	1
	Newark	0	5	8
	St. Mary's, Overey	0	3	4
	Waverley	1	4	8
Sussex	Lewes	10	1	0
	Shulbrede	0	12	0
	Tortington	2	0	0

[1] *Recepta forinseca* have not been taken into consideration.

		£	s.	d.
Warw.	Wroxall ...	0	13	4
Westm.	Shappe ...	0	13	4
Wilts.	Amesbury ...	15	10	7
	Bradenstoke ...	2	6	8
	Edindon ...	7	0	10
	Farleigh ...	1	18	1
	Lacock ...	1	1	10
	Malmesbury ...	5	8	6
	Stanley ...	1	10	0
	Wilton... ...	24	3	6
Worc.	Bordesley ...	5	1	7

		£	s.	d.
	Evesham ...	18	3	4
	M. Malvern ...	4	9	5
	P. Malvern ...	0	18	6
	Pershore ...	18	8	5½
	Worcester Cath.	26	7	8
Yorks.	Jervaulx ...	1	0	0
	Nostell... ...	0	10	2
	Pontefract ...	0	10	10
	Roche	0	10	8
	Selby	2	6	8

The curial income of all the monasteries given in the above table amounts to £1,250 12s. 6¼d.; the gross temporal income of the same monasteries slightly exceeds forty-four thousand pounds. The curial income, therefore, is a little less than three per cent. of the gross temporal income. If we suppose that the curial income of the remaining monasteries bears the same proportion to their gross temporal income the grand total of the curial income would be about three thousand five hundred pounds. But, inasmuch as the receipts from Courts and from admission fines of nineteen of the monasteries in the above table, with a gross temporal income of £7,500, work out at nine, and not three per cent. of the gross income, I conclude that the grand total of the curial income of the Valor Ecclesiasticus ought to be estimated at least at £4,000.

The proportion of the curial income in the V. E. varies in different monasteries. In some cases the curial income represents more than ten per cent. of the gross temporal income; it is so in Shaftesbury, Sherborne, Dorset; Hulme, Norfolk; Bruton, Glastonbury, Minchin Bockland, Muchelney, Somerset. In Hulme the income from Courts equals one-seventh of the gross temporal income; in Sherborne it exceeds one-seventh; in the small monastery of Minchin Bockland it is equivalent to almost one-fourth. But the curial income of some other monasteries is less than one-tenth of one per cent. of the gross temporal income (Lincolnshire, Hagnaby; Surrey, St. Mary's, Overey). Differences like these in the amount of the curial income may mean either that the curial income entries did not include the same items in the different surveys, or that the figures of the curial income given in the V. E. are not very trustworthy; or it may be that both these conditions prevail. It would be easy for the monks to manipulate the figures of curial income, inasmuch as they were not called upon to make a statement as to a *fact*, the revenue of a particular year, of the last year for instance, but only to give an *estimate*, the income of an average year (*communibus annis*), and the Commissioners had no time to verify the monastic valuation. If we compare the figures of the curial income in the V. E. with those of the later surveys, and the accounts made by the Augmentations Court, our doubts respecting their accuracy will be confirmed; for there are very important points of difference between the two sets of figures. Not infrequently the later official valuation is much higher than that of 1535, and here we have ground for believing that the figures of 1535 were less than the actual value. But converse cases are found in which the later valuation is lower than that of 1535. The small amount of curial income in many monastic surveys must not be wholly attributed to the manipulation of the monks and mistakes of the Commissioners; in some cases the total given was small because it embraced only a part of the receipts which are in other surveys included with greater totals. Sometimes everything was reckoned; curial fees, hundredal profits, heriots, reliefs, admission fines; but in other cases, where the curial income entered was from one to two shillings, only the amerciamenta were taken into account. It is, therefore, impossible to define the place that admission fines occupy in the curial income, or the extent to which the curial income in the Valor Ecclesiasticus is *landed revenue* proper. In Somersetshire the admission fines are much higher than the revenue to which the name 'perquisita curiae' is given, but we do not know whether this was so in the returns for other counties in which the admission fines, even where they are mentioned, are not distinguished from the other curial income. And in several cases we have ground for supposing that the admission fines were not included in the curial income at all.

CHAPTER III

AGRICULTURAL INCOME

Total of
rural
landed
revenue. THE foregoing calculations enable us to form an idea of the rural landed revenue of the monasteries. The gross temporal income amounts to about one hundred and twenty thousand pounds ; of which about fourteen thousand was derived from urban rents and farms ; about two and a half or three thousand from artisans' tenements, mills, and fisheries, and about four thousand from the curial income. This would leave about one hundred thousand pounds as the amount of the rural landed income. It is just this part of the monastic revenue that is most important in the study of English economic history.

Kinds
of rural
landed
income. The rural income from land of the monasteries may be considered from several points of view. It was derived from entire manors, from separate tenements, from the demesne in hand and from the payments of tenants. Among the last may be distinguished the rents of freehold, copyhold, and leasehold and payments for tenements held at the will of the lord at common law. With regard to the income from the demesne in hand, this may be divided into that derived from arable land, from meadow, pasture and wood. An accurate distinction of all these revenues is found only in a very few surveys in the Valor Ecclesiasticus, and the totals for the various kinds of rural landed revenue can be only approximately calculated. By the amount of this or that particular revenue in some surveys, we can form a guess at the corresponding amount in other surveys. The survey of Godstow, in Oxfordshire, affords one of the rare examples in which the different kinds of temporal income from land are distinguished in almost all the possessions of the monastery. The survey is divided into two parts ; a detailed description of the demesne in hand, and the different kinds of tenants' payments ('terre dominicales monasterii in manibus abbatisse ;

maneria terre et tenementa in diversis locis et comitatibus '). Some possessions (Wolvercote and Woodstock) of the monastery are called manors, others are not. But strangely enough the possessions to which the name of 'manor' is given are in their revenues much less like manors than some of the possessions to which this name is not applied (for instance, Sandford cum Kyngs Clere). The terms 'redditus' and 'firma' are applied to the payments of tenants. Speaking generally, 'redditus' is the same as 'redditus assisus', the fixed rent of freehold and copyhold, and more rarely the fluctuating payments of tenants at the will of the lord of the manor; the term 'firma' generally means a leasehold rent. But even in the careful and detailed survey of Godstow the words 'redditus' and 'firma' are not always used in their strict sense. In Ludwell the term 'redditus' is applied to a leasehold rent (de redditu unius virgate terre dimisse ad terminum annorum per indenturam); and in Blechenden the term 'firma' is applied to the tenure at the will of the lord. It is, therefore, difficult to come to a conclusion as to the legal nature of the tenure when the payment is characterized only by the word 'redditus' or 'firma'. But in the survey of Godstow, along with the payments, clear indications concerning the legal character of the tenure are given; the tenants are divided into liberi tenentes, tenentes custumarii, tenentes ad voluntatem domini, tenentes per copiam curie, firmarii.

It seems to me that, in the rural landed income, the most important difference observed is that between the payments of the tenants and the income from the demesne in hand. If we take the total of the income from land to be a hundred thousand pounds, we shall have no need to calculate separately the total of each one of the two component parts; it will be sufficient to define one of them. Which of the two then is more easily defined? It seems to me that it is easier to define approximately the amount of the income from the demesne in hand, both because it is much smaller than the payments of the tenants, and because it is more readily separated from the gross temporal income. If we wished to calculate the payments of the tenants it would not be sufficient to separate them from the income from demesne ; we should have to deduct from them the non-rural revenue and the revenue not derived from the land, i. e. the urban, the industrial, the mining, the fisheries, the market revenues, the profits of the mills and the curial revenue. All these special revenues are distinguished in only a few of the surveys ; and even in some of these it is impossible to establish the exact amount of the income from demesne. On the whole, there are not many cases in the Valor Ecclesiasticus in which it would be possible to define the exact total of the tenurial payments, and the conclusions drawn from such cases can hardly be extended to all the monasteries. Of course, some kinds of revenue not derived from land occupy only a very modest place in the monastic budget ; and we shall make but a slight error if, provisionally, we consider them as non-existing in those surveys in which they are not separated from the tenurial payments. This, however, cannot be done with regard to the revenue from mills, and still less with regard to the urban revenue, for the amount is much too great to be left out of consideration. At the same time it is not often that we can single out the urban revenue with certainty. Even the legal distinction between a small town and a large village is not quite clear, and the economic distinction between the urban and rural revenue is still more vague. In each individual case it would be incumbent on us to indicate what particular items should be classified as ' urban ' income, and such classification must be largely matter of opinion. In estimating the payments of tenants the following method might, perhaps, be adopted :—Where the revenue from demesne in hand is given separately we might add together the remaining temporal revenues, and from their sum deduct one-sixth for urban and other non-landed revenue ; for it has been already shown that the £120,000 of the temporal income of the monasteries includes, roughly speaking, £20,000 of urban and other non-landed revenue, &c. ; but, of course, in doing so we are taking for granted that the urban and non-landed revenue is not already included in the demesne income.

Income
from
demesne.

Instead, however, of making these somewhat long calculations it is simpler to establish an approximate total for the income from demesne ; this also involves some difficulties, but they are less serious than those encountered in calculating the tenurial payments. Only the income of the demesnes of which it is distinctly said that the monks held them in their own hands must be considered as home farm income. In some surveys it is said, at one and the same time, that the demesne is in the hands of the monks and that a *firma* is received from it ; the term 'firma', however, is generally applied to leasehold rents. This seeming contradiction can be explained by the supposition that the term 'firma' is used in the very wide sense of 'exitus, proficua ', and the demesne must be considered as held in the hands of the monks.[1] We will consider as income from demesne all income that is said to be received from 'terrae dominicales in manibus abbatis sive prioris ', and only such income. Then it seems to me we shall only be in danger of diminishing and not exaggerating the actual amount of the income from home farms, for it is possible and sometimes probable that, in some surveys, by the words 'terre dominicales valent ', or in 'terris dominicalibus ', is meant the income from the demesne in hand.[2]

The danger of exaggerating the income from demesne will still exist, but it will depend upon quite other features of the survey. In the Valor Ecclesiasticus by income from demesne is meant, for the most part, only the rural

---

[1] The following are instances of the term 'firma ' being applied to the 'demesne in manu '. Chertsey, Surrey, ii. 56 : 'firma terrarum pratorum pascuorum et pasturarum modo in manibus dicti abbatis existentium per annum ut per declaracionem de particulis inde examinatam £16 3s. 4d.' Bordesley,Worc., iii. 271 : Bydforde manor. The income from the demesne is described in three entries. In two, the expression 'firma terrarum dominicalium' is used without further explanations. But in the third case it is said : 'in firma terrarum dominicalium in manibus propriis occupatarum £8 2s. 8d.' The survey of Magna Malvern, Worc., iii. 238, 'Powycke messor et Pyam,' is quite clear. The demesne is divided into two parts : one is in the tenants' hands, the other in the prior's hands ; to both the term 'firma ' is applied. 'In firma terrarum dominicalium in manu tenentium ad voluntatem domini £33 5s. 10½d., in firma terrarum dominicalium in manu domini prioris per annum £13 6s. 8d.'

[2] In some surveys the only demesne mentioned is not directly called the demesne in hand, but there can be no doubt that it was so. An instance can be found in the survey of Beauchief, Derb., or Newenham, Beds.

income and the landed income. But in some surveys the demesne income includes the revenues from urban monastic sites and also other profits than those from land ; for instance, receipts from mills or fisheries.[1] They ought, of course, to be deducted from the account ; this, however, cannot be done, for the amount is unknown. But such non-rural and non-landed incomes are less often found in the revenue from the demesne than among the tenurial payments ; and this is one of the reasons why it is more convenient to calculate the revenues from the home farms and not the tenurial payments. When calculating the demesne receipts it is necessary to add an explanation concerning the revenue from the woods. This is mentioned often enough in the Valor Ecclesiasticus and in most cases is given in separate entries. The monks generally kept the woods in their own hands, and the wood receipts ought not in any case to be classed with the tenurial payments. The most accurate way would be to calculate the income from woods apart from the demesne and add its total to the total of the income from demesne. This I have done wherever the nature of the survey permits. Such cases, however, are comparatively rare. One reason of this is that in many of the surveys in which the wood receipts are given separately, the income from demesne is not distinguished from the tenurial payments. In the table that follows, the amount on the left signifies the receipts from the demesne in hand, the one on the right the income from woods.

				£	s.	d.	£	s.	d.
Beds. ...	...	Harwold ...	...	11	0	0	1	13	4
		Merkyate ...	...	15	3	$3\frac{1}{2}$	2	0	0
		Woburn ...	...	53	9	8	7	6	8

[1] The surveys of St. Mary, Leicester, and St. Michael, Stamford, may serve as instances in which the revenue from sites of the urban monasteries was included in the income from demesne. But often the Commissioners did not consider monastic sites as being capable of yielding any profit at all. Thus the urban sites of Bury St. Edmunds, Huntingdon Priory and Worcester Cathedral are considered as profitless. The usual formula used in such cases is : 'firma situs monasterii nichil quia reservatur in manibus prioris et monachorum ibidem et nullum proficuum inde provenit.' In the survey of Sawtre, Hunts., the income from fisheries ('piscariae cum piscacionibus ') is included in the demesne receipts. In the survey of Furness, Lanc., the revenue from mills is included among the receipts from demesne ('situs abbathie cum pomariis molend' et certis clausis eidem abbathie adiacen' et ad usum proprium occupat' £2 0s. 0d.').

County	Monastery		£	s.	d.	£	s.	d.
Bucks.	Ankerwyke	...	4	13	4	1	13	4
	Lavenden ...	...	14	12	6	1	12	0
	Missenden ...	...	6	8	0	20	0	0
	Nutley	...	26	18	4	5	0	0
Dorset	Cerne	...	70	17	10	6	0	0
	Shaftesbury	...	19	8	4	38	4	5½
	Sherborne ...	...	24	10	0	1	7	10¼
	Tarrent	...	25	1	8	2	19	4
	Middleton ...	...	116	8	11½	3	15	6
Gloucester ...	Tewkesbury	...	37	6	8	1	12	8
Hereford ...	Wormesley...	...	17	19	6	0	8	0
Kent	St. Radegund's, Dover		23	1	8	1	0	0
Lincoln	Alvingham	...	20	0	0	10	0	0
	Newsome ...	...	13	5	0	0	6	8
	Revesby	...	28	17	6	20	0	0
	Staynesfield	...	15	0	0	5	0	0
	Stixwold	...	4	0	0	1	0	0
	Willoughton	...	10	0	0	1	9	6
Middlesex ...	Syon	...	20	15	6	33	19	4
	Westminster	...	4	5	4	57	19	0
Norfolk ...	Shouldham...	...	21	12	10½	1	10	0
	Walsingham	...	57	0	10¾	9	15	4¾
	Westacre ...	...	44	14	8	4	0	0
	W. Dereham	,,	44	4	8	3	6	8
Northants ...	Finneshed ...		4	19	4	10	0	0
	Pipewell	...	19	13	8	7	0	0
Oxon.	Rewley	...	8	13	8	0	10	0
Somerset ...	Henton	...	17	10	0	3	6	8
	Witham	...	60	0	0	5	15	2
Surrey ...	Chertsey	...	16	3	4	21	7	0
	Merton	...	3	6	8	20	14	0
	Newark	...	18	18	9	2	5	0
	St. Mary's, Overey...		2	0	0	5	11	0
	Waverley ...	...	16	14	10	0	16	8
Wilts.	Wilton	...	21	7	8	10	11	8
Worcester ...	M. Malvern	...	21	6	8	1	11	8
	P. Malvern	...	8	1	8	0	4	10
Yorks.	Roche	...	17	0	0	4	0	0

The monasteries in this table had a total income from demesne of £986 12s. 5¼d. and a total income from woods of £336 13s. 4¾d. The gross temporal income of these same monasteries amounts to about sixteen thousand two hundred and fifty pounds; but if from this sum we deduct one-sixth for the non-rural and non-landed revenues a little more than thirteen thousand five hundred remains. The income from demesne, together with that from the woods (£1,323 5s. 10d.), amounts to about 9¾ per cent. of this remainder; 7¼ per cent belonging to the income from demesne and 2½ per cent. to the income from the woods. Nine-tenths, therefore, of the rural revenue from the land represent the tenurial payments.

The number of monasteries in the table is but small, and the conclusions drawn from it need of course to be ratified and confirmed. We must therefore have recourse to those more numerous surveys in which the demesne revenues are divided from the tenurial, but the wood receipts are not mentioned at all. In some cases the absence of income from woods may mean that as a matter of fact there was no such income, but in other cases the absence may have been caused by the revenue from the woods being included in some other account. It is of course impossible to say whether it should be looked for in the income from demesne or among the payments of tenants; we can only form more or less plausible conjectures concerning its amount. In the table below, the amounts of the income from the demesne in hand are stated.[1]

			£	s.	d.				£	s.	a.
Beds.	Bushmead	...	10	0	0	Notts.	Rufford	...	19	16	8
Bucks.	Burnham	...	11	0	2		Shelford	...	26	2	3
Devon	Canonleigh	...	1	16	0		Thurgarton	...	30	0	0
	Hartland	...	45	0	0		Welbeck	...	20	13	2
Glouc.	Lantony	...	32	9	3		Worksop	...	9	17	8
	Winchcombe	...	142	1	8	Oxon.	Thame...	...	3	3	3
Hereford	St. Guthlac	...	0	13	8		Wroxton	...	10	1	4
Hunts.	St. Neots	...	20	16	8	Salop	Buildwas	...	20	9	8
	Sawtre...	...	33	6	4		Haghmond	...	19	19	4
Kent	Dartford	...	26	18	4		Lilleshall	...	16	0	0
	Horton...	...	5	0	0		Wombridge	...	6	13	4
Lanc.	Furness	...	104	15	8	Somerset	Athelney	...	3	17	0
Leic.	Garendon	...	44	7	8		Barlinch	...	5	11	9
	Kirby Beller	...	14	0	0		Bruton...	...	10	0	0
	Launde...	...	113	0	0		Minchin Bockland		5	17	8
	St. Mary	...	41	0	0		Muchelney	...	8	6	0
	Ulverscroft	...	18	6	8		Taunton	...	15	11	9
Linc.	Ailesham	...	9	0	0		Worspring	...	24	3	0
	Greenfield	...	12	13	0	Staff.	Croxden	...	36	16	8
	Hagnaby	...	32	0	0		Dieulacres	...	8	18	6
	Markby	...	19	0	6		Roncester	...	23	16	0
	Sixhill ...	...	26	13	4	Suffolk	Bury St. Edmunds		25	13	4
	Spalding	...	50	0	8		Redlingfield	...	17	5	0
	Stamford, St. Michael's		9	14	7		Woodbridge	...	8	0	0
	Swineshed	...	46	7	4	Sussex	Battle ...	...	20	0	0
Norfolk	Langley	...	20	8	0		Michelham	...	25	11	0
Northants	Ashby ...	...	31	6	8		Robertsbridge...		27	3	0
	St. Andrews	...	17	0	0		Shulbrede	...	25	6	8
	St. James	...	13	10	0		Tortington	...	8	0	0
	Sulby ...	...	133	6	8	Warw.	Warwick	...	25	7	0
Notts.	Lenton...	...	20	3	4		Wroxall	...	22	0	0
	Newstead	...	13	6	8	Westm.	Shappe	...	16	7	8

[1] I have intentionally omitted from this table the cases where one general total is given for the wood and the curial income taken together.

			£	s.	d.				£	s.	d.
Wilts.	Amesbury	...	10	9	5	Yorks.	Marton...	...	21	0	0
	Kington	...	5	6	8		Meaux ...	...	24	0	0
	Malmesbury	...	8	0	0		Newburgh	...	16	0	0
Yorks.	Fountains	...	183	6	8		Nostell...	...	41	0	0
	Jervaulx	...	72	11	8		Pontefract	...	34	1	2
	Marrick	...	21	0	0						

The monasteries in the above table have a total income from demesne of £2,102 7s. 1d. The gross temporal income of these same monasteries amounts to about £18,800. If we deduct from it one-sixth for the urban and non-land receipts, about £15,700 will remain. The income from demesne slightly exceeds one-eighth of this remainder. We do not know how much income from woods is included in the total £2, 102 7s. 1d. If we consider the income from woods as a part of the income from demesne, then £2,102 7s. 1d. is the minimum for the income from demesne of all the monasteries in the table. For this figure represents the total income from demesne only on the supposition that not a single wood receipt is included in the tenurial payments; every wood receipt included in the tenurial payments will *pro tanto* increase the total of £2,102 7s. 1d.

The percentages of both tables differ but slightly. If we suppose that in the remaining monasteries the demesne receipts bore the same proportion to the payments of the tenants, then according to the first table the income from demesne of all the monasteries that I have studied would amount to ten thousand pounds, and according to the second, to twelve thousand five hundred pounds (if we take a hundred thousand to indicate the rural revenue from the land). Perhaps it would be safer to take a figure nearer to ten than to twelve and a half thousand, for in the case of some monasteries only the profit from woods are given and the income from the demesne is not mentioned, and in the case of others no entries are made of the income either of the wood or the demesne.[1] About ninety thousand pounds fall to the share of tenurial payments.

Total of income from demesne.

Large and average numbers are important and instructive to the economic historian. It is important to remember that

[1] For Norwich Cathedral, Bodmin, Launceston, Horsham, only the income from woods is mentioned. For Maiden Bradley, Kyme, Horsham, Totnes, Montacute, no entries are made of income either from the wood or the demesne.

L 2

on the eve of the Dissolution the system of farming the monastic demesnes was still alive and yielded an income of about
£10,000 ; it is no less instructive to know that the tenurial payments exceeded the income from demesne by about nine times
its amount. But such large averages may obscure and cloak
the real and varied character of the actual economic situation,
unless they are accompanied by figures *typical* of this or that
group of monasteries. According to the averages, the demesne
in hand gave the monks one-tenth of their whole rural income
from land ; whereas some monasteries had no demesne in hand
at all. There were also many whose income from demesne
was very small compared with the payments of the tenants,
and others whose income from the home farm composed
a large, and in exceptional cases even the greater part of
their rural income from land. Let us now compare the
payments of the tenants and the demesne receipts of a few
monasteries ; those instances have been taken in which it was
possible to exclude the ' non-landed ' and the urban revenues.
The first amount after the name of the monastery indicates
the income from demesne together with the income from
woods; the second indicates the tenurial payments. St. Peter's,
Westminster, Midd., £62 4s. 4d. + £2,350 0s. 0¾d. ; Evesham,
Worc., £33 3s. 4d. + £982 4s. 6½d. ; Merton, Surr., £24 0s. 8d.
+ £640 13s. 4½d. ; Shaftesbury, Dors., £57 12s. 9½d. + £958
5s. 1½d.; Chertsey, Surrey, £37 10s. 4d. + £492 19s. 8¾d. ;
M. Malvern, Worc., £22 18s. 4d. + £265 16s. 1¼d. ; Henton,
Soms., £20 16s. 8d. + £200 5s. 4d. ; Rewley, Oxon., £9 3s. 8d. +
£86 1s. 5d. ; Newark, Surrey, £21 3s. 9d. + £127 19s. 4½d. ;
Thurgarton, Notts., £30 0s. 0d. + £167 18s. 0¼d. ; Westacre,
Norf., £48 18s. 4d. + £187 18s. 5¼d.; Fin., Northants, £14
19s. 0d. + £43 14s. 8d. I cannot include the two surveys of
Launde, Leic., and Warwick Priory, for in them the different
kinds of ' non-landed ' and urban revenues are not all
separately given. In the survey of Launde the urban and
curial revenues only are given separately ; the payments of
the tenants yield £162 8s. 5½d., and the income from the
demesne in hand is valued at £113. In the survey of the
small priory of Warwick, in which the total receipts are

divided into income from demesne and tenurial payments, the former is double the latter; the corresponding figures being £25 7s. 0d. and £12 15s. 10d. There is a long chain of intermediate differences linking those monasteries which have no home farm to those whose budget in its greater part is based on an income from that source.

On the whole, however, the bulk of the rural revenue from land was yielded by the rents of the tenantry. These payments call for much more remark than the income from demesne, which represented only a very small part of the monastic budget. The historian approaches this sum of ninety thousand pounds with a series of questions ; he would like to divide it into parts, to put it into definite shape, and to see in it, if not a vivid picture of the economic life of the numerous monastic tenants, at all events the chief outlines of such a picture. How are the payments of the tenants distributed between the *firmae*, the fixed rents of freehold and copyhold and the fluctuating payments of the tenants at the will of the lord ? How often was the relation of the monks to the land nothing but a title to a fixed payment ? What were the rents paid by the different kinds of tenants ? How much of it was paid in work, in kind, in money ? Is it possible to estimate the acreage of the tenancies from the amount of payment ? What was the approximate number of the tenants of these monastic lands ? What was their social status ? How can they be divided according to the size of their tenancies ? To what extent were the monastic lands concentrated on a small area or scattered in many distant localities ? How were they divided into whole manors and separate tenancies ? How was the land divided between the demesne and the tenancies within the monastic manors ? This chain of questions could be considerably lengthened if it were worth while to do so. But it is not ; for with only the Valor Ecclesiasticus at our disposal it is only possible to give a somewhat definite picture of that part of the land which remained in the hands of the monks, and not of the part in the possession of tenants. The tenurial payments are in the great majority of cases very briefly described. Only an answer to the most general

Payments of the tenants.

questions can be got from the Valor Ecclesiasticus, and even this will be merely approximate.

Manors and tenancies. My impression is that in the monastic territory entire manors predominated over separate tenancies. The manors, of course, were of various sizes, and a large tenancy might exceed a small manor in size. But on the whole the prevalence of manorial revenues in the monastic budget shows that the monasteries derived a larger income from the letting of big farms than from small plots or from titles to rent scattered about in different places. I speak intentionally of my 'impression' and not of a numerical inference, for it is not always easy to distinguish that which is a manor from that which is not a manor in the Valor Ecclesiasticus. The word ' manerium ' is not used at all in the Glastonbury Survey,[1] although most (32) of the estates from which the monastic income was derived were undoubtedly manors, for their income is divided into the demesne farm, tenurial rent and curial income—(I here provisionally treat the income from woods as part of the demesne farm). In a smaller number of estates (19) the demesne farm is not mentioned,—the income is divided into rents and curial receipts; in three cases it consists of tenurial payments only—London, Bristol, Byndon. What are these nineteen estates ? Are they or are they not, manors ? Some of these estates are undoubtedly manors (e. g. Netylton, Deveral Langbrigge, Est Moncketon): not only is the amount of income arising from them equal to that which would arise from entire manors and include the curial receipts, but in an official survey of a later date, made by Pollard and Moyle, the rents given in the Valor Ecclesiasticus are divided into the demesne farm and the payments of the tenants. For instance, in the Netylton survey the Commissioners of 1535 show only the rent (£31 8s. 11¼d.) of the tenants and do not mention the farm of the demesne ; in the Pollard and Moyle survey the rent of the tenants is shown to be £21 9s. 11d., and in addition the farm of the demesne is given as £10 0s. 6d. On the other hand we must not take for granted 'entire manors' in all cases in

---

[1] Goderihay is the only exception in which we find an entry 'firma manerii cum dominicalibus '.

which the word 'manor' is used.   The word 'manerium' has
a variety of meanings in the Valor Ecclesiasticus, especially in
the combination 'firma manerii'.   The 'firma' of a manor
may signify payment for the whole manor, for the manorial
demesne, for the site of a seignorial hall.   Sometimes the words
'manerium' and 'firma manerii' have different meanings in
one and the same survey.[1]   Sometimes the words 'such and
such a manor brings in such and such an income' do not
signify at all that the monastery is the lord of the manor, but
only that the income in question is received from the manor
in question.[2]   And when the two words 'firma manerii' are
used to describe some place we can only guess their true
meaning.   Therefore, any one desiring to find the relation
between entire manors and separate tenancies must confine
himself to individual instances, and must take only those
surveys in which the term 'manerium' is used in a clear
sense.

Almost all whole manors yield a larger income than
separate tenancies.   In some cases all, or almost all, the rural
income from land of a monastery consists of the revenues of
whole manors, e. g. Edington (Wilts.) or Shaftesbury (Dorset).
In the surveys of Blackborough, Walsingham, Westacre
(Norfolk), Faversham (Kent), the separate tenancies give a
smaller though considerable part of the income.   I can point to
only one survey where there is reason to suppose that separate

---

[1] The use of the term 'manerium' is instructive in the survey of
St. Augustine, Canterbury.   Several times the income from a certain place
is divided into two parts ; one being made up of 'redditus et firme cum
perquisitis curie', another of 'manerium ibidem'.   In two places both
revenues are farmed by one person (Ryple, Langdon) ; then the characteristic formula is used 'manerium ibidem cum redditu insimul ad firmam
dimissum'.   'Manerium' in this survey stands for a part only of the
monastic possessions in the place in question.—In the survey of M. Malvern,
Worc.,the word *manerium* is used in three senses ; several times it means in
the headings ' an entire manor ', as for instance, ' dominium sive manerium
de Longney.'   Sometimes, in Powycke for instance, it means the demesne
of the manor ; in Powycke the *firma manerii* is divided from the payments
of the tenants.   Sometimes, for instance in Longney just mentioned, it
stands for the seignorial mansion alone ; in Longney the *firma manerii* is
distinguished not only from the payments of the tenants, but even from
money paid by the farmer for the demesne.

[2] Here is an instance, Horsham, Norf. iii. 366 : 'manerium de Heverlonde
valet in quadam annuitate 1. 6. 8.'

tenancies predominate over whole manors : I refer to the
case of Bradenstoke, Wilts., but even here the matter is not
absolutely clear. Most of the manors belonging to a monastery were generally situated in the same county as the
monastery, but the monastic manors were seldom contiguous.
Large monasteries possessed manors in many counties.
St. Peter's, Westminster, had manors in Gloucester, Worc.,
Midd., Surrey, Bucks., Oxon., Berks., Essex, Notts. Even a
monastery of moderate size, W. Dereham, Norf., had manors
in five counties, viz. Norf., Camb., Suff., Yorks., Linc.
Individual tenancies were still more scattered. The individual
tenancies of Maiden Bradley, a monastery in Wiltshire,
yielded only a small income, but they were scattered in
small portions over five counties, viz. Wilts., Dorset, Soms.,
Hants, Sussex. In some places the monastery received an
income of only one shilling, or even sixpence, as, for instance,
Mortwery, Soms., and Mere, Wilts. ; separate tenancies might
be scattered even if they were situated in the same county.
All the separate tenancies of the monastery of Cokesford were
situated in Norfolk, but they were in nine different localities,
and they brought in only seven pounds of income.

The Law of Mortmain renders a map of monastic possessions
a sort of guide to the economic story of the monasteries,
preserving the memory the earliest donations and the latest
acquisitions, the most important, and the smallest increments of
the land area. The surveys that present the economic side of
monastic life on the eve of the Dissolution throw a sidelight,
too, on its earliest history. They indicate that the monastic
lands were acquired much more often by donation than by purchase or exchange, although no doubt some gifts of land were
only secret sales, mortgages, and exchanges. Only the Anglo-
Saxon kings could give entire hundreds to the monasteries ;
in later times the grants became smaller. Poor people would
give small pieces of land or small rents ; a rich person might
give whole manors, but often we find him confining his gifts
to separate tenancies. Large or famous houses attracted
pilgrims from various counties ; a God-fearing donor made it
his object to give his land not to the neighbouring, but to his

favourite house. The more reasons he had to fear God the more strict and careful was he in his choice of advice and advocate in view of the Last Judgement. Thus the landed revenue dwindled in out-of-the-world places, and flowed by the well-trodden pilgrim roads to religious centres, in accordance with the text: 'To him that hath shall be given, and from him that hath not shall be taken away even that he hath.' This is the reason why Christchurch, Canterbury, acquired lands in Devonshire and Norfolk, and Westminster Abbey acquired land in Nottinghamshire and Worcestershire.

In 1535 the manor was divided as formerly into demesne and tenancies, but already this division had lost the meaning that it had in former times. The home farms had ceased to depend upon the work of the tenants.

Holdings and manorial demesnes.

The lords of the manors for the most part entirely ceased to cultivate their demesnes themselves. There is no reason to believe that monastic lands were in any exceptional position as compared with the lands of secular lords; we can only conjecture that they kept the demesne in their own hands more frequently than did the latter. But with the cessation of the week-works and boon-works the division of a manor into demesne and tenancies did not wholly cease or lose its meaning; and consequently we cannot disregard the question of the relation between the demesne and the tenancies of monastic manors. Speaking generally, the demesne did not disappear, but only passed into new hands. The lord of the manor seldom divided up the demesne into separate plots of land to be let to local tenants. Usually the demesne and its buildings, sometimes even together with the live and dead stock, passed into the hands of one farmer.[1] An instance can be found in the survey of Battle, Sussex. This monastery owned twenty-two whole manors, and only in one of them did the monks keep the demesne in their own hands; in nineteen the demesne was farmed by one person; in one, Dengemershe, by two persons; and in another case, that of

---

[1] In the V. E., entries are made of land and stock leases but they are very rare. The following is an instance: Amesbury, Wilts, ii. 95: Chadelworth in firma terr' dnicalium cum firma stauri ibm £6 13s. 4d.'

Wachenden, by three.   Not infrequently the farmer of the
demesne was entrusted with the collection of the tenants'
payments ; then he became the farmer of the manor and the
connexion of the lord with the manor was limited to receiving the payment agreed upon.   The demesne continued to
be farmed upon a scale much larger than the tenancies.
On the whole it can also be said that the demesne area
became an area of leases for years, in distinction to freehold, copyhold and tenure at the will of the lord which
prevailed on the remaining part of the manor.   We do not
of course, find a lease for years at common law on every
demesne.   We learn occasionally from the V. E. that a
demesne was let by copy of the court roll.   The abbey of
Evesham held the manor of Offenham ; part of its demesne
remained in the hands of the abbot, the other part was
leased by copy.   The same monastery held the manor
of Ombresley, where all the demesne was leased by copy.
Another Worcestershire monastery, M. Malvern, held the
manor of Powyck Messor and Pyxam ; part of the demesne of
this manor was retained by the lord of the manor and part
was let to tenants at the will of the lord.   On the other hand
we come across leases at common law for a term of years on
separate tenancies.   But the bulk of the monastic demesne
was leased for terms of years, and the bulk of the monastic
lands leased for years consisted of manorial demesnes.

The Valor Ecclesiasticus does not enable us to establish the
relation between the area of demesne land and the area of the
tenancies. We can only compare the income from the demesnes
with that from the tenancies. For this comparison we must
pick out those surveys in which the income from demesne is
accurately distinguished from tenurial payments, at least in some
of the manors ; such surveys are few, and almost all of them
refer to the southern and western counties.   In order not to
complicate the calculations by the income from woods I have
taken only those manors in which no entries of wood sales are
made ; it is possible, however, that in some manors this was
included in the income from demesne.   In the following list
the amount on the left stands for the income from demesne,

that on the right for the payments of the tenants; the name is that of the manor:—

SHAFTESBURY, DORSET.

	£	s.	d.	£	s.	d.
Ludyngton ...	20	0	0	24	18	11
Henton ...	9	1	4	34	7	0
Felsham ...	8	6	8	54	10	10
Kyngeston ...	14	6	8	19	11	2
Stower ...	6	13	4	36	5	7
Chesylborne	20	0	0	17	17	1
Canndell ...	5	6	8	4	8	0
Melbury ...	15	11	8	37	12	9
Almere ...	2	12	0	5	10	10
Kelveston ...	10	0	0	21	6	8

TEWKESBURY, GLOUC.

	£	s.	d.	£	s.	d.
Teynton ...	13	0	0	18	7	10
Welneford ...	5	6	8	19	4	$2\frac{1}{4}$
Kyngeston ...	13	13	8	14	3	9
Tarraunte, Mon.	13	15	0	13	7	6
[illegible] ...	10	[illegible]	[illegible]	[illegible]	[illegible]	[illegible]

CHRISTCHURCH, CANTERBURY.

	£	s.	d.	£	s.	d.
Monketon ...	61	13	4	29	4	$10\frac{1}{2}$
Addysham ...	22	16	8	41	3	$1\frac{1}{2}$
Bekesborne ...	11	13	4	5	12	$1\frac{1}{2}$
Chartham ...	26	13	4	19	1	$11\frac{1}{4}$
M. Chart ...	28	0	0	37	18	$5\frac{1}{8}$
Appuldore ...	55	2	9	38	6	0
Mersham ...	16	0	0	18	14	$3\frac{3}{4}$
Holyngborne	11	0	0	53	1	$9\frac{1}{4}$
W. Clyff ...	14	10	0	30	5	$0\frac{1}{2}$
Chayham ...	5	0	0	6	6	8

BATH, SOMERSET.

	£	s.	d.	£	s.	d.
Weston ...	38	9	4	26	8	6
Northstock ...	12	8	2	10	0	0
Forde ...	22	0	0	29	18	$8\frac{1}{2}$
Combe ...	11	2	8	8	2	$1\frac{1}{2}$
Southstocke	10	7	5	9	10	$2\frac{1}{2}$
Pryssheton ...	12	7	0	15	18	9
Staunton ...	4	2	0	6	0	5
Corston ...	12	5	6	13	5	6
Lyncomb ...	13	6	8	20	1	$3\frac{1}{2}$
Hameswell ...	15	0	0	20	12	6

GLASTONBURY, SOMERSET.

	£	s.	d.	£	s.	d.
Strete ...	8	0	0	39	9	10
Aisshecote ...	4	0	0	25	8	5
Shapwyke ...	27	0	0	36	13	$11\frac{1}{4}$
Wythis ...	12	14	10	3	2	6
Greyngton ...	1	10	0	17	19	0
Daltyng ...	10	0	0	30	15	$11\frac{1}{2}$
Mellez ...	6	6	8	36	7	$7\frac{1}{2}$
Badecomb ...	6	0	$10\frac{1}{4}$	25	2	$10\frac{1}{4}$
Est Pennard	2	0	0	49	0	$10\frac{3}{4}$
Myddelton ...	6	3	0	17	2	$4\frac{1}{2}$
Hamme ...	9	12	$9\frac{1}{2}$	40	9	$2\frac{1}{2}$
Estrete ...	4	0	0	6	17	10
Uplyme ...	2	16	8	23	1	5
Wynterbourne	12	0	10	15	5	0
Badbury ...	12	3	4	17	12	$10\frac{1}{2}$
Grutlyngton	5	18	0	15	18	$1\frac{3}{4}$

HENTON, SOMERSET.

	£	s.	d.	£	s.	d.
Norton ...	20	2	0	28	7	4
Peggelege ...	26	13	4	8	2	7
Longleate ...	5	0	0	17	10	[illegible]

ST. THOMAS'S, STAFFORD.

	£	s.	d.	£	s.	d.
Frodeswall ...	2	0	0	6	17	7
Penford ...	4	0	0	5	18	$7\frac{1}{2}$
Drayton ...	1	6	0	5	18	2
Mere ...	2	0	0	5	13	3
Apeton ...	1	9	8	3	4	2
Coton ...	4	0	0	6	0	0

LEWES, SUSSEX.

	£	s.	d.	£	s.	d.
Atlyngworth	7	6	8	7	15	$3\frac{3}{4}$
Imberhorne	7	6	8	14	6	1
Langney ...	20	0	0	22	3	$7\frac{3}{4}$
Newtimber ...	3	6	8	5	6	8
Carleton ...	10	16	8	9	14	5

AMESBURY, WILTS.[1]

	£	s.	d.	£	s.	d.
Bulteford ...	24	10	0	29	14	0
Melkysham	19	0	0	69	7	$8\frac{1}{2}$
Wallope ...	9	3	4	35	19	$4\frac{1}{4}$
Wygley ...	2	6	8	6	18	$10\frac{1}{2}$
Chadelworth	6	13	4	7	9	1
Falley ...	5	18	4	6	10	3

[1] The income from pastures is included in the demesne.

EVESHAM, WORCESTER.

	£	s.	d.	£	s.	d.			£	s.	d.	£	s.	d.
Moreton Abb.	5	0	0	10	12	8	Seynbury	...	2	14	0	18	16	6
Wykwanforde	13	2	8	13	18	2	Burghton	...	4	0	4	36	10	3
Kynwarton...	3	19	6	4	8	9	Bradwett	...	10	0	0	21	2	6
							Swell	...	7	0	0	5	11	8

The income from demesne of all the seventy-eight monasteries in this list amounts to £938 17s. 11¾d., and the receipts from tenancies to £1,628 10s. 7⅞d.; the demesne thus brings in about three-fifths of the sum yielded by the tenancies. The relation between the profits from the demesne and those from the tenancies varies considerably for different monasteries and also for different manors of the same monastery; these differences are especially great in the county of Somerset, as is clear from the instances just given, and on this account we must take a great many cases if our calculations are to be accurate. The above table is insufficient, for it contains only a few manors and those unequally distributed. But I think that the list may have some value as a series of standard cases.[1] The income from woods is not mentioned in any of the manors in this table, and the income from pasture is mentioned in a few only, in spite of the fact that some of the manors derived a considerable revenue both from woods and pastures. On the whole we may regard with much confidence the conclusion that the profits from demesnes amounted to about three-fifths of the sum received from the tenancies : and, as in the whole monastic income the receipts from entire manors were evidently greater than the receipts from separate tenancies, we are justified in believing that the payments of the demesne tenants amounted to a considerable sum, hardly less than a quarter of all the tenurial payments.

Revenue from ordinary tenancies.

Anyhow, the bulk of the rural income from land consists of the revenue from tenancies and not from demesne. It would be very important if we could classify the rural revenue according to the legal nature of the tenure; if we could establish the amount of receipts from freehold, copyhold, leasehold and from tenures at the will of the lord at common law; if we could get an idea of the general features at least of

[1] Cf. Savine, English village of the Tudor age, 393-7 (Russian).

the social status of the monastic tenantry. But it is seldom
that we find in the Valor Ecclesiasticus exact indications of the
legal nature of a tenure, and more rarely still that a particular
group of holdings is given an entry to itself. Generally
the words ' firmae ' and ' redditus ' are used in connexion with
the tenancies ; and the word ' assisus ' is often added as a
definition of the word ' redditus '. Unfortunately these words
cannot be taken as strictly technical terms, for in different
passages they have different meanings. ' Firma ' is generally
applied to the rent of a leasehold ; but there are instances
in which it stands for the income from the home farm,
or even for the rent of a copyhold.[1] ' Redditus ' generally
signifies the rent of a freehold, a copyhold or a tenure at the
will of the lord at common law ; but it can also mean the
leasehold rent and the income from the demesne in hand.
' Redditus assisus ' means a fixed rent ; but it may refer either
to freehold or copyhold or to both together. ' Redditus ad
voluntatem domini ' is applied to tenure at the will of the
lord ; but these may either be customary or common law
tenures. Such expressions as ' redditus liberorum tenentium,'
' redditus custumariorum tenentium,' ' redditus terrarum dimissarum per copiam curie,' ' firma terrarum dimissarum per indenturam,' 'firma terrarum dimissarum pro termino annorum,' have
a definite meaning ; but often in spite of the use of these
definite terms the income from tenancies of two or three kinds
is joined in one entry. The V. E. will not entirely satisfy
any one who hopes to glean from it statistics of tenancies and
tenants in the English village of the sixteenth century ; the
necessary evidence can only be found in the manorial surveys.
From the Valor Ecclesiasticus I could extract information on
one question only, viz. on the comparative position of the
freehold and customary tenure in the manorial revenue, but
this information refers only to some eight monasteries and some
seventy manors. However, considering the importance of the
question I give even this scanty evidence. I have chosen only
those manors in the description of which a special entry is

---

[1] Here is an instance : Merkyate, Beds., iv. 209 : ' Kamelton etc. in
reddit' et firm' dim' divers' person' per cop' cur' £2 10s. 2½d.'

made of freehold rents; but I have not excluded the manors in the description of which the word 'nichil' stands against the words 'redditus liberorum tenentium'. The names given in the list are the names of manors; the figure on the left is that of the freehold rent, that on the right the rent of customary tenants.

Freehold and copyhold payments.

BUCKFASTLEIGH, DEVON.

	£	s.	d.	£	s.	d.
Buckfastleigh	0	4	6	50	0	11
Brent ...	8	6	7⅝	87	17	3
Churchstowe	2	14	8¼	17	7	8
Engleburne...	0	9	0	10	7	2
Sele... ...	0	17	3½	15	19	8¼
Bottokysburgh	1	15	5½	6	6	8
Trysme ...	0	7	2	5	9	0½

CANONLEIGH, DEVON.

	£	s.	d.	£	s.	d.
Netherton ...	0	2	6	8	14	9¾

BURSCOUGH, LANC.

	£	s.	d.	£	s.	d.
Burscough,&c.	6	1	4	37	0	0

GODSTOW, OXON.

	£	s.	d.	£	s.	d.
Walton ...	0	4	0	8	3	0
Fencott ...	0	16	2	1	1	2
Sandford ...	0	10	2	12	16	6
Cheryngton	4	5	0	1	14	0

AMESBURY, WILTS.

	£	s.	d.	£	s.	d.
Bulteford ...	0	8	6	29	5	6
Melkysham	24	4	10½	45	2	10
Madyngton...	0	4	0	11	19	10
Wygley ...	0	18	4	6	0	6½
Kentbury ...	1	12	8	18	1	7
Chadelworth	1	12	1	5	17	0

LANTONY, GLOUC.

	£	s.	d.	£	s.	d.
Hempstede...	0	13	0	27	0	9¾
Brockworth	0	11	0	23	6	0
Paynysweke		nl.		6	2	6
Harfeld ...		nl.		5	8	1¾
Prestbury ...		nl.		3	14	4
Collysbone...	0	8	7	3	0	1
Ailberton ...	11	11	4	7	11	8
Ocle... ...	1	1	8	4	6	0

	£	s.	d.	£	s.	d.
Wesbury ...	2	2	3	4	19	9
Froma ..	0	0	2	11	8	4
Falley ...	2	12	10¾	2	18	8½
Alvington ...	2	0	0	24	16	9
Borowghyll...		nl.		1	12	6
Reddegrove	0	13	3	2	6	8
Tedryngton...		nl.		2	0	0
Turkedene ...		nl.		3	16	4
South Cerney	0	19	9	12	3	11
Widmarshmore		nl.		11	13	9¾
Cheryngton...	0	13	6	7	11	4
Henlowe ...		nl.		18	6	3½
Stannton ...	1	7	2	2	3	2½

EVESHAM, WORCESTER.

	£	s.	d.	£	s.	d.
Wolbarowe	0	11	6¾	11	1	11½
Ombresley ...	0	5	7½	95	9	9¼
Tadlyngton	0	1	9	22	16	2
Moreton ...	0	6	8	10	6	8
Badby ...	3	7	6¼	50	12	5
Salford Abbatis	1	6	8	5	18	8
Wetheley ...	0	5	6	2	15	6
Kynwarton...	0	2	11	4	5	10
Wytlaxford...	4	0	0	0	8	0
Seynbury ...	0	10	0	18	6	6
Burghton ...	1	1	8	35	8	7
Bradwett ...	0	2	0	21	0	6
Malgaresbury	0	7	0	15	11	4

WORCESTER CATHEDRAL.[1]

	£	s.	d.	£	s.	d.
St. Jonys ...	1	15	5	23	6	8½
Crowle ...	1	0	10	9	8	1
Tyberton ...	0	5	0	13	18	5
Hymulton ...	0	12	4	23	13	7¼
Bradwas ...	0	5	7	31	19	11½
Hallowe ...	0	9	2	18	10	9
Grymley ...	0	13	10	44	13	11½
Wolverley ...	2	8	2	22	2	0¾
More ...	1	16	4	25	18	9½
Newenham...	2	2	6	32	4	11
Tedynton ...	0	12	2	30	10	11

[1] In the survey of Worcester Cathedral the 'custumarii tenentes' and 'tenentes ad voluntatem domini' are separated from each other. In the manors where both these classes are found I have added their rents into one general total.

	£ s. d.	£ s. d.		£ s. d.	£ s. d.
Cleve ...	0 17 0	25 3 2	Alston ...	1 13 5¼	23 17 8¾
Herforton ...	0 13 5	17 5 8	Stoke ...	1 3 0	34 9 2
Cropthorn ...	0 16 1	22 1 8¾	Cudston ...	3 6 8	4 9 8
Chorlton ...	0 18 0	11 10 0	Bredycote ...	0 5 9	1 8 10
Overbury ...	1 7 2	33 4 6	Ancrede ...	0 15 0½	0 18 0

The rent of the customary tenures [1] of all the manors in the list amounts to £1,310 10s. 10d., and the rent of the freehold amounts to £116 14s. 8⅜d., i. e. less than one-eleventh of the first total. The list, of course, is only an illustration. But even from this it is clear that the rents of customary tenures were infinitely more important to the monks than the receipts from the freehold, and that the customary tenants were the most numerous class of the monastic peasantry. There is no need to insist on the importance of this conclusion, which is not at all confined to the case of monastic lands. I will only remind those who attempt to calculate the approximate area of monastic lands that the prevalence of customary tenures must be taken into account. The freeholders paid less for their lands than the copyholders; the higher the percentage of freehold in an area of land for which a given amount of rent is paid, the larger the area. But the V. E. shows that the rents of freeholders who were in 1535 tenants of the English monasteries were much less than the rents of copyholders. And though the relation of freehold to the general area of monastic lands was larger than that of the freehold rents to the general monastic income, the prevalence of customary tenure on the monastic lands compels us to regard with suspicion any very high computation of the area of the monastic lands.

The *firmae* of the leaseholders, the rents of freeholders and copyholders, the rents of tenants at the will of the lord, constitute the bulk of tenurial payments. The sum that represents payments called by other names is very small; and it includes payments of a local character which cannot well be dealt with in a general sketch. But some of these payments of local character are curious, and the amount by no means

Tenurial payments of a local character.

---

[1] Perhaps we should say together with the rent of the tenures at the will of the lord.

measures their interest for us. Such are the payments connected with the system of works. In the Valor Ecclesiasticus
we find entries of payments called the sale of works, the works
of the customary tenants, work-silver, autumn works. These
payments are not common, and they are always much lower than
the rents of the tenants. Nevertheless, they are very interesting as a survival of an old state of things. The descriptions
of work-payments are generally made in a very summary
way, and it is difficult to see the meaning of the corresponding
figures of the income. Do they signify the money-valua-
tion of the work actually performed by the tenants, or the
money that was paid by the tenants in respect of work
unperformed? In one instance only, the entry is clear and
detailed. Some of the tenants of Faversham, a monastery in
Kent, continue to perform work in the fields and do a great
deal of it.[1]

The 'movable rents' (*redditus mobilis*) of the Survey also
call for remark. They are not often found, and their amount
is very small. But there is reason to believe that a 'movable'
rent means rent *paid in kind.* Now payments in kind are not
rare at all in the Valor Ecclesiasticus, and they not infre-

---

[1] The expression 'vendicio operum' is found more often than any other
formulae. Sometimes the words 'custumariorum tenentium' are added to
it. Here are my instances—Taunton, Soms., i. 169: Vicus canonicorum
£0 7s. 6d., Fons Georgii £1 2s. 10d. Abbotsbury, Dorset, i. 229: Wotton
£0 12s. 7d., Portesham £0 2s. 11d. Polslo, Devon, ii. 315: Tuddheys
£0 12s. 10d. Canonleigh, Devon, ii. 328: Rockebear £0 13s. 8d.
Frithelstoke, Devon, ii. 335: Frithelstoke £0 10s. 0d. Torre, Devon, ii.
361: Torremohun £0 9s. 4d. Gloucester, St. Peter, ii. 409: Upledon
£1 8s. 1½d.; 411, Standisshe £0 15s. 10d., Churcham £0 0s. 11d.; 413,
Ullingeswicke £0 6s. 8d. Barnewood et Croneham £0 11s. 2d. Lantony,
Glouc., ii. 423: Hempstede £0 2s. 8d.—'Vendicio operum' is mentioned,
but not separately, in many manors of the survey of Plympton, Devon.
Very similar to this formula is 'Werkesilver' in the survey of M. Malvern,
Worc. iii. 238: 'Powyck Messor et Pyxam £0 7s. 11d.' We know that
in the bailiff's accounts the words 'vendicio operum' are applied to such
works as were not performed because they were not wanted, and instead
of which payment was required from the tenants according to the valuation
fixed by custom. In the survey of Cirencester, Glouc. ii. 468, the expression 'exitus operum custum' ten' ' (Cirencester £1 0s. 0d., Mynty
£1 0s. 0d.) is twice found. Less often is used the formula 'opera custumariorum' or 'opera autumpnalia'. Shirborne, Dorset, i. 282: Thorneford
£0 10s. 10½d. Buckfastleigh, Devon, ii. 369: Hethfyld £1 10s. 1½d.,
Patrikstowe £1 8s. 0d. Butteley, Suff., iii. 419: Chesilford £0 1s. 0d.,

quently amount to a considerable sum. These, however, are
included in the demesne farm, while the 'movable' rents are
the payments for tenancies. It is true that nowhere in the
Valor Ecclesiasticus is there an explanation given of the term
'redditus mobilis', nowhere is it said that it is a payment
in kind; but this sense of the term can be established from
other authorities. As the entries of rent in kind are rather
scarce we must take into consideration all the movable rents,
however small their amount.[1]

Definite information is given in the Valor Ecclesiasticus Payments
about the payments in kind, most often in corn, but sometimes in kind.
in eggs, poultry, cattle. Sometimes the entry is so short that

---

Boyton £1 9s. 1½d. ; 420, Debenham £0 0s. 8d.—Only in the survey of
Faversham, Kent, i. 82, did I find a quite definite indication of the fact that
the tenants really performed such works; it is the 'principall maner of
Faversham'. Part of the manor was in the hands of the monks ; the
description of the remaining part of the manor begins thus: 'Item receyvid
for the yerely ferme of the resydue of the same maner in corne cattall money
and for *custume* of 22 acres dim' rod' of lande belongyng to the same
maner that is, to witt in eryng sawyng the said acres with whete ryppyng
carying into the barnes of the said maner' and taffing of the same whete
done by the tenants of the same man' yerely by the tenure of their landes
£36 0s. 0d.' Thus the works are called here 'custume'. The word
'custume' is mentioned once more in the description of the same manor,
in the section of 'rent of uplonde belonging to the said manor of Faversham'; it is possible that here also 'custume' signifies the works actually
performed. Information concerning the works or work-payments is also
found in the Part. for grants, e. g. n. 994, m. 2, Shaftesbury, Lyddyngton,
35 H. VIII ; n. 129, m. 2, Cirencester, Latton and Esye, 36 H. VIII;
n. 993, m. 4, Shaftesbury Combe, 34 H. VIII, n. 1, Hertland, 37 H. VIII.
  [1] I found an explanation of the term 'redditus mobilis' in some of the
Particulars for grants—(1) n. 102, m. 4, 36 H. VIII : 'parcella poss' Johis
comitis Bathon. Castrum manerium de Whittyngdon Salop.' Among
other rents is mentioned the 'redditus mobilis ibm viz. in firma gallinarum dim' Edwardo ap Roberte per copiam curie £0 10s. 0d.'; (2) n.
818 : 'redditus mobilis ut de precio 38 gall' provenientium de redditu
diversarum personarum in Baschurche Aicton et Prescott qualibet gallina
appreciata ad 1½d. in toto per annum £0 4s. 9d.; (3) n. 995, mm. 6–7,
38 H. VIII : 'precio gallorum et gallinarum de redditu mobili £0 2s. 6d.,'
in Leigh manor, Wilts. Here are instances of 'redditus mobilis':
Tavistock, Devon, ii. 382 : 'manerium de Conwyck £0 13s. 6d.' Many
manors of the survey of Butteley, Suffolk : Butteley £0 1s. 6d., Tangham
£0 3s. 3½d., Wandesden £0 1s. 1d.; Chesilford £0 0s. 1½d., Bawdesey
£0 0s. 7½d., Boyton £0 0s. 7½d., M. Glernham £0 0s. 9d., Stratford
£0 0s. 10d., Debenham £0 2s. 1d., Thorp £0 0s. 5d., Harlyston £0 1s. 6d.
Sibton, Suff. iii. 434 : Sibton £0 2s. 3d., Glernham £0 6s. 3½d. Leiston,
Suff. iii. 437 : Culpho £0 1s. 4d. Campsey, Suff., iii. 415 : Overhall
£0 1s. 6d.—It is well known that the freeholders not unfrequently paid their
rent in kind, in pepper, in wax; '12 rent hennes' are mentioned in the
survey of Faversham, Kent, i. 85, Elynden.

it is impossible to say from what land the revenue in kind is received, whether from demesne or tenements, from a short lease or from a tenure of longer duration. In the survey of Robertsbridge, Sussex, corn payments are mentioned amounting to £17 14s. 9d.; for every kind of corn the quantity and price are given. It is remarkable that two kinds of wheat are noted. In all the following examples the quantity of corn is given in quarters; w. = wheat, r. = rye, b. = barley, o. = oats, p. = peas, m. = malt; the price per quarter is given in shillings and pence. Here is the rent in corn for Robertsbridge : 27 w. at 6/11 + 10 w. at 6/8 + 12 m. at 4/0 + 16 b. at 3/4. The names of the estates from which the rent is derived are also given in the survey, but it is not known what kind of estates they were, whether manors, granges, or separate tenancies. The abbey of St. Augustine, Canterbury, occupies, of course, the first place in the Valor Ecclesiasticus by the amount of its payments in kind, both absolute and relative. In the survey of this monastery the spiritual revenue is not always distinguished from the temporal ; they have, therefore, to be taken together. Out of the gross income of £1,684 4s. 1¾d., £309 7s. 0d. is brought in by the receipts in kind, which are made up as follows : 550 w. at 6/8 + 634 b. at 3/4 + 4 p. at 6/8 + 50 rams at 2/0 + 87 sheep at 1/0 + 32 rabbits at 0/2 + 40 pigs at 3/4 + 1 boar at 6/8 + 6 rolls of cheese at 8/0. Payments in kind come mostly from the leased granges and manorial demesnes ; but the farmers of one rectory and two mills also pay in kind. The second place in regard to the absolute amount of payments in kind is taken by the Lancashire monastery of Furness. The payments are spread over many localities and their variety is striking. Here are the products and their valuation as received by the monastery : 52 quarters of wheat = £20 8s. 0d. ; 64¼ quarters of barley = £16 1s. 3d. ; 372 quarters of oats = £44 9s. 4d.; 80 loads of turf = £4 0s. 0d.; 206 hens = £0 17s. 2d. ; 30 capons = £0 5s. 0d. ; 54 geese = £0 9s. 0d. ; 62 calves = £9 6s. 8d. ; 150 rams = £7 10s. 0d. ; 26 stones (*petrae*) of butter = £0 13s. 0d. ; 60 stones of cheese = £2 0s. 0d. ; 24 stones of wool = £2 8s. 0d. ; several prices are indicated for the same product; for instance, five different

valuations are given for oats.   Out of a gross temporal income
of £763 0s. 10d. the payments in kind amount to £108 9s. 5d.
The payments from demesne are not set out separately from the
payments of tenancies, and no doubt to these latter belong some
of the payments in kind.   There are, however, two places,
Northend and Bolton, that are directly called tenancies.   The
only instance that I know of, in which large rents are undoubtedly paid in kind by customary tenants, is found in the
survey of Worcester Cathedral.   Here the payments in kind
are considerable indeed : 244¼ w. at 5/4 + 26 r. at 4/0 + 202 b. at
3/4 + 13 0. at 2/0 + 2¼ p. at 2/8 (and more peas at £1 11s. 8d.)
+ 1 boar at 6/8. Most of these payments arise from the demesne ;
but in three manors the *firma* of the demesne is paid in money
only, and payments in kind are received from customary
tenants.[1]   All the remaining payments in kind that I have
noted, small and great, come from manorial demesnes or
granges.   Granges are more often found in the northern
counties.   The monastery of Rufford, Notts., received half
its income from granges in corn :—14 w. at 5/0 + 14 b. at 3/0 +
14 0. at 1/8 + 12 r. at 3/8 + 2 p. at 2/0.   The monastery of
Whitby received from the grange of Stanby 30 w. at 5/0 +
32 0. at 1/4.   The monastery of Welbeck received from some
granges 28 w. at 5/0 + 33 b. at 3/0 + 13 r. at 3/8 + 9 0. at 1/8.

The payments in kind have a considerable place in the temporal revenues of the monasteries of Middleton, Shaftesbury,
Cerne, Dorset ; M. Malvern, Worc. ; Wilton, Wilts.   I give
below the rents in kind received by these monasteries.[2]   Such

---

[1] These manors are Bradwas, Hallowe, and Grymley.   The most
interesting is the entry in Bradwas, iii. 221 : ' In terr' dnic' ad firmam
dimiss' £2 0s. 0d.   In redditu custumar' tenentium ibm communibus
annis 26¼ quarteria frumenti et de 5 quarteriis frumenti et 4 quart' siliginis
provenientibus de tercia garba terrarum dnic' ibm 2¾ quarteria ordei
2½ quart' pulc' precii cuiuslibet quarterii frumenti 5/4 siliginis 4/0 ordei
3/4 et pulc' 2/8.   In toto communibus annis £9 8s. 2d.' (the total is
wrong ; it ought to be £9 18s. 6d.).   Thus, here a part of the rents in kind
paid by the customary tenants is still received from the demesne.

[2] In referring to these monasteries I have followed the order of the proportion which the payments in kind bear to the gross temporal income.   In
the case of Middleton this proportion is about $\frac{1}{16}$, Wilton about $\frac{1}{7}$; St. Augustine's, Canterbury, is even higher.   It is not difficult to gather that rents
paid in kind and *firmae* prevailed chiefly in the southern and south-western
monasteries.   This can be only partly explained by the fact that the

facts as these show how certain parts of the old manorial régime remained unaltered in some places. It is curious, too, that the payments in kind disappeared from the tenancies much earlier and more completely than from the demesne, although the reverse might have been expected. In a small peasant household such a survival as payment in kind would seem more natural than in the business of a farmer on de-mesne who not infrequently had large pecuniary means at his disposal. As a matter of fact, however, monastic freeholders and copyholders paid their rent in kind in exceptional cases only while the farmer of the demesne often paid in corn. This observation will not of course apply without modification to the manors of secular lords. There were many mouths to be fed in a monastery and the need of corn would be greater than in the household of a secular lord. The monks, more-over, were more used to payments in kind, because a con-siderable part of their income consisted of tithe, which was generally paid in kind. References to the peculiar conserva-tism of spiritual corporations, or to the desire of the monks to have as little as possible to do with the laity, may perhaps be open to question, but it is possible that such tendencies as these had also something to do with a certain lack of progress to be observed in the monastic economy. Such considerations, however, while they may explain the reason why the monks received more payments in kind than did the

southern and south-western monasteries are described more fully than the other. Probably the older economic conditions were longer pre-served in the south and south-west. It must, however, be explained that neighbouring monasteries might manage their lands in quite different ways. The monastery of St. Augustine, Canterbury, received payments in kind worth more than three hundred pounds; but in the survey of Canterbury Cathedral, which was much richer, the rent in corn is mentioned only once (i. 10: 'Addysham de ordeo provenien' de tenent' ibm £7 1s. 8d.').

Middleton   ...   73$\frac{13}{16}$ w. at 5/4 + 83$\frac{5}{8}$ b. at 2/8 + 97$\frac{1}{8}$ o. at 1/4
Shaftesbury ...   202$\frac{1}{2}$ w. at 5/4 +154 b. at 2/8 +216 o. at 1/4
Cerne   ...   93$\frac{5}{8}$ w. at 5/4 + 97$\frac{7}{8}$ b. at 2/8 + 96$\frac{1}{2}$ o. at 1/4
M. Malvern ...   62 w. at 5/4 + 30 b. at 3/4 + 31 o. at 1/8
        Besides cattle and poultry worth £1 10s. 3d.

Wilton, 183$\frac{29}{48}$ w. at 5/0 + 231$\frac{7}{16}$ b. at 3/0 + 110$\frac{7}{16}$ o. at 2/0 ; 62 capons at 3d., 110 hens at 2d. ; 105 geese at 4d., 800 pigeons at 1s. 3d., a calf at 3s., 30 woolfells at 3d., 1$\frac{1}{2}$ pounds of pepper at 1s., 8 loads of hay at 3s.

lay lords, do not by any means serve to explain why the monks received more rent in kind from the demesne than from tenancies. Here we are evidently face to face with a fact common to all seignorial households. By the sixteenth century the lords had accustomed themselves to receiving from their tenants nothing but money ; but with regard to the demesne they could not give up the idea that it must supply them with all the products necessary for every-day life. They therefore often insisted on the farmer of the demesne paying not in money but in corn, hay, poultry and cattle.

I cannot allow myself to hazard a suggestion as to the extent of the area of land, of which the tenurial payments amounted to ninety thousand pounds ; neither will I venture to apportion this sum between the different kinds of tenure. It may of course be stated with confidence that the rents of the freehold formed but a small portion of the payments of the tenants. But it is much more difficult to estimate the rents of copyhold, the *firmae*, the payments of tenants at the will of the lord at common law. Assuming, however, that we do succeed in apportioning the tenurial payments between the different classes of tenures, how are we to translate revenue into area ? The simplest plan, of course, would be to ascertain the average income derived from one acre, but how is this to be done ? In the V. E. we find the acreage of only a few home farms and leaseholds. The same kind of evidence with regard to freeholds and copyholds would have to be sought elsewhere, a laborious task which has not yet been attempted. There is yet another difficulty which meets us when we try to arrive at the average income per acre brought in by the peasant tenancies, and that is the complicated nature of a peasant holding. Even in the detailed manorial surveys and field maps the acreage is stated only of such land as is in the actual occupation of each peasant. The various rights of common are not and cannot be expressed in units of area. And the difficulty cannot always be evaded by a reference to the fact that meadows, pastures, woods, and wastes were technically included in the manorial demesne. In the demesne surveys we do indeed sometimes come across an indication

Area of monastic lands.

of the area of commons; and a few cases of the kind may even be found in the Valor Ecclesiasticus (i. 330, Balneth), but much more often the area of the commons is not given in figures. Among these rare indications of the area of commons large figures are, however, to be found, so that to neglect this part of the monastic land would lead to error in calculating the total area of the monastic lands. Pollard and Moyle's survey of Glastonbury affords a very instructive illustration of this. The Commissioners of 1535 do not mention the commons at all, but Pollard and Moyle describe them and give approximate details of their area or boundaries; their figures are as follows: circuit 16 miles + 300 a. + circuit 1 mile + circuit 24 miles + 2,000 a. (Budleigh common, but part of it is occupied by wood), + circuit 1 mile + 900 a. + 318 a. + 80 a. The enumeration cannot be called complete. Pollard and Moyle do not mention the commons in Domerham and Idmiston, and yet the commons there covered a large area and are described in detail by the well-known terrier of 1518 (Harl. 3961). However cautious we may be in translating circuit into area, still we must allow that the commons occupied a very considerable area. The lack of evidence concerning the commons does not, of course, prove that the income from these lands had not been taken into consideration. It might have been included in the general total of the income from demesne. But in the case of Idmiston we know for certain that the Valor Ecclesiasticus entirely omits the revenue derived from commons. Further, it is just in these cases that it is particularly difficult to judge of the area by the income, for the commons and wastes often included a quantity of unprofitable and useless land.—And lastly, the area of monastic lands held by individuals also is not easily expressed in figures. The evidence of the V. E. goes to show that very great differences of income existed according to the locality and the kind of land.

Income from an acre.

The nuns of Merkyate, Beds. (iv. 209), let out part of their demesne. One farmer paid £2 1s. 8d. for 192½ acres of arable land, that is to say 2⅔d. per acre; another paid £0 6s. 8d. for 20 acres of arable land, i. e. 4d. an acre. And Ivy Church, a monastery in Wiltshire, received £0 1s. 4d. for

2 acres of arable land in Stratford, i. e. 8*d*. per acre (ii. 97). Pasture land was on the whole considered of more value, but there are cases where its valuation varied quite as much. The Malmesbury monks received 8*d*. an acre from the farmer.[1] In Queddysley (ii. 423), a manor in Gloucestershire, the monks received as much as 1*s*. 8*d*. per acre from the farmer for 20 acres of pasture. About the same rate per acre was received by another monastery in Gloucestershire for a small piece of pasture in Brompton.[2] Canterbury Cathedral (i. 8) received about £0 16*s*. 0*d*. for 8 acres of pasture in Harbaldown, i. e. 2*s*. per acre. Meadows were considered even more valuable, and the rents for them varied still more. The Cumberland monastery of Holme Cultram (v. 282) received the income of a pound only for 20 acres of meadow in Sevalle Cowbyer. The same income was received by the monastery of Hinchinbrook for 20 acres of meadow in Huntingdon (iv. 255). The Gloucestershire monastery of Lantony received twice as much (2*s*. per acre), for its meadows in M. Baryngton and Queddysley (80 acres, 18 acres, ii. 423). The nuns of Merkyate, Beds., received £2 13*s*. 4*d*. for eight acres of demesne meadow, i. e. 6*s*. 8*d*. per acre (iv. 209).

Since the rents of arable land vary from 2⅝*d*. to 8*d*., the rents of pasture from 8*d*. to 2*s*., and the rents of meadow from 1*s*. to 6*s*. 8*d*., we require a large amount of statistical evidence in order to find the average income of an acre of arable, of pasture and of meadow respectively. Since, too, the leasehold rents vary from 2⅔*d*. to 6*s*. 8*d*., we require evidence in like abundance with regard to the nature of the occupation of the land for which the rent is received before we can speak of the average income of an acre of leasehold. In neither case is evidence forthcoming. The same considerations are applicable to freehold, copyhold and tenure at the will of the lord.

[1] 'Cowfold exitus pastur' et cert' terr' vocatarum Cowfold Marshe et le Breche continentium per estimac' 40 acras precio acre 8ᵈ. occupat' ad usum dci monasterii sic nuper dimissarum Edwardo Hungerford armigero per indenturam.' The pasture in the park of Westparke is valued at 6*d*. an acre, in the park at Cowfold at 8*d*.; but it is possible that these parks remained in the hands of the monks.

[2] Gloucester, St. Peter's, ii. 412 : 'in firma herbagii cuiusdam pasturae 2½ acr. £0 4*s*. 0*d*.'

The revenue from the monastic demesne in hand is treated
in the Valor Ecclesiasticus in much the same varied way
as the payments of the tenants; but, on the whole, it is
much clearer to us than the latter. And what evidence there
is, is much easier to supplement. The Commissioners who suppressed a house were compelled to make a detailed inventory
of the monastic goods; some of these inventories and suppression accounts are still extant. Very soon after the
Suppression, the Augmentations Court made new surveys
of most of the monastic demesnes. The officials wished to
know what price they were to ask for the demesne from
any one who applied to them for a farm or a sale. Many
such surveys are still extant (Paper Surveys[1]), and I was
able to use this valuable and compact evidence which amply
repays investigation.

The description of monastic home farms in the Valor Ecclesiasticus can be called definite only in comparison with that of
the tenancies. In many surveys of 1535 neither the demesne
nor the income from it is mentioned at all. When these
surveys are very short, as is the case with those for Hants,
we are obliged to put them aside entirely. But it is more
difficult to decide what to do with regard to those detailed
surveys in which nothing is said either about the demesne in
hand or even the monastic site; Christchurch, Canterbury;
Montacute, Soms.; Hulme, Norf., may be taken as instances.
In such cases may we conclude from the silence of the survey
that no home farm existed? It is difficult to give a definite
answer. I think it is more probable, at least in some cases
—for instance, Christchurch, Canterbury—that the monks in
1535 did not keep their demesne in their own hands. But
the terminology of the Valor Ecclesiasticus is very arbitrary, and even the words 'firma manerii' may stand for
income from the demesne in hand. And for this reason these
surveys also cannot be used to any purpose. Sometimes

---

[1] One of the Augmentations' men boasted before Cromwell that he
personally measured the demesne of the monastery of Furness whilst the
Suppression Commissioners took the area on trust. (Gairdner, xii. ii.
205, 3 July, 29 H. VIII.)

the monastic demesne is separated from the rest of the monastic land, but it is not said whether it remains in the hands of the monks or is let out to tenants.[1] An investigator cannot make use even of such surveys as that of Croyland (iv. 85), for there the Commissioners only state that the monks kept a part of the demesne in their own hands, but they do not give either the amount of its area or income.

But even such entries as show the demesne *in manu* separately can only be worked to a limited extent by the statistician. The Commissioners often give only the total of the income from demesne; for instance, Spalding (Linc.), Lilleshall (Salop), Wroxall (Warw.). Such figures may be useful in establishing the place of the demesne revenue in the temporal budget of the monasteries but are useless for any other purpose. Such cases as Boxgrove, Sussex (i. 306), or Croxton, Leic. (iv. 150), are of more use ; for there, besides the income, the general area of the home farm is also given. Surveys in which the area is apportioned into the different kinds of land are even more definite, but they vary considerably. Some of them give the area of each kind of land in acres, but give only one total for all the income from demesne.[2] There are some surveys in which the income and the area of some one kind of land, arable or meadow for instance, are given, whilst the other kinds are joined together in one general total.[3] Sometimes the area of pasture is not expressed in the same way as that of other kinds of land : the area of arable and

[1] Such surveys may be either very short or fairly detailed. In the surveys of Gresley, Repingdon, Derb. ; Chicksand, Newenham, Wardon, Beds. ; Burne, Sempringham, Linc. ; only the total of the demesne is given. In the survey of Staynesfield, Linc., the demesne, apart from the wood and warren, is divided into fifteen portions, and for every portion its area and income are given (comp. Wendling and Wymondham, Norf.).

[2] Alvingham, Linc. iv. 58: 'prior et conventus habent terras dominicales infra precinctum monasterii in manibus suis propriis 80 a. terre arabilis 100 a. prati et 100 a. pasture que valent inter se per estimacionem communibus annis £20 0s. 0d.' ; cf. Willoughton, Linc.; Carlisle, Cumb.; Nun-Ormesby, Linc.

[3] Worksop, Notts.: 'profitts in occupacon of the demayne—medows, 30 a. = £3 6s. 8d.; arable landes, pasture, and closynge, 160 a. = £5 16s. 0d.; also in oppen groundes and plews, 200 a. = £0 15s. 0d.' Lacock, Wilts., ii. 115 : 'de annuo redditu et valore 247 acr. terr' errabill' dnical' domine ibm per annum £4 2s. 4d., de redditu 123½ acrar' prator' et pastur' domine dnical' suar' ibm per annum £11 2s. 6d.'

meadow is given in acres, and that of pasture is defined by the number of cattle that graze or can graze upon it.[1]

Acre incomes in the V. E.   The distinction of the different kinds of land is not always observed throughout the area of the demesne. Not infrequently separate plots of land are simply called 'land' or 'closes', and only in exceptionally favourable cases can the perplexed reader tell with certainty whether they refer to arable, meadow, or pasture. The fact is, the surveys most desirable for the purposes of the economic historian are pretty rare in the V. E.; I mean, surveys in which the whole area of the demesne is given in acres, the whole land divided into the different kinds, and the income of every plot of land stated. I give below the examples that I noted in the V. E. In the first column is given arable land, in the second pasture, and in the third meadow.

	a.	£ s. d.	a.	£ s. d.	a.	£ s. d.
Cirencester, Glouc. ...	1210	=11 3 4	480=	6 13 4	503	=30 13 4
Lantony, Glouc. ...	102	= 4 5 o	130=	10 16 8	160	=16 o o
St. Neots, Hunts. ...	360	= 9 o o	230=	6 16 8	30	= 4 10 o
Bollington, Linc. ...	80	= 2 13 4	20=	o 6 8	30	= 2 o o
Greenfield, Linc. ...	90	= 2 5 o	115=	5 15 o	43	= 2 16 o
Hagnaby, Linc. ...	70	= 4 o o	180=	18 13 4	140	= 9 6 8
Swineshed, Linc. ...	145½	=19 14 o	85=	6 13 4	150	=20 o o
Wallingwells, Notts. ...	60	= 1 10 o	80=	2 3 4	26	= 2 6 8
Burcester, Oxon. ...	390½	= 6 10 2	139=	6 6 11	10	= o 10 8
Studley, Oxon. ...	180	= 3 o o	134=	6 14 o		*nl.*
Redlingfield, Suff. ...	148	= 7 8 o	120=	8 o o	18½	= 1 17 o
Amesbury, Wilts. ...	290	= 4 16 8	15=	1 1 o	22	= 2 4 o
Ivy Church, Wilts. ...	19	= o 6 4	3=	o 2 o	31	= 2 11 8
Totals ...	3,145	= 76 11 10	1,731=	80 2 3	1,163½	=94 16 o

Thus, the totals are as follows:—3,145 a. arable = £76 11s. 10d.; 1,731 a. pasture = £80 2s. 3d.; 1,163½ a. meadow = £94 16s. od.; and, the valuation of an acre being calculated to one-tenth of

---

[1] Thetford canonicorum, Norf., may serve as an instance: 'Diversi redditus et firme in Thetford cum firm' 107 acr' terr' arabil' ibm ac libertate faldag' ac pastur' 500 ovium matric' 100 vervic' et 300 hoggastr' in occupacione prioris ibm valent per annum £17 2s. 4d.' The entry is curious also because the area of the demesne *in manu* is separately stated in the description of the manor, but the income from the demesne *in manu* is not separated from the whole manorial income. (Comp. Thetford monachorum and Thetford monialium.) Similar difficulties are encountered with the arable. Sometimes both meadow and pasture are given in acres, and the arable land—or part of it—in virgates of unknown size. A good instance is found in the survey of Dorchester, Oxon. The bulk of the arable land consists of 7½ virgates, the meadow and pasture are given in acres; besides these 'closes' are also mentioned.

a penny, we have: 1 a. arable $= 5 \cdot 9d.$; 1 a. pasture $= 11 \cdot 1d.$; 1 a. meadow $= 19 \cdot 6d.$ If this short list were the only evidence, we should be compelled to acknowledge that the arable land far predominated over the pasture and meadow, for its area exceeds that of both these taken together. We could affirm, moreover, that an acre of arable land in 1535 was worth $6d.$, an acre of pasture twice as much, and an acre of meadow thrice as much. But the table is very short, and stands in need of strong confirmation.

Now, there is abundant evidence, worthy of attentive study, Income to be found in the ' Paper Surveys', by which the information per acre in the Paper contained in the V. E. can be checked. It is not possible to Surveys. work statistically through all the Paper Surveys. The whole land is not always divided into the different kinds : some pieces of ground are simply called ' closes ' or ' lands ' (Worksop, Notts., Exch. Augm. O. Misc. b. v. 399, p. 339 ; St. Bees, Cumb., ib. p. 105). If the pasture were a common one, in some instances nothing is said about its area (P. Marlow, Bucks., ib. v. 406, f. 4), or it is only said how many cattle the monks might keep thereon (Swyne, Yorks., ib. v. 401, p. 383). Nevertheless, the Paper Surveys give much more information than the Valor Ecclesiasticus. As in the table above, the sites and the woods were not taken into account if they were mentioned in the survey. In the references the first figure means the volume of the series of the Exchequer Augm. Office Misc. books, the second is the folio or the page of the volume ; two cases are taken from other series of records, but for them the full reference is given.

Monastery.	Arable.				Pasture.				Meadow.			
	a.	£	s.	d.	a.	£	s.	d.	a.	£	s.	d.
1. Bushmead, Beds.[1]	410	= 11	3	4	18⅓	=	5	9	8	11	— 0	18	8
2. Elstow, Beds. ...	228	= 5	14	0	209	= 10	9	0	136	= 9	0	4
3. Merkyate, Beds.	185¼	= 7	16	0	10	=	3	6	8	37½	= 1	16	8
4. Wardon Park grange, Beds.	420	= 10	10	0	203	=	9	15	0	40	= 2	0	0
5. Lavenden, Bucks.	220	= 5	10	0	118	=	2	1	8	20	= 2	0	0
6. Missenden, Bucks.	231	= 4	5	6	90	=	1	17	4	23	= 2	7	8
7. Notley, Bucks. ...	110	= 2	15	0	101	=	5	2	4	35	= 5	7	4
8. Aconbury, Heref.	120	= 1	0	0	123½	=	2	7	4	30½	= 3	1	0

References and Date of Survey.

1. 402, 4.   2. 402, 7.   3. 402, 11.   4. 402, 1.   5. 402, 17.
6. 406, 9.   7. 406, 12.   8. 399, 155 ; Sept., 28 H. VIII.

[1] Besides this there was pasture valued at 14s.

Monastery.	*Arable.*				*Pasture.*				*Meadow.*			
	a.	*£*	*s.*	*d.*	*a.*	*£*	*s.*	*d.*	*a.*	*£*	*s.*	*d.*
9. Clifford,[1] Heref.	184 =	3	1	4	100 =	3	0	9	45¼ =	4	12	1
10. Wigmore, Heref.	144 =	1	14	0	64¼ =	4	9	4	54¼ =	4	14	4
11. Horton, Kent ...	34½ =	1	3	0	33 =	1	13	0	24½ =	1	12	8
12. Leeds, Kent ...	100½ =	5	0	6	196½ =	7	11	4	31 =	4	18	8
13. Swinfield, Kent ...	65½ =	5	6	6	73 =	4	17	4	18 =	1	16	0
14. Croxton, Leic. ...	320 =	21	3	4	353 =	31	8	8	37½ =	4	10	10
15. Leic. St. Mary ...	56 =	2	16	0	157½ =	18	17	8	103 =	10	15	0
16. Olveston, Leic. ...	300 =	7	10	0	317½ =	24	18	4	115 =	9	18	4
17. Bokenham, Norf.	120 =	3	0	0	29 =	2	8	4	168 =	7	0	0
18. Langley,[2] Norf. ...	134 =	2	4	8	30 =	1	3	10	1 =	0	2	0
19. Louth Park, Norf.	340 =	5	13	4	232 =	14	4	0	251 =	12	11	0
20. Ashby, Northants	341 =	7	2	1	553 =	23	0	10				
21. Catesby, Norths.	161 =	4	0	6	788½ =	50	7	0¼	83 =	6	18	4
22. Northampton, St. James	152 =	3	16	0	19½ =	2	0	0	38 =	5	14	0
23. Pipewell, Norths.	150 =	4	13	0	167 =	13	19	4	29 =	3	7	8
24. Sewardesley, Nth.	105 =	2	12	6	5 =	0	10	0	10 =	2	0	0
25. Stamford nuns, N.	209½ =	3	13	1	64 =	5	1	9	20 =	2	0	0
26. Sulby, Northants.					1229½ =	127	15	6	58 =	6	14	0
27. Brewood, Salop...	75 =	1	7	0	188½ =	5	5	2	22¼ =	1	14	0
28. Lilleshall, Salop	157 =	3	12	4	331½ =	12	8	10	35½ =	3	4	0
29. Roncester, Staff....	70 =	1	18	2	201 =	27	6	0	20 =	2	18	0
30. Ronton.[3] Staff. ...	79 =	2	12	8	121½ =	6	14	4	39 =	3	7	4
31. Dureford, Suss. ...	195 =	7	2	0	58 =	2	18	0	21 =	1	18	0
32. Erdbury, Warw.	56 =	1	10	9½	145½ =	8	9	5¼	31 =	2	15	10
33. Henwood, Warw.	30½ =	0	15	3	93 =	6	6	4	6½ =	0	15	2
34. Wroxall, Warw.	127 =	6	7	0	257¼ =	14	4	2	12 =	1	1	2
35. id. W. le Frene ...	40 =	1	0	0	78 =	1	13	4	6 =	0	10	0
36. P. Malvern, Worc.	50 =	2	10	0	82½ =	6	2	4	9 =	1	1	0
37. Westwood, Worc.	113 =	5	2	4	157 =	7	4	2	27½ =	4	5	0
38. Coverham, Yorks.[4]	44 =	1	14	8	39 =	2	12	0	77½ =	6	19	0
39. Kirklees, Yorks.	60 =	1	17	8	117 =	2	17	2	27 =	1	17	8
40. Monk-Bretton,[5] Yk.	32 =	7	3	4	76 =	3	9	4	101 =	6	1	8
41. Whitby,[6] Yorks.	66 =	4	6	8	296 =	12	9	4	30 =	2	0	0

References and Date of Survey.

9. 399, 137. 10. 399, 161; July, 31 H. VIII. 11. 402, 29. 12. 406, 17. 13. 406, 19. 14. 399, 175; Oct., 30 H. VIII. 15. 399, 179. 16. 399, 171; June, 28 H. VIII. 17. State P. D., Suppr. pap. 3, 20. 18. Ib. 3, 30; 28 H. VIII. 19. Ib. 3, 41; 28 H. VIII. 20. 399, 246; May, 28 H. VIII. 21. 399, 234; April, 28 H. VIII. 22. 399, 286; May, 28 H. VIII. 23. 399, 290. 24. 399, 236; May, 28 H. VIII. 25. 403, 15; 29 H. VIII. 26. 399, 342; Nov., 30 H. VIII. 27. 400, 13; Sept., 28 H. VIII. 28. 400, 1. 29. 400, 104. 30. 400, 108; March, 28 H. VIII. 31. Rent et S.; Portf. 15/32; Aug., 28 H. VIII. 32. 408, 308; July, 28 H. VIII. 33. 400, 318; Aug., 28 H. VIII. 34. 398, 70; 28 H. VIII. 35. Id. 36. 400, 348; Aug., 28 H. VIII. 37. 400, 352; Aug., 28 H. VIII 38. 401, 37. 39. 401, 195; Nov., 31 H. VIII. 40. 401, 237; Nov., 30 H. VIII. 41. 401, 391.

[1] In the survey the meadow is described thus:—(13¼ a. = £1 2*s.* 1*d.*) + £3 10*s.* 0*d.* We may be allowed to assume that the second piece of meadow was of the same quality as the first.

[2] Besides this there was pasture worth 14*s.*

[3] The monks have also in their hands 'Heth howse graunge, 97 a. arable, pasture, meadow = £3 6*s.* 0*d.*'

[4] To the demesne there belongs also 18 a. close = £1 10*s.* 0*d.*

[5] To the demesne there belongs also 6 a. close.

[6] To the demesne there belongs also Dovehowse close, 40 a. at 8*d.*

The monasteries in the list possessed altogether 6,235¾ a. arable = £182 3s. 6d.; 8,691½ a. pasture = £497 15s. 11½d.; 1,852¾ a. meadow = £156 4s. 5d. An acre of arable on the average is valued at 7d., an acre of pasture at 13¾d., an acre of meadow at 20¼d. The relation between the areas of arable, pasture and meadow is entirely different in the two lists. In the first, the arable land takes up more than half of the whole area of the demesne; in the second list, the pasture occupies more than half of the area of the demesne. The meadow land in the first list takes up more than a sixth of the whole area, and in the second list it is less than an eighth; but the valuations of the different kinds of land are very similar in both lists. The valuation of the Augmentations Court for all the kinds of land is higher than that of 1535; the valuation of the pasture is raised by almost one-fourth, the valuation of arable by a little less than one-fifth, the valuation of meadow land only by about one-thirtieth. This result is important when we come to criticize the Valor Ecclesiasticus. When we compared the Valor Ecclesiasticus with the Paper Surveys (pp. 60–6) we saw that the valuation of the monastic demesnes, made by the officials of the Augmentations Court exceeded the corresponding valuation of 1535 by a little more than one-tenth. The two lists given above show that the difference in valuation depended upon two causes.

To some extent the Augmentations officials defined the area itself differently. But even in cases where they agreed with the Commissioners in the calculation of the area of demesne, the later valuation was, acre for acre, higher. The difference in the two valuations of the different kinds of land is not so great as to exclude the possibility of drawing valid inferences from both lists. In both, the arable land is the cheapest and the meadow land the most valuable; in both, the pasture is about twice and the meadow land about three times as expensive as the arable land. In both lists the valuation of one and the same kind of land varies very considerably in different monasteries. In the V. E. an acre of arable land is valued at 2⅓d. for the monastery of Cirencester, and at 2s. 8d. for the monastery of Swineshed. In the Paper Survey an acre of

arable land is valued at 2*d.* for the monastery of Acorneby,
and at 19½*d.* for the monastery of Swinfield.

Sown land and fallow. Evidently the difference in the proportions of arable,
meadow, and pasture land in the various monasteries was
even greater than the difference in the income or valuation
of each kind of land. Thus the list of thirteen monasteries
taken out of the V. E. does not by any means yield results
analogous to those yielded by the list of forty-one monasteries
taken from the Paper Surveys. But, even so, some reservations must be made. For instance, with regard to arable land,
which consisted of sown land and fallow. Was the fallow included in the area of the arable land? Not always, by any
means. Forty-six acres of arable land are mentioned in the
Yorkshire survey of Ellerton; it is all sown, and the fallow is
not mentioned at all.[1] In other cases the fallow is included
in the area of arable land, and occasionally direct mention
of it is made. The monastery of Cirencester, Glouc., observed the two-field system on their land; both fields, the
sown and the fallow, are surveyed in the Valor Ecclesiasticus.[2] In the survey of Bokenham, Norf., the Augmentations officials indicate separately the area of arable land
and the area of sown land; in the manor of Hollwyke
almost all the arable land surveyed is sown, but only a
third of that adjoining to the monastery itself.[3] Indirect

[1] Exch. Augm. O. M. b. 401, 47–9.
[2] V. E. ii. 467: 'Exitus 1080 acr' terr' arabil' iacen' super Montes apud
Cirencester' ad grangias de Burton et Spyring spectan' in man' abbatis
monasterii reservat' pro cultura et pastura bidencium qua 540 sunt annuatim in cultura et 540 jacent annuatim warrectate et quelibet acra jacens
in cultura—cum pastura terre warrectate appreciatur ad 4*d.* et sic in
toto £9 0*s.* 0*d.*'
[3] Suppr. Pap. v. 3 ff. 20–1: 'the demaynes now in thandes and occu-
pacion of the prior there . . . arable 120 a.=£3 0*s.* 0*d.*' Out of these
120 acres 14 were sown with wheat, 20 a. with barley, 6 a. with oats and
peas. The monks also tilled the land in the manor of Hollwyke which
consisted of 49 a. at 6*d.* an acre of arable land, and 9 a. at 10*d.* an acre of
meadow. Of the 49 acres of arable land 42 acres were sown. The survey
negatives any suggestion that the cost of the crop is included in the
valuation of the arable land. The crops are valued in the survey *apart*
from the valuation of the land, and exceed it even at the highest figure.
The land itself is valued only at 6*d.* per acre. The crop of wheat sown on
an acre is valued at 6*s.* 8*d.*, of barley and oats at 3*s.* 4*d.* The crop is
valued apart from the land also in the Part. f. gr. n. 782 (37 H. VIII,
parcella monasterii Redyng, manor of Whittebury) together with the

indications are also found. Where the survey divides the arable land into three fields of about the same size, we may conclude that the monastery follows the three-field system, and that the whole of the arable land is described.[1] In the survey of Bushmead we read concerning a certain piece of ground that it has about 300 acres when it is under crops ; the surveyor was interested in all the arable land and not in the crops only.[2] I am inclined to believe that both in the V. E. and the Paper Surveys the arable land and not the crops are generally described, and that the area of the arable land was diminished but very little by disregarding the fallow. But the area of arable land might be also exaggerated in the survey. It is possible that not the whole of the land that is called arable in the survey was actually tilled, and distinct confirmation of such doubts is found in the Glastonbury terrier of 1518, in the description of Domerham, a manor in Wiltshire. The land is divided into arable and pasture, and the former is mentioned in three places. In two of them, however, the reservation is made that not the whole of the land mentioned is under cultivation. In one place only a little more than half of the land is under cultivation, and the rest is used as pasture for sheep ; in another, almost the whole of the land called arable was actually used as pasture for sheep.[3] A comparison of the two surveys of the Westwood home farm

'stock of the ferme : barley sowne 40 acres 4s. 0d. each, otes sowne 20 a. 2s. 8d. each.' Evidently not only the crops but also, to some extent at least, the cost of tillage was included in the valuation of the crops. According to Fitzherbert, to the acre two bushels of rye or wheat must be sown, four or five of barley, three of oats (Fitzherbert, surv. 34, 13, 14). Even in a year of dearth the value of corn sown is much lower than the valuation of crops. The nuns in St. Sexburghe, Sheppey, however, sowed four bushels of wheat to the acre. Exch. Treas. Rec. v. 154, f. 84 dorso (27 H. VIII).

[1] E. g. Kenilworth, Warw., Augm. O. M. b. 400, 118–19 : arable, Priorsfelde 70 a.=£0 16s. 8d., Wyndmille felde 80 a.=£0 16s. 8d., Firsey felde 66 a.=£0 13s. 4d.

[2] Ib. 402, 4 : 'Plasworth felde not severall but when it is sowen containeth by estimacion 300 acres.'

[3] Harl. 3961, ff. 148–87 : 'Terre arabiles : (a) apud Bolesborgh 188 a. unde coluntur iam 100 a. vel minus et residuum ad pasturam bidencium ibm quas Johes Rade modo tenet pro redditu £2 ; (b) apud Elyngford 167½ a. ; (c) apud Twohide 142 a. unde coluntur singulis annis circa 5 a. et residuum pro pastura bidencium dni cum la downe.'

suggests the same doubts with regard to the Valor Ecclesiasticus and the Paper Surveys. In the V. E. all the demesne
described in detail is divided into pasture and meadow ; in the
Paper Survey the three pieces of pasture of the Valor Ecclesiasticus are called arable land.[1] They evidently were either
pasture that became arable land, or arable land that became
pasture. The Domerham case makes the latter suggestion the
more probable. Land tilled for a long time continued to be
called arable even after it had been converted into pasture.
This may have been the result of habit merely, or have been the
outcome of a desire to evade the Acts against conversion. Whatever the reason was, the number of acres given in the survey does
not always agree with the area that was actually being tilled.

Proportion of arable to pasture. Reservations must also be made with regard to pasture.
The rural economists of the sixteenth century distinguished
the ' enclosed' or ' several' pasture from the common pasture.
Many monasteries had pastures of both kinds, and it is important to learn whether both were entered in the demesne
surveys. Very often no indication at all is given in the survey
itself as to this. ' Several' pastures were of great importance
to a monastery and were surveyed with more detail. In cases
where both the common and the ' several' pastures are mentioned in the survey, the amount of the area is generally given
only for the latter. As less attention was paid to the commons
it is quite likely that their existence was occasionally ignored
through inadvertence : indeed, in some cases it can be clearly
shown that such omissions did occur.[2] We may therefore
believe that the ' pastures' of the surveys are for the most
part ' several' pastures. On this point, however, there is
a difference between the Valor Ecclesiasticus and the Paper

---

[1] V. E. iii. 276. Among the pieces of pasture are mentioned : Brode
felde, £2 0s. 0d., Boycote felde £1 3s. 4d., Bankamushylle £2 0s. 0d. In
the Exch. Augm. O.· M. b. 400, 352, the arable land consists of three
pieces : Banamyshyll 36 a., Braddefelde 44 a., Boycotefilde 33 a.

[2] In the Exch. Augm. O. M. b. 398, 70, the pasture of the monastery of
Wroxall is surveyed. 257¼ acres are divided into nine allotments ; eight
allotments are called ' clausurae'. The commons, therefore, are not taken
into consideration at all, although there was a considerable extent of
them. Among the monastic inventories in Exch. Treas. Receipt, v. 154
the Wroxall inventory is also preserved. It has an entry : ' Comons and
wast 200 a.'

Surveys. From the Paper Surveys I can give at least one instance in which not only the income but also the area of the common pasture is given;[1] I know of no such case in the Valor Ecclesiasticus. The comparative fullness of the Paper Surveys tells in favour of the supposition that some of the pastures were common, while in the more condensed V. E. it is otherwise. And if in the Paper Surveys the proportion of pasture to arable land is much greater than in the Valor Ecclesiasticus, this may to a certain extent be explained by the fact that the Paper Surveys sometimes introduced the commons into their pasturage totals, while the Commissioners of 1535 confined themselves to the 'several' pastures.

Nevertheless, in spite of all these conjectural reservations, we have before us an economic fact of great importance. Arable land occupies a very considerable part of the area that the monks kept in their own hands; it was very little, if at all, less than the area of the 'several' pastures. As agriculturists the monks carried on a large, or at any rate a fair-sized business. Now if the conversion of arable land into pasture had become general under the first two Tudors, then in these thriving monastery farms it ought to be in much greater evidence than in the small homesteads of the peasants, who tilled the land for their own subsistence and were fettered on all sides by communal regulations. The monasteries had also reasons of their own for giving up corn-growing and taking to grazing; or else for leaving the demesne to a farmer. The Dissolution was not an entirely unexpected event for the monks. Particular dissolutions under Wolsey must have produced an impression upon them and inspired them with apprehension as to their future; and when the situation became complicated by a breach with Rome these apprehensions must have become intensified. The great uncertainty of their position would naturally make them reluctant to invest new capital in land or even to carry on the old business, to under-

The monks and the agrarian revolution.

---

[1] Catesby, Northants, Exch. Augm. O. M. b. 399, 234: 'Severalle pastures in 10 closes, 253 acres 2 roods 32 poles = £16 18s. 3¼d. Item ther is in pasture in one ffellde called Highfelde not enclosed, wherin the tenaunts of Catesby have comon with certen nomber of cattalle and the same conteyneth in acres of pasture 535 a. arented at £33 8s. 9d.'

take expensive repairs of their numerous buildings, to keep up
a large staff of labourers, horses, and oxen. On the eve of
the Dissolution we find them endeavouring to draw in their
capital; they cease to repair their buildings, employ fewer
labourers, and reduce the amount of their tillage; they sell
off their stock, let out all they can, and substitute less costly
sheep for their expensive cattle. Both the Valor Ecclesiasticus
and the later surveys represent the monastic agrarian economy
at a time of exceptional conditions; the monks seeking to
convert into money as much as possible of their possessions,
while the Government tried in every way to prevent them
from doing this. Under such conditions the figures of
monastic tillage become eloquent. In spite of the fact
that pasture was twice as valuable as arable land, that monasteries were in a large way of business, and that they had
particular reasons to reduce the amount of their arable, yet
up to the last the monks tilled almost as much land as they
kept for grazing purposes. Doubtless it would only be by
comparison of the sixteenth-century methods with those of
earlier date that we could appreciate the tendency of agricultural development; but the condition of the monastic agriculture on the eve of the Dissolution is a serious warning to us
not to form exaggerated ideas concerning the agrarian revolution of the sixteenth century.

Situation of the monastic home farms.

The monks generally grew their corn in one place, namely,
on the land adjoining their monastery. Cases in which the
demesne in hand was distributed among many manors are
seldom found in the Valor Ecclesiasticus. Even in these
rare cases, arable land is generally found only in the manor
attached to the monastery; it is the pastures which are
scattered. Doubtful cases are, however, occasionally found :
the monks kept in their own hands the lands of several
manors, but it is not clear what kind of land it was. The
Edindon *Bonhommes* kept in their own hands the land of
six manors (ii. 140-1); in Beynton it was pasture, but no
explanations are given about other manors. The large
northern monasteries had not infrequently several, sometimes
many granges (*grangiae, logiae*); five of those belonging to

Jervaulx are named, and twenty-one belonging to Fountains (v. 241, 253). In the brief entries of the Valor Ecclesiasticus it is not stated on what lines the northern granges were conducted, but the existence of large stocks of grain and cattle, attested by the Suppression Account of Fountains, leads us to suppose that to a large extent it was a corn-growing business.[1] It is very probable that the monks of Middleton tilled the land of several manors themselves.[2] A quite clear indication of the fact that the monks used to grow corn themselves in several manors I found in one survey only—that of Lewes priory (V. E. i. 329-30), where the monks kept in their own hands 200 acres of arable in the manor of Swanbergh, 90 acres of arable in the manor of Ballysden, 440 acres of arable in the manor of Falmer; all the arable land being valued at one shilling an acre. In the manor of Balneth the monks also kept in their hands a demesne of 120 acres ; it is possible that part of it was arable land. It is possible, too, that there was some arable land in the demesne of the manor of Southover et Kyngeston.

According to the Paper Surveys, too, the arable land is generally concentrated in one place. In a small minority of cases the arable land is divided into two parts, one being adjacent to the monastery and the other to some grange. Such are the surveys of Wardon (Beds.), Wroxall (Warw.), Swyne (Yorks.).[3] In the survey of Worksop (Notts.) no arable land on the demesne is mentioned, all the monastic arable being evidently attached to the grange of Lathes, which is described with much completeness.[4]

---

[1] The Suppression Account is published in the Mon. Ebor. 143-7.

[2] V.E. ii. 249-51. The monks kept in their hands the demesne land in Myddelton, Huysshe, Sydlyng, Holewey, Holswurthe, Est Ryngsted, La-Lee, Wullond. In six cases the formula ' in terris pratis pascuis pasturis in occupacione abbatis' is used, and ' terre' in such a combination of words generally means arable land.

[3] Exch. Augm. O. M. b. 402. 1; 398. 70; 401. 381 (cf. Part. f. grants 529, m. 1).

[4] Ib. 399. 339-44: 'Graungia de Lathes near to the scite havyng a house mete for a hynde to dwell therein an oxehouse an hayehouse and two barnes a yarde oon litill garden one litill crofte, Myrecrofte 2 a., Thommecrofte 2½ a., Lambecrofte 3 a., Lathefyld close 28 a., Whynneclose adjoyning Lathefeld 20 a., adjoynyng it Arnoldeparke well sett with yonge

Systems of
tillage. Direct evidence concerning the system of tillage is rare.
I have already mentioned the instructive information about
the two-field regulation on the large demesne of the monastery of Cirencester (V. E. ii. 467); we also possess quite
definite information about the monastery of St. Sexburghe,
Sheppey, Kent. The nuns had on their demesne the three-
field system, but already somewhat complicated. The Commissioners supressed the nunnery on March 27th, 1536.
In the preceding autumn 50 acres were sown with wheat,
4 bushels to the acre; 6 acres were sown with beans, 4 with
peas, 7 with oats. Barley had not yet been sown, but almost
the whole of it was threshed for seed. Barley was much more
important than oats in the household, 36 acres were going to
be sown with it; 18 qrs. had been left for seed—that is to
say, 4 bushels to the acre. The third field ' of 50 acres and
more' remained fallow; wheat was going to be sown on it
next autumn. It is curious that the nuns sowed tares for
horse food; the Commissioners found 4 acres just sown, and
at the end of March the tares of the last year had not yet
been all consumed.[1]

As to the systems of tillage on monastic land, we have to
be content for the most part with indirect evidence, and we
have such evidence for the two-field and three-field systems.
It is instructive that the information about the two-field
system on the Cirencester lands does not stand alone : in the
Glastonbury terrier of 1518 the demesne arable land of
many manors is divided into two fields (Grutleton, Winterborne, Aisshbury, Gomeldon, Idmyston); it must, however,
be stated that the demesnes were leased. For Grutleton we
also possess additional information as to the existence of the
two-field system. In the two fields of arable land we find
leys; when the field was fallow the leys could not be mown,

okes 3 a., 3 closes in Nether Tonnefeld 80 a., Cootefeld 30 a., Conygre
wodd set with yong ookes 3 a., Howthe close 3 a.'
    [1] Exch. Treas. Rec. M. b. v. 154, f. 84 dorso : ' Barley redy thresshyd
for sede 18 qrs. Barley to thressh by estymatys 3 qrs. Tares for horse
meate. 50 acres of whete redy sowne with $\frac{1}{2}$ qr. on every acre in sede
tyme. Sowne 6 a. of beanes. Sowne 4 a. of pease. Sowne 7 a. of otys.
Sowne 4 a. of tares, 36 a. of falowe for barley, 50 a. of falow and more for
whete falow the next yere.'

because it was left for pasture in the same manner as the fallow. When the field was sown, grass could grow under cover of the corn crop and could be mown. It is pointed out in the terrier that the leys were mown every other year.[1] This means that the turn was a two-years one : one year the field was sown, the next left fallow. In the Paper Surveys are also found some cases of arable land being divided into two fields ; but more often we find there the division into three fields.[2] We must not think, of course, that only the two-field and three-field systems were adopted on the monastic demesne. Fitzherbert points out that under peculiar local conditions more complicated rotations of arable and pasture were possible.[3]

In the history of demesne farming no small part must be given to the attempts of the lords and farmers to free the demesne from the communal restrictions and to separate the demesne arable from the peasants' open fields. The Paper Surveys give us some idea as to how far the monks succeeded in doing this. Several monasteries had the whole of their arable land in an open field as formerly.[4] The survey does not always say in so many words that all or nearly all the monastic arable land is situated in the open field, but this is evident from the plots being widely scattered, and from the smallness of the plots or strips.[5] Sometimes the survey points

The home farm and the village community.

[1] Harl. 3961, Grutleton, ff. 5–13, 'Prata: Inmede 30 a. in scparali + la mershe in campo boreali $17\frac{1}{2}$ a. alternis annis falcabiles + aldemede in campo occidentali 11 a. alternis annis falcabiles. Arable : campus borealis 128 a. + campus occidentalis $90\frac{1}{2}$ a.'

[2] Leicester St. Mary, 399. 179: '56 a. in 2 campis.' Wroxall, Warw., W. le Frene 398. 70 : '40 a. in 2 campis.' Aconbury, Heref., 399. 155 : '120 acres in 3 fields of 40 acres each.' Olveston, Leic., 399. 171 : 'terre arabiles 300 a. in tribus separalibus campis de Olveston.' Kenilworth, Warw., 400. 118 : 'Priorsfelde 70 a. + Wyndmylle felde 80 a. + Firsey felde 66 a.' Westwood, Worc., three fields in 36 a., 44 a., 33 a. respectively. Lavenden, Bucks., 402. 17, three fields in 75 a., 65 a., 80 a. respectively.

[3] For instance, Surv. 37, and generally the section about the improvement of soil. It is hardly necessary to say that in the works of agricultural writers of the second half of the sixteenth century and the beginning of the seventeenth (Tusser, Norden, Markham), the more complicated systems of tillage are described more clearly.

[4] Exch. Augm. O. M. b. 399, 286 : terre arabiles ibm in communibus campis in manu abbatis 152 a. = £3 16s. od.' Northampton St. James.

[5] This is how the demesne arable land of the Priory of Swyne was described soon after the Dissolution (Part. f. grants, n. 529, m. 1, 31 H. VIII), all the arable land being valued at 6d. an acre: '10 a. ar. in Cotedale, $3\frac{1}{2}$ a. ar. super Humpkyns, 5 a. ar. in les Fossebutts, 21 a. ar.

out that a part of the arable land is situated in the open field, but does not tell us where the rest of the arable land is.[1] Other cases are more enlightening, and the survey says definitely that one part of the arable land is enclosed and the rest remains in the open field : thus it was in the demesnes of Monk-Bretton and Nunmonkton. The survey of Monk-Bretton is especially interesting : 209 acres of arable land consist of eight enclosed plots ; the remaining 29 acres are called flatts, and are evidently strips or groups of strips in the open field.[2] Other monasteries had apparently been for some time more successful, and had enclosed not only all their arable land but all their demesne.   According to the Paper Surveys this was the state of things in several Yorkshire houses —Coverham, Ellerton, Kirklees, Whitby, and in a Staffordshire house, Ronton.[3]   Many and varied were the manorial regulations which existed at the same time even on the lands of lords belonging to the same class of society.

in Keldale, 7 a. ar. in Keldale, 5 a. ar. in 15 peciis vocatis little butts, 5½ a. ar. iuxta Chery crofte syde, 5 a. super eandem furlong in diversis locis, 11½ a. super les Kirke landes, 11 a. ar. super le fosse, 9 a. in campo predicto in diversis locis, 3½ a. subtus Willok Myre, 4½ a. apud Fosse brigge, 11 a. apud le furlonge de Fosse brigge pred' in diversis locis, 16 a. in diversis locis subtus Wolbrugh hedge, 17 a. inter le More Yate et Coniston Yate, 5 a. vocate Humkenes, 26 a. apud Hoggelane ende, 3 a. iuxta villam de Swyne, 6 a. apud Uphousegarth, 16 a. ar. in diversis locis, 22 a. ar. voc' le falowes subtus villam Milnefelde, 4 a. ar. voc' le falowes super les Humkyns, 20 a. ar. apud Compton Dyke in 2 locis, 7 a. ar. iuxta le Thorne, 17 a. ar. in Colmandale, 8 a. ar. in le Combe Noke in diversis locis, 27 a. ar. in Foxom, 5 a. ar. in le West felde apud les Wraye butts, 41 a. a retro le Pighill in diversis locis, 6 a. apud Milkester butts, 11 a. apud le West Wells, 37 a. apud le Carre syde in diversis locis, 8 a. ar. et pasture apud le Brome hill.'

[1] Notley, Bucks., Augm. O. M. b. 406. 12 : 'arable : Whyndeyardes 10 a. (at 10d.), a feld stony and very baren 20 a. (at 4d.), 80 a. in the comen felde at Crendon (at 6d.).'   Missenden, Bucks., ib. 406, 9.   There were seven whole 'fields' of arable land, 160 acres on the whole, the valuation of which varies from 3d. to 12d.   The remaining 71 acres are situated in two open fields : Myddel Wyde felde 27 acres in seven plots, in Buryfeld 44 acres in sixteen plots.   It is curious that at Buryfeld there was arable land of five different prices, from 1d. to 8d.

[2] Monk-Bretton, ib. 401. 237.   The following is a description of the flatts : 'Fevell 2 a., nine lands 2 a., Lynghyll flatt 4 a., Shawflatt 2 a., Hungeryehyll 2 a., Endworthebroke 1 a., Essett 1 a., four lyttle flatts in tholdefeld 3 a., four rye flatts in the comon felds.'   Nunmonketon, 401. 247 (=253=286) ;

[3] Ib., Coverham, 401. 37 ; Ellerton, 401. 47 ; Kirklees, 401. 195 ; Whitby, 401. 391 ; Ronton, 400. 108.

As to meadow land the monks had a strong desire to Communal
retain it exclusively in their own hands, and to preserve meadows.
it from any encroachment on the part of the peasant community, seeing that it was the most valuable kind of land.
But even as regards meadow, the separation of demesne from
tenancies had not been accomplished everywhere by the time
of the dissolution. In some places the communal meadows
formed part and parcel of the monastic manors until they
passed over to the Crown. Communal meadows are twice
mentioned in that part of the 1518 Glastonbury terrier which
has come down to us: in the manors of Badbury and Idmiston
the demesne meadow consisted of strips in the communal
meadow. The nuns of Catesby were bound, according to
an ancient custom, to leave on one of their meadows some
loads of hay for the local tenants.[1]

In the case of pastures also the separation of demesne Monastic
from tenancies was still far from being accomplished. Our rights of
common.
authorities mention both the communal and the several
pasture, but it is difficult to establish their comparative importance as regards the demesne. Very often the authorities
do not explain at all the nature of the pasture rights, and
it is impossible to say with certainty whether the land was
common or in the exclusive use of the monks. We can
draw a definite conclusion concerning the separation of the
demesne pasture when it is enclosed or ' several' (*pastura clausa, p. separalis*); but the term ' unenclosed pasture'
has no very definite meaning, inasmuch as unenclosed land
might be both severally and communally used. For instance, it is difficult to form a definite opinion as to certain
land belonging to the monastery of St. Neots which in the
Valor Ecclesiasticus is called ' pastura jacens ad largum'.[2]
The lack of evidence as to the monastic rights of common

---

[1] Harl. 3961, ff. 99–113: Badbury, ' 53 acre 1 pertica in communibus
pratis'; ib. ff. 137–46: Idmyston, ' prati 16 a. in communibus pratis.'
Catesby, Augm. O. M. b. 399. 234: ' ther is in mede 83 a. wheroff in one
mede called Netherfeld wheryn the seid tenauntes of Catesby have by
prescripcon certen loodes of haye yerely 75 a., and in Catesby felde 8 a.'

[2] V. E. iv. 262. Monastic pasture is divided into two parts: ' pastura
inclusa precio cujuslibet acre 12*d.*, pastura jacens ad largum 140 acre
quelibet acra 4*d.*'

does not necessarily mean that such rights did not exist.
Nothing is said either in the V.E. or the Paper Surveys about
the rights of common belonging to Erdbury, and it had really
no such rights; this is definitely settled by the inventory, made
soon after the Dissolution, in which there is a special entry
'comons none'.   Neither in the V. E. nor in the Paper
Survey of Wroxall is anything said about rights of common ;
yet such rights did exist, for the inventory makes note of
200 acres in the entry for wastes and commons.[1] In the
case of commons, a monastery had only a part of the landed
income.   In order to get a definite idea of the commons we.
must know more about them than we do about the land which
was in the exclusive use of the monks ; we must know, besides
the area and the income appertaining to any given monastery,
what part of the general income from the common was comprised in the monastic income. But as a matter of fact we know
less about commons than about the land that was exclusively
monastic.   In some instances our authority only says that a
monastery had in such and such a place rights of common,[2]
but does not make known what the area of the commons was,
or what income accrued therefrom to the monastery and to
other commoners.   In the inventories made after the Dissolution we sometimes do find a similar formula ; the Commissioners say that the monastic rights of common are according to the rate of their demesne or are such as other tenants
have.[3]   But the rights of common might be distributed in
different places in quite a different manner ; for instance, in
the inventories just mentioned there is a case in which they
were distributed in such a way as cannot well be regarded
as typical of the monastic economy.   The inventory of the

---

[1] Erdbury, V. E. iii. 56; Augm. O. M. b. 408. 308-9; Exch. Treas.
Rec. v. 154. 56-64. Wroxall, V. E. iii. 89; Augm. O. M. b. 398. 70;
Exch. Treas. Rec. ibm.   Henwood, Warw., is a case similar to that of
Wroxall, V. E. iii. 79 ; A. O. M. b. 400. 318, Exch. Tr. Rec. ibm.

[2] Croxton, Augm. O. M. b. 399. 175 ; 'the abbey has all the comons for
almaner cattall belonging to the same within the ldp of Croxton.' Clyfford,
ib. 399. 137 ; Aconbury, ib. 399. 155; Parva Marlow, ib. 406. 4 ; Worksop,
ib. 399. 339 (' Romwodd—tharbage therof is common ')) ; Pinley, Exch.
Treas. Rec. v. 154. 56-64.

[3] Exch. Treas. Rec. M. b. v. 154: Bradley, Warwick St. Sepulchre's,
Olveston, Grace Dieu, Langley, Pollesworth, Stoneleigh.

monastery of Henwood mentions a common containing 210
acres; its 'soil' belongs to the house of Henwood, its
'common' (evidently the right of pasturage) to the neighbouring villages, and the wood growing upon it to Westminster
Abbey; the Henwood nuns, however, can use the wood for
fuel and repairs.[1] Often enough the authorities indicate only
the size of the commons, and in doing so they sometimes give
not the area of pasture, wood or waste, but their perimeter, from
which we have to discover the area. In other cases the area is
stated for a part of the commons, some general indication
being given concerning the rest. But, of course, there are
definite statements of the area of commons to be found as
well.[2] The fullest information about the commons gives their
area and the amount of the monastic common rights; the
latter being expressed either in money or in the number of
cattle a monastery may keep on the commons. The extent
of monastic rights of common is, however, sometimes given
by itself, without any indications as to the area.[3]

[1] Ib., Com' Warr', ii. 56–64, n. 4. 'Comons 210 a. the soyle wherof
belongethe to the howse of Hynwood and comon to the townshipps
adjoynyng and the wood upon the same belongithe to the abbey of
Westm.' ; Hynwood house can take for itself ' tymber to repayre the howse
and te[neme]nts and to buren within the priorie'. The description of the
Domerham demesne in the Glastonbury Terrier of 1518 (Monasticon, i.
16–21 ; Harl. 3961, ff. 137–46) shows very clearly how variously the rights
of pasture might be distributed between lords and different groups of
tenants in a mountainous and sheep-rearing district. I do not mention this
example in the text, because the Domerham demesne used to be let out.
[2] Exch. Tr. Rec. M. b. 154: 'Ulverscroft common in the forest of
Charnewood which is 20 mylls aboute or more, with all maner of catell
without nombre.' On such an area a very great number of cattle could be
fed; it is no wonder that another monastery in Leicestershire also had
rights of pasture in the forest of Charnewood. I have already mentioned
(p. 166) that in the Glastonbury survey of Pollard and Moyle the circuit of
the commons is often given instead of the area—an indication of part of
the area is given for Pollesworth (Exch. Tr. Rec. M. b. 154) : ' comon acc'
unto the rate of ther demenes as other tenants have and also a grette
comon wherapon the wood dothe growe by est' 60 a. grownd and above.'
The general area of commons is given in the inventories of Garendon
450 a., Henwood 210 a., Wroxall 200 a., Tortington 80 a., Boxgrove 60 a.
(ibm., and Suppr. Pap. v. 3, n. 128).
[3] Catesby, Exch. Augm. O. M. b. 399. 234 : ' 535 a. arented at
£33 8s. 9d.' Amesbury, V. E. ii. 93 : 'in pastura ad 374 oves in com-
munia pro qualibet ove 1d.' Ivy Church, ii. 96 : ' pastura super
communem brueram ad 140 oves quelibet 1d. ob.' Lavenden, Exch.
A. O. M. b. 402. 17 : ' Comen for abbots shepe valued 7s. 6d.'

It is only when the survey definitely speaks of the non-existence of commons on the monastic territory that we can affirm with certainty that the monks succeeded in separating all their pastures from the peasant holdings. Such cases, however, are rare ; I can only mention Erdbury, Warwickshire ; Coventry Charterhouse, Warwickshire ; and Hastings, Sussex. It is possible, and even probable, that entire separation had been accomplished in cases where all the pasture mentioned in the survey is enclosed and the common pasture is not mentioned at all. Such cases are St. Mary's, Leicester ; Ronton, Staffordshire ; Coverham, Ellerton, Kirkleys, Nunmonketon and Whitby, Yorkshire.

In two instances we find interesting information as to the way in which the monks freed their land from the communal restrictions by agreement with the commoners. No division of land was made, but the monks annually paid the commoners a sum agreed upon for the waiver of their rights of common. In Kenilworth they paid to the local parson £0 6s. 8d. that he might allow them to keep in severalty three pieces of arable. The nuns in Stamford paid annually £1 0s. 0d. to the parishioners of St. Martin, in Stamford, for the same permission with regard to three pieces of pasture.[2]

Monastic sheep-farming   In the Valor Ecclesiasticus we find a good deal of information about monastic sheep-farming; unfortunately, however, such information is not always quite clear. The entries generally give the name of the place where sheep are kept and their number ; they divide the sheep into classes and give the income received per head from each class. At first sight the entries seem definite enough, but there are some very important points which remain obscure, so that the entries can be interpreted in different ways. The land on which the sheep are fed may be in the exclusive occupation of the monks, or these may have only rights of pasture similar to those of other commoners. The monks may themselves breed sheep on their own pasture, or they may take sheep

---

[1] Exch. Treas. Rec. M. b. 154 ; Warw. n. 3, 5 ; Suppr. P. v. 3 n. 128, n. 3 ; Exch. Augm. O. M. b. 399. 179 ; 400. 108 ; 401. 37 ; 401. 195 ; 401. 247 ; 401. 391.   [2] Ib. 400. 118 ; 399. 274=403. 23.

for grazing or let out the pasture itself to a grazier. Even the entry giving the number of sheep may be interpreted in different ways. The number may be that which was actually fed on the spot, or the entry may be taken to mean that no more than that number of sheep mentioned could be fed on the pasture.[1] If a monastery has only the rights of pasture, the reference to a certain number of sheep may signify both the extent of such rights and the number of sheep actually fed upon the pasture.

I noticed in the V. E. only thirteen descriptions of monastic sheep-farming. This, of course, does not signify that other monasteries did not rear sheep, but only that the 'Instruction' left a great deal of latitude to the Commissioners of 1535 and that they performed their duties in various ways. Some of the Commissioners found it necessary to make a return of the monastic income from sheep-farming; the majority confined themselves to a short return of the income from the home farm. Seven returns of sheep-breeding come from Dorsetshire, three from Norfolk, and one occurs in each of the returns for Gloucestershire, Wiltshire and Sussex.[2] The presence of seven large monastic sheep-farming businesses in the Dorset returns testifies, of course, to the fact that many sheep were kept in the county, and that the monks occupied a very important place among sheep-breeders. But the absence of entries about sheep-farming in the returns for Somersetshire and Suffolk does not necessarily indicate that the monks in these counties had no sheep.

The Dorset returns occupy an exceptional position in the Valor Ecclesiasticus. The Commissioners describe the sheep-farming of all the monasteries in the county with the exception of two small cells, Cranborne and Holme. The total number of sheep, or pastures, that have been counted is very considerable ; of the former, more than twenty-five thousand head. In the returns of other counties nothing similar is to

---

[1] The Glastonbury terrier of 1518, Harl. 3961, Domerham, ff. 148–87: 'Pastura separalis pro dno in Alyngford 325 a. ubi sustineri possint 500 multones si clausure bene claud' et sustin'; Pastura montana in Twohide 147 a. ubi sustentari possint 500 multones et ultra.'
[2] I mean the surveys of Winchelcombe, Wilton and Lewes.

be found.   The three Norfolk entries concerning sheep-farming relate to three monasteries which are all situated in one
locality, Thetford (Thetford monachorum, Th. canonicorum,
Th. monialium): and of these, only the 'monks' had many
sheep or pastures.   In the Thetford returns the following
formula is found: ' Manerium valet in firmis cum firma terrarum arabilium et libertate faldagii et pastura ovium ibidem in
occupacione prioris.' [1]   The 'libertas faldagii' and 'pastura
ovium' are different things; 'libertas faldagii' means, in this
case, first of all, the payments for pasturage, and 'pastura'
means a certain area of pasture.   Sheep of 'the monks' are
mentioned in eleven places, and their total number is 5,800
head, but it is difficult to say whether we are to take literally
the numbers of head given, as all of them are exactly round
numbers.   The canons and nuns are said to have sheep only
in Thetford itself—the canons 800 head, and the nuns 60.

Conceal-
ment of
monastic
goods.

Much more definite is the information about the monastic
cattle-breeding which we get from the Crown inventories.   At
the Suppression the Augmentations officials made returns not
only of the revenues but also of the goods of the monasteries,
including the monastic cattle.   When they say that the monks
had 100 cows or 200 sheep the meaning of such a statement is
clear: the reference being to the actual number of cows and
sheep, and not to the rights of pasture or to the area of pasture.   But to what extent may we base our ideas of the
monastic economy on the condition of things at the time of
the Suppression?   Is it not possible that substantial changes
have taken place with regard to the monastic live stock
even during the short interval between the compilation of the
Valor Ecclesiasticus and the Suppression?   The catastrophe

[1] The well-known statute of 25 H. VIII, c. 13, s. 10, gives some idea of
sheep-farming in Norfolk and Suffolk.
[2] The Thetford returns may be compared with the description of the
demesne belonging to the Norfolk house of Buckenham, V. E. iii. 316:
'Manor' de Vet' Bokenham valet in redd' et firmis cum firm' 47 a. arabil'
248 a. pastur' et 10 a. prat' ac libertate faldagii et pastur' 400 ovium
matric' in occup' prioris £48 15s. 2¾d.'   According to the Suppr. Pap. v.
3 ff. 20–1, it was a demesne 'in manu prioris'; the income from pasture
was composed of two parts: 168 a. of pasture at 10d., and 'for the fold
course of 400 shepe £1 6s. 8d.'

could not have been entirely unexpected by the monks; no special sagacity was needed to foresee the proximity of the end after having witnessed the partial dissolutions under Wolsey, the breach with Rome, and the visitations of 27 H. VIII. After the dissolution of the smaller monasteries it must have been clear to the monks of the large houses that their time also was short. Even a fatalist seldom remains inactive on the eve of a *débâcle*, and the most timid souls in a critical moment will take decisive action, sometimes without any hope of success, simply at the bidding of their instinct of self-preservation. As the end drew near, therefore, the English monks took steps to conceal all that could be concealed.[1] Everybody recognized the inducements to such a course—the Government, the monks themselves, the neighbours —all acted accordingly. The interests of the monks generally coincided with those of the local population and were always opposed to those of the Government. The neighbours natu rally were quite ready to acquire as great a part as possible of the monastic property at the lowest possible price; the Crown just as naturally wanted the whole of it. The local population therefore helped the monks to conceal their goods, and the Government agents were bidden to frustrate such designs. The Government accused the monks of treason, and expressed more or less feigned indignation at the 'immorality' of the people who were destroying their own house, that very house which the Government wished to wipe off the face of the earth.[2] But even the most zealous Treasury officials and the most fervent accusers of the monks understood the inevitableness of the monastic 'immorality', and thought out measures that would prevent not the immorality itself, but only such consequences as would bring a loss to the Crown. The Dissolution Statutes annulled all monastic grants made *mala fide* on the eve of the Suppression. The Government instructed the Augmentations officials to make strict search for goods concealed and to seek out everything that it was possible to find; the Augmentations Court to the end of its short life

---

[1] Cf. Gasquet, ii. 278-86. [2] 27 H. VIII, c. 28, s. 4.

never ceased its examination of the supposed concealers.[1] The reports of the Commissioners and Augmentations officials are full of complaints about the endless concealments by the monks made in anticipation of the Dissolution ; and among these series of accusations and denunciations one seldom meets with a word of praise for the monastic management of the demesne.[2]

As early as Wolsey's days complaints were made about the behaviour of the monks who were threatened with dissolution. In 1529 Wolsey learns from Norfolk that the monks of St. Benet's (= Hulme) fear a dissolution and therefore manage their affairs carelessly; and that it is necessary on that account to impress upon them that they must not give away their lands or conceal their movables.[3] The complaints become more numerous as we approach the general Dissolution. Some denunciations contain general complaints about monastic behaviour, others accuse particular monasteries. In October, 1538, Freman, an Augmentations official, writes to Cromwell from Lincolnshire advising him to suppress the monasteries not singly but simultaneously throughout the country. After the downfall of the smaller houses we find Government agents persuading the large monasteries to surrender of their own free will. Freman adds ironically that there is not the slightest need to persuade the monks, for they are all ready to surrender themselves without being asked. They surrender, however, not to the Crown, but to the local population : they let out their lands, sell off their stock and hide away their jewels. The Dissolution ought, therefore, to be proceeded with as soon as possible. At the same time a complaint comes to Cromwell from Nottinghamshire ; the greedy monks of Worksop are selling off all their cattle, their grain, their wood, and the other local monasteries are following their

---

[1] Statutes 27 H. VIII, c. 28, s. 4, 31 H. VIII, c. 13, ss. 5-8, Instructions. Gairdner, x. 721, xi. app. 15, xiv. 1189-90. Instances of examinations from the Augmentations records are given by Gasquet, ii. 283-6.

[2] Gairdner, xiv. 78 : Jan., 30 H. VIII, Petre to Cromwell. Petre acknowledges that the Malmesbury monks have much cattle, that the shrine is in good order, and that the monks do not let out their demesne to farmers.

[3] Brewer, iv. 5415.

example.[1] Other informers speak of separate monasteries ; in Abingdon all the monastic buildings except the Church have fallen into decay. In Bordesley the abbot has sold the crops to his servants, and felled part of the wood. The nuns in Romsey, Hants, having heard of the Dissolution hastily let out their lands and sell their goods. The Glastonbury monks have concealed and stolen so many Church ornaments and plates that a new abbey might be built with the value thereof. A man to whom the demesne of the monastery of Whitby was promised reports that the abbot has sold a part of his cattle and concluded several secret leases.[2] The worst case, as Cromwell's correspondents assures him, is one where the monastery would seem to have been stripped. The famous Layton, in July, 1538, took over the Berkshire monastery of Bisham ; he writes to Cromwell that only a few vestments, very few vessels and household utensils were left ; there were no cattle with the exception of a few milch kine, and no corn at all ; the abbot sold everything in London, and if only another year were given him no doubt he would sell the monastery itself with all the monastic lands.[3] If one may believe the informers (and we may do so to a considerable extent), the local population took whatever the monks had left. From the time that the latter signed the formal surrender, or rather from the time that they were convinced of the inevitableness of the end, all their concern for the safeguarding of the property had ceased. The neighbours then yielded to the natural wish to seize the unguarded property, and the poorer people especially were tempted to take part in the plunders of Dissolution. The Augmentations Court strove in every way to save the property which now belonged to the

[1] Gairdner, xiii, ii. 528, Freman to Cromwell, 3 Oct., 30 H. VIII ; ib. 726, Hercy to Cromwell, 31 Oct., 30 H. VIII.
[2] Gairdner, xiii, i. 332, Ryche to Cromwell, Feb., 29 H. VIII ; ib. 1343, Evance to Cromwell, July, 30 H. VIII ; xiii, ii. 352, Lyster to Cromwell ; xiv, ii. 232, Pollard, Moyle, and Layton to Cromwell ; xiv, i. 576, Jenny to Cromwell, March, 30 H. VIII.—Exactly the same kind of complaints had also been heard before at the wholesale suppression of small monasteries by the Act of 27 H. VIII, c. 28. For Marham, Blackborough, Shouldham, Crabhouse, vide Gairdner, x. 563, Rich. Southwell to Cromwell.
[3] Gairdner, xiii, i. 1239.

Crown. It ordered the monks to carry on the household vigorously and in the usual way up to the last day before the Suppression; it hastened to find a farmer or a bailiff for the demesne. In spite of all this, however, the inhabitants of the neighbourhood succeeded in obtaining monastic property, sometimes not without the friendly help of the monks. In January, 1538, three Augmentations officials complain to Cromwell that the monks and the inhabitants of the neighbourhood helped each other in the plunder of the monastic property.[1] In June, 1537, Pollard writes to Cromwell about the monastery of Bridlington that the greater part of the monastic stock had been taken by the poor people of the locality before he arrived, and scarcely anything remained to be sold. In December, 1538, the Bishop of Dover complained to Cromwell that at Lewes the buildings in which the monastic goods were stored were being broken into. A short time before, the visitor London had written to Cromwell saying that in Warwick only the well-to-do people had helped him to guard the monastic property, and that the poor people came from town and country night and day to carry away anything there was to take, as long as any doors, windows, iron, glass, lead remained: and he repeated his complaints a little later.[2]

In January, 1542, an inquisition was begun in the Augmentations Court concerning the plunder at the suppression of Hayles, a Gloucestershire abbey. A number of people confessed that they had carried off from the monastery or bought for next to nothing a variety of things, as glass, lead, locks, and wood-carving. One of the depositions is curious; the witness had received his story from a serving-woman. One evening some kind of locks were brought to her master from the monastery. She then reproached him: ' Why do you receive thus this stuff?' The master replied: ' Hold thy peace, for it is there now catch that may catch.'[3]

The monastic cattle had been gradually disappearing before

[1] Gairdner,xiii, i. 101-2, Layton, Southwell, and Lestraunge to Cromwell: ' What falsehood in the prior and convent, what bribery, spoil and ruin contrived by the inhabitants, it were long to write.'
[2] Gairdner, xii, ii. 92; xiii, ii. 1059; ib. 757 et xiv, i. 150.
[3] Gairdner xvii. 8.

the Dissolution, together with the rest of the stock. From a private letter at the end of the year 1538 we can see to how great an extent some of the monks were restricting their sheep-farming in consequence of the rumours of a dissolution ; this letter refers to Launde, a priory in Leicestershire. There had been on the demesne, together with Whatboro field, about two thousand sheep, but now not more than five hundred can be found, and half of these do not belong to the monks ; the Prior had kept on the commons of Loddington fields as many as five hundred sheep, but now there is not one. Neither is there now to be found a single sheep in Frisby, whereas there had been a whole flock ; in the last days before the Suppression the prior secretly took away several milk kine and a bull.[1]

For these reasons the inventories made after the Dissolution cannot be regarded as truly representing the normal monastic husbandry. In some places, of course, the monks duly managed their estates in the old way up to the very day of the surrender ; some out of fear of Cromwell's severity, and others in hope of a good pension. But often we find in the inventories only fragments, which for some reason were saved until the final cataclysm. Nevertheless, in spite of all this, the inventories are a valuable source of information ; they at all events give us a minimum estimate of the monastic household in the sixteenth century. If we have nothing else to rely upon except these inventories, we cannot establish the exact dimensions of the monastic demesne farming ; but we can affirm with tolerable certainty that they exceeded those indicated by the Suppression inventories. It is with reference to the monastic live stock in particular that the inventories become an important addition to the evidence of the Valor Ecclesiasticus ; they confirm the conclusion drawn from premises of a general character as to the casual nature of the V. E. descriptions. The inventories mention considerable flocks in those counties for which the Valor Ecclesiasticus gives no separate account whatever of sheep. Thus the nuns of the house of Sheppey in Kent—

Monastic cattle.

[1] Gairdner, xiii, ii. 1122, J. Smythe to F. Cave ; cf. Gasquet, ii. 284.

whose gross temporal income slightly exceeded a hundred pounds—appeared at the time of the suppression to have a very considerable number of cattle; they had 17 horses, 132 oxen, cows, bulls, and calves, 43 pigs, 2,325 sheep. The inventory contains some curious details; oxen are divided into 'country', and western (i. e. the breed from the western counties), lean and fat, workers and those sold for meat. The monastery followed the three-field system, and tilled about 50 a. in each field; oxen were used for work, but the inventory clearly indicates that horses also worked in the fields. However, sheep were of more importance in this monastery than cattle. The inventory proves that in spite of the high valuation of arable land in Kent, even a comparatively small monastery could have as many sheep as a large Dorsetshire house, and that the silence of the Valor Ecclesiasticus does not by any means prove that sheep-farming was not carried on.[1] As we have only a few instances before us, we cannot make any extensive generalizations; it is worth noting, however, that live stock of different kinds, with a much higher percentage of horned cattle, are found in some of the northern counties. The Suppressors found in March, 1537, on a grange of Whalley, in Lancashire, 84 head of horned cattle, 160 sheep, 10 pigs, 12 working horses.[2] On the demesne of Fountains, a large Yorkshire abbey, the horned cattle even exceeded the number of sheep: only 1,326 sheep of every kind are mentioned in the inventory, and 2,356 oxen, bulls, cows and calves.[3] The large number of horned cattle evidently depended upon the monastery having many

---

[1] Exch. Treas. Rec. M. b. v. 154, f. 84 *dorso* (Inventorye of Sheppey taken on 27 March, 27 H. VIII).—The nuns in *Catesby*, Northts., had at the suppression 1,124 sheep, valued at £200, and 110 cows, bulls, and oxen worth £96 (St. Pap. Dom., Suppr. Pap. v. 3 f. 68).

[2] Ib. f. 75 dorso: 'The graunge 50 draughte oxen, 6 steris of 4 yeres, 8 steris of 3 yeres, 12 steris of one yere, 80 ewes, 80 hoggeshepe, 10 swyne, 12 horses for the ploughe and carte.'

[3] Burton, ff. 143–7. 'Horned cattle: bulls 49, oxen 536, cows 738, heffers 151, young steers 151, bovicali or young whys 142, stirketts 242, calves 347. Sheep: hurts 50, multones 421, ewes 535, hogs 320. Pigs: boars 5, swine 9, porci 18, porculi 18, suckling pigs 30. Horses: emissarii 5, equi ad stabulum abbatis 6, equi ad bigam 6, equae 37, equi unius anni et dimidii 4, fillies unius anni et dimidii 11, pulli 17.'

granges and a considerable corn-growing area, for which much manure and working power were needed ; a large number of cows indicates that the monks managed a large dairy farm.[1]

But other monasteries proved to be in possession of much fewer cattle at the time of the Suppression.[2] The monastery of Merevale, Staff., had cattle in three places : 10 working horses, 12 working oxen, 9 cows and a bull, 80 sheep, 14 pigs and a boar. The very small monastery of Brewood had only one horse and that was probably a very inferior one, for it was valued at 4s. only. The abbey of Lilleshall, Salop, had cattle in two places : 18 oxen, 25 cows,

[1] In innumerable sixteenth-century complaints about conversions and enclosures, much is said about sheep which ' are eating up people '. Much less attention is paid to cows. Conversions for the enlargement of dairies however were possible, for there existed large dairies working with a view to the foreign market. In the Patent Rolls of Henry VIII we not infrequently come across permissions to export cheese. In 1534 a curious complaint was made to Parliament about the high prices and the exportation of butter and cheese ; on the continent victuals are cheaper than in England ; the exportation of cattle ought to be entirely forbidden, and also the exportation of victuals when prices exceed a certain level. ' Such (that in) yeres past have kept their landes in tillage . . . do put away their tillers and servants to convert their grounds arrable into several . . . and make dayry houses, trustyng yet that the same restraint (measures against exportation) shall not be enforced, that the said butter and cheese and other vitalls by such unlawful engrosyng and carying of the same over the sea shall shortly be inhanced to hye and unreasonable prices' (Gairdner, vii. 58). The Statute of 25 H. VIII, c. 2, is probably an answer to the petition. We can infer with considerable probability that dairy farms were not rare in the North. In the demesne inventories of Durham Priory for 1464, horned cattle were of great importance in many manors (Surtees Soc., lviii. 118, 120, 186–91, 207–8). In the hundred of Clitheroe in Lancashire large allotments of land are called in the sixteenth century ' vaccariae ' (Farrer, 294–8). When at the beginning of the seventeenth century Norden speaks of cattle in the northern counties, he mentions the cows first, then the horses, and last of all the sheep (Norden, 107–8, article 24). From the letter of the Mayor of Kingston-upon-Hull to Cromwell, we see that there were many dairies in this town, and that a great income was derived from butter (Gairdner, xiii, i. 1026, May, 30 H. VIII). Of course dairy farms existed not only in the North ; in the third decade of the century a large quantity of butter and cheese was exported to Flanders from Norfolk and Suffolk ; Brewer, iv. 3649.

[2] Exch. Augm. O. Misc. b. v. 172. The inventories were drawn up in 30 H. VIII by two commissioners, ' Th. Ligh doctor in the lawe and W. Cavendishe auditor.' Nearly all the monasteries are situated in the central counties. I take the monasteries in the order in which they are placed in the book.

and two bulls, 23 calves, 40 sheep and 25 pigs. The priory
of St. Thomas, Stafford, had cattle in two granges : 24 oxen,
9 cows, 8 calves, 5 horses, 15 pigs, 6 'wynter bests'(?), 210
sheep. The abbey of Dieulacres, Staff., had 6 oxen, 3 horses,
13 pigs, 60 sheep. The monastery of Darley, Derb., had
cattle in two places : 38 oxen that were harnessed in pairs,
10 cows, 9 horses, 52 pigs and 60 sheep. The monastery of
Dale, Derb., kept its cattle in three places : 16 oxen, 11 cows,
15 bullocks, calves worth £1 6s. 8d., horses worth £1 6s. 8d.,
27 pigs, sheep worth £3 13s. 4d. The monastery of Repton,
Derb., is said to have only 3 cows and 10 horses. The priory
of Grace Dieu, Leic., had cattle in two places : 24 oxen, 18 cows,
and two bulls, 18 calves, 11 horses with a foal, 63 pigs, 24 bee-
hives ; there is no mention of sheep. The abbey of Pipewell
possessed 6 oxen, 39 cows and a bull, 100 calves, 280 sheep,
30 'great hogges', 40 'small stores'. The urban monastery
of Barnwell, Camb., evidently had no sheep at all. In all
the inventories not only the number of cattle but also the
price for which they were sold is indicated.[1] In three
Huntingdonshire inventories there is given only the valuation

---

[1] The sale prices of the inventories are on the whole much lower than
the prices of cattle given in Rogers's table for the corresponding period
(Rogers, iii. 172 sqq., Conclusions, iv. 331 sqq.). The low level of prices
in the inventories may be attributed to various causes. It was much
easier for the monks to sell the best kind of cattle ; the cattle that were
left were probably not tended with much care before the surrender ;
probably only the cattle of an inferior kind are found in the inventories.
If a large sale takes place in a small market prices inevitably fall. Besides,
the Suppressors often sold the whole stock to the person into whose
hands the demesne had passed. It is, of course, possible also that the
Suppressors may have been unfair in their valuation of the stock ; though
I have not found any place where this was evidently the case. The
relative prices of cows, sheep and pigs of different sex and age are almost
the same in the inventories and in Rogers's tables ; but there is a great
difference in the prices of horses. In the inventories they are as a rule
cheaper than cows, and their average price does not amount even to 10s. ;
in Rogers's tables horses are generally much more expensive than cows.
Nearly all the evidence collected by Rogers is derived from a one-sided
source, as he himself points out (iv. 214, 331, 335), that is, from the prices
for good cattle given by rich purchasers. This is especially so with regard
to horses ; in Rogers's tables riding-horses are most numerous, and those
often of a very high quality, whilst the monasteries at the time of suppression had only draught-horses. In Rogers's tables the price of a draught-
horse differs considerably from that of a good riding one. Under 1531-2 are
mentioned the prices paid in Durham ; £0 17s. 0d., £8 16s. 0d., £1 0s. 0d.
Under 1538-9 the prices vary from £1 6s. 8d. to £5.

of the cattle found in the monasteries at the time of the
Suppression. All the cattle in Huntingdon are valued at
£58 5s. 8d., those in Sawtre at £84 12s. 4d., those in Stonely
at £17 5s. 0d.[1]

In these same inventories we find some curious information Stores of
as to the stores of grain preserved by the monasteries. From corn.
these alone it is difficult to judge of the extent of the monastic
demesne farming, for before the surrender the grain stores
would be diminished by theft or by secret sales; and also
owing to the inventories having been drawn up at different
times of the agricultural year, when part of the grain
might have been bought. But the figures of the inventories do enable us to form an opinion about the relative
importance of the different kinds of corn in demesne
farming, and in the diet of the monastic population.
Besides corn, the inventories also mention the stock of hay.[2]
Grain is given in quarters and the prices in shillings and
pence.

[1] Cleop. E. iv. 336-40, 'certyfycate of J. Goodryk, W. Legh, Th Comber
comyssyoners.'

[2] I have not included in the list below some kinds of corn which are
very rare in the Suppression inventories. 1. Merevale, '12 strykes
myskelen worth 4s., 2 strykes pese and barley.' A stryke is a bushel
(Rogers, iv. 207). Myskelen is a mixture of rye and wheat (New Ox.
Dict., s.v. maslin). It is very strange that its price is so low here.
2. Brewood, 1 qr. of munkecorn worth 8s. (New Ox. Dict., s.v. mongcorn).
3. St. Thomas's, Stafford, 11 qrs. of 'rye and monkecorne', at 6s. 8d.
4. Lilleshall, 10 qrs. of dredge, at 3s.

Monastery.	Wheat.	Rye.		Wheat and Rye.	Barley.
	qrs. s. d.	qrs.	£ s. d.	qrs. s. d.	qrs. s. d.
Fountains	135	30			90
Sheppey St. Sexb. ...	2¼				3
Merevale	60 at 5 8 and 20 at 6 8	4 at	7 0	20 at 5 0	60 at 3 4
Brewood	1 at 6 2				
Lilleshall		14 at	6 8		20 at 4 0
Stafford St. Thomas	3 at 7 0	12 at	6 8		44 at 3 4
Dale...	3 at 8 0	5 at	7 0		11 at 4 0
Dieulacres		10½ bz. = 1	1 0		90 at 4 4
Darley				7 at 8 0 and 4 at 7 0	
Repton	1 at 8 0	2 at	7 0		15 at 4 0
Grace Dieu	22 at 6 0	4 at	6 0		64 at 3 4
Pipewell	6 at 4 6	6 at	4 0		55 at 2 4

Continued on next page.

The table given in the note suggests interesting conclusions. Thus, the stores of barley were the largest: the totals of the entries of the table show that there was more barley than wheat and rye taken together. The malt given in the list is also chiefly barley malt; in Sheppey only were there 20 qrs. of wheat malt. There was much less rye than wheat, nevertheless there was a considerable amount of it, and of course in the monasteries they ate not only wheaten but also rye bread. There was much less oats than barley; and the smallness of the corn stores of St. Sexburge, Sheppey, agrees with the figures of the crops in the inventory of the same place, where we find 36 acres of barley and only 7 of oats. The abundance of peas—in the figures of which beans are probably included—attracts our special attention.

Bread of the Tudor age. It will help to make the meaning of the table more clear, if we compare it with other evidence concerning the food of the people in the time of the Tudors. Rogers expressed the opinion that the consumption of rye much decreased in the sixteenth century and even in the fifteenth century. But his prices of corn, like his prices of cattle, are derived from a one-sided source; they are the sale prices of rich corporations who did not find it necessary to buy much rye.[1] England under Henry VIII, and even under

Monastery.	Malt.	Oats.		Peas.		Loads of hay.
	qrs. s. d.	*qrs.*	*s. d.*	*qrs.*	*s. d.*	*£ s. d.*
Fountains		136				392
Sheppey St. Sexb....	36	2				160
Merevale	12 at 6 8			12 at	4 0	50 at 3 4
Brewood		1 at	1 8	1 at	2 8	10 at 1 6
Lilleshall				10 at	6 8	30 at 2 0
Stafford, St. Thomas		10 at	2 8			32 at 2 0
		3 at	1 4			
Dale	6 at 4 0	159 bz. =		9 at	4 0	16 at 2 0
		£11 19 0				
Dieulacres... ...				12 at	4 0	29 = 3 0 0
				7 at	2 8	
Darley				6 at	4 0	50 at 2 0
Repton	4 at 5 0			rick for		10 at 2 8
				£4 0 0		
Grace Dieu ...		28 at	2 4	47 at	2 8	72 at 2 8
Pipewell	10 at 2 8			30 at	3 0	for £2 13 4

[1] Rogers, iv. 219. Rogers himself points out the one-sidedness of his evidence (iv. 213), although he scarcely appreciates the importance of this fact.

Elizabeth, could not be called the happy land of white bread. In the North of England during the sixteenth century rye was used in the army in almost the same quantity as wheat.[1] It is true that in the Patent Rolls of Henry VIII hardly any licences to export rye are found, while there are many licences for the exportation of wheat, barley, and malt. But rye was imported into England. If we may take the figures of 1596 as a criterion, then at the end of the sixteenth century much more rye than wheat was imported into London.[2] Rye however was also sown in England in the time of the Tudors. When Fitzherbert speaks of winter crops he mentions wheat and rye together; Tusser also often mentions rye. Even at the beginning of the seventeenth century rye held an important place in the treatise of Markham, although he decidedly prefers wheat to rye.[3] In the sixteenth, and even in the seventeenth century, white bread was the bread of the rich, or at least of the well-to-do people. Even rye bread was not

---

[1] Dasent, i. 360. Two London merchants take a Crown contract to supply 2,000 quarters of rye in Berwick and Newcastle, March, 1546. Dasent, i. 548: For the army at Berwick were appointed—490 barrels of wheat in flour and 592½ qrs. in grain, 55 barrels of rye in flour and 67 qrs. in grain, 422 qrs. of beans, 2,801 qrs. of hops, 1,546½ qrs. of malt, Nov., 1546. Dasent, viii. 351: In March, 1575, it was permitted to bring from Lynne to Berwick 1,000 qrs. of wheat, 1,000 of rye, and 500 qrs. of malt.

[2] The following is one of the rare permissions to export rye: Brewer, iii. 3,062, '1 license to the inhabitants of Harwich to export 80 qrs. of wheat and 120 qrs. rye' (15 H. VIII). The statistics of corn imported into the port of London from Mich. to Dec. 31, 1596, State Pap. Dom., Eliz., v. 261, n. 3: the English imported from abroad 14,375 qrs. of wheat and 22,180 qrs. of rye, the foreigners 2,881 of wheat and 3,985 of rye.

[3] Fitzherbert, Husb., 17, 18: Tusser, passim; Markham, Husb., passim, concerning the superiority of wheat, ch. viii. H: 'Wheate being a richer grain than rye, it is a small husbandrie to sow more rye or maslin than for your house, if you be assured that your ground will beare wheate well.' When in 1542 the king complains of the increase of corn prices, he singles out wheat and rye as an especially clear example (Proclamation concernynge corne, quoted by Cunningham, i⁴. 543), and supposes that a great quantity of rye is being sown. In Whalley and Worksop the monks give rye bread to the poor, V. E. v. 230, 176; and also in Coventry Charterhouse, iii. 54. In Kenilworth, Warw. (iii. 66), and Fountains, Yorks. (v. 254), the bread for the poor is 'ex frumento et siligine'. But wheat bread is more often mentioned in the V. E. in connexion with the common doles. 'Panis albus' is mentioned in the survey of Bridlington and Thurgarton (v. 121, 152).

accessible to all, for rye approached wheat in price. True, in Bury, in 1589, rye bread was given even in a house of correction,[1] but when Tusser praises the advantages of several over champion, he says among other things that only in the several places do they bake wheat, mastlin and rye bread, and in the open country they have to confine themselves to bean bread. According to Harrison it is only the rich who eat white bread, and their households eat rye and barley bread, and in time of scarcity oats, peas and bean bread; the peasants eat barley and oat bread, the artisans and poor workmen always eat horse food—oats, peas, beans and lentils. Norden, who travelled all over England, tells us that at the beginning of the seventeenth century in out-of-the-world localities the cottagers live on oaten bread, sour milk and goats' milk. Another witness, a very trustworthy one at the beginning of the seventeenth century, the agriculturist Markham, says that in Leicestershire, Lincolnshire, Nottinghamshire and many other counties they eat bread made of peas. In his guide-book for housewives, he advises them to feed only their own families on wheat bread; the servants ought to have 'brown' bread made from a mixture of barley, peas, wheat or rye and malt.[2] In the year of

---

[1] Regulations of a house of correction at Bury in 1589 (Eden, iii, app. vii).

[2] Tusser, 62, 23, 'the tone is commended for grain: yet breade made of beanes they doo eate;—the tother for one loafe have twaine—of mastlin, or of rie or of wheate.' Harrison, i. 153, 258–9; Norden, 106–7, art. 22; Markham, Husb., Ch. 7 F: 'people eat lentils also.' Markham, Houswife, 125–8: 'Your best cheat bread is also of wheat only. . . . For your *browne* bread or bread for your hinde servants which is the coursest bread for mans use, you shall take of barley two bushels, of peas 2 pecks, of wheat or rie a peck, a peck of mault.' Markham gives some curious information about the kinds of flour, *ib.*: (*a*) simple—rye, wheat, (*b*) mixed—rye and wheat, rye, wheat and barley, rye and barley. Mixed bread is characteristic both of the cooking and the agriculture of the period. The mixtures had their technical names, for instance, Markham, Husb., 26, 'mastlin is blend corn, wheat and rye mixed together.' Cf. V. E. iii. 287, 'panis de 25 quart' mixtelionis.' Rye used to be mixed with wheat not only for baking but also for seed (Tusser, 16, 11 and 15, 12–13). Tusser, however, does not approve of such a mixture. Markham, on the contrary, advises the sowing of peas and beans together: if one does not succeed the other will certainly grow (Markham, Husb., ch. 5, c. 3). Several kinds of such mixed corn are given in the monastic inventories: wheat and rye, pese and barley, dredge. I think that the rye and the munkencorn

scarcity, 1622–3, the Privy Council limited the production of barley malt because barley was needed for the poor people's bread.[1] In the year of scarcity 1630–1, in Norfolk, it was not so much wheat and rye as barley that was sold to the poor at a diminished price.[2]

It remains to consider the monastic income from the woods. I have already given the amount of this according to the V. E., for the monasteries in the surveys of which the wood and the demesne receipts are given separately (pp. 144–145). The income from woods of the forty-one monasteries of that list was found to be about $2\frac{1}{2}$ % of the temporal income from land. But not infrequently the Valor Ecclesiasticus gives the amount of the income from woods also for those monasteries in whose surveys the receipts from the demesne in hand arc not clearly distinguished.[3] Let us examine the cases of this latter kind. The figure signifies the amount of the income from woods.

Income from woods in the V. E.

Beds.			£	s.	d.				£	s.	d.
Beds.	Elstow ...	...	10	0	0	Norfolk	Norwich Cath....		8	6	8
	Newnham	...	4	12	0		Wendling	...	0	6	8
	Warden ...	...	23	4	0	Somerset	Bath	...	4	6	8
Cornwall	Bodmin ...	...	3	0	0		Glastonbury	...	70	18	3½
	Launceston	...	4	0	0	Suffolk	Ixworth	...	0	10	0
Hereford	Aconbury	...	4	0	0	Surrey	Bermondsey	...	8	19	0
Hunts.	Huntingdon	...	1	3	4	Worc.	Bordesley	...	13	6	8
	Ramsey ...	...	43	16	4		Evesham	...	14	18	4
Kent	Malling ...	...	19	6	0		Pershore	...	13	0	0
Linc.	Louth Park	...	4	13	4		Westwood	...	13	6	8
Midd.	London St. Barth.		6	13	0		Worcester Cath.		12	1	8
Norfolk	Horsham	...	20	0	0	Yorks.	Selby ...	...	8	0	0
	Hulme ...	...	10	19	4						

in the inventory of St. Thomas, Stafford, is also some such kind of mixture.

[1] Proclamation: 'barley is in time of scarcitie the bread corne of the poor,' St. Pap. Dom. Jas. I, v. 133, n. 52, quoted by Miss Leonard, 145 (Early Poor Relief).

[2] Leonard, 188–91, Norwich Court books: '6 March, 1631, the corn delivered to the poor to be two parts barley, one wheat and one rye.' St. Pap. Dom. Car. I, v. 192, n. 19: 'for the most part in every towne throughout the hundreds of W. and E. Flegg, Happing, Tunstead, a sufficient quantity of barley and buck is set aside to be issued to ye poor at a reasonable rate.'

[3] In many of the Devonshire and Warwickshire surveys the income from woods is mentioned, but joined in one general total with the curial income; for instance, Kenilworth, Warw., 'et de £1 13s. 4d. de vendicione boscorum perquisitis curie et aliis exitibus et proficuis casualibus.'

The income from woods for all the 25 monasteries of the list amounts to £323 7s. 11½d., and the gross temporal income is a little more than £13,500. If we deduct from the gross temporal income one-sixth for the urban and non-landed revenue, about £11,250 will remain. The income from woods constitutes about 2·9 % of this remainder; it is somewhat higher than that in the first list, but the difference between the two lists is very small. If we suppose that in the other monastic households the income from woods was the same, then the total income from woods of all the monasteries would be from two and a half to three thousand pounds.

This figure must be regarded with suspicion, not only because it is arrived at from the consideration of a minority only of the monasteries, but because the Commissioners of 1535 used different methods when defining the income from woods of various monasteries. Sometimes they omitted the wood used in the monastery itself; sometimes they valued all the woodland products brought into the monastic household: so that the monks paid the Tenth on all the fuel, brushwood and timber used for internal needs of the house and did not yield one penny of income to the monks. When it is not stated in the survey whether the wood for the monks' own use is included in the total of the income from woods, the reader of the V. E. does not know whether he has before him the whole of the woodland receipts of a given year or only that part which was derived from sales.[1]

Sometimes the Valor Ecclesiasticus gives also, besides the amount of the income from woods, the acreage of all monastic

---

[1] Louth Park, iv. 57: 'et etiam 4 a. bosci prostrati annuatim infra precinctum monasterii ad usum abbathie que valent inter se £4 13s. 4d. per estim' coibus annis.'   Hulme, Norf., iii. 341: 'in bosco expendito in hospicio de crescencia infra monast' coibus annis £10 19s. 4d.'   In the survey of Christchurch, Canterbury, the wood brings in no income at Addysham, Ikham, Amery Court, Copton, Appuldore, Ebbeney, Rokynge, Holyngborn, Myltonhall, Stysted, Panfield, Borelygh, Illygh; the usual formula is—'de vendicione boscorum ibm. nichill quia reservantur pro focali manerii'.   Cf. Worcester Cathedral, iii. 221: 'manerium de Wolverley in proficuis boscorum nichill quia reservantur ad usum focali mon'.' Middleton, man' de Myddelton, i. 249: 'in bosc' expendit' infra hospicium abbatis £1 13s. 4d.; man' de Stykelane, i. 250, in vendicione bosci £2. 2s. 2d.'   Horsham, Norf., iii. 365: 'in bosco tam vendito quam expendito in hospicio prioratus £20 0s. 0d.'

woods or of a part of them; in that case it is possible to judge
of the quantity and value of the land occupied by woods.
The income from the wood land is defined in different ways:
The surveyor most frequently divides the yearly revenue from
woods by the number of acres of all the monastic woods, and
so gets the average income of an acre of wood. But sometimes the small part of the whole wooded area which was
to be felled is singled out in the accounts for the year and the
woodland receipt is divided by the number of acres felled;
and, of course, under this proceeding the income of each acre
of wood is very high.[1]

When the income from woods is distributed over the whole
of the woodland area, we find that the woods of some Northamptonshire houses appear to be the most profitable. 284 acres
belonging to Peterborough are valued at 2s. an acre, 471 acres
at 20d., 51 acres at 18d., 3 acres at 16d.; but for the large
Fiskerton wood an income of only £41 1s. 6½d. is shown.
The monastery of Pipewell is said to have 84 acres bringing
in an income of 20d. per acre, and Fineshade 120 acres also
at 20d. per acre. We more often find the income from woods
of 1s. an acre. In the case of the two richest monasteries in
Middlesex only part of the wood was measured in acres.
St. Peter's, Westminster, has 445 acres, St. John of
Jerusalem, London, 232 acres, and all this woodland seems
to bring in 1s. an acre. In the case of three monasteries in
Middlesex the area of all the woods mentioned in the survey
is given: Clerkenwell 24 a., St. Thomas Acon 111 a., St. Mary
Graces 388 a.; all this woodland seems to bring 1s. an acre.
The Valor Ecclesiasticus gives the same income from the
woods of three monasteries in Surrey, and two in Beds.;
and the area is also shown for all the woods mentioned in
the survey: St. Mary Overey 111 a., Bermondsey 179 a.,

---

[1] The excerpts given above from the survey of Louth Park, Linc., may
serve as an example of a case where the whole wooded area of a monastery
is not given, but only that part of it which must be felled in the course of
the year. No doubt we have a similar case in the survey of Kirkstead,
Linc., iv. 34: 'in boscis coibus annis 5 acres ad annuum valorem £13 6s. 8d.'
An income of £2 13s. 4d. falls to each acre. When the income from
woods is distributed in the Val. Eccl. among the whole wooded area, it is
never more than 2s. per acre.

Chertsey 427 a., Caldwell 70 a, Elstow 200 a. A still lower valuation of the income from woods is found in a few cases in small areas only, and it may be explained by the fact that it refers to undergrowth or shrubs.

Woods in the later surveys.   The scanty evidence of the V. E. concerning the management of the woods must be supplemented from other sources. At the time of the Suppression it was the duty of the Commissioners and Suppressors to describe the woods as well as other demesne lands. The Suppression Accounts therefore contain some information as to the area, age and value of the monastic woods. The Augmentations Court appointed special officials to manage the woods; and this specialization of the forestry would seem to furnish a reason for the fact that the Paper Surveys give less attention to the woods than to the arable land, meadow and pasture; yet in them, also, there is to be found some valuable information about the monastic woods. The Glastonbury survey of Pollard and Moyle even gives the turn in which the various portions of the wood were felled, and this information may be compared with the evidence of the Glastonbury terrier of 1518. When woods that used to be monastic passed again into private hands the forester put in charge was required to give an account of the value of the woods on these lands, and this account was added to the other official records of the alienation in the so-called ' Particulars for Grants '. Thus the latter contain also some information about the monastic woods.

I begin with the Suppression Accounts of seven Leicestershire monasteries, ten in Warwickshire and one in Rutland.[1] *Bradley* : ½ a. of wood more than 20 years old, 5½ a. of wood more than 12 years old.—*Olveston* : 19 a. of wood 5 years old, not very valuable ; 203 a. of good young wood with oaks from 50 to 60 years old, valued at £305 6s. 8d. ; this is evidently the price that the Crown would ask for the wood if sold to be cut. On the commons there was wood worth £24.—*Kirby Beller* : On the demesne in different places there is wood worth £20, and in the fields underwood

[1] Exch. Treas. Rec. M. b. v. 154.

worth £4.—*Ulverscroft*: On the demesne the wood is scattered and worth £23. There are 10 a. of thick wood one
year old, 42 a. 30 years old and more, 170 a. of 50 years old
and more, 30 a. of 80 years old and more, 207 a. of 100 years
and more. All this wood is valued at £745.—*Garendon*: On
the demesne there is scattered wood worth £25. There are
10½ a. of thick wood less than 20 years old, 2¼ a. of 50 years
and more, 536 a. of 100 years and more; the whole of this
wood is valued at £649 13s. 4d.—*Grace Dieu*: 20¾ a. of
wood 7 years old and less, 15 a. 30–50 years old, 15 a.
50–80 years, 56 a. 80–100 years, and 89 a. of 100 years and
more; the whole of this wood is valued at £79.—*Langley*:
29 a. of wood of 12 years and less, 11½ a. of 30 years, 43 a.
60–80 years, 11½ a. 80–100 years, 20 a. of 100 years and
more; the whole of this wood is valued at £96 13s. 4d.—
Pollesworth: 108 a. of wood about 100 years old, together
with the trees scattered over the demesne are valued at
£114 10s. 0d.—*Maxstoke*: There are in the park 6 a. of wood,
30 years old and less, worth £2; 94 a. of 100 years and more,
worth £62 13s. 4d. In the parish of Maxstoke there are
86½ a. of wood, 12 years old and less, worth the sum of
£20 13s. 0d. On the demesne there are scattered trees worth
£1.—*Henwood*: 14 a. of wood 80 years old(?), worth, if
sold at 16 years' growth, £2 6s. 8d.; 16 a. of wood 16 years
old, already sold by the monks for £3 6s. 8d.; 30 a. of
100 years and more, valued at £30. The trees scattered on
the demesne are worth £1.—*Charterhouse, Coventry*: 6 a. of
wood 7 years old, worth £3 6s. 8d. if sold at 16 years' growth;
1½ a. 3 years old, worth £0 13s. 4d. if sold at 16 years' growth.—
Pinley: there is no wood except that growing on the demesne
and the copyhold.—*Stoneleigh*: 328 a. of wood 8 years old and
less, which will be worth £108 6s. 8d. if sold at 14 years' growth.
There are 60 a. of wood 14 years old, worth £15 16s. 8d.;
160 a. of wood 100 years old and more, worth £160.—
St. Sepulchre's, Warwick: 2 a. of wood 60 years old, worth
£2; 1½ a. of wood 7 years old, worth 10s.—*Wroxall*: 22 a. of
wood 7 years old and less, which will be worth £56 13s. 4d.
if sold at 20 years; 72 a. of wood 100 years old, worth £79 6s. 8d.

The wood on the demesne and waste is worth £26 13s. 4d.—
Studley : 46 a. of 6 years and less ; at 14 years' growth it will
be worth £23 0s. cd. ; 21 a. of wood 10 years old, worth
£12 13s. 4d. ; 1¼ a. of 16 years old, worth £0 12s. 6d. ; 28½ a.
of 20 years, worth £18 10s. 0d. ; 27 a. of 60 years, worth
£27.—*Broke* : 20 a. of 7 years and less ; 208 a. of very old
wood, about 200 years, but it has no good timber.

Less detailed is the information about woods in the Suppression Accounts of several Sussex monasteries. The whole
of the wood is stated to be more that 20 years old. Tortington,
60 a. at 13s. 4d. ; Boxgrove, 60 a. at 10s. ; Hastings, 100 a. at
3s. 4d. ; Michelham, 80 a. at 13s. 4d. ; Shulbrede, 100 a.[1] The
monastery of Buckenham in Norfolk was found at the time
of the Suppression to be in possession of 111 a. of wood ; 100 a.
were valued at £2 an acre, 5 a. of 20 years old were valued at
£6 13s. 4d. ; 6 a. of unknown age were valued at £26 13s. 4d.,
i. e. at £4 8s. 6⅔d. an acre.[2] The priory of Huntingdon,
according to the Suppression Account, had no wood. The
monastery of Sawtre had 422 a. of wood, and the revenue of
an acre was valued by the tenants at 1s.[3]

Information concerning woods is very rare in the Paper
Surveys (Sulby, Westwood, Coverham, Bushmead, Lavenden) ;
the figures of landed area given there are small, and we cannot
be certain that they indicate all the monastic wood. But in
the rental of Kirkstead, Linc., the area and age of each allotment of monastic woods are given, as well as the gèneral
income from all the wood. Eleven allotments contain 419 a.

---

[1] State Pap. Dom., Suppr. Pap. v. 3, n. 128.
[2] ib., ff. 20–21. I found a higher valuation only in Pollard and
Moyle's survey of Glastonbury, in which 60 a. of timber are valued at
£290 10s. 0d. Thorold Rogers says (iv. 369) that in 1540 and 1542 he
came across wood-sales in which the price of an acre went up to £5 6s. 8d. ;
but he gives neither the place nor his authority. These cases do not
appear in his table. In the tables (Fuel, iii. 255–77) there are altogether
very few cases of wood-sales for felling ; for 1500–1582 three cases only
(1500, 1503, 1560).
[3] Cleop. E. iv. 336–40, Entry for Huntingdon : ' woods none saving
trees growing about the hows for the defens of the same hows.' In the
Suppression Accounts for Notts. and Yorks., 30 H. VIII (Cleop. E. iv.
f. 357–8), only the number of acres is given : Worksop 112, Monkbretton
168 and 400 oaks, St. Andrew, York, nothing. Bellalaund 274, Rievaulx
341, Kirkham 146, Ellerton 9.

of wood from one to a hundred years old; the yearly income from the wood is £20, i.e. a little less than a shilling an acre.[1] In the Paper Surveys for Sewardesley it is stated that 80 a. of undergrowth are divided into 7 allotments, and that each year one of them is felled and the average income derived from this is £2. In the Paper Surveys for Ashby it is explained that the demesne wood is sufficient for the needs of the local tenants only.[2]

The Particulars for Grants describe chiefly the land which was in the hands of the farmers and tenants, and we get from them an idea as to the woodland of those manors on which it was not included in the demesne *in manu*. Not infrequently we come across an indication that there is no wood to be sold, and that there is hardly wood enough for ' housebote, hedgebote, firebote, ploughbote, cartebote ', for the tenants or the demesne farmer.[3] Sometimes the wood is divided into two parts, one of which is to supply the needs of the local inhabitants and is therefore not valued ; in such cases the Particulars for Grants, when describing the wood do not indicate its area in acres but give the number, kind and age of the trees. It is possible that this was done when a manor had only copses, hedges and separate trees. The monastery of Tewkesbury had a manor, Leigh, in Wiltshire, the net income of which was valued at £22. It seems that on the manor were found 2,200 oaks and 100 elms, 60 and 40 years old. Of these 700 were left to the farmer of the manor of Asheton Keynes, which was joined to the manor of Leigh for the *visus franci plegii* ; among them 500 were for firebote and 200 for housebote ; these were not valued at the sale. The remaining 1,500 trees are valued :

[1] Harl. 144, f. 47 dorso.

[2] Sewardesley, Exch. Augm. O. M. b. 399. 236: 'de valore 80 a. subbosci in Nunewodd al' Henwodd qui dividitur in 7 copic' qualibet copicea ad finem 7 annorum ultra custum' claus' et sepin' eorundem tam per visum comiss' decime (but in the V. E. nothing is said about the wood), quam per visum comiss' dni regis nunc et sic dict' boscus valet coib' annis vendend' £2.'—Ashby, ib., 399. 246.

[3] Part. for Grants, n. 1085, m. 2: 'Landes in Marsche Chappell and Markholme, Linc., parcell of the poss' of the late priorye of Nunormesbye. The trees growing in the hedges about the sayd landes wyll barelye suffice for stakes for hedgeboote to repayre and meynteyne the sayd hedges and fences therefore not valued.' Cf. Part. for Grants, n. 995, m. 4, n. 129, mm. 11–14.

500 trees at 2*d*., 500 at 4*d*., 500 at 8*d*.[1] The monastery of
Shaftesbury had a manor in Wiltshire, Lyddyngton, the net
income of which was valued at £39 14*s*. 11½*d*. This manor
had 300 oaks and elms 60 and 80 years old ; only 60 trees are
valued at 6*d*., the remaining 240 are to be used for housebote,
ploughbote, cartbote by the farmers of the demesne in accordance with the agreements and by the tenants under the local
custom.[2] Sometimes only the wood that has been valued
is mentioned ; for instance, 230 ash trees at 1*s*. on the demesne
of the manor of Wykeham, that belonged to the monastery of
Spalding.[3] In some of the Particulars for Grants, the reckon-
ings both according to acres and by the number of trees are
found side by side. In 37 H. VIII the king exchanged some
lands with the Earl of Bath ; the king gave to the earl three
manors that used to belong to the monastery of Dunkeswell ;
in two of them the wood is counted by trees, and in the third
by acres.[4]

Upon the whole we must confess that the management
of the woods in the sixteenth century to a great extent
remains unexplained. The *perpetual turn* was very well
known ; the wood being divided into sections, and one section,
the oldest, being sold each year. But the age at which the
trees were sold would seem to be very young according
to our notions. The authorities say that a wood is divided
into 20, 16 and 14 sections, even if it consists of the slow-
growing oak. It is not quite clear how with such an arrangement, trees of 100 or even 200 years old could be preserved.
The separate treatment of timber is worthy of notice, but
it is not always clear whether timber means trees grown in
forest, or merely the larger trees among smaller wood or in
the meadows, fields and pastures. This point, however, is
also obscure with regard to the young wood. Perhaps the

---

[1] Part. for Grants, n. 995, mm. 6–8, 37 H. VIII.
[2] Part. for Grants, n. 994, mm. 2, 10. Cf. ib., n. 54, m. 3 ; n. 217, m. 3.
[3] Part. for Grants, n. 546, m. 1.
[4] Part. for Grants, n. 102, mm. 8–9. The reckoning by trees is followed
in the manors of Hackpen and Shelden, by acres in the manor of Boleham.
The wood is reckoned by acres only in the Part. for Grants, n. 102, m. 5,
and n. 129, m. 4.

great differences in the valuation may to some extent be explained by differences in density. From the Glastonbury terrier of 1518 we are able to judge of the distribution of a wood into allotments on several manors of the abbey. In Netylton there were 36 a. of wood of which 5 a. may be sold annually at 6s. 8d. an acre ; the wood therefore is divided into 7 allotments and is sold very young. In Kyngton there are 400 a. of wood divided into 16 allotments, and the income from an allotment 16 years old is valued at 13s. 4d. per acre.[1] In Crist-Malford there are 361½ a. of wood consisting of oak and ash ; under proper management 20 a. may be sold yearly at 10s. per acre. In Ayshbury out of 275 acres of oak and ash 36 a. may be sold every third year at 18s. an acre ; the wood is clearly divided into 24 allotments. In Domerham there are 441 a. of wood in 5 places; the area of wood was defined by measurement and not by inspection ; the wood according to local custom was measured by the 18-foot perch, and the arable land, meadow, and pasture by the 15-foot perch. Under proper management in Domerham 20 a. of wood 20 years old might be sold annually at £1 an acre.[2]

According to Pollard and Moyle's survey, the woods on the manor of Glastonbury were managed in a somewhat different way.[3] The manor had three parks : Norwood, Wirrall, and Sharpham. In Norwood, 172 a. of wood 20 years old are mentioned, valued at £1 an acre ; if we are to take the entry literally, then the whole wood was of the same age. But

---

[1] 'Kyngton. Est ibm quidam boscus voc' Haywode cont' 400 a. bosci et subbosci ubi vendi possint quolibet anno 25 a. subbosci si copis' bene preservetur et supervideatur precio acre £0 13s. 4d. et sic qualibet copis' recrescet in 16 annis.'

[2] 'Domerham. In boscis predictis vendi possint quolibet anno 20 a. in copisiis ibm. de subbosco ex etate crescencie 20 annorum ultra clausur' copis' pdc' alloc' q' val' singulis annis £20 cum vetustis arboribus et shrud querc' ad mearem(ium) non aptis simili modo vendi copis' pdce bene custod' usque crescenc' 5 annorum. Et sic in 20 annis omnes bosci recresc' si ista ordinacio bene et diligenter observetur.' Some points are not clear to me in this entry; I do not know how 440 acres can be divided in 20 allotments of 20 acres each; nor how the 'growth of 20 years' can be reconciled with the 'growth of 5 years'. May we suppose, as a solution of the difficulty, that the woodland area was divided into two parts with a different number of allotments ?

[3] Mon. i. 11.

in those days the wood used to be sold every 16 years, and Pollard and Moyle do not explain how it is that this wood was allowed to grow for 20 years. Again, if we take the entry literally, then the whole of the 172 acres in the park of Norwood was sold at once, 20 years earlier than the time of Pollard and Moyle's survey. In the park of Wirrall there were 60 a. of good timber ('fayre tymbre') very highly valued at £290 10s. 0d. In the park of Sharpham, the trees are separated from the wood; as many as two hundred oaks fit for timber are scattered about the park, worth about two shillings each. There are also 80 acres of wood 'well sett with okes, asshes and maples'; previously it used to be felled once in every 14 years; the surveyors valued each acre at 6s. 8d.; the wood might be sold yearly for the sum of £1 10s. 0d.; evidently by this casual wood-sales are meant. Unfortunately, Pollard and Moyle's survey only increases our confusion instead of dispelling it.

Debts of the mona-steries.   It has often been stated that long before the Dissolution the monasteries were suffering from a prolonged economic crisis. Instances of great liabilities in the case of individual monasteries are found very early. As the Dissolution drew nearer, it is said, the indebtedness increased, so that at the time of the actual dissolution many if not all of the monasteries had become hopelessly insolvent. To prove this, one author refers to the fact that, after the monastic liabilities have been met, the Crown receipts from the sales of monastic goods are found to be very small, if we exclude from the reckoning the bells, roofs, gold and silver plate and jewels.[1] But it may be doubted whether this is the right view of the matter. That the monasteries had great liabilities just before the Dissolution is very improbable even from a general point of view. Institutions and corporations that are uncertain of their existence from day to day do not readily obtain a large credit. The interest of the monks in the economic welfare of their house from the time they realized the weakness of their position naturally became slack, and that interest may have ceased

[1] Home and For. R., 1864, Jan., 170, 175–7, 187 ; Brewer, H. VIII, i. 50 ; Gasquet, i. 28.

entirely when they were convinced of the proximity of the
catastrophe.   They would no longer shrink from running
into debt ; it would now be to their advantage to use to the
utmost all their credit, to leave the monastery, to carry off
carefully concealed sums of money, and to throw on the
Crown administration the heavy burden of their debts.   But
the proximity of the Suppression was not a secret to the
neighbouring population, and the local capitalists became
rather sceptical with regard to the chance of recovering
money lent to the monks.   The monks might assure their
neighbours as much as they liked that the interests of other
people would not suffer by the Suppression ; the neighbours
had, nevertheless, serious grounds for fearing that many
of the contracts into which the monks entered on the eve
of the Dissolution would be declared void, as having been
contracted in bad faith.   The monks did not find it always
easy, just before the final catastrophe, to find farmers who
would agree to pay at once large admission fines on condition
that very low annual rents should be inserted in the indenture.
The Paper Surveys at least show that the lands managed by
the monks in 1535, at the time when the Valor Ecclesiasticus was being compiled, often remained in monastic
hands until the very moment of the Suppression.   In
order to get a certain amount of cash against the day of
need, or occasionally, perhaps, even for current expenses,
the monks resorted not so much to borrowing as to selling,
either secretly or openly, some of their movables.   A
monastery might become poor, the goods of the house might
quickly disappear, and at the moment of the Suppression
the value of the household stuff and the agricultural stock
might not suffice to meet the monastic debts, even though the
monks had not in the later years increased their old liabilities
by a penny.   In order to judge of monastic indebtedness we
must compare it not with the Crown receipts from monastic
movables, but with the annual income of the monastery.

   In the letters of Cromwell's correspondents indications are
often found of the indebtedness and poverty of the monasteries. Sometimes the complaints are expressed in very general

terms. For instance, in December, 1535, Layton writes that the monastery of St. Andrew's, Northampton, is greatly in debt. In the spring of 1538 the Bishop of Dover visited the houses of the midland and western counties: he reports that next year only a few of the monasteries will be able to balance their accounts, and that in a very short time poverty will compel all of them to surrender their houses to the Crown.[1] Occasionally exact figures of the monastic liabilities are given. In April, 1536, the abbot of Athelney implores Cromwell to help him, as otherwise law-suits and bankruptcy threaten the monastery; the monks are utterly unable to pay all their debts at once; the most that they can pay is a hundred pounds a year. A long list of debts and of creditors is added, and there are 57 of the latter. The total amount of debts is given as £869 12s. 7d., but the real total is £860 2s. 7d.; besides this there is thrice mentioned in the list 'ode money'.[2] The gross income of the monastery according to the V. E. was about £290, the net £210. Therefore the amount of the liabilities must be considered as very great. But in Cromwell's correspondence the mention of indebtedness to such an extent is somewhat exceptional; his informants are generally concerned even when the total liability of the monastery approaches its annual income. The visitor, Legh, who suppressed the monastery of Muchelney, complains of the spoliation of monastic movables: only the roofs and bells are intact, and they are so only because, being heavy, it was difficult to take them away. No hospitality is shown, and hardly a servant or labourer is kept. In all probability the receipts from the sale of the movables of the monastery were far from covering its debts, the total of which the visitor calculates at about £400. Legh, of course, finds this a large sum. It is less than one year's income, however: according to the V. E. the gross income was about £510, the net £450. Another visitor speaks reproachfully of the £400 liabilities of such a monastery as Bath Abbey, whose income according to

---

[1] Gairdner, ix, 1005 ; xiii. i. 1052-3.
[2] Harl., 604, f. 63. The letter is printed in Mon. ii. 407-8, and by Archbold, 29-33.

the V. E. was more than £700 gross, and more than £600 net.[1]
The total debts of the monastery of Reading at the time of
the surrender exceeded those both of Muchelney and of Bath ;
but £500 was less than a quarter of the gross annual income.[2]

Another source of information respecting the liabilities of
monasteries is found in the Suppression Accounts.[3] In some
of these only the monastic creditors are mentioned, in others
the debtors to the houses are also given. In the majority of
cases only the totals of the debts are given, e. g. *Lancashire* :
Burscough, £86 3*s*. 8*d*. ; Cartmell, £59 12*s*. 8*d*. ; Cockersand,
£108 9*s*. 8*d*. ; Conishead, £87 17*s*. 3½*d*. ; Holland, £18 18*s*. 10*d*.
Leicestershire : Bradley, £4 6*s*. 8*d*. ; Garendon, £142 11*s*. 7*d*. ;
Kirby Beller, £63 13*s*. 4*d*. ; Langley, £19 15*s*. 0*d*. ; Olveston,
£47 ; Ulvescroft, £66 11*s*. 0*d*. *Rutlandshire* : Broke, £4 13*s*. 4*d*.
Sussex : Boxgrove, £42 10*s*. 6¼*d*. ; Hastings, £12 13*s*. 4*d*. ;
Michelham, £26 9*s*. 1*d*. ; Tortington, £12 6*s*. 8*d*. *Warwickshire* : Coventry Cath., £9 5*s*. 5*d*. ; Erdbury, £50 18*s*. 11*d*. ;
Henwood, £27 18*s*. 10*d*. ; Maxstoke, £196 12*s*. 5½*d*. ; Pinley,
£14 12*s*. 7*d*. ; Pollesworth, £27 3*s*. 4*d*. ; Studley, £122 0*s*. 4*d*. ;
St. Sepulchre's, Warwick, £133 14*s*. 9*d*. ; Wroxall has no debts.
In some of the inventories the Commissioners, who used to
gather information not only about the creditors of but also
about the debtors to the houses, do not mention the latter at
all, but give only the total of the monastic debts—e. g. Derb.,
Darley, £142 0*s*. 2*d*. ; Salop, Lilleshall, £26 6*s*. 8*d*. ; Staff.,
Dieulacres, £171 10*s*. 6*d*. ; St. Thomas, £235 19*s*. 7*d*. I will
not take it upon me to interpret the meaning of the silence
of such inventories : it may be that the monasteries had no

---

[1] Archbold, 33.

[2] Gairdner, xiv, ii. 136, Moyle to Cromwell, Sept., 31 H. VIII. In the
case of Bordesley the debts (£200) constitute about a half of the annual
income. Gairdner, xiii. i. 1343 ; Evance to Cromwell, July 30, H. VIII.

[3] The Suppression Accounts are found in Exch. Augm. O. M. B. vv. 172,
404 (ff. 218–51), 494 ; Exch. Treas. Rec. M. b. v. 154 ; St. Pap. Dom.,
Suppr. Pap., v. 3, n. 128 ; Cleop. E. iv. 336–40, 342–3, 357–8. For
Grace Dieu and Stoneleigh the debts are given in two inventories ; the
figures do not coincide, but the difference between them is small : £12 2*s*. 3*d*.
and £16 2*s*. 0*d*. for Gracedieu, and £212 19*s*. 10*d*. and £219 8*s*. 6½*d*. for
Stoneleigh. May we suppose that the larger figure signifies the total
monastic debts and the smaller the excess of the debts over the amount
due to the house ?

debtors, or that the figure given as that of the debts indicates the excess of the debts over the amount due to the House. Two lucky monasteries—Ellerton, Yorks., and St. Andrews, York—had neither creditors nor debtors. These were small monasteries, and their economic integrity may be explained by their lack of money, and the consequent absence of credit. More curious are those cases in which the account mentions neither creditors nor debtors, owing to the abbot having received permission both to collect the sums due to the House and to satisfy the creditors. We find this at Worksop (Notts.), Bellalaund (Yorks.), Kirkham and Rievaulx. It is hardly likely that such permission was without advantage to the abbots. The clearest conception of monastic liabilities is to be obtained from those inventories which take into account both the creditors and the debtors. In the following examples the first amount gives the total due from, the second the total due to the house : Cambs., Barnwell, £125 5s. 8d., £129 15s. 6½d.; Derb., Dale, £24 11s. 6d., £1; Repton, £63 1s. 2½d., £76 3s. 4d. ; Hunts., Huntingdon, £244 19s. 9½d., £103 0s. 4d.; Sawtre, £168 15s. 0d., £67 13s. 4d.; Stonely, £9 2s. 0d., £8 2s. 6d.; Northants, Pipewell, £90 6s. 4d., £4 7s. 4d.; Warw., Merevale, £150 2s. 6d., £101 8s. 5d.; Yorks., Monkbretton, £83 12s. 4d., £5 3s. 4d.

In the Exch. Augm. O. M. b. v. 494, the entries respecting debts are more detailed. Two monasteries of medium size— Hayles, Glouc., and Wherwell, Hants,—are found to have neither creditors nor debtors : they had only to pay £23 1s. 7½d. and £16 18s. 2d., the current debts to the merchants for food supplies. At Amesbury, Wilts., and St. Mary, Winchester, the Suppressors granted to the prioress and the abbess respectively the privilege of receiving money due to their house and paying off the debts ; at Amesbury, however, they had only to pay the provision bills, viz. £20 14s. 5½d. The creditors of the cathedral of St. Swithun, Winchester, demanded £197 10s. 0d., and besides this the canons had to pay £8 for their provision bills ; there was only one debtor to the house, the Bishop of Winchester, who owed them £100. The abbey of Winchcombe, Glouc., had four creditors—Rowl. Morton,

£13 6s. 8d.; Anth. Ayleworth, £20; President of Corpus Christi, Oxford, £20; J. Alayn, Kt., £536. The current debt amounted to £15 3s. 4d. The house had only one debtor— the executors of the Lord of Berkeley, who owed £26 13s. 4d. for the ward that the late lord had bought from the monks. The abbey of St. Peter, Gloucester, had creditors who demanded £326 10s. 0¾d., and the current debts were £77 5s. 8¾d. The debtors to the house owed £149 10s. 6½d., one of whom, J. Ap. Rees, had not paid £50 of farm rent due for the cell of St. Guthlac, Hereford ; three other persons had not paid the £40 they owed on agreement ; W. Cockes, 'husbond-man,' had not yet paid £20 for cattle and stock he had bought from the abbot, and several farmers were still in arrears to the extent of £39 10s. 6½d.

The entries for Malmesbury, St. Augustine's, Bristol, Ciren-cester, are very much alike. The Suppression Commissioners entrust the head of the house with paying part of the debts, the remainder being evidently taken up by the Crown. The abbot of Malmesbury compounded with all the creditors with the exception of three, and for this purpose he received £70 4s. 4d. from the Commissioners. The three creditors were : the 'widow of K. Audelett, who demanded £180 (she had two monastic bonds worth £730, but of this £530 had already been paid) ; Anth. Hungerford, Kt., £23 ; W. Button, Gent., £63. Only one debtor to the house is mentioned—Sir H. Longe—he signed a bond for £210, but had already paid £50 on it; the Commissioners transferred the right to receive the remaining £160 to K. Audelett. The abbot of St. Augustine's, Bristol, promised to satisfy all the creditors with the exception of two who demanded £74; moreover, the monastery had current debts amount-ing to £58 10s. 2d. The debtors to Cirencester, Glouc., owed £34 15s. 0d., and the current debt was £9 5s. 2a. Evidently the abbot, by an agreement with the Commis-sioners, took upon himself to pay the debts to the sum of £145 15s. 11d.; besides this, £118 14s. 8d. of debt remained.[1] The monks of Tewkesbury owed £36 8s. 4d. for fish: they

[1] The entries for Cirencester and Tewkesbury are not quite clear.

let a mill and the rectory of Teynton to W. Bush, and took from him £60 in money, but neither admitted him nor returned the money ; a third creditor demands £115. The monastery has also some debtors : Raaf Northwood ought to pay £100 admission fine for the manor and rectory of Teynton, but as yet has paid only £40, and he asks that this sum be returned to him if the indenture should eventually be declared void. Geo. Throgmorton, gent., had not paid £29 14s. 4d. of the amount that he promised to pay for admission to the cell of Deerhurst.

Even more detailed is the information about the debts of 16 monasteries in Exch. Augm. O. M. b. v. 404, ff. 218–51.[1] The one most deeply in debt is Stoneleigh, Warwickshire ; it owed £219 8s. 6½d., which was distributed between thirty-six creditors ; some of the debts mentioned in the list are very old ; during seven years the monks did not pay for cattle bought from Cecil Higgins, and during ten years they had not made up their minds to return £10 which they borrowed from Th. Hogges ; a debt to W. William was older still. A third of the whole amount of debts consists of money loans ; the rest are unpaid bills and wages. Very great expenses were incurred for malt (i.e. for beer) ; the debt for malt at the time of the surrender appears to be £75, and almost the whole of it was purchased during the years 27 and 28 H. VIII ; judging from these unpaid bills the monks used in two years more than 150 quarters of malt.

Thus the evidence on the liabilities of single houses confirms our supposition, based on general considerations, that at the Suppression the monastic property was not encumbered with enormous debts, if we consider only as ' enormous ' such debts as consume the income of several years. Such cases as that of Athelney are exceptional ; the next to Athelney in the amount of its liabilities is St. Sepulchre's, Warwick ; the demands of its creditors equal the gross income of

---

[1] The account was made by ' G. Gyffard and R. Burgoyn, the Kyngs commissioners, by the vertue of the Kynges commyssyon to them directed 24 Aprell, 28 H. VIII ' ; some sheets of the document are lost. The monasteries whose debts are described therein are situated in Northampton, Warwick, Leicester, Rutland.

two and a half years. We seldom come across monasteries having debts which are more than one year's but considerably less than two years' gross income (Stafford St. Thomas, Maxstoke, Henwood, Stoneleigh). More frequently we read of monasteries whose debts are more than half a year's but less than a year's gross income, as Huntingdon, Burscough, Cartmell, Conishead, Garendon, Langley, Ulverscroft, Pinley and Studley. Furthermore, monasteries are found whose debts amount to a very small portion of their annual income, as Charterhouse, Coventry, St. Peter's, Gloucester, Malmesbury, Tewkesbury; while others either have no debts at all, as Ellerton, St. Andrew's York, Wroxall, Wherwell; or have debts less than the amount due to them, as Repton, Barnwell. We could not, of course, leave monastic debts out of consideration, but it is evident that they did not seriously affect the financial results of the Dissolution.

CHAPTER IV

MONASTIC CHARITY

ALONG with the horses and the sheep, with the monastic liabilities and the money due to the houses, the Suppressors numbered the monks and the population that was dependent upon the monasteries. Behind the pounds and shillings, behind the carts and oxen, we can discern the men and women who were the immediate victims of the catastrophe. We are not, of course, quite safe in judging of the monastic population of the sixteenth century merely from the figures of the Suppression Accounts.[1] The influx of new monks and also of new servants must have decreased considerably during the later years of monastic history, and even the old population did not remain without change until the last. Those who had nowhere to go of course remained. Some others remained too. Many of them stayed through affection for their house, or because they hoped to obtain a good pension. But the monks were under suspicion of treason, and the hope of a pension might not be so strong as the fear of prison or of gallows. The more cautious of them naturally sought to escape while they were still safe, if only they could succeed in finding some refuge. As to laymen, it is likely enough that the monks in order to cut down expenses decreased their staff of officers and servants. On the other hand, it is just as likely that in later years they created new and well-paid offices for their influential neighbours in order to gain their favour

---

[1] Perhaps we may be permitted to doubt the exactness of the commissioners' survey. On July 28, 1536, the commissioners of Warwickshire write to Cromwell and ask him not to dissolve the nunnery of Pollesworth which has but 12 nuns (Cleop. E. iv. 244), but according to their official account (Exch. Treas. Rec. v. 154, f. 56) it has 14 nuns. It is possible, however, that in a private letter the commissioners gave round numbers.

or even in return for cash. Some of the monastic retinue may
have departed of their own accord, when they have found
remunerative employment elsewhere, in order not to be without
a home after the Suppression.   In three cases it seems we are
able to note an actual decrease in the monastic population.
The Commissioners of 1535 wrote that the ' coquinarius ' of the
abbey of Winchcombe fed 26 monks.   The house surrendered
at the very end of 1539 and then the Suppressors found there
an abbot and 17 monks.[1] According to the survey of 1536
the nunnery of Grace Dieu, Leic., had 15 nuns, a prioress, and
a population of 48 other people ; according to the Suppression
Account of 30 H. VIII the number of nuns remained the same
but the rest of the population is said to be less than in 1536—
only 42.[2]   In Broke, the only Rutland monastery, the Suppressors found only a prior, eight servants, and one corrodian ;
the last two monks went to the monastery of Kylyngworth.[3]

It is quite possible, and even probable, that in the last days
before the surrender fewer people lived within monastic walls
than at the time of the Valor Ecclesiasticus, not to speak of
times still more remote.   This, however, does not impair the
evidence of the Suppression Accounts.   The figures of the
Suppressors embrace that part of the whole monastic population which remained on the spot to the end, and was directly
affected by the catastrophe ; they furnish us with a minimum
for our estimate of the total of this population.   Many of the
Suppression Accounts also contain information about the lay

List of the
population
of the
mona-
steries.

---

[1] V. E. ii. 450 : ' officium coquinarii redditus pro diettis 26 fratrum sive
commonachorum in eodem cenobio degentium viz. pro quolibet eorum 12*d*.
pro septimana.' Exch. Augm. O. M. b. v. 494, pp. 75–80. At the end
of December, 1539, the commissioners assigned a pension of £140 to the
abbot and £250 to the 17 monks.

[2] Exch. Treas. Rec. M. b. v. 154. The Commissioners of 1536 found
the following population in Grace Dieu : ' 15 nuns with the priores and
48 persons havyng their lyvyngs of the same house wherof yomen 1,
hynds servants 26, women servants 9, persons havyng ther lyvyng of the
same house by purchase 3, persons fownde of almes 9.' In the Suppression Account (30 H. VIII, Exch. Augm. O. M. b. v. 172, pp. 76–83)
pensions are assigned to the prioress and 15 nuns. The entry about
laymen is not quite clear. The prioress has 3 servants. The monastery
has 35 servants of whom 8 are women. Moreover, some money is paid
to 4 poor folk having corrodies.

[3] Exch. Treas. Rec. M. b. v. 154, ff. 64–5.

people who lived in the monasteries; in these, men and women
are sometimes distinguished, the servants and the poor, adults
and children; and occasionally the office of the servants is indicated. When Parliament gave to the Crown the monasteries
with a net income not exceeding £200, a general Instruction was issued before the Dissolution as to the manner of
describing them. Besides questions about the monks, the
number of clergy among them and the number of those
who wish to give up Holy Orders, the Instruction prescribes
also the following question:—'How many servants, hinds
or other dependents belong to the house?' The question
about the laymen is expressed in almost the same words
in the Instruction to the Leicestershire Commissioners ap-
pended to their survey: 'Nombre of servantes hynds and
other persons having their lyvyngs of the same house.' In a
short Suppression account of several Lancashire monasteries
the population is divided into two parts: (1) religious persons,
(2) servants and others having lyving.[1] But while in the
Leicestershire and Warwickshire accounts servants are distinguished from persons 'found of' alms and from priests, in the
Lancashire account all non-religious persons are comprised in
one total. Therefore in a general table we have to be satisfied
with one general total for laymen. It may even be doubted
whether the Suppression Accounts of 31 H. VIII, of which I
have made use (Exch. Augm. O. M. b. v. 494), take into consideration all the non-religious population; they mention only
officers, servants, and priests; they do not mention persons
found of alms, nor the schoolboys. Probably the Suppression
Accounts for Huntingdon, Sawtre, and Stonely do not give the
actual population of the monasteries in 1536, but the number
of servants that they kept in average years.[2] However, the

---

[1] Gairdner, i. 721; Exch. Treas. Rec. M. b. v. 154, f. 48; Cleop. E.
iv. 342-3.

[2] Cleop. E. iv. 336-40. I do not venture to speak with certainty about
these three cases. On the one hand the words 'commonly kept, ac-
customally kept, most commonly' stand by the side of the number of
monastic servants. On the other hand, in Huntingdon and Sawtre the
servants are divided into yeomen and hinds; it may be that, for both, the
number of people who actually lived in the monasteries is given. (Huntingdon, 34 servants commonly kept, wherof yomen 10, hynds 24.)

table below will enable us to form some idea of the number of monks and persons who lived upon the monasteries. The figure to the left indicates the monks or nuns, and that to the right the laymen who lived in the house.[1]

County	Monastery	Monks	Laymen	County	Monastery	Monks	Laymen
Derby.	Dale	16	30	Leic.	Ulverscroft	9	40
	Darley	15	57	Nthts.	Pipewell	14	44
	Repton	10	24	Rutl.	Broke	1	11
Glouc.	Cirencester	17	110	Salop	Lilleshall	12	43
	St. Peter's, Gloucester	30	86	Soms.	Bristol St. Augustine	12	46
	Hayles	22	70	Staff.	Brewood n.	5	8
	Tewkesbury	39	144		Dieulacres³	13	30
	Winchcombe	18	90		Stafford St. Thomas	7	29
Hants	Christchurch, Twyneham	22	63	Sussex	Boxgrove	9	28
	Wherwell	25	48		Dureford	9	24
	Winchester St. Mary n.²	23	20		Hastings	4	6
Hunts.	Huntingdon	13	34		Michelham	9	29
	Sawtre	7	22		Shulbrede	5	13
	Stonely	8	22		Tortington	7	12
Lanc.	Burscough	5	42	Warw.	Coventry Charterhouse	13	21
	Cartmell	10	38		Erdbury	7	36
	Cockersand	22	57		Henwood n.	7	7
	Conishead	8	41		Maxstoke	8	26
	Holland	5	26		Merevale	11	45
Leic.	Bradley	3	6		Pinley n.	5	8
	Garendon	15	79		Pollesworth n.	15	38
	Grace Dieu n.	16	48		Stoneleigh	12	46
	Kirby Beller	9	36		Studley	9	30
	Langley n.	6	17		Warwick St. Sepulchre	4	8
	Olveston	7	33		Wroxall n.	6	11
				Wilts.	Amesbury n.	34	37
					Malmesbury	22	54

In the 52 monasteries of the list there were 631 religious persons and 1,973 laymen. The gross income of St. Augustine's, Bristol, is not known in the V. E.; if we omit it in our reckoning we shall find that in 51 monasteries with the gross income of about £14,400 there were 630 religious persons and 1,927 laymen. We notice a great difference between the houses of monks and nunneries. Ten nunneries with 143 nuns and 242 laymen have a gross income of about £1650. Forty-

---

[1] The references to the Suppression Accounts were given on p. 213, note 3. In most cases in the accounts the number of religious persons is given, followed by the words 'besydes the prior' or 'with the prior'. In such cases I have everywhere added one to the number of monks. n. means nunnery.

[2] I have not counted 12 women who received aid from the monastery (Exch. Aug. O. M. b. 494, p. 11: 'almes to 12 pore women called £4 0s. 0d. by yeare').

[3] In this monastery 30 servants are mentioned. Besides alms are ' gyven to landers (=laundress) and 8 pore women there £1 6s. 8d.' (Exch. Augm. O. M. b. 172, 41-9), I have not counted these women ; perhaps they did not live in the monastery.

one houses of men with 487 monks and 1,685 laymen have about £12,700 gross income. The nunneries in the table are, on the average, only half as rich as the men's houses, but the average number of religious persons in them is larger; therefore the share of the gross income that falls to the lot of a monk is more than twice as much as that which falls to the lot of a nun. The difference between the two groups in their relation to laymen is also considerable. The number of laymen who obtain their living in men's houses is three and a half times as great as the number of the monks themselves; the monks are evidently very well off, they have many servants and sometimes keep a considerable number of indigent people. The nunneries are much more modest; the number of laymen who obtain their living there is less than the double of the number of nuns. Whatever the social position of the ordinary nun may have been before she took the veil, it was evidently only in a few of the rich houses that they could live like great ladies and do no manual work at all.

The foregoing table does not entitle us to calculate the whole number of religious persons and of laymen obtaining their living from the monasteries, unless the figures given may be regarded as typical of the whole country. But we are to some extent justified in so regarding them. Monasteries of different sizes and in different localities are included in the table; and these 52 monasteries constitute about one-eleventh of the whole number of monasteries that I have considered; and their gross income is about one-eleventh of the gross income of those same monasteries. If we take the number of religious persons and laymen of this list to constitute one-eleventh of all the religious persons and monastic laymen, we shall find that before the Dissolution there were about 7,000 religious persons, and that the number of laymen who obtained their living within the monastic walls did not amount even to 25,000. This estimate of the total number of religious persons approaches very nearly the figures given by Dr. Gasquet.[1] He affirms that the Suppressors found in

---

[1] Gasquet, ii. 237, 241, 322-3. Dr. Gasquet points out that the chief authorities for his calculations were the surrenders and the pension books.

the monasteries about 8,000 religious persons. If from this number we exclude the friars, of whom I have taken only the Maturins into account, a little more than 6,000 will remain : and to this number we must add the Knights Hospitallers, whom Dr. Gasquet has not mentioned at all in his work. I entirely disagree, however, with the hagiographer of the English monks as to the number of monastic laymen. Dr. Gasquet affirms that the number of people who depended upon the monks, or otherwise earned their living in the monastic service, was probably at least ten times as great as the number of monks themselves[1]; but he gives no proofs whatever for this assertion. His expressions, ' dependents, livings,' are borrowed from the instruction to the Commissioners who surveyed the monasteries at the Suppression. But the very returns of these Commissioners show that the number of laymen living within monastic walls immediately before the Dissolution was only three times as great as the number of monks. Certainly these laymen did not include all the people dependent upon the monastic revenue ; but in considering the economic influence of monasteries one's attention is, of course, directed first to the people found within the monastic gates at the last moment of the monastic history.

The Suppression Accounts divide monastic laymen into groups. The persons who received wages are mentioned separately, and the women among them are reckoned separately from the men. In the accounts for Leicestershire and Warwickshire the men are divided into two groups, hinds and servants ; in the Sussex accounts they are divided into ' hinds ' and ' wayting servants ' ; yeomen evidently belong to the upper class and very likely they are the personal servants of the monks, the hinds being the agricultural labourers. About women it is often said that they work at the dairy. Speaking generally,

Laymen in the monasteries.

Unfortunately, however, he does not give references, and to verify his calculations one would have to do over again the work done by him ; a task for which I had not the time.

[1] Gasquet, ii. 323. It must be noted that this statement of Dr. Gasquet's can hardly be reconciled with his much more trustworthy calculations concerning the small monasteries. With reference to the Suppression Accounts of 21 monasteries he calculates the average number of monks in a small house to be 8 and of laymen 27 (Gasquet, ii. 282; cf. ii. 208).

the lay administrators of monastic estates—stewards, bailiffs, auditors, receivers—are not mentioned in the Suppression Accounts, which enumerate only the persons receiving wages and hired for a comparatively short time, and not the officials who were appointed under the convent seal, mostly for life, and received fees (*feoda*); but in the Suppression accounts of St. Sepulchre's, Warwick, and Erdbury, mention is made of 'other persons havyng fees extra ordinem by covent seale'. The return for Erdbury is curious also because two yeomen are said to receive wages by covent seal, and thus the distinction between the wage and the fee, between labourer and official, seems to have died out.[1] The priests and chaplains who were not monks occupy a special place; they were necessary in nunneries but were also found in men's houses (Maxstoke). The remaining laymen did no work for the monasteries, but merely helped to consume the monastic income; not all of them, however, were fed by the monasteries without return. Some of them were corrodians by purchase, and there are also mentioned corrodians by covent seal; it is possible that the latter also bought their living; in the list I have placed them in one group with the corrodians who are evidently such by purchase, and with those who are called in the account simply corrodians. The words ' persons founde of almes' are applied to the poor; and the words ' persons havyng lyvynge by promise ' seem to have the same meaning. The poor children are sometimes counted separately.

Monastery.			Yeomen or waytyng servants.	Hinds.	Women servants.	Corrodians, c. by purchase, c. by covent seal.	Persons found of almes.	Children found of almes.	Priests.
Leic.	Bradley...	... ...		3	2			1	
	Olveston	... ...	7	22	4				
	Kirby Beller	... ...	16	17	1	2		14	
	Ulverscroft	... ...	20		3	1	2		
	Garendon	... ...	11	45	11	2	5	5	
	Grace Dieu	... ...	1	26	9	3	9		
	Langley	... ...		10	4	2			1
Warw.	Pollesworth	... ...	8	17	9		1		3
	Maxstoke	... ...	9	12	3				2

[1] There is one such yeoman also at Maxstoke; '9 yeomen servants, on havyng a yerly stypend by covent scale.'

Monastery.	Yeomen or wayting servants.	Hinds.	Women servants.	Corrodians, c. by purchase, c. by covent seal.	Persons found of alms.	Children found of alms.	Priests.
Warw. Erdbury¹	19	5	2		6		
Henwood	1	2	3				1
Coventry Charterhouse²	6					12	
Pinley		3	4	1			
Stoneleigh³	15	21	2	5	2		
Warwick St. Sepulchre⁴	2			3	1		
Wroxall		7	3				1
Studley	6	20	4	1			
Suss. Tortington⁵	2	8	2				
Boxgrove	10	8	2			8	
Hastings	4		2				
Michelham	18	11					
Shulbrede	5	6	2				
Dureford⁶	8	12	4				

When the cathedral of St. Swithun, Winchester, and the Monastic abbey of St. Peter, Gloucester, surrendered to the Crown servants. (14 Nov. and 2 Jan., 31 H. VIII) they were not suppressed but only reformed. The Commissioners allowed some of the former monks and servants to remain, and from the new staff, which was smaller than the old, we can get an idea of the grand style of life that prevailed in the large and rich monasteries. In St. Peter's, Gloucester, at the time of the surrender, thirty monks were found, but among them were four Oxford students ; there were also eighty-six servants. After the reduction of the staff the Commissioners left 27 canons and 20 officers of the household (clerke of the kitchyn, fowle cater, cooke, undercoke, 2 scolyons, panter, underpanter, waterman, butler, under-butler, baker, under-baker, bruer, underbruer, porter at thall door and verger, underporter, common barbor, 2 wayterers in thall, elemosiner),

¹ This is what is said about six persons found of alms : 'other ympotent persons and chyldren fownd of almes, 6.' I have not included in this table two persons of whom it is said 'other persons havyng fees extre ordinar'.

² I have not included in the table three ' converses professed '.

³ I have not inserted in the table one man, ' oon havyng an annyte by covent seal.'

⁴ I have not included in the table two ' other persons havyng fees extra ordin' by covent seal 2.

⁵ I have omitted 'a prior quondam ' having a pension of £10 by re-signation.

⁶ Also in Dureford the old prior who had resigned is omitted.

Three servants were given to the steward; the guardians were each allowed to keep a servant at their own expense. In St. Swithun's, Winchester, 19 officers of the household were left (the same as at St. Peter's, Gloucester, except the elemosiner), their wages (amounting to £33 6s. 8d.) were assigned to them, and 1s. 4d. a week each for the table; moreover, 12 servants were given to the guardian (wages £23 13s. 4d. and £20 0s. 0d. for livery), and four members of the chapter were allowed to keep a servant each at their own expense.[1]

In modest and remote houses the 'servants' were different. In the inventory of St. Sexburge, Sheppey, a nunnery in Kent, a list of hired servants and their wages is given. A good many people, about forty, were fed by the nunnery, but few of them were household servants. The nuns kept in their own hands a fairly large demesne and for it they needed workmen. For themselves they kept only a few servants, all, it seems, hired by the year ; many of them receive their wages in livery and others in pasture. If we exclude three priests, 28 men and 8 women were 'servants in wages'. The duties of all are not indicated, and even when this is done, only three can be definitely called officers of the household: J. Cocke, butler, R. Welshe, brewar, Ellyn at my lady's (= the abbess) fynding ; all the rest are employed on the demesne farm : carpenter, carter, two cowherds, thatcher, horsekeeper, malter, three shepherds.[2]

---

[1] Exch. Augm. O. M. b. v. 494, pp. 93-101, 1-9.

[2] Exch. Treas. of Receipt M. b. v. 154, ff. 85-6 : 'Names of the servants now in wages: Mr. Eglestone by yere (amount not mentioned). Mr. Whyte £1 6s. 8d. and lyvere. J. Cocke butler £1 6s. 8d. (wherof to pay ¼) and livere. Alyn Sowthe bayly for closure and hys servant £6 13s. 4d. and two lyveryes. J. Mustarde £1 0s. 0d. a kowes pasture and lyvere. W. Rowet carpenter £2 0s. 0d. and lyvere. Th. Thresher £1 3s. 4d. The carter £1 13s. 4d. R. Dawton £1 13s. 4d. R. Gyllys £1 6s. 8d. and lyvery. The kowherd £1 10s. 0d. J. Bartnar £1 8s. 0d. R. Welsh brewar £1 0s. 0d. A thatcher £1 13s. 4d. and a hosecloth. W. Nycolls £1 0s. 0d. J. Andrew £0 13s. 4d. J. Putsawe £0 13s. 4d. and a shyrt redy made. Geo. Myllar £1 1s. 8d. Rob. Rychard horsekeeper £1 0s. 0d. J. Harryes frencheman £0 13s. 4d. and a shyrt. J. Gyles the oxeherd £0 14s. 0d. and a payre of hoses and a payre of shoys. R. Gladwyn for to take malt £1 6s. 8d., he hath ben here 8 weeks. Dorothe Sowthe the baylyfs wyfe £2 0s. 0d. and lyverye. Ales Barker £0 13s. 4d. and lyvere.

The Suppression Accounts do not include all the people who obtained their living (either partly or entirely) from the monastic revenue. The Commissioners did not reckon the lay administrators along with the people dependent on a monastery, either because the stewards, bailiffs, receivers, and auditors did not live in the monastery itself, or perhaps because the Commissioners did not wish to place persons of important or high social position on the same level with cooks and horse-keepers. Neither did the Commissioners enter in the accounts all those who received monastic alms; they counted only those who lived exclusively on monastic charity. This charity, however, was not limited to keeping the old or the poor in monastic almshouses, or to the education of children in the monastic school. The monasteries also dispensed money, clothing, and victuals, fed the hungry on appointed days, gave hospitality to wayfarers of various social positions. Such doles, given once for all or periodically, were considered a very important element of monastic charity.

It was just at the period of the Dissolution that it was for the first time forbidden not merely to ask for alms but even to give them; this was the doing of the same Parliament that handed over to the Crown the monasteries with an income not exceeding two hundred pounds. Gatherings of people in the places where kindhearted benefactors or their executors fed all who asked for food ('commen and open doolis') were recognized as especially dangerous. An exception, however, was made for monasteries; they were allowed, as of old, not only to accept impotent corrodians but also to give food, clothes, and money on the days fixed by custom or by the donors.[1]

Charitable expenses of the monasteries.

Ales Fykkers £0 13s. 4d. and lyvere. Gladwyns wyfe £0 13s. 4d. and lyvere. Ellyn at my ladyes fyndyng. Emme Cawket £0 12s. od. and lyvere. Rose Salmon £0 12s. od., she hath ben here a month. Marget Lambard £0 13s. 4d. and lyvere. Syr J. Lorymer curat at the paryshe church £3 16s. 8d. Syr J. Ingram chaplen £3 3s. 4d. Syr Tho. Feldar chaplen £3 3s. 4d. J. Gayton shepard £2 13s. 4d. J. Pelland shepard £1 0s. 0d. J. Marchant shepard £0 13s. 4d. and pasture for 40 shepe. J. Helman £0 16s. od. and 10 shepes pasture. J. Lammyng sheppard £1 0s. od.'

[1] 27 H. VIII, c. 25, s. 28.

The Valor Ecclesiasticus is a much more abundant and many-sided source of information concerning monastic charity than the Suppression Accounts. For a whole series of monasteries the Commissioners of 1535 give not only the number of persons relieved, but also the amount of the alms, the dates of distribution, the kind of victuals or things given to the needy. Still for all this the Valor Ecclesiasticus does not give a complete idea of monastic charity ; the evidence which it contains about alms was recorded and taken into account not because the Government desired to collect information about the charitable work of the monks, but because without it the net income of the monasteries could not be defined. The charitable expenses of the monasteries were partly compulsory, partly voluntary. Even laymen in Tudor times used not infrequently to spend large sums of money in liberal hospitality, and from time to time gave food to all who appeared at their doors asking for alms ; it was but natural that both the well-to-do and the poor of the sixteenth century should expect still greater liberality from the rich monasteries. Thus the monasteries of the sixteenth century often did, and had to do charitable work without being otherwise compelled thereto by any one ; but many of their acts of charity were not the outcome of piety, pity or respectability, but of legal obligation. The innumerable gifts of land and income from land, that were showered upon the monasteries to the end of their long history, were seldom given to the monks unconditionally. No donor could expect the provisions of his gift to be carried out faithfully for ever unless he gave something to the monks. But having left them one part he might well expect that they would manage the other part with more conscientiousness and with more regard to his wishes than he could expect from a layman, especially where the relief of the poor was concerned. If a monastery were obliged to spend a certain part of a grant upon the poor, its relation to that part is that of trustee and not of owner. The statesmen of 1535 had not the audacity to tax that part of the monastic revenues which the monks distributed to the poor under the will of a donor. The Statute concerning the

Royal Tenth orders the Commissioners to tax voluntary alms, but they were instructed to deduct from the gross income the annual and perpetual alms given in compliance with any foundation or governmental ordinance.

This compulsory charity, in connexion with the acquisition of new revenue by a monastery, was not always of recent origin. A considerable part of the monastic property consisted of appropriated rectories, and two Statutes at the end of the fourteenth and the beginning of the fifteenth century require, in the event of such appropriation, that the monks should bind themselves to distribute therefrom to the poor not less than the latter had been receiving (15 R. 2, c. 6, 4 H. 4, c. 12). The Valor Ecclesiasticus shows that when an appropriation took place the donor or the bishop of the diocese entered into a formal agreement with the monks respecting the amount of compulsory almsgiving. Among its possessions, the abbey of St. Peter, Gloucester, owned the rectory B. Marie 'ante portas Gloucestric'; at the time of its appropriation the abbot and the bishop of the diocese agreed that the rectory should keep up its former payments, out of which twenty-five yards of cloth were annually given to clothe five poor parishioners. A similar course was also taken by the same prelates when the rectory of Holy Trinity was appropriated.[1] At the appropriation of the rectory of Lantryssen in Glamorganshire, it was not the local bishop but the lay donor, Hugo Despenser, who made the agreement with the monks.[2] Thus the Commissioners of 1535 had to distinguish between compulsory and voluntary alms, the former only being declared free of tax. It was natural that frequent

---

[1] V. E. ii. 416: 'Super appropriac' ecclie B. Marie ante port' abbe Glouc' ex ordinacoe Waltheri Froncettor quondam abbatis mon' pdcti et epi Wigorn' loci illius ordinarii Elemos' viz. in precio 25 virg' panni lanei distributi 5 pauperibus parochianis pro togis inde fiendis.' About the rectory of Holy Trinity ibm., comp. Lilleshall, iii. 198, elemosina de Holme, and esp. Sulby, iv. 301, elemosine. Cf. V. E. ii. 459. Sometimes *appropriacio* signifies the agreement made at the appropriation. Vide V. E. iii. 241, Great Malvern: 'elemosina per appropriacionem ecclie parochialis de Powyck.'

[2] V. E. ii. 476, Tewkesbury, Glouc. In the same survey a similar instance is found with regard to the alms of the rectory of M. Marlow, Linc., V. E. ii. 474.

disputes should arise between the Commissioners and the taxpayers. When the monks possessed any document under which they were bound to give certain alms they of course showed this document to the Commissioners, although it might be the will of King Arthur himself, or of Lucius, the first Christian king of the Britons or of Barnulf, king of Mercia. The Commissioners probably looked at the ancient charters with great reverence for the signatures of the ancient kings and exempted the monks from the tax.[1] But when the monks had no document to show, they attempted to evade the tax by referring to some good and immemorial custom. Occasionally the Commissioners were persuaded and did not put a tax on the alms ; more often, however, they refused to enter in their exemption list the alms which the monks could not trace back to the definite instructions of a certain donor. In Furness the Commissioners refused to take into consideration the traditional maintenance of thirteen poor corrodians. Moreover, they occasionally did not recognize some expenses that were most undoubtedly compulsory. For instance, the Winchester Commissioners refused to exempt the monastic expenditure upon poor children and poor scholars in spite of the remonstrances of the monks, and of the fact that the 'scholar' of those days was little better than a beggar. The monks pointed out that the expenditure upon poor scholars was called alms, but the Commissioners did not listen to them ; and Gardiner explained to Cromwell that there was a great difference between the relief of the poor and the education of children ; the poor would die without

---

[1] V. E. i. 147, Glastonbury : 'Et in denariis solut' pro elemosina annuatim distributa div' pauperibus ex ordin' et fundac' div' fundatorum viz. incliti regis Arthuri Lucii Britonum primi regis Christiani Kenwalchi Kentivi et Henrici regum Gwenere regine et Ider principis Edgari Athelwolsey Athelbaldi & Ethelrede regum necnon plurimorum regum et al' benefactorum prout per inspeccoem fundac' coram commissionar' dni regis ostens' £140 16s. 8d.' ii. 411 : 'Glouc' St. Peter, Elemosina distributa per ordinacionem Barnulphi quondam regis Marciorum.' But the Commissioners did not recognize the expenses of the priory of St. Catherine, Lincoln, for the hospital of St. Sepulchre (iv. 34), although the monks referred to the wills of definite donors. It may be that the monks could not produce the documents or that the Commissioners did not consider their documents genuine.

the alms but the children could do without a school.[1] Speaking generally, the entries of monastic educational expenditure are very few in the Valor Ecclesiasticus. The Commissioners do not mention schoolboys even in those cases where there was no doubt about their existence. When the monasteries of Lilleshall, Garendon, Ulverscroft, were suppressed, children were found there, but the V. E. does not mention the fact.[2]

Even those educational expenses which were entered in the primary survey were not infrequently crossed out in the diocesan returns, although they were enjoined upon the monks under the will of a particular donor and might be called alms. Both in Gloucester and in London the Commissioners made no objection to the alms given by the monks of the abbey of St. Peter, Gloucester, to the adult poor under the will of Barnulf, king of Mercia, but they crossed out the monks' expenditure upon thirteen poor schoolboys, although in this case too the monks referred to the will of King Barnulf. The monastery of Winchcombe, Gloucester, had a grant from a widow on condition that part of the income should be used to support the teacher of the grammar school and for the keep of six schoolboys and the other part for the benefit of her soul and for doles to the poor. The monks had the documents to prove this and the expenses for the poor were allowed, but those for the school were disallowed.[3] *Educational expenses.*

The refusal to allow educational expenses cannot be explained by disbelief in the monks' testimony, for at the Charterhouse, Coventry, the Commissioners allowed a very considerable charity although the monks could not name the particular donors

---

[1] Gairdner, viii. 654, ix. 1070, n. 3.

[2] In Lilleshall at the time of the suppression were found ' 4 gentylmens sones and their scolemaster' for some reason reckoned with the servants (Exch. Augm. O. Misc. b. v. 172, pp. 21–31). Exch. Treas. Rec. M. b. v. 154: ' Garendon chylderen founde of almes 5, Ulverscroft chyldren for the chappell there 14.'

[3] Gloucester, St. Peter, V. E. ii. 411 : ' Standisshe 13 pauperes scolares vocat' le childern de le Almery.' Winchcombe, V. E. ii. 459–60: ' fundacio et ordinacio dni Johanne Huddlestone.' In the margin there is a characteristic remark: ' nota pro elemosina inter pauperes quod allo'r et resid' disallo'r.' In the same survey the expense of six small boys who sing in the chapel is entered, but it also is omitted in the final returns.

for the whole of the alms; but the expenses on twelve poor schoolboys were not allowed, in spite of the fact that the monks produced some charters of English kings who had made the grants for the express purpose of education. There were, in fact, twelve schoolboys in the monastery, and at the time of the suppression that was the very number found there.[1] In other monasteries, too, the expenses for keeping schoolboys though entered in the primary surveys were crossed out on revision (for instance, Coventry Cathedral, Ixworth). The abbot of Westminster paid £26 13s. 4d. annually to the divinity lecturers at Oxford and Cambridge under the will of Margaret, Countess of Richmond, but he did not even venture to enter this expense in the survey, and only petitioned— probably without much hope of success—against the payment of the tenth on this money.[2] Only a few entries concerning poor schoolboys were allowed to remain at the revision.

The monastery of Sherborne kept three children at the local grammar school. The monastery of Tewkesbury gave cloth for the clothing of sixteen poor schoolboys, and kept some other poor boys who were also at school; there could not have been many of them, as only £3 11s. 8d. was spent upon them.[3] Norwich Cathedral had a school of its own where thirteen boys were taught; the Cathedral priory fed them and hired for them a teacher and a guardian. Worcester Cathedral also fed fourteen schoolboys, even their bread and beer allowance being given in the survey. An entry of alms in Oseney Abbey, Oxford, is somewhat curious: £1 6s. 8d.

---

[1] Exch. Treas. Rec. M. b. v. 154, Coventry Charterhouse: ' 12 children browte up in vertue and lernyng fownd ther of almes.'

[2] V. E. iii. 51, 483; i. 418. The monks at St. Peter's, Gloucester, kept a lecturer in divinity in the house itself and paid him £6 13s. 4d. by order of the king; but this expense was not tax-free (ii. 418). For some reason, however, a similar expense in Worcester Cathedral is exempt from tenth. iii. 224: ' in feodo magistri Rogi Neckeham professoris theologie custodis carnerie iuxta palatium Wigorn' £10 16s. 8d.'

[3] V. E. ii. 284: ' In elemos' pro exhibic' 3 scolarium in scola grammaticali apud Shirborne ex fundac' Alfrici Thornecombe.' ii. 483: ' Elemos' distrib' certis paup' scolar' ad num' 16 ut in panno laneo ill' vestiend', £7 13s. 4d. Elemos' distrib' certis paup' pueris ex ordinac' fundat' limitat' tam in eorum esculent', poculent' et al' necessariis quam in exhibic' eor'dem puer' ad studium, £3 11s. 8d.' I believe that the thirteen boys kept in Bridgewater Priory were also schoolboys (i. 209-10).

spent on the 'consolation' of poor students.[1]   In the monastic
surveys I found no mention of student monks, of whom there
were considerable numbers both at Oxford and Cambridge ;
but in the suppression account of the monastery of St. Peter's,
Gloucester, it is remarked that of its thirty monks, four
were students at Oxford, and a like number of Oxford
students were found at the time of the suppression in the
cathedral-priory of St. Swithun, Winchester.[2]   Wherever the
Valor Ecclesiasticus gives information concerning the outlay
for the relief of the poor, it is only the expense of food and
clothing that is taken into consideration.   The expenses or the
schoolboys vary considerably in the cases just mentioned.
Sometimes a pound a year or thereabouts is spent on each
boy (as at St. Peter's, Gloucester, Coventry Cathedral, Bridgewater) ; sometimes a pound and a third (as at Norwich Cathedral, Sherborne, and Bridgewater).   The charge for each boy at
Ixworth costs £1 13s. 4d., but it is possible that the fees of the
schoolmaster are included in this amount.   The cost of the
food alone to Worcester Cathedral for each schoolboy was
almost two pounds, but these were probably adults, for the
large allowance of a gallon of beer per day was given them.
At Charterhouse, Coventry, the cost per boy was £2 10s. 0d. ;
these also were possibly adults.   It costs the monasteries about
the same amount to keep a poor adult.   At Evesham and
Athelney the annual cost of each was one pound, at Norwich
a pound and a third, at Holme Cultram £1 8s. 0d., and more
than two pounds at Bridgewater and Lenton.   For keeping
thirteen poor the Nostell monks paid to the hospital of
St. Nicholas, Pontefract, £46 17s. 7½d, i.e. about £3 10s. for
each.   It may be, however, that this amount was not spent

---

[1] iii. 287 : 'Elemos' dat' 13 pueris commorantibus infra mon' erudiendis
in scola grammat' voc' Le Almery Scole vid' quolibet eor'dem iuxta rat'
£1 6s. 8d. ; pro victu et vestitu ac pro vadiis cujusdam magistri ad docend'
dc' pueros, £2 13s. 4d. necnon pro vad' cujusdam serv' attend' sup' de'
pueros, £1 0s.0d., sic fundat' p' Hilbertum quondam epm Norwici.'   iii.227:
'Elemos' pro 98 panibus voc' monke loves et pro 9 pan' voc' yoman
Paste loves septimanatim delib' 14 scolar' elemosinar' ex ordin' scor'
Oswaldi et Wolstani, £12 11s. 4d. pro 84 lagenis cervicie septim' delib'
pdc' scolaribus £6 13s. 4d. pro victual' emptis pro pdc' scholar'
£6 13s. 4d.'   Oseney, ii. 216, pro consolacione pauperum scolarium in
Universitate Oxoniensi.   [2] Exch. Augm. O. Misc. b. v. 494, pp. 101, 2.

exclusively upon the Nostell corrodians.[1] The monastery of
St. Peter's, Westminster, spent more than any other upon each
pauper relieved; fifteen people cost about £72 a year.[2]

Some of the surveys are so full of detail that they enable us
to grasp the principal methods of monastic charity. I will
quote the case of Norwich. Twelve poor men live in the
Cathedral; they eat in the monastic dining-hall at a cost of
6½d. per head per week. Besides this, the monastery spends
more than £28 on their hospital of St. Paul, Norwich.
' Poor sisters' live continually in the hospital, and other poor
come daily to the hospital to pray for the soul of the founder
and of course to be fed. Several times a year the monks give
bread and money to all the poor who come to pray for the
soul of the founder, Bishop Gilbert; £2 2s. 0d. in money is
distributed, and also as much bread as can be made out of
26 quarters of grain. The doles on Maundy Thursday, the
day of the Last Supper, are mentioned separately; it was
a holiday for the poor, and the monks endeavoured to show
their obedience to the commandment of humility not only by
the ceremony of washing the feet of the poor, but also by offer-
ing them a liberal feast. This day cost the Cathedral £10 in
bread, fish, beer and money distributed.[3]

In large monasteries where a certain proportion of income
and expenditure was appropriated to the various offices, there
was almost always an almoner, but to his office there was
generally assigned only a small part of the monastic income,
and not the whole of this was used in compulsory poor relief.
In the allotments to other offices the alms were sometimes more
considerable. Out of the budget of about £1,500 at Tewkesbury,

---

[1] V. E. iii. 252, i. 206, iii. 287, v. 283, i. 208, 209, v. 149. 63.
[2] V. E. i. 420.
[3] V. E. iii. 287. Cf. i. 251-2, iv. 274-5. Two Ramsey abbots bequeathed
doles sufficient for almost a thousand poor (960). This is the ' fundacio ' of
one of them, Johannis Tichmarch : ' in elimos' data 800 iuxta ratam 120 pro
100 pauperibus tam infra villam ibm morant' quam alien' supervenientibus
quibuscunque in festo Omnium Scorum cuilibet eorum obolum £2 0s. 0d.'
The poor ' fratres ' similar to those of Ramsey are also found in the abbey
of Chertsey (ii. 57). There were thirteen of them there, they also received
a fixed money allowance—not £0 2s. 6d. but £0 5s. 0d. In Chertsey
there were even ' half fryers ' who received half as much as the ' fratres '.
The alms at Whalley, v. 230, and at Sulby, iv. 301, are also curious.

the budget of the almoner was only £55 11s. 2d., and
of this the compulsory alms were £16 8s. 8d. only. Out of
the budget of some £800 at Selby, Yorks., only £15 16s. 7d.
went to the almoner, and of this sum only £10 was spent on
compulsory alms; whilst in the budget of the bursary the
alms for the poor amounted to £13 11s. 8d. Out of the
budget of Bury St. Edmund, Suff., which amounted to more
than £2,000, the gross income of the almoner is not more than
£43 10s. 4½d., and of this only £15 8s. 9d. is for compulsory
alms; they are more considerable in the budgets of the
sacristan, abbot and treasurer; they are very much larger
in the budgets of the hospitaller and cellarer: viz. £86 14s. 5d.
and £191 19s. 1d. It is possible that the almoner also supervised the alms attached to other offices, but in that case he
would not dispense them independently but under the directions of others.

It is impossible to judge of the whole monastic charitable List of
budget from the Valor Ecclesiasticus, for not all the alms charitable expenses.
were entered in the Commissioners' returns. But the Valor
Ecclesiasticus enables us to judge of the magnitude of the
charities that were allowed to go tax free. In the list below
are given the alms of more than two hundred monasteries
whose total income amounted to more than half of the
monastic revenue:—

Beds., Wardon, £17 2s. 1d.—Bucks., Burnham, £4 13s. 4d.;
Missenden, £1 12s. 0d.; Nutley, £1 2s. 6d.—Chesh., St. Mary,
Chester, £10 3s. 0d.; St. Werburgh, Chester, £14 0s. 0d.;
Combermere, £12 13s. 4d.; Norton, £29 0s. 0d.—Cornw.,
Bodmin, £2 12s. 0d.; St. Germans, £4 10s. 0d.; Launceston,
£7 8s. 10d.—Cumb., Carlisle, £11 7s. 8d.; Holme Cultram,
£10 0s. 0d. — Derb., Gresley, £0 18s. 4d.; Repingdon,
£10 7s. 3d. — Dev., Buckland, £0 18s. 0d.; St. Nicholas,
Exeter, £0 1s. 1d.; Totnes, £0 5s. 0d. — Dors., Hindon,
£0 16s. 8d.; Cranborne, £0 10s. 0d.; Middleton, £54 5s. 8d.;
Shaftesbury, £13 1s. 11d.; Sherborne, £18 2s. 5d.; Tarrent,
£3 0s. 0d. — Glouc., Flaxley, £2 10s. 0d.; St. Oswald,
Gloucester, £0 19s. 4d.; St. Peter, Gloucester, £114 11s. 11½d.;
Lantony, £40 5s. 6d.; Tewkesbury, £36 0s. 10d.; Winch-

combe, £11 8s. 4d.—Heref., Aconbury, £0 14s. 7d. ; Brom-
field, £0 3s. 4d. ; Clifford, £0 13s. 4d. ; Dore, £1 16s. 0d. ;
Wigmore, £3 8s. 8d. ; Wormesley, £0 9s. 1d. — Hunts.,
Huntingdon, £9 5s. 4d. ; St. Neots, £4 0s. 0d. ; Ramsey,
£47 3s. 2¼d. ; Sawtre, £0 2s. 4d.—Kent, Bilsington, £1 0s. 0d. ;
Boxley, £0 6s. 8d. ; St. Augustine's, Canterbury, £30 0s. 0d. ;
Christchurch, Canterbury, £39 6s. 4½d. ; St. Gregory, Canter-
bury, £10 6s. 8d. ; Dover, £13 19s. 2d. ; Faversham, £10 0s. 0d. ;
Horton, £1 16s. 8d. ; Leeds, £5 0s. 8d. ; St. Sexburge, Shep-
pey, £3 7s. 0d.—Lanc., Burscough, £7 0s. 0d. ; Furness,
£11 10s. 0d. ; Hornby, £4 0s. 0d. ; Penwortham, £8 13s. 4d. ;
Whalley, £121 18s. 10d.—Leic., Croxton, £8 2s. 0d. ; Garendon, £5 0s. 0d. ; Grace Dieu, £2 0s. 0d. : Launde, £3 6s. 8d. ;
Ulverscrofte, £1 13s. 0d.—Linc., Axholme, £1 3s. 0d. ; Bardney, £3 10s. 5d. ; Belvoir, £5 1s. 4d. ; Crowland, £17 6s. 8d. ;
Freston, £1 17s. 2d. ; Kyme, £17 0s. 8d. ; St. Catherine's, Lincoln, £2 3s. 4d. ; Newstead, £2 4s. 8d. ; Revesby, £1 7s. 0d. ;
Spalding, £8 8s. 7d. ; St. Michael's, Stamford, £0 6s. 4d. ; Stixwold, £7 5s. 4d. ; Thornholm, £9 0s. 0d.—Midd., Charterhouse, London, £5 2s. 4d. ; Clerkenwell, London, £1 14s. 0d. ;
Elsing Spital, London, £10 0s. 0d. ; Haliwell, London,
£6 3s. 11d. ; St. John of Jerusalem, London, £56 11s. 1d. ;
St. Mary Bishopsgate, London, £3 8s. 4d. ; St. Mary Graces,
London, £3 10s. 0d. ; Syon, £5 1s. 5d. ; St. Peter's, Westminster,
£103 18s. 5d.—Norf., Beeston, £2 13s. 8d. ; Cockesford,
£14 13s. 4d. ; Horsham, £4 11s. 0d. ; Hulme, £5 18s. 8d. ;
Ingham, £1 7s. 8d. ; Langley, £6 8s. 3d. ; Norwich Cathedral,
£89 7s. 5d. ; Thetford canons, £0 11s. 8d. ; Thetford monks,
£8 11s. 0d. ; Walsingham, £2 3s. 2d.—Northants, Ashby,
£127 18s. 0d. ; St. Andrew's, Northampton, £6 16s. 2d. ;
De la Pré, Northampton, £1 6s. 8d. ; St. James's, Northampton,
£7 19s. 4d. ; Pipewell, £4 0s. 0d. ; Sulby, £2 18s. 9d.—Notts.,
Blythe, £3 6s. 8d. ; Lenton, £17 1s. 8d. ; Newstead, £4 0s. 0d. ;
Shelford, £2 6s. 8d. ; Thurgarton, £6 8s. 1d. ; Wallingwells,
£2 6s. 8d. ; Welbeck, £8 16s. 8d. ; Worksop, £23 17s. 8d.—
Oxon., Burcester, £7 4s. 2d. ; Dorchester, £2 0s. 0d. ; Eynsham, £12 15s. 4d. ; Godstow, £19 16s. 7d. ; Oseney,
£8 15s. 4d. ; Rewley, £2 0s. 11d. ; Thame, £0 13s. 4d. ;

Wroxton, £7 10s. 0d. — Salop, Haghmond, £8 13s. 4d. ;
Halesowen, £3 7s. 4d. ; Lilleshall, £7 3s. 4d. ; Shrewsbury,
£3 13s. 8d. ; Wenlock, £8 5s. 0d. ; Wombridge, £2 13s. 4d.—
Soms., Athelney, £28 7s. 7d. ; Barlynch, £5 9s. 0d. ; Bath,
£10 9s. 2d. ; Bridgwater, £32 5s. 4d. ; Bruton, £16 6s. 8d. ;
Cleeve, £27 10s. 0d. ; Dunster, £0 14s. 8d. ; Glastonbury,
£145 16s. 8d. ; Keynsham, £10 15s. 0d. ; Montacute,
£23 8s. 7½d. ; Muchelney, £11 3s. 0d. ; Taunton, £40 19s. 0d. ;
St. John, Wells, £3 6s. 8d. ; Worspring, £10 0s. 0d.—Staff.,
Roucester, £1 17s. 4d.—Suff., Brusyard, £10 2s. 0d. ; Butley,
£10 16s. 8d. ; Eye, £7 19s. 0d. ; Flixton, £2 16s. 8d. ;
St. Trinity, Ipswich, £1 16s. 0d. ; Ixworth, £20 15s. 0d. ; Redlingfield, £9 0s. 0d. ; Sibton, £3 12s. 9½d. ; Wangford,
£2 13s. 4d. ; Woodbridge, £0 6s. 0d.—Surr., Bermondsey,
£14 8s. 8d. ; Chertsey, £14 16s. 6d. ; Merton, £5 0s. 0d. ;
Newark, £3 6s. 8d. ; Shene, £43 12s. 10d. ; Waverley,
£4 10s. 5d.—Suss., Battle, £5 2s. 10d. ; Boxgrove, £3 15s. 8½d. ;
Lewes, £34 11s. 0d. ; Tortington, £1 6s. 8d.—Warw., Coventry
Cath., £33 18s. 6d. ; Charterhouse, Coventry, £77 6s. 9d. ;
Erdbury, £3 13s. 0d. ; Kenilworth, £23 17s. 7d. ; Maxstoke,
£10 1s. 8d. ; Merevale, £11 16s. 8d. ; Nuneaton, £6 17s. 4d ;
Pinley, £1 9s. 4d. ; Pollesworth, £2 12s. 8d. ; Studley,
£4 6s. 3d. ; Wroxall, £1 0s. 0d.—Westm., Shappe, £5 17s. 10d.
Wilts., Amesbury, £3 3s. 0d. ; Bradenstoke, £13 5s. 0d. ;
Farleigh, £2 13s. 4d. ; Ivy Church, £2 0s. 0d. ; Lacock,
£9 14s. 9d. ; Maiden Bradley, £3 0s. 0d. ; Stanley, £4 0s. 0d. ;
Wilton, £20 16s. 8d.—Worc., Bordesley, £0 18s. 8d. ; Evesham, £55 3s. 8d. ; Great Malvern, £50 9s. 2d. ; Pershore,
£10 15s. 1d. ; Worcester Cathedral, £60 10s. 0d.—Yorks.,
St. Agatha's, £13 15s. 2½d. ; Bridlington, £22 6s. 8d. ; Coverham, £3 0s. 0d. ; Egglestone, £3 18s. 4d. ; Ferreby, £2 5s. 7½d. ;
Fountains, £20 5s. 0d. ; Gisburn, £24 5s. 4d. ; Grosmont,
£2 0s. 0d. ; Haltemprice, £2 0s. 5d. ; Handale, £4 19s. 8d. ;
Helagh Park, £0 1s. 11d. ; Jervaulx, £23 18s. 0d. ; Knaresborough, £0 10s. 8d. ; Marrick, £9 4s. 7½d. ; Marton,
£2 0s. 0d. ; Meaux, £16 3s. 4d. ; Middlesborough, £2 12s. 0d. ;
Monk-Bretton, £0 3s. 4d. ; Mountgrace, £0 5s. 0d. ; Mount
St. John, £5 0s. 0d. ; Newburgh, £11 17s. 10d. ; Newland,

£6 10s. od.; Nostel, £66 8s. 3½d.; Nunmonkton, £3 18s. od.; St. John's, Pontefract, £14 7s. 7d.; Roche, £1 os. od.; Selby, £25 8s. 4d.; Swine, £7 11s. 4d.; Warter, £10 16s. 4d.; Whitby, £25 13s. 4d.

This list includes 210 monasteries having a gross income of nearly ninety thousand pounds. The alms free of the 'tenth' tax amount to about £2,700, i.e. 3 per cent. of the gross income. But there are a great many monasteries in the V. E. where alms are not mentioned at all in the survey. Excluding those with an income of less than £50, as not being rich enough to be charitable, more than a hundred monasteries may be found in the V. E. that did not dispense any alms free of Tenths. I give the instances that I discovered :—

Beds., Bushmead, Caldwell, Dunstable, Elnstow, Merkyate, Newenham, Woburn ; Bucks., Lavenden; Chesh., Birkenhead, Vale Royal ; Cornw., Tywardreath ; Cumb., Lanercost; Derb., Beauchief, Dale ; Dev., Buckfastleigh, Canonleigh, Dunkeswell, Ford, Frithelstoke, Hartland, Pilton, Plympton, Polslo, Tavistock Abbey, Tavistock Priory, Torre; Glouc., Deerhurst, St. Leonard Stanley ; Heref., St. Guthlac ; Hunts., Stonely ; Kent, Combewell, St. Radegund Dover, Langdon, Malling, Muttlinden ; Lanc., Holland ; Leic., Kirby Beller, St. Mary, Leic., Olveston; Linc., Alvingham, Bollington, Greenfield, Hagnaby, Hevening, Kirkstead, Legbourne, Louth Park, Markby, Neubo, Newsome, Nocton Park, Nuncotton, Nunormsby, Sempringham, Sixhill, Swineshed, Thornton, Tupholme, Vaudey, Wellow, Willoughton ; Midd., St. Helen's London, St. Bartholomew's London, Minories London, St. Thomas of Acres London, Stratford-at-Bow ; Norf., Blackborough, Bromholm, Hickling, Pentney cum Wormgay, Shouldham, Thetford nuns, Wendling, Westacre, W. Dereham, Wymondham ; Northants, Fineshade ; Notts., Beauvale, Felley, Mattersey, Rufford; Oxon., Studley ; Salop, Buildewas, Chirbury ; Soms., Henton, Minchin Bockland, Templecombe, Witham ; Staff., Croxden, Dieulacres, Hulton, Ronton, St. Thomas Stafford, Stone, Trentham; Suff., Leiston ; Surr., Reigate, St. Mary Southwark, Tandridge ; Suss., Hastings, Michelham, Robertsbridge ; Warw., Alcester,

Warwick; Wilts., Edingdon, Eston; Worc., L. Malvern, Westwood, Whiston; Yorks., Hampole, Thinningthwaite.

In this list there are 113 monasteries whose total income is more than twenty-two thousand pounds. Taking the two lists together, we shall find that the monastic alms composed less than $2\frac{1}{2}$ per cent. of the gross income. But it must be remembered that the Commissioners of 1535 did not record all the monastic alms and not even the whole of the compulsory alms, but only the alms free of 'Tenth'. One can hardly doubt that they treated in different ways the very same kind of charitable expenses, recording them in the case of some monasteries and not in others. In the second there are nine monasteries whose gross income is more than five hundred pounds: Buckfastleigh £505, Edindon £522, Vale Royal £540, Southwark £657, Thornton £731, St. Bartholomew's London, £763, Tavistock Abbey £911, Plympton £931, St. Mary, Leicester £1,057. Can we believe that these monasteries gave nothing at all to the poor under the wills of their benefactors? In the Commissioners' returns for Devonshire, Staffordshire, and Bedfordshire (if we exclude Wardon) hardly any alms are mentioned. It is difficult to believe that none of the Devonshire and Staffordshire monasteries bestowed any prescribed charity. It is much easier to suppose that the Commissioners of these two counties refused to exempt from the Tenth, alms such as in other counties were allowed to go free. The fiscal motive is especially evident in the surveys of hospitals, whose chief purpose was to help travellers, the sick and the poor; works of charity made a great drain upon their budget. These alms, however, are either not mentioned at all in the surveys of the hospitals, or only a very small amount of them is entered by the Commissioners. I will instance the largest London hospital—St. Mary's, Bishopsgate. It is said to have distributed £3 8s. 4d. in alms, but at the suppression in 1539 the number of persons relieved at this hospital was thirty-four, and it used probably to be more.[1] One cannot, of course, think that all the charitable expenditure of these hospitals was voluntary

[1] Gasquet, ii. 511, with a reference to Exch. Acc. 253, 12.

and that not one of the founders specified the purposes for
which the revenues given by him were to be used. Whenever
the administrators of the hospital endeavoured to procure the
entry in the survey of all its compulsory expenses for the
relief of the poor the Commissioners crossed out the items,
for by taking into consideration all the expenditure the Crown
would gain too little out of its Tenth. The small Yorkshire
monastery of Northallerton, with a gross income of £59, spent
£28 a year on the relief of twelve persons; this expenditure is
crossed out in the survey in spite of a definite indication given
as to its compulsory nature.

Monastic hospitality. It is impossible, from the Valor Ecclesiasticus, to judge of
the voluntary charitable expenses of the monks. In particular
instances, the charitable expenditure, entered in the primary
survey but omitted in the diocesan returns, may be very
considerable, and may equal, or even exceed, the alms free of
tax. The latter at Christchurch, Canterbury, are given as
£39 6s. 4½d., the taxed alms are £38 6s. 4d. : the corresponding figures for St. Augustine's, Canterbury, are £30 and
£16 5s. 0d.; for St. Peter's, Westminster, £103 18s. 5d. and
£161 13s. 4d.; for Furness, Lanc., £11 10s. 0d. and £21 13s. 4d.;
for St. Catherine's, Lincoln, £2 3s. 4d. and £21 13s. 4d. But
compared with the whole monastic budget the alms entered in
the Valor Ecclesiasticus, even if we include the taxed alms,
appear to be very small. And only the smaller part of
these alms was spent on corrodians; the compulsory monastic
alms consisted chiefly of common and open doles on holidays
and commemoration days. Poor corrodians are mentioned
in the case of a few houses only, and in comparatively small
numbers. Five at Lenton, Notts.; six at Evesham, Worc.;
eleven at Athelney, Soms.; twelve at Christchurch, Canterbury;
thirteen both at Furness, Lanc., and Nostel, Yorks.; eighteen
at St. Peter's, Westminster, and twenty-four at Whalley, Lanc.
Where the V. E. does not mention monastic corrodians, it does
not follow that there were none. They may have lived in other
houses. In the surveys of Garendon, Grace Dieu, and Erdbury,

---

[1] V. E. v. 85 : ' ex fundacione domini episcopi Dunelmensis.'

the Valor Ecclesiasticus mentions only the common doles, but
the Commissioners at the suppression found there corrodians
also (5, 9, and 6).   But even in these cases the number of
poor corrodians is less than the number of monks ; even if we
count the schoolboys in Garendon, Grace Dieu and Erdbury,
there are only 25 poor persons to 38 monks, and in other
monasteries the proportion was still smaller according to the
Suppression Account.   There can be no doubt that the number
of poor living on the liberality of a particular monastery was
smaller, and probably much smaller than the number of the
monks.   If in judging of the charitable work of the monks we
confine ourselves to the corrodians, we shall have to admit
that in their latter days the monasteries in this way did
very little to alleviate the acute distress of their time.
Even the Tudor apologists for the monks confirm by their
silence the justice of this remark.   They are obliged to speak
not of the almshouses or asylums of the monasteries, but of
monastic hospitality.   When the Visitors and Suppressors
complain of the decay of monastic charity, they speak of the
absence of 'hospitality'.   Certainly the word has a wide
meaning, but it primarily means intermittent assistance given
sporadically to the poor and to travellers.[1]   When these same
apologists wish to show how important the charitable work
is, they speak of the wildness of the country in which the
monastery is the only safe place of refuge.[2]   One of the chief
arguments of modern apology for English pre-Reformation
monasticism is furnished by the evidence given by Robert
Aske.   At his examination he tells at some length how necessary and dear to the population of the northern counties
are the disappearing monasteries ; and of all the aspects of
monastic charitable work the most important in his eyes seems
to have been that of 'hospitality'.   When the monasteries
disappeared, then hospitality also disappeared. Many northern

---

[1] Archbold, 68.   Legh to Cromwell: ' I founde thabbot very necligent
in admynystracion—and in manor no servauntes mayntenyd or hospitalite
kept.'
[2] Exch. Treas. of Rec. M. b. v. 154: 'Ulverscroft stendith in a wilder-
nesse in the forest of Charnewood, and refressith many pore people and
wayefaryng people.'

monasteries were situated in mountainous or wild districts, where the monks alone could give 'refreshment' to people; the corndealers and pilgrims in the North found a refuge in the monasteries, without which it would have been impossible for them to continue their journeys.[1] When Brinklow, the emigrant and ex-friar, praises the kindness of the monks as compared with the harshness of the lords who seized upon the monastic parishes, he refers chiefly to monastic hospitality and the common doles.[2] The revolutionary monk who met his death gloriously in the fighting line, and was one of the earliest authors of the Roman Catholic version of Reformation history, does not speak of corrodians but praises the monastic hospitality and the liberal common doles.[3]

Corrodians proper.

Corrodium signifies food, and in a special sense monastic food allowances; people receiving such an allowance had to live either in the monastery itself or near it. Spelman believes that the founders were entitled at common law to maintain one corrodian in the monastery. The king had the right in a great many (119) monasteries of sending one or two corrodians, and Spelman concludes from this that such monasteries were founded by the Crown.[4]

Fuller also speaks of the right of the founders to send a certain number of their poor servants into the monastery.[5] In the

---

[1] Gairdner, xii, i. 901, Aske's examination, art. 23=E. H. R. v. 561-2. Cf. Gasquet, ii. 91-100, 131-2.

[2] Brinklow, ch. 14: 'Of lordes that are parsons and vicars. The monkes kepte hospitalyte and helped their pore frinds . . . and as toching the almesse that they dealt and the hospitalyte that they kepte, many thowsandes were well releved of them.'

[3] Sanders, 147: 'Vitingus pro abbatum consuetudine ad 300 domesticos sustentabat (if, as Sanders says, there were as many as a hundred monks in Glastonbury, the number of domestics is very probable) atque in iis multos nobilium filios, plurimos praeterea ad literarum studia in academiis alebat; hospitalitatem in omnes peregrinos exercebat quacunque causa transeuntes: ita ut 500 aliquando, eosque equites, eodem tempore reciperet: quartis ac sextis feriis, elemosynas amplas certasque pauperibus undique ex vicinis pagis concurrentibus distribuebat atque haec etiam fuerat aliorum, fere angliae caenobiorum ac abbatum *ditiorum* consuetudo.' Considerably later Spelman affirmed that many thousands of poor people lived in monasteries as corrodians (Spelman, *Sacr.* 129). The authorities of the sixteenth century are of course much more trustworthy.

[4] Spelman, *Glossar.*, v. corrodium al' corredium. 'Alimenti modus qui in aliquo monasterio alicui conceditur,' &c. As to early *corrodia* vide Pollock and Maitland, ii. 134-5.   [5] Fuller, 326.

Valor Ecclesiasticus *corrodia* are seldom found, and then mostly given to one person, very rarely to two. Here are the instances which I have noted: the figures stand for the amount of the corrodia :—Bed., Wardon, £2 13s. 4d. ; Cheshire, Vale Royal, £3 6s. 8d.: Cornw., Tywardreath, £3 6s. 8d. ; Derb., Dale, £1 6s. 8d. ; Dors., Bindon, £2 13s. 4d ; Cerne, £6 13s. 4d. ; Middleton, £11 13s. 4d. ; Sherborne, £5 0s. 0d. ; Glouc., St. Peter's, Glouc., £14 6s. 8d. ; Hunts., Ramsey, £5 10s. 8d.; Kent, St. Gregory's, Canterbury, £2 13s. 4d. ; Linc., Spalding, £7 10s. 0d. ; Norf., Thetford Monks, £4 11s. 3d. ; Salop, Lilleshall, £3 0s. 0d.; Shrewsbury, £11 0s. 0d. ; Wenlock, £10 0s. 0d.; Soms., Glastonbury, £5 0s. 0d. ; Montacute, £2 13s. 4d. ; Staff., Burton upon Trent, £3 6s. 8d. ; Trentham, £2 0s. 0d.; Surr., Chertsey, £3 6s. 8d.; Merton, £4 10s. 0d.; Wilts., Malmesbury, £10 0s. 0d. ; Stanley, £9 13s. 4d.[1] ; Wilton, £5 3s. 4d.[2] ; Worc., Bordesley, £2 13s. 4d.; Evesham, £4 0s. 0d. ; Worcester Cathedral, £5 16s. 0d. ; Yorks., Nostell £2 13s. 4d.: Selby £3 6s. 8d. ; Warter £0 10s. 0d.   In the surveys of Cerne, Middleton, St. Peter's Gloucester, Spalding, Malmesbury, Shrewsbury and Stanley, two corrodians are found in each case ; in the survey of Wilton four corrodians are mentioned, and in other cases one in each. Nearly all the corrodies are paid by the king's appointment or to the king's servants ; only in one instance, that of St. Gregory's, Canterbury, is an appointment by the founder mentioned (i. 16 : Magistro Leonardo Hethrington servienti domini archiepiscopi fundatoris nostri nomine corrodii £2 13s. 4d.) ; in the surveys of Warter and Stanley it is not said by whom the corrody is appointed. Occasionally the period for which it is granted is mentioned : at Vale Royal

---

[1] ii. 115 : 'Pencion' solut' Johi Fysshar pro corrodio suo per annum £4 13s. 4d., Georgio Bregus idem.' But I did not consider as a corrody the following entry : 'et solut' 3 pauperibus Edithe Lowce Agneti Merler et Johanne Maynarde cuilibet illarum ann' £1 6s. 8d. pro corrodiis suis et ordin' fundatoris.'

[2] The entry is unusual, ii. 112 : 'in annua sol' priori Ederos £0 18s. 4d. priori sci Dionisii £2 16s. 8d. priori sci Johis iuxta Wilton £1 8s. 4d. pro 4 corrodiis suis.' It may be that the priors had the right to appoint corrody. I have not counted the following entries as corrodies: 'Bulbridge in quadam penc' sive augmento vicario de Bulbridge ut in precio unius corrodii panis et s' vicie per annum £1 0s. 0d.'

and Malmesbury a corrody is granted for life; at Thetford
to two people 'for two lives'; at Warter and perhaps
at Selby, 'sibi et heredibus suis.'[1] The average worth of
a corrody is more than the annual monastic outlay of alms
for one pauper. The corrodies were evidently given to people
of a higher social status and occasionally to people who probably were not poor. Among those in receipt of corrodies is
a doctor at Ramsey, priests at Dale and Nostell, a gentleman
at Thetford, esquires at Evesham and Worcester Cathedral,
the king's servants at St. Peter's Gloucester, St. Gregory's
Canterbury, Wardon, Thetford and Selby; one of the king's
servants, receiving a very large corrody from the monastery of
St. Peter's, Gloucester, had a servant of his own (ii. 418: 'Corrodium Johannis Pye servientis dni regis unacum esculentis
suis et pro famulo suo £10 0s. 0d.'). Evidently some of the
corrodies mentioned in the Valor Ecclesiasticus had ceased
to be paid in kind and had become money payments.[2]

Corrodians
by pur-
chase. The Valor Ecclesiasticus by no means mentions all those
who received monastic corrodies. The Suppression Accounts
often mention corrodians in monasteries where they were not
noted by the Commissioners of 1535. Corrodians are found in
nine of the Suppression Accounts which I used (pp. 224–5),
but in the corresponding surveys in the V.E. the corrodies are
not once mentioned. Possibly the Commissioners of 1535 knew
of the expenditure on corrodies but did not consider it as tax
free and therefore omitted it; why they should tax the corrodies, if they knew about them, will be readily understood from
some instances. Thus, in the Suppression Accounts of Grace
Dieu and Garendon the receivers of the corrody are called
corrodians by purchase.[3] These people were of no expense
at all to the house. They sought within the monastic walls,

[1] Warter, v. 126: 'Soluc' cuiusdam corod' Wmo Babthorpe et hered'
suis imppm ann' solut' £0 10s. 0d.'; this is a very poor allowance and not
sufficient to live upon. Selby, v. 13: 'Rico Trice servienti dni regis pro
corrodio annali per dnm regem conc' imppm per annum £3 6s. 8d.'
[2] Nostell, v. 63: 'Denar' annuatim solut' de corrod' per dnm regem
concesso,' &c.
[3] Exch. Treas. Rec. Misc. b. v. 154: 'Garendon: persons havyng corrodies by purches 2. Gracedieu: persons havyng ther lyvyng of the same
hows by purchase 3.'

not free food but comfortable and healthy quarters, which they purchased. Rich and pious old men went into a monastery to spend the remainder of their lives ; they gave to the monks a certain sum of money and entered into a formal agreement (under covent seal) in which sometimes the food to which they were entitled was stated with minute detail. In a survey of 31 and 32 H. VIII of Grace Dieu, curious details are preserved concerning corrodians of precisely this sort. A husband and wife gave £20 to the nuns in Grace Dieu in 23 H. VIII, for which the latter promised to feed the couple for life, and give them bread, meat, ale and small ale, fuel and pasture for four cows and two pigs ; evidently the old people had migrated to the monastery with their own cows and pigs.[1]

But even if we include in the population dependent upon the monastic revenue all the corrodians, the number will not be sufficiently great to cause any substantial modification of our views about the economic influence of the monasteries. Another class of persons, omitted in the Suppression Accounts, and known almost exclusively through the Valor Ecclesiasticus, appears to be of greater importance; I mean the lay administrators of the monastic estates, stewards, bailiffs, receivers and auditors. The Suppression Accounts pass them over because they did not generally live in the monastery itself; they did not receive immediate assistance from the Suppressors, as they retained their former fees. On the other hand, the Valor Ecclesiasticus speaks only of these higher officers because, out of all the monastic expenditure for administrators and labourers, the Commissioners of 1535 were permitted to make tenth-free only the perpetual fees of the receivers, bailiffs, auditors and stewards. *Lay administrators.*

[1] Exch. Augm. O. M. b. v. 294 : 'Computus Georgii Giffarde receptoris curie augment' in comitat' Ntht., Leic., Warw.' Mich. 31 H. VIII–Mich. 32 H. VIII, ff. 78–80: 'In corrodio Wmi Berfote et Johanne uxoris eius quibus nuper priorissa de Gracedieu et conventus in consideracione 20 l. eis solut' per lras suas indentatas 23 Junii, 23 H. VIII, dederunt quoddam corrodium pro termino vitae eorum et eorum alterius diutius viventis viz. qualibet septimana 10 panes conventuales et 7 lagenas cervisie conventualis et unam lagenam minoris cervisie vocate smalle ale et quolibet anno 8 carectat' focalium ac herbagium et pasturam pro 4 vaccis per totum annum ac victum pro 2 porcis per totum annum et quolibet die carnum unum ferculum,' &c.

Fees of the officials.

The amount of the fees of these officers is given in a great many surveys, but here again we must make some reservations. The figures of the fees in the Valor Ecclesiasticus almost always stand not for the whole of the monastic expenditure on the lay officials, but only for the money which the monastery was bound by agreement to pay directly into their hands. Besides these money payments, the monastery had to incur considerable expense for food, livery and travelling expenses of the officials and their servants. Occasionally the monks endeavoured to introduce everything into the survey. In the budget of Christchurch, Canterbury, we find very heavy travelling expenses for the warden of the manors and for the auditor, who travelled in various counties with a retinue of eight people, but this entry was crossed out at the revision.[1] The nuns of Godstow petition against the payment of the Tenth on the amount of expenditure for the meals of their lay officials, but it is hardly likely that even they themselves had any hope of success.[2] Some cases are, however, found, though rarely, where the expenditure for food and the travelling expenses of the officials entered in the survey were allowed to pass tenth-free, either owing to inadvertence or on account of some special consideration. I found such leniency exercised in the surveys of Amesbury, Wilts.; Syon, Middlesex; and of Norwich Cathedral.[3]

---

[1] i. 16: 'Pro expenc' unius monachi monasterii pdci officio custodis maneriorum eiusdem monasterii fungentis anglice dicti the Warden of the manners annuatim bis cum auditore dci monasterii et eorum 8 servientibus equitantibus per comitatus Norf. Suff. Oxon Bucks Essex Surr. Sussex et Kanc. ad recipiendum firmas redditus et revenciones maneriorum terrarum et tentorum ad dcm monast' pertin' in comitatibus pdctis et in com' Devon ac civitate London exist' per annum ad minus £43 6s. 8d.'

[2] ii. 196: 'We most lowly beseche to be alowyd for dietts of our generall receyvors, auditors, stywards and bayliffs £13 6s. 8d.' It must, however, be added that, strangely enough, the travelling expenses of the receiver-general remained untouched in the same survey, ii. 191.

[3] Amesbury, ii. 95 : 'Generalis receptor, auditor, deputatus senescalli' receive fees of £24 2s. 0d.; other money besides fees is spent on them. 'In denariis alloc' annuatim pro expensis receptoris cum 2 famulis suis cum al' ei venien' et auditoris ac subsenescalli terr' cum 2 servien' pro eorum esculentis qualibet septimana £0 6s. 8d. £17 6s. 8d.' Besides, 16s. for clothes for each of 6 bailiffs are included in the survey. Syon, i. 426: 'Thome Watson senes' omnium poss' mon' pdci pro feodo suo in denariis £5 0s. 0d. et pro mans' s' ad 16d. per septimanam et 3 servient' s' cuiuslibet eorum cuiuslibet ad 12d. septimanam £11 5s. 4d., ac pro liberatura sua et cleric' 30s. necnon pro feno et provend' pro 4 equis £6 in

Such entries cannot, of course, be regarded in the same light as entries in which only the fees, in the narrow sense of the word, are given. Other entries excite our suspicions by the small amount of the administrative expenditure. True, there might be a considerable difference between two monasteries in the cost of administration. The lands of some were scattered, those of others concentrated within a small area. In some houses the monks themselves could take part in the administration of the landed estates, in others the whole management was in lay hands. In some districts the lay officials were unimportant people content with small pay; in others they were men of high position accustomed to big fees. In two monasteries in one and the same county, with about the same annual gross income, the expenses of administration differ considerably. Sixhill and Stixwold were both situated in Lincolnshire, not far from each other; the annual income of Sixhill was £169 18s. 8d., of Stixwold £163 1s. 2½d.; administration in the former appears to cost £4 6s. 8d., in the latter £17 10s. 0d. No matter how great the difference is between two sets of figures, there is no need to consider both wrong; the expenditure on administration may be found ranging between 10 and 1 per cent., but 5 per cent. may be taken as a fair average.

But much more considerable and much more surprising deviations from the average are found in the Valor Ecclesiasticus. Holme Cultram, a monastery in Cumberland, had a gross income of £535 3s. 7½d., and the fees of the administrators were said to be only £5; Nostell, a monastery in Yorkshire, had the gross income of £606 9s. 3½d., and the fees of the administrators were said to be only £7. Most probably, in this case, that part of the fees which was tenth-free was not

---

toto £23 15s. 4d. Johi Morres gen' recept' mon' pdci pro feodo in denariis 5 l. et pro mensa sua et 2 servientium s' per annum £8 13s. 4d. ac pro liberar' et clic' suorum 30s. necnon pro feno et provend' pro 3 equis per annum £4 10s. 0d. in toto £19 13s. 4d. Johi Mynne audit' £6 13s. 4d. pro liberat' sua et cleric' 30s. in toto £8 3s. 4d.' It may be that indulgence was exercised because the chief steward in Syon was Cromwell himself. Norwich Cathedral, iii. 288 : ' J. Heydon mil' cap' sen' ' receives the fee of £3 6s. 8d., but £10 more is spent upon him ' pro liberatura sua et expensis equorum suorum.'

entered in the survey. In the survey of Catesby only the chief steward, Cromwell, is mentioned; not a word is said about bailiffs and other administrators, though Cromwell did not, of course, manage these lands himself. I thought it more advisable not to include such cases as this in my long list giving the amounts of the monastic expenditure on lay administration.

List of fees.　Beds., Caldwell, £7 6s. 8d.; Harwold, £4 13s. 4d.; Newnham, £12 3s. 4d.; Woburn, £16 3s. 4d.—Bucks., Ankerwyke, £4 6s. 8d.; Lavendon, £3 5s. 0d.; Missenden, £7 6s. 8d.; Nutley, £15 3s. 4d.—Chesh., Birkenhead, £8 3s. 4d.; St. Werburg, Chester, £31 0s. 0d.—Cornwall, Launceston, £18 11s. 0d.—Derb., Beauchief, £9 13s. 4d.; Dale, £3 0s. 0d.; Repingdon, £12 6s. 8d.—Devon, Buckfastleigh, £12 16s. 0d.; Hartland, £11 15s. 0d.; Newenham, £11 6s. 0d.; Plympton, £14 12s. 0d.; Tavistock, £27 11s. 2d.; Torre, £12 0s. 0d.; Totnes, £5 13s. 4d.—Dorset, Cerne, £33 16s. 8d.; Shaftesbury, £67 7s. 0d.; Sherborne, £32 8s. 1d.; Tarrent, £17 2s. 6d.—Glouc., St. Peter's, Gloucester, £80 11s. 4d.; Lantony, £36 2s. 8d.; Tewkesbury, £55 19s. 3d.; Winchcombe, £21 11s. 2d.—Heref., Aconbury, £5 13s. 4d.; St. Guthlac's, £10 17s. 8d.; Wigmore, £29 0s. 0d.—Hunts., St. Neots, £8 13s. 4d.; Ramsey, £130 11s. 6d.; Sawtre, £4 0s. 0d.—Kent, St. Augustine's, Canterbury, £59 18s. 0d.; Dover, £15 6s. 8d.; Faversham, £23 14s. 8d.; Malling, £12 7s. 5d.; Sheppey, £6 0s. 0d.—Lanc., Cartmell, £20 0s. 0d.; Cockersand, £27 0s. 0d.; Furness, £62 4s. 4d.; Horneby, £3 13s. 4d.; Whalley, £48 3s. 4d.—Leic., Croxton, £37 5s. 4½d.; Garendon, £11 16s. 8d.; Kirby Beller, £3 16s. 8d.; St. Mary's, Leicester, £23 5s. 0d.; Olveston, £3 10s. 0d.; Ulverscroft, £3 6s. 8d.—Linc., Bardney, £16 10s. 0d.; Bollington, £11 6s. 8d.; Crowland, £64 5s. 10d.; Hagnaby, £2 13s. 4d.; Kirkstead, £24 6s. 8d.; Kyme, £4 0s. 0d.; Louth Park, £9 13s. 4d.; Neubo, £4 10s. 0d.; Newsome, £6 13s. 4d.; Revesby, £9 16s. 4d.; Sempringham, £10 10s. 0d.; Sixhill, £4 6s. 8d.; Stixwold, £17 10s. 0d.; Thornton, £27 16s. 8d.; Willoughton, £16 13s. 4d.—Midd., Haliwell, £18 0s. 0d.; St. Bartholomew's, London, £17 0s. 0d.; Stratford at Bow, £8 0s. 0d.; St. Peter's,

Westminster, £194 2s. 4½d.—Norf., Hickling, £6 16s. 8d.; Horsham, £10 0s. 0d.; Hulme, £31 13s. 4d.; Langley, £8 4s. 0d.; Norwich Cathedral, £57 11s. 8d.; Shouldham, £4 6s. 8d.; Walsingham, £10 15s. 0d.; Wendling, £2 4s. 8d.; Wymondham, £17 0s. 0d.—Northants, Fineshade, £4 6s. 8d.; St. Andrew's, Northampton, £15 4s. 4d.; Pipewell, £20 10s. 0d.; Sulby, £12 0s. 0d.—Notts., Lenton, £17 15s. 4d.; Rufford, £18 10s. 0d.; Thurgarton, £15 6s. 8d.; Worksop, £11 0s. 0d. —Oxon., Eynsham, £47 1s. 8d.; Godstow, £23 1s. 4d.; Rewley, £6 6s. 8d.; Studley, £7 6s. 8d.; Wroxton, £8 6s. 8d.; —Salop, Buildwas, £11 13s. 4d.; Haghmond, £13 0s. 0d.; Lilleshall, £26 8s. 8d.; Shrewsbury, £33 3s. 4d.; Wombridge, £2 10s. 0d.—Soms., Barlynch, £19 10s. 0d.; Bath, £23 10s. 0d.; Bruton, £26 16s. 8d.; Glastonbury, £124 2s. 1¼d.; Keynsham, £30 0s. 0d.; Montacute, £16 13s. 3¼d.; Taunton, £25 5s. 4d.; St. John's, Wells, £4 13s. 4d.—Staff., Hulton, £6 0s. 0d. Ronton, £4 6s. 8d., Rocester, £9 13s. 4d.; St. Thomas's, Stafford, £11 13s. 4d.; Stone, £3 6s. 8d.; Tutbury, £18 13s. 4d. —Suff., Bury St. Edmunds, £130 4s. 0d.; Flixton, £5 13s. 4d.; Ipswich, £7 6s. 8d.; Ixworth, £7 13s. 4d.; Leiston, £10 0s. 0d.; Redlingfield, £4 0s. 0d.—Surr., Bermondsey, £15 16s. 8d.; Chertsey, £29 10s. 0d.; Merton, £23 3s. 4d.; Newark, £14 6s. 8d.; St. Mary Overey, £16 6s. 8d.; Waverley, £6 11s. 8d.—Suss., Battle, £47 11s. 6d.; Lewes, £62 5s. 4d.; Michelham, £11 2s. 0d.; Robertsbridge, £7 16s. 8d.—Warw., Kenilworth, £21 16s. 8d.; Merevale, £15 6s. 8d.; Nuneaton, £19 13s. 4d.; Pollesworth, £7 6s. 8d.; Studley, £8 3s. 4d.; Wroxall, £3 6s. 8d.—Wilts., Bradenstoke, £15 6s. 8d.; Edindon, £22 10s. 0d.; Kington, £6 13s. 4d.; Lacock, £14 13s. 4d.; Malmesbury, £44 0s. 0d.; Stanley, £12 0s. 0d.; Wilton, £16 13s. 4d.—Worc., Bordesley, £11 7s. 0d.; Evesham, £72 16s. 7d.; M. Malvern, £29 4s. 8d.; Pershore, £46 0s. 8d.; Worcester Cathedral, £45 4s. 10d.—Yorks., St. Agatha's, £9 16s. 8d.; Bridlington, £20 13s. 4d.; Fountains, £48 13s. 4d.; Gisburn, £22 3s. 4d.; Jervaulx, £33 13s. 4d.; Meaux, £9; Newburgh, £28 6s. 8d.; Pontefract, £23 0s. 0d.; Roche, £9 6s. 8d.; Selby, £46 0s. 0d.; Whitby, £22 0s. 0d.

The expenditure on administrators' fees in all the 156

monasteries in the above list amounts to £3,481 13s. 3½d., and the gross income of the same monasteries is a little less than seventy thousand pounds; about 5 % therefore of the gross income is spent upon fees. This figure appears to be very small, but the V. E. gives only a part of the expenditure on a part of the administrative staff. The inferior officials and workmen hired for a definite period of time are omitted in accordance with 26 H. VIII, c. 3; the statute admits the perpetual fees of sheriffs and judges; but the official Instruction disregards them; the money for food, travelling and livery of stewards, auditors and receivers is very seldom included in surveys. The administration of their landed estates cost the monasteries much more than 5 per cent. of the gross income.

Number of lay officials.

The Valor Ecclesiasticus enables us to judge not only of the cost, but even of the number of the administrative *personnel*. In order to make the figures more convincing, one has but to compare them with the numbers of other sets of persons dependent upon the monastic budget, with the number of the monks themselves, or with the number of the inferior officials and labourers. I therefore have counted up the lay administrators in those monasteries for which the Suppression Accounts give the number of religious persons, and (vide table on p. 221) the figures are as follows:—Derb., Dale, 2; Repton, 5; Glouc., Cirencester, 25; St. Peter's, Gloucester, 44; Hayles, 7; Tewkesbury, 47; Winchcombe, 15; Hunts., Huntingdon, 8; Sawtre, 2; Stonely, 3; Lanc., Burscough, 4; Cartmell, 7; Cockersand, 16; Conishead, 7; Holland, 2; Leic., Garendon, 7; Grace Dieu, 6; Kirby Beller, 5; Langley, 2; Olveston, 4; Ulverscroft, 3; Northants, Pipewell, 13; Salop, Lilleshall, 13; Staff., Dieulacres, 4; St. Thomas, Stafford, 10; Suss., Boxgrove, 2; Dureford, 4; Hastings, 2; Michelham, 6; Shulbrede, 3; Tortington, 7; Warw., Coventry Charterhouse, 2; Erdbury, 7; Henwood, 2; Maxtoke, 7; Merevale, 8; Pinley, 2; Pollesworth, 5; Stoneleigh, 6; Studley, 5; St. Sepulchre, Warwick, 2; Wroxall, 2; Wilts., Amesbury, 17; Malmesbury, 22.

In these 44 monasteries there were found, in 1535, 371 administrators receiving perpetual fees; a little later, at the time of the suppression, 527 religious persons were found in them. It is of course possible that some officials are omitted in the Valor Ecclesiasticus, especially bailiffs, and that consequently the total of 371 ought to be slightly increased, but on the other hand the number of religious persons in the monasteries was somewhat greater in 1535 than at the time of suppression. Besides, plurality existed in the monastic administration. Enterprising auditors served in several monasteries contemporaneously. The monks vied with each other in trying to secure influential peers and statesmen as their chief stewards; in 1535 the Earl of Shrewsbury served as steward or chief steward in eleven monasteries. Thus in the monastic system of administration the officers were less numerous than the offices, and there can be no doubt that in 1535 there were fewer lay officers than monks. Not all of these officers lived entirely at the expense of the monastic budget. When monastic estates were scattered, a special bailiff was not infrequently kept for the management of some small estate, and for the collection of some income in a place remote from the monastery; such work as this took up but little time, and the monks would give to the bailiff or receiver only a small remuneration, which to him would be but a subsidiary source of income. Among the 44 officers mentioned in the survey of St. Peter's, Gloucester, were 16 persons—15 bailiffs and 1 steward—who received less than ten shillings. Among them N. Capenor received 4s. and had to collect £12 17s. 1¾d. of monastic revenue in Longforde; W. Davys received 3s. 4d., and had to collect £7 5s. 8d. of monastic revenue in Tyverton; J. Taynton received 2s. and had to collect £7 os. 8d. of monastic revenue in Tyverton. True, the duties of such bailiffs were sometimes exceedingly simple. J. Corbett had nothing more to do than to collect annually from a Norwich priest £4 out of the parish revenues; for this he received 6s. 8d., which seems liberal enough remuneration. There are individual cases in which it is difficult to understand why a monastery should have continued to hold its distant and scattered property. Thus, the Cheshire monastery of Birkenhead had estates in Lancashire that brought in an income of

15s. 2d. ; of this sum the monastery had to pay 10s. to the king, and 13s. 4d. to a special bailiff who collected the rent. Unless the Valor Ecclesiasticus has mistaken the facts, these estates actually cost the monastery 8s. 2d. a year.

Duties of lay officials.

The Commissioners of 1535 were allowed to enter in the survey only the stewards, bailiffs, receivers and auditors. A large monastery might have other officials as well, but their fees were not exempt from the tenth-tax. The monks of Canterbury Cathedral did introduce into their account (i. 16) their marshal, doctor, four attorneys-general ('apud West-monasterium, in scaccario regis, in civitate London, infra Cantuariam') and their Westminster solicitor, but the expenses on all these officials were disallowed at the revision. Stewards were chiefly, if not entirely, the representatives of monastic jurisdiction as chairmen or judges in the monastic courts. The numerous bailiffs were administrators in the proper sense of the term ; they supervised all the work in places where the monks had demesne in hand, and where all the land was let out they took care that the farmers and tenants committed no waste, cut down no wood, did not overfeed the pasture or catch too many fish. If a monastery had to do repairs anywhere, the bailiff drew up the estimate and looked after the workmen ; he used often also to collect the tenurial payments, and was called 'ballivus sive receptor', 'ballivus sive collector redditus.' Not the whole of the manorial revenues found its way to the monastery, for a part thereof was used on the spot to meet the current local expenses. The surplus of revenue from large areas was collected by special receivers, and the control over these, and the book-keeping were entrusted to the auditors. The economic year began at Michaelmas, and the local revenues were sent to the monastery either once or twice a year—at Michaelmas or Lady Day. Before each accounting term came round, the monastic estates were visited by the auditor, who verified the local accounts and helped the bailiff to write up the current account; and if any changes had occurred in the manor, either with regard to the tenants or the amount of the payments, he made a new survey. With, or after the auditor came the receiver, who, having received the money either from the bailiff or direct from the tenants, brought it to the monastery. In some large monasteries the chief supervision of the local households was entrusted to a special 'warden of the manors' (*custos maneriorum*). The warden of the manors of Canterbury Cathedral went round the monastic estates twice a year, along with the auditor and a retinue of eight people. The big houses had several stewards and receivers, but even the richest monasteries were content with one auditor. The larger monasteries had separate receivers for different counties in addition to the receiver-general, and the chief steward stood at the head of all the other stewards. It is hardly likely that the chief stewardship (*capitalis senescalleria*) had attached to it any constant and definite duties: it was probably what we should call a sinecure; it was frequently held by a peer, and often several monasteries had the same chief steward. The monastery needed him not for his work, but for his influence, and especially at critical times, when it would be important to have a strong man at the Court, in the Privy Council, in the waiting-room of Wolsey or Cromwell. The chief steward usually had an assistant (*subsenescallus deputatus senescalli, senescallus omnium possessionum*), who carried out the actual curial work and not infrequently received larger fees than his chief. Some great landowners had in each of their big honours a chief as well as an ordinary steward. Rich monasteries having many manors had to hold courts accordingly. A steward who had only one court to hold received but a small salary, especially if the manor was small, but the position of a steward who held many courts and had to travel from manor to manor was much more important.

The lay administrators were a very miscellaneous set of people, and it would be a great mistake to suppose that they were all of a docile and easy-going character, or lived exclusively on monastic liberality. Of course, many of the bailiffs on individual manors differed but little from well-to-do peasants, and looked upon their abbot with reverence and awe; but some of the stewards were not infrequently richer *Social status of lay officials.*

and more influential than their 'masters', while even insignificant monasteries had sometimes great personages as their stewards. On the Isle of Sheppey, at the mouth of the Medway, stood the nunnery of St. Sexburge, which had a gross income of £170 2s. 7d. The Valor Ecclesiasticus mentions four of its officers—receiver, auditor, under-steward and chief steward; but for some reason nothing is said about the bailiff, although the nuns had a fairly large demesne in hand and paid their bailiff a rather large fee. It may be that he did not hold his office in perpetuity by covent seal, but was engaged by the year. The chief personage was 'our highe stuard', Thomas Cheyney, knight, who received £3 6s. 8d. a year. There can be no question as to his having been dependent upon the nuns, for he was their landlord as well as their officer, and they paid him a considerable rent (£0 11s. 11d.) for some lands in the manor of Minster. He had a law-suit with the nuns about Rogge Marshe, probably a large area of land, for its income is valued at £10. The fee of £3 6s. 8d. constituted but a small part of Cheyney's income. He probably had a good deal of land, for when he bought from the Crown the site and adjoining lands of that very nunnery (St. Sexburge, Sheppey) he did not pay in money, but gave in exchange two manors in Sussex. Cheyney received a fee not only from the nuns in Sheppey, but also one of £2 from the Archbishop of Canterbury, whose chief steward he was. This, however, did not lessen his independence with regard to Canterbury Cathedral, for the canons complain in 1535 that he had taken from them some land worth £5. Cheyney had, of course, more influence than the country nuns for whom he acted as steward. As early as 17 H. VIII he was one of the six 'gentlemen wayters'; in 31 H. VIII he was 'Warden of the Cinque Ports and Treasurer of the King's household', and in 32 H. VIII a privy councillor. It is hardly likely that Cheyney had time to preside often in the monastic court, nevertheless there was between the poor nunnery and this *grand seigneur* an intimate connexion which was made very evident after the Dissolution, for we find that on December 12, 1537, Cheyney received by the King's Letters Patent in fee simple the whole monastic site and the three monastic manors of Sexburge, Picstocke, and Minster, and thus the ' servant ' took the place of his 'masters'.

Persons of even greater importance than Sir Th. Cheyney Peers. are found among the chief stewards and simple stewards: the list contains the names of many leading peers, e.g. Suffolk, the King's brother-in-law, Norfolk and Cromwell himself. These, however, were often connected with a large number of monasteries. To take a few instances : Charles, Duke of Suffolk, was the chief steward of only two monasteries, Ose-ney, Oxon., £4 (the figure indicates the fee) and Bermondsey, Surrey, £3 6s. 8d. Thomas, Duke of Norfolk, in 1535 the most influential person in the kingdom after Cromwell, was chief steward of four monasteries and one diocese— St. Augustine's, Canterbury, £6 13s. 4d.; Combe, Warw., £3 6s. 8d.; Langley, Norf., £3 6s. 8d.; Bury St. Edmunds, Suff. ('capitalis senescallus libertatis de Bury'), £13 6s. 8d., Episcopatus Norwicensis, £2 0s. 0d. The Earl of Derby was connected with seven monasteries : St. Sepulchre, Warwick, cap' sen', £2 0s. 0d.; St. Werburgh, Chester, sen' mon', £2 0s. 0d.; St. Mary, Chester, sen' mon', £1 6s. 8d.; Whalley, Lanc., £5 6s. 8d.; Penwortham, sen' prioris, £3 6s. 8d.; Furness, sen' in Yorks. et Lanc., £10 0s. 0d.; Cartmell, cap' sen', £2 0s. 0d. The Earl of Rutland was connected with six monasteries : Haliwell, Midd., cap' sen', £3 6s. 8d.; Crowland, Linc., cap' sen', £5 0s. 0d.; Neubo, sen' mon', £2 0s. 0d.; Peterborough, Northants, sen' in Norf., £5 0s. 0d.; Kirkham, Yorks, cap' sen', £5 0s. 0d.; Newstead, Notts., sen' prioratus, £1 0s. 0d. The Earl of Wiltshire was also connected with six monasteries : Clive, Battle, Robertsbridge, Clerkenwell (London), St. Peter's (Westminster), Halesowen, and with the See of Canterbury. The abuse of plurality is most striking in the case of the Earl of Shrewsbury, who held the steward-ship of eleven monasteries, while in a twelfth, St. Werburgh, Chester, his office is not named. Here is his list : Wilton, Wilts., £5 10s. 0d.; Beauchief, Derb., £2 0s. 0d.; Shrewsbury, Salop, £3 6s. 8d.; Buildwas, £2 13s. 4d.; Haghmond, £2 13s. 4d.; Lilleshall, £2 13s. 4d.; Wenlock (he receives

£8 6s. 8d. along with his two helpers); Tutbury, Staff., £3 6s. 8d.; Welbeck, Notts., £3 0s. 0d.; St. Werburgh, Chester, Chesh., £2 0s. 0d.; Vale Royal, £4 0s. 0d.; Combermere, £4 0s. 0d. Thomas Cromwell, the King's Secretary, held offices in many monasteries—he was steward in five and in one college; they are: Michelham, Suss., £2 0s. 0d.; St. Peter's, Westminster, £7 13s. 4d.; Syon, £3 6s. 8d.; New College, Oxford, £4 0s. 0d.; W. Dereham, Norf., £2 0s. 0d.; Catesby, Linc., £2 13s. 4d. From Butley and Holme Cultram Cromwell also received fees (£3 6s. 8d. and £6 13s. 4d.), but his office is not mentioned; the second fee was not tax-free. From Peterborough he received an annuity for life of £3 6s. 8d., and from Osney £2 0s. 0d. pro benevolencia.

Local gentry.

The connexion between the monasteries and the local gentry was, perhaps, even more important. This connexion in the case of knights, esquires and simple gentlemen was not so extensive as in that of the influential peers, but precisely because it was so limited it became the stronger and more intimate. The local people were able to give more time to the monastery, they came to know the monastic household intimately and took a very important position in monastic circles. As an instance I would point to the Kentish Haleses, John and Christopher[1]. True, their position was not a simple one; they were not only Kentish gentlemen (in the V. E. they are called armigeri) but also important State officers: John was Baron of the Exchequer; Christopher was Attorney-General. Their considerable official position no doubt gave them increased weight in the monastic world, but their monastic connexions preserved a local character notwithstanding, and were limited to Kent. John Hales held the chief stewardship of Canterbury Cathedral, for which he received the very large fee of £26 13s. 4d. Christopher was steward in the same monastery (senescallus alte curie), but received much less— only £2 13s. 4d.; he was, however, connected with other monasteries in Kent. He occupied the same office (senescallus alte curie) in the abbey of St. Augustine, Canterbury, with the fee of £6 13s. 4d., and there he also looked after the park

[1] V.E. i. 16, 17, 18, 22, 25, 26, 33, 42, 53, 59, 105.

of Chystlett (£4). He held the stewardship or chief stewardship in four other Kentish monasteries, and in one college in Kent —St. Gregory (Canterbury), Horton (Dover), St. Radegund's (Dover), Cobham—from which he received £10 0s. 0d. The Abbey of St. Augustine, Canterbury, had to pay to John and Christopher and their heirs the considerable rent of £10 0s. 0d. for their lands in Littleborn. The survey does not say what kind of rent it was; but with regard to St. Gregory, Canterbury, and the women's hospital of St. James, Canterbury, John Hales was the landlord, and as such raised the rent of the monastic holdings in the manors of Dungeon and Tannington. John had also another privilege connected with the hospital : after the death of each prioress he had the right to a ' relief ' of £0 10s. 11½d. The connexion of the Haleses with the Kentish monasteries brought its fruits after the Dissolution. The monastic lands acquired by Christopher were chiefly lands of the Kentish monasteries, of which he held the stewardship, St. Augustine's, Canterbury, and Christ Church, Canterbury.[1]

From the Valor Ecclesiasticus it is difficult to judge of the number of gentlemen among the monastic officers. Attached to the names of many officers are the words ' miles, armiger, generosus ', but it must not be supposed that this was invariably the case; no doubt knights and gentlemen were to be found among the monastic officers to whom the V. E. does not give any of these titles. Generally speaking, the use of the terms ' miles,' ' armiger,' and ' generosus ' is very vague in this survey : sometimes they are attached to the name of a person and sometimes not, even when it is the name of a conspicuous person like Sir W. Kingston or Sir E. Baynton ; they are never, or scarcely ever, added to such well-known names as Willoughby, Danby, Fauntleroy, Fitzjames, Sackville. If in any given group of monasteries we count all the officers to whose names the V. E. adds the titles of ' miles, armiger, generosus ', we shall obtain only the minimum of the actual number of gentlemen-officers. In the test-reckoning below

Gentlemen among monastic officers.

[1] Grants, Dec. 24, 1538, Mar. 8, 1539, Jan. 13, 1548, cf. Sept. 10, 1545 (Jas. Hales).

I counted only the stewards, and those with the titles 'dominus, miles, armiger, magister' composed half of the whole number in counties situated in different parts of England. In my list I give only the names of monasteries and stewards :

Dorset. Bindon, Dnus Dawbeney. Cerne, Dnus Dawbeney. Middleton, Th. Denys miles. Shaftesbury, Dnus Dawbeney, Dnus Sandys, J. Styleman. Shirborne, J. Gilbert, Th. Denys mil., Egid. Strangeweys mil., J. Horsey miles.

Leicestershire. Croxton, Dnus Hastings, Th. Waldram, J. Uvedale, H. Lacy, Marm. Tunstall. Launde, Comes Huntyngdon, Th. Waldram, J. Gifford miles. Leicester St. Mary, Comes Huntyngdon, R. Temple, Rad. Pexall.

Lincolnshire. Bardney, J. Husey, J. Hennye, Th. Moygne, Ant. Messendyn, J. Littlebury. Crowland, Comes Rutland, J. Husee miles, Dnus Husee, J. Littlebury, R. Ogle, Th. Maydell, W. Parr mil., J. Warner, Th. Hutton ar., W. Assheley. Lincoln St. Catherine's, Dnus Husee, Ant. Missenden. Revesby, Dnus Husee, mag. Th. Hennege, Th. Gildon, J. Brigge, J. Littlebury. Sempringham, Dnus Husee, J. Comberworthy. Thornton, Rob. Turwytt mil., J. Huse mil., W. Askew mil., W. Turwytt mil., J. Constable mil., Rad. Glikere, W. Constable, Th. Hatclyffe, Edw. Skypwyth, J. Hennege, J. Wenteworthe, Th. Moygne, Ant. Messendyn, G. Flynton, G. Seyntpole, J. Rudde, Leon. Leythorpe.

Norfolk. Blackborough, J. Shaxton. Crabhouse, J. Valenger. Hulme, W. Hubberde mil., W. Hare. Norwich Cath., J. Heydon mil., Andr. Robyns, J. Corbett, Th. Reve, Th. King, Geo. Wynston. Thetford monks, St. Draper. Walsingham, Rog. Townsend mil. (idem Castleacre, Pentney, Westacre). Wymondham, Comes Sussex, W. Hare.

Somerset. Athelney, Dnus Dawbeney, J. Cuff. Bath, J. Scuse ar., Walt. Denys mil. Bridgwater, H. Powlet ar. Bruton, J. Brygges mil., Marchio Exeter. Hinton, J. Boneham ar., Walt Hungerford mil., Keynsham, W. Kingston mil., Montacute, Amis. Powlett mil., J. Horsey mil., Rob. Byrte, J. Cuff, J. Williams. Muchelney, Amis. Powlet mil. Taunton, N. Wadham miles, Rog. Yorke serviens ad legem. Witham, N. Fitzjames.

Suffolk. Bury St. Edmunds, Th. Dux Norfolk, Th. Wing-feld ar., Rob. Paiton mil., Dnus Morley, Clam. Higham, Jac. Bullen mil., J. Plowdon, J. Cornewales mil., H. Lucas. Butley, Th. Russhe mil. Leiston, Th. Wingfeld mil. Sibton, W. Rowes mil.

Sussex. Battle, Thomas Comes Wiltes', Edw. Baynton mil., Tyrrell de Heron gen., N. Carne mil., J. Baker attornatus ducatus Lanc., Ric. Sakevile. Lewes, J. Covert, W. Connyngesby, magister Wynkfeld, Ric. Tempest mil., Th. Thatcher, Michelham, mag. Th. Crumwell, Egid. Fynes ar., R. Sackvile gen. Robertsbridge, Comes Wiltes', N. Tufton, Geo. Marser.

Worcestershire. Bordesley, Gilb. Talbot mil., G. Throkmorton mil., Rog. Sparry. Evesham, Geo. Throkmorton mil., W. Cokesey. Magna Malvern, W. Kingston mil., Rog. Wygston ar., Geo. Blounte ar., Ph. Draycote, Th. Rocke, Ric. Warnecombe. Pershore, Gilb. Talbot mil., Dan. Courtt, J. Bruggis. Worcester Cathedral, Rob. Wye, J. Pakynton ar.

The above list contains 111 names, half of which are followed by a title showing that the bearer is at least a gentleman. Of course, all the stewards bearing the title of armiger or miles were not necessarily local land-owners or land-owners at all, but all of them in their habits and opinions belonged to the class of country gentlemen, and many actually had lands in the neighbourhood ; some of the stewards who had no title undoubtedly belonged to the same class. I did not find the title of miles, armiger or generosus attached to the names of auditors, receivers or bailiffs. This does not, of course, signify that gentlemen never held such offices, but that they were few if any at all. A special knowledge and experience was required from auditors which could hardly be expected in a squire, and the offices of receiver and bailiff were associated with much drudgery and were evidently considered unsuitable for a gentleman. When a *grand seigneur* held a stewardship, especially a chief stewardship, he never performed his curial duties if he could possibly hand them over to his deputy; nevertheless his official position enabled a squire to become well acquainted with the monastic estates and to feel at home within the monastic walls; and this was one of the causes which contributed to the success of the Dissolution. When the monastic estates came into the market, the squires knew not only to whom they should address themselves, but knew also what particular estates to ask for; thus they easily selected the most profitable portions for themselves.

Gentlemen farmers.

And such official ties were not the only ones which connected gentlemen with the monasteries. Gentlemen were to be found among the monastic farmers. As the Valor Ecclesiasticus seldom gives the names of the farmers, I can only give a few instances. Among the farmers of Burcester priory in Oxfordshire five are called gentlemen and two esquires (Ric. Banaster gentilman, Edw. et Th. Denton gent., Eg. Reede gentilman, Ric. Langeston armiger, Anth. Cope armiger, J. Goodwyn gentylman). Among the rather numerous farmers of the monastery of Merkyate, Beds., one only, Reginald Dygby, who farmed the rectory of Colleshull, is called gentleman. Among the many farmers of Battle Abbey, Sussex, there are only two gentlemen, J. Toke and Ric. White. This, of course, does not mean that there were no more gentlemen to be found among the farmers, for the title of 'generosus' is not added even to such a highly respectable name as W. Wyatt. Supplementary evidence concerning gentlemen farmers may be found in the Royal Patents by which the monastic lands were granted to various people. If the land in question had been let by the monks and the lease had not expired, the King could grant only the reversion; the Patent often gives the farmer's name.

I will give a few instances in which the farmers were gentlemen. In January, 1516, Sir H. Bourchier, Earl of Essex, leased for 96 years the manor of Gladfen Hall from the Priory of Lees, Essex, at the annual rent of £6. In November, 1532, Dame Elizabeth Audley leased from the Abbey of Sawtre, Hunts., the manor of Narford for 99 years at the yearly rent of £6 13s. 4d. In October, 1531, Sir J. Gage, the King's Vice-Chamberlain, leased the lands in Chetyngle for 40 years from the abbey of Robertsbridge at the annual rent of £4.[1] Although the number of these gentlemen farmers was

[1] Grants, June 25, 1537, Dec. 16, 1537, April 24, 1539.

not great, still the fact of their existence is of considerable interest for us. Their presence on the monastic lands shows that the gentry were not content with their important share in the administration of the Church estates, but sometimes participated in the more active working of the farms. Even before the Dissolution economic initiative had, on monastic territory, to a considerable extent passed from the monks to the gentry.

Among the gentry named in connexion with the mona- Founders
steries a special place is occupied by the families of founders and
and benefactors. In the minds of the people of the sixteenth factors.
century there still existed the idea that the donors had imposed certain obligations upon the monasteries with regard to the management of their grants, and that after the Suppression all monastic properties ought in justice to be returned to their donors.[1] When the descendants of a founder asked that this or that monastic land should be granted to them they were careful to point out that they belonged to the family of the founder. The legislators were consequently compelled to grapple with this view of the situation ; and the Dissolution Act contains a proviso with regard to the rights of founders (27 II. VIII, c. 28, ss. 3, 16 : cf. 31 H. VIII, c. 13, s. 4 ; 34 & 35 H. VIII, c. 19, s. 1). It is there laid down that although the Dissolution is not to deprive the founder of the revenues he had hitherto received from the monastery, yet it does not create for him any new rights. This declaration, however, was concerned only with cases of a fixed income. The representatives of founders or donors could have a right to a certain monastic office or rent. Spelman affirms that the founder had the right to one corrody in his monastery if it had not been founded in frankalmoign. It was evidently such definite rights as these that were recognized and protected by Parliament. But along with these there existed other and wider claims which the monks seem not infrequently to have admitted. Fuller says that founders could

---

[1] About the rights of donors, cf. 13 E. i. c. 41 ; Co. Lit. 13 ; Blackstone, Comm. ii, ch. 15, p. 256. In the curious episode of the surrender of the priory of Christchurch, London, the king himself refers to the right of the founders (25 H. VIII, c. 33). It is true that in this case the founders were the king's ancestors.

send to their monasteries several poor servants to be fed there, and that only a few of such corrodies were recognized by the Crown at the Dissolution.[1]

Gentlemen as guests. At times, gentlemen who had no claim to belong to the roll of benefactors, made great use of the monastic hospitality. When a poor patrician had nowhere to go to he went to a monastery, where if anywhere he might expect to be kindly received. Dr. Gasquet mentions the case of a son of the Duke of Buckingham, who pitifully confesses that previous to the Dissolution he had lived with his wife and seven children for four years at the expense of a monastery. Soon after the Dissolution, Brinklow said—probably with some rhetorical exaggeration—that idle gentlemen never left the abbeys, and that the horses of important people were continually fed in the monastic stables.[2]

Gentle pupils of the monks. Neither was the educational charity of the monks exclusively democratic. Many of their pupils were quite poor and of humble birth; but the children of gentlemen also were sometimes taught in the monasteries. When under examination in the Tower, Aske referred with regret to the time when the children of gentlemen could be educated in the monasteries. At the time of the surrender, there were found in the abbey of Lilleshall in Shropshire four sons of gentlemen with their teacher.[3] Dr. Gasquet mentions the fact that in the school of the Winchester nuns there were twenty-six daughters of lords, knights and gentlemen, among whom were a Plantagenet and others bearing the names of Tichborn, Pole and Tyrrell. He adds that many other schools held in the nunneries of Barking, Ringsmead, Nuneaton, Northampton Delapré, Wintney and Shouldham were as a matter of fact schools for ladies. The teachers also were of a good stock. Dr. Gasquet points out that in the houses just mentioned, as well as others such as the Norfolk nunneries of Bungay, Campsey and Thetford, most of the nuns had been, according to the episcopal

---

[1] Fuller, 326.
[2] Gasquet, i. 34; Brinklow, ch. 14.
[3] Gairdner, xii. 901, art. 23=E. H. R. v. 562; Exch. Augm. O. M. b. v. 172, f. 21–31.

visitations, members of the best local families—Willoughbys, Everards, Wingfields and Jerminghams.[1]

Notwithstanding its fragmentary character, the evidence contained both in the V. E. and in the Suppression Accounts leads us to regard with some suspicion statements concerning the immense social influence of monasticism in England. Some Roman Catholic historians of the present day are given to representing their Church as a democratic institution, especially in countries where the Roman Catholics are in a minority and are not often found among the dominant classes of society. Dr. Gasquet assures us that the English Reformation was a rising of the rich against the poor ; that it made the rich richer still, and took from the poor their last mite ; that its effect was that of a wedge driven into the very heart of the nation, which for ever divided the rich from the poor and established a cleavage between classes and masses. He depicts the age of Roman Catholicism as an age of social harmony in which the Church acted as a general peacemaker, and the monks invariably marched at the head of those who loved the poor. In his book on the Dissolution the social work of the monks is especially eulogized. He speaks of the monastic property as the sacred heritage of the poor ; he says that all modern charity is but a trifle compared with the work so much better done by the monks. He thinks that the stigma attaching to pauperism originated with the Dissolution. In pre-Reformation times poverty was honoured. Those who were responsible for the Dissolution hastened to put the brand of shame and even crime upon the poverty which they themselves had created. The opinions of the Benedictine abbot-president concerning the legislation subsequent to the Dissolution are but little less vehement than the indignation of Karl Marx. According to Dr. Gasquet the beneficial economic influence of the monks extended far beyond their charity ; he maintains that they kept a great many servants and labourers ; he even finds it possible to assert that the lay population fed by the monasteries was at least ten times more

Dr. Gasquet's view.

---

[1] Gasquet, Monastic life, 177-8, H. VIII and Mon., ii. 220-2.

numerous than the monks themselves. The well-being, also, of a very large class of monastic tenants was, in his opinion, closely dependent on the fate of the monks, who in their kindness took the low rents and admission fines fixed by immemorial custom, and did not seek to extract the very last penny from their tenants. The presence of the monks was a very great benefit to all the surrounding district, for the monks spent nearly all their income on the spot, and were a profitable *clientèle* to the neighbouring merchants and artisans. As the monasteries were scattered all over the country, their large income was distributed with reasonable equality among the population of the whole kingdom. In all these respects the Dissolution prejudicially affected the masses. Along with the monks, all the lay population of the monasteries were thrown out of their routine of life, and largely increased the numbers of the proletariat so cruelly persecuted. Until the Dissolution the tenants were protected by immemorial and unalterable custom ; the Dissolution storm swept away the custom and left the weak to the tyranny of the strong. The landlords who took the place of the monks were heartless men who sought to raise all the rents and brought the tenants face to face with evil times. All the surrounding population suffered too, for the bulk of the monastic revenues now flowed into other channels. In the first years after the Dissolution the revenues were collected into the chests of London treasurers and spent there. Tradespeople whose living was dependent on monastic purchases were now left without customers. Even after the monastic lands had passed into the hands of private people the situation was but slightly improved, for the rich landlords spent their revenues at Court.[1]

The evidence contained in the V. E. and the Suppression Accounts is not sufficient to enable us to examine every single assertion of this theory, but we learn enough to form an opinion respecting some essential portions of it. The people who lived exclusively at the expense of the monasteries were

---

[1] Gasquet, H. VIII and the Mon., *passim*, especially ii. 323, 494, 504–6, 510, 515, 523–4.

neither so numerous nor so plebeian as is affirmed by the
Roman Catholics.   According to the Suppression Accounts,
the number of monastic laymen was only three times as great
as the number of the monks.   It is true that these accounts
do not take into consideration the administrative staff, the
stewards, receivers, auditors, and many of the bailiffs; it is
also highly probable that the monastic population immediately
before the Dissolution was less than normal.   We have grounds
for believing that, on the whole, the number of monastic
laymen including the administration was about four times
as great as that of the monks.   If we suppose that by the
time of the Dissolution the monastic population had decreased
by one-fifth of its usual number in the sixteenth century, even
then the number of monastic laymen will work out at but five
times the number of monks.   If my calculations are correct,
the number of mouths which were fed by the monasteries may
be put at about thirty-five thousand; for the total number of
professed religious persons (with the exception of friars) was
about seven thousand.   This multitude was not composed
chiefly of paupers, but of officers and working-men, many
of whom could find employment even after the Dissolution.
Of all the many forms assumed by monastic charity, the
evidence of the sixteenth century attaches most importance
to the common doles.   True, the Valor Ecclesiasticus ignores
the alms that were taxed; but the tenth-free alms constituted
less than three per cent. of the monastic budget, and most of
these represented food for the poor on certain holidays or
commemoration days; it is very difficult to believe that the
taxed alms greatly exceeded the amount of the alms which
were tenth-free.

Of the people whose existence most closely depended on
the monastic budget by no means all were members of the
lower strata of society.   Some of the monks themselves were
gentlemen; and the nuns often came from good families.   The
so-called corrodians were a miscellaneous population; some
of them were well-to-do people who had themselves made
a grant to the monastery and were on that account welcomed
and allowed to spend the rest of their lives within its walls; Aristocratic
elements
in the
monastic
popula-
tion.

and the inferior courtiers and officials also might enter monasteries as corrodians by the king's appointment. In the monastic schools, too, not only the children of the poor, but also those of gentlemen were educated, and it is possible that in the girls' schools the daughters of noble families were even more numerous than those of the poor. Monastic hospitality was not affected by class prejudice. The doors of the monastic kitchen were wont to open quite as widely before a rich knight as before an old beggar. The most honourable offices of the monastic administration—the stewardships— were very largely bestowed upon gentlemen, knights and peers, who thus had excellent opportunities not only of becoming thoroughly acquainted with monastic life, but also of influencing it. Gentlemen not infrequently farmed the monastic lands, and, on the whole, occupied an altogether substantial position in the monastic world before the Dissolution. I am afraid Dr. Gasquet's picture is more typical of the democratic Roman Catholicism of the present day than of the English monasteries in the sixteenth century.

Social sympathies of the monks.   The monasteries could not be democratic institutions. Up to the very eve of the Dissolution, Roman Catholicism was the religion of an overwhelming majority of Englishmen, and the Roman Catholic community was almost co-extensive with the nation itself. The monks could not be guided exclusively by the interests of the masses; such a line of conduct would have been directed against one part of the most faithful children of the Church, and would in consequence have met with serious opposition from the upper and middle classes, who were much more influential than the apprentices, small peasants, agricultural labourers and vagrant paupers. The monks themselves belonged to very varied social strata; and it is idle to talk of the unanimity of their views and interests. Some monks lived in abbeys like Glastonbury, which had a gross income of £3,500; others in priories like Byrkley with a gross income of five pounds. The abbots of the principal monasteries sat in the House of Lords; and, as the heads of great establishments, naturally considered themselves very important personages and the superiors of their numerous servants, labourers, and tenants. Even the ordinary monks of large monasteries lived in great comfort, prayed in a church both grand and beautiful, dined in a large refectory, worked in the comfortable galleries of the inner cloister, walked within the high walls of their own carefully tended gardens amidst such beauties and amenities as may still be seen in the oldest colleges of Oxford and Cambridge. The monks of the poorer provincial houses, on the other hand, had scarcely money enough to live upon, had to perform manual work and kept but few servants and labourers. Judged by the standard of income, they were on a par with the average small farmer. The friars were beggars and tramps, who could readily sympathize with the proletariat of the day. But however heterogeneous the interests of the professed 'religious' might have been, the majority of them could not but sympathize with the upper and middle classes, in a way altogether at variance with anything like a democratic spirit.

In a society full of discord between classes so various, the Roman Catholic Church failed to remain thoroughly and sincerely democratic because it was as it still is the Church of general unity. It undoubtedly expressed sympathy with the masses and the poor, but at the same time it continued to be on good terms with the few and the rich. It enjoined simplicity, poverty, privations, but at the same time it knew how to find excuse for riches and luxury. In the great drama of class warfare it was compelled to shift its fighting-place or to stand between the hostile camps. It was stronger abroad than at home. It became bold and mighty when it girded itself with a sword against the infidels; in the hard struggle for life among its own children it confined its energies to a policy of pious appeals to love and mercy.

APPENDIX

TABLE OF MONASTIC INCOME

The following table is based on the ' Valor Ecclesiasticus '.

The monasteries are arranged in the alphabetical order of counties and names. Four counties (Berkshire, Cambridgeshire, Essex, Hertfordshire), for which the net monastic income alone is known from the ' Liber Valorum ', are placed after the rest.

The first column contains the names of the monasteries. The second gives the gross general income ('general' means spiritual *plus* temporal). The third shows the net general income ('net' in the sense of 28 H. VIII, c. 3, and the 1535 instructions to the Commissioners). The fourth indicates the gross temporal income. The fifth contains the net temporal income. The sixth refers to the page and volume of the V. E. [Record Commission]. Where the figures of the temporal income are wanting, it is because they could not be distinguished from the general income.

a = abbey, c = cathedral, co = commandry or preceptory, n = nunnery, p = priory.

A = Augustinians.
B = Benedictines.
Bethl = Bethlemites.
Bon = Bonhommes.
Bridg = Bridgettines.
C = Cistercians.
Ch = Carthusians.
Cl = Cluniacs.
Fr = Franciscans.
G = Gilbertines.
P = Praemonstratensians.
Trin = Trinitarians.

	£	s.	d.	£	s.	d.	£	s.	d.	£	s.	d.	
BEDS.													
Bushmead p A	81	13	5½	72	13	9½	81	13	5½	71	13	9½	iv. 200–201
Caldwell p A	148	15	10	109	8	4	73	12	6	61	1	8	iv. 189–190
Chicksand p B	230	3	4½	212	3	5½	182	16	8½	172	9	9½	iv. 194–195
Dunstable p A	402	13	9½	344	12	5½							iv. 206–208
Elstow a B n	325	2	0¾	284	12	10¾	139	17	8¾	122	5	2¾	iv. 188–189
Harwood p A n	46	13	2	40	8	2	26	13	2	21	15	2	iv. 204
Merkyate p B n	143	18	5	114	16	1	53	10	5	42	17	1	iv. 209–210
Newnham p A	343	15	5	293	5	11	156	3	2	135	15	3	iv. 187–188
Wardon a C	442	11	11	389	16	6¼	410	13	4¼	386	5	4½	iv. 193–194
Woburn a C	430	13	11½	391	18	2½	390	13	11½	366	13	5	iv. 212–213
BUCKS.													
Ankerwyke p B n	45	14	4	32	0	2	45	5	0	37	10	10	iv. 222
Bittlesden p C	162	1	2	125	4	2¼	130	1	2	114	1	0	iv. 237–238
Burnham a A n	91	5	11½	51	2	3¾	72	3	11½	55	13	1	iv. 220–221
Ivinghoe p B n	22	6	7	14	3	1	17	10	11	14	14	1	iv. 227–228
Lavenden a P	91	8	3½	78	13	8	61	5	8½	56	11	0	iv. 241–242
Little Marlow a B n	37	6	11	23	3	7¼	26	8	10	19	16	6	iv. 250
Medmenham a A...	24	17	2	20	6	2	18	6	5	14	3	1	iv. 251
Missenden a A	285	15	9	261	14	6¼	198	15	8	183	4	8	iv. 246–247
Nutley a A	495	18	5½	437	6	8½	177	9	1½	136	16	6¼	iv. 232–234
Snetteshall p B	24	0	0	18	1	11	23	10	2	17	15	7	iv. 228–229
CHESHIRE.													
Birkenhead p B	102	16	9½	91	2	11½	19	19	3	11	5	11	v. 212
Chester St. Mary's p B n	99	16	2	66	18	4	74	6	2	60	0	8	v. 206
Chester St. Werburgh' a B	1104	14	2½	1030	5	6	751	9	1½	706	16	11	v. 205–6
Combermere a C...	258	6	6	225	9	7	181	2	10	161	9	9	v. 216–17
Norton a A	258	12	8	180	7	6½	113	3	8	82	8	4½	v. 209–210
Vale Royal a C	540	6	2	518	19	8	239	1	9	225	9	5	v. 208–209

		CORNWALL.			
Bodmin p A	289 11 11	270 0 11	217 9 11	200 17 11	ii. 400–401
St. Cyrus p Cl	11 1 0	10 15 0			i. 196
St. Germans p A...	243 3 0	227 4 8	119 11 4	109 11 4	ii. 405
Helston	14 7 2½	12 16 4	14 7 2½	12 16 4	ii. 393
Launceston p A	392 11 2¼	354 0 11¼	233 2 6¼	213 13 6¼	ii. 402–403
Tywardreath p B	151 16 1	123 9 3	51 18 3	42 11 7	ii. 396
		CUMBERLAND.			
Armthwaite p B n	19 2 2	13 12 0	13 2 2	13 1 2	v. 291–292
St. Bees p B	149 9 6½	143 6 2½	79 4 6½	79 1 2½	v. 11
Celder a C	64 3 9	50 9 3½	48 15 0	40 15 0	v. 264
Carlisle c p A	482 8 1	418 3 4¾	150 2 3	129 12 7½	v. 274–276
Holm Cultram a C	535 3 7½	477 19 3½	370 17 0½	365 7 7½	v. 282–283
Lanercost p A	79 19 0	77 11 11	28 10 10	26 18 10	v. 277
Seton p B n	13 17 4	12 12 0½	8 4 8	8 4 8	v. 265
Wetheral p B	128 7 2¾	117 12 10¾	57 12 2¾	49 11 2¾	v. 10
		DERBY.			
Beauchief a P	157 11 2	126 4 3	77 0 0	64 5 0	iii. 172–174
Breadsall p A	13 0 8	10 17 9	7 14 0	5 11 1	iii. 156
Dale a P	182 4 1	145 4 11	130 4 2	124 11 6	iii. 155–156
Darley a A	285 9 11½	258 13 10			iii. 153–4
Derby King's Mead p B n	21 18 8	18 6 2	19 8 8	16 6 2	iii. 157
Gresley p A	39 13 8	31 6 0	26 15 8	24 6 4	iii. 163
Repingdon p A	167 18 2½	118 8 6[illegible]	73 9 11½	57 12 11½	iii. 162–163
Yeveley and Barrow co.		93 19 4½			iii. 168
		DEVON.			
Barnstaple p Cl	130 6 9	123 9 7	114 0 1	107 2 11	ii. 354
Buckfastleigh a C	504 10 8⅜	466 9 4[illegible]	435 16 5⅝	422 18 5⅝	ii. 368–370
Buckland a C	279 0 2⅜	241 19 1[illegible]	213 10 2⅜	202 16 2⅜	ii. 378–379
Canonleigh a B n	216 3 0½	197 4 8	166 18 6½	159 13 5	ii. 328–330
Carswell p Cl	28 16 4	25 19 1			i. 196

DEVON (*continued*).

	£	s.	d.	£	s.	d.	£	s.	d.	£	s.	d.	
Cornworthy p A n	66	16	5	63	2	10	26	12	7	24	19	3	ii. 366
Dunkeswell a C	309	13	11	290	5	3	290	4	7	271	8	2	ii. 304–5
Exeter St. Nicholas p B...	161	8	1	147	12	0	109	18	9	104	1	9	ii. 313
Frithelstoke p A...	142	1	4	127	2	4	76	14	3¼	71	4	7¼	ii. 335
Hartland a A	309	0	10¼	292	8	2¼	150	1	2¼	136	12	4¼	ii. 333–335
Newenham a C	240	1	2	227	17	10	209	12	8	198	2	8	ii. 301
Pilton p B	63	15	7	56	12	8½	29	2	8	22	18	8	ii. 355
Plympton p A	931	0	4⅛	898	0	8⅛	459	17	9⅝	443	13	5⅝	ii. 375–378
Polslo p B n	179	10	4¼	164	8	11¼	98	18	4¼	88	3	7¼	ii. 315
Tavistock a B	911	4	11¼	842	3	4¼	712	10	5¼	670	10	7¼	ii. 381–383
Tavistock p A	65	1	9	60	10	11	37	16	5	33	5	7	ii. 384
Torre a P...	425	4	7¼	398	8	11½	268	12	2¼	253	18	10¼	ii. 361–362
Totnes p B	153	16	8	134	9	2½	81	6	8½	75	6	2½	ii. 367–368

DORSET.

	£	s.	d.	£	s.	d.	£	s.	d.	£	s.	d.	
Abbotsbury a B	483	1	9¾	414	18	11¾	392	3	1¾	382	1	3¾	i. 227–230
Bindon a C	236	8	9¾	155	16	7¾	185	8	9¾	144	16	7¾	i. 239–241
Cerne a B...	622	7	10¾	514	12	6¼	559	19	2¾	509	2	7¾	i. 253–257
Cranborne p B	49	5	1	31	18	4½	21	0	0	14	16	8	ii. 485
Ford a C	394	4	4½	373	8	2½	371	11	0½	356	15	4½	ii. 299–300
Holme p Cl	16	9	4	14	3	8							i. 196
Middleton a B	715	9	10½	579	0	9	588	3	10½	557	17	8½	i. 248–252
Shaftesbury a B n	1324	14	7	1149	10	3	1210	18	5	1109	11	5	i. 276–280
Sherborne a B	743	14	1⅝	673	3	10⅞	652	15	7⅝	613	1	2⅝	i. 281–285
Tarrent a C n	239	10	10	214	4	9	217	13	6	196	1	10	i. 265–267

DURHAM.

	£	s.	d.	£	s.	d.	£	s.	d.	£	s.	d.	
Durham c p B	1572	14	0½	1328	15	2	1106	8	2½	1007	19	9	v. 301–303
Finchale p B	146	19	2	122	15	11	86	5	6	72	18	11	v. 303–4
Jarrow p B	40	7	8	38	14	4	20	14	4	19	14	4	v. 304
Wearmouth p B	26	18	4	25	8	4	8	13	4	7	13	4	v. 304

					GLOUCESTER.								
Cirencester a A	1325	12	8	1045	16	4¼							ii. 463–71
Deerhurst p B	158	2	6¾	134	8	0¾							ii. 484
Flaxley a C	129	14	8½	112	3	1							ii. 486
Gloucester St. Oswald's p A	140	9	1	90	10	2½	60	9	1	37	0	6½	ii. 487
Gloucester St. Peter's a B	1744	11	0½	1419	12	4	1473	13	2	1331	12	3	ii. 409–18
Hayles a C	407	10	7	360	5	9							ii. 453–6
Lantony p A	849	7	1	723	17	11¼	577	9	2	526	1	10½	ii. 423–30
Stanley p B	126	0	8	106	17	0	42	9	4	39	7	8	ii. 419
Tewkesbury a B	1478	7	11½	1319	6	5½	1057	15	3½	990	4	2	ii. 471–83
Winchcombe a B	812	3	2¼	759	11	11¼	710	5	2¼	685	19	8¾	ii. 456–61
					HANTS.								
Badersley co	131	14	1	118	16	7							ii. 26
Beaulieu a C	428	6	8¼	326	13	2¾							ii. 19
Bromere p A	200	5	1½	154	14	1½							ii. 18
Hyde a B	993	9	5	865	1	6¾							ii. 3–4
Letley a C	160	2	9½	100	12	8							ii. 19
Motisfont p A	167	15	8½	124	3	5½							ii. 16
Quarre a C	184	1	10	134	3	11							ii. 24
Romsey a B n	528	8	10½	393	10	10½							ii. 16
Southampton St. Denys p A	91	9	0	80	11	6							ii. 19
Southwick p A	324	17	10½	257	4	4							ii. 21
Titchfield a P	280	19	10½	249	16	1							ii. 21
Twyneham p A	543	6	0¼	312	7	0¼							ii. 18
Wherwell a B n	403	12	10	339	8	7							ii. 7
Winchester St. Mary a B n	245	17	2½	179	7	2							ii. 4
Winchester c p B	1762	19	2	1507	17	2¼							ii. 2–3
Wintney p C n	59	1	0	43	3	2							ii. 13
					HEREFORD.								
Aconbury p A n	78	18	1½	66	3	10½	51	1	1½	44	14	9½	iii. 17–18
Clifford p Cl	49	11	11	42	4	2	26	5	3	21	18	7	iii. 30
Dore a C...	87	0	0	75	14	0	65	13	4	59	16	8	iii. 33

		£	s.	d.	£	s.	d.	£	s.	d.	£	s.	d.	
Hereford (*continued*).														
Flanesford p A		15	8	9	14	8	9	15	8	9	14	8	9	iii. 17
St. Guthlac's p B		189	2	1½	169	19	6½	134	11	5½	115	15	6½	ii. 420–1
Lymbrook p A n		23	17	8	22	17	8	19	11	0	18	11	0	iii. 40
Wigmore a A		316	13	5½	267	2	10⅛	183	19	7½	151	18	5½	iii. 202–4
Wormesley p A		89	3	9	73	10	2	37	17	5	32	16	3	iii. 29
Huntingdon.														
Hinchinbrook p B n		19	9	2	17	1	4	17	17	10	16	0	0	iv. 255–6
Huntingdon p A		232	7	0½	187	15	6¼	126	11	4½	101	12	6¼	iv. 253–5
St. Ives p B		69	0	8	0	18	2	41	3	4				iv. 272
St. Neots p B		256	1	3¼	241	11	4¼	192	13	11¼	183	18	7¼	iv. 261–2
Ramsey a B		1849	8	4¼	1643	4	10	1786	9	8¼	1632	19	4¼	iv. 271–5
Sawtre a C		199	11	8	140	13	11	159	11	8	104	13	1	iv. 265–7
Stonely p A		61	5	7½	44	13	9½	36	18	10½	24	9	2½	iv. 258
Kent.														
Bilsington p A		122	0	8	81	1	6¼	122	0	8	91	17	10¼	i. 50–1
Boxley a C[1]		218	19	5	204	4	6	195	12	9	183	13	3	i. 79–80
Canterbury St. Augustine's a B[2]	*a*	1733	9	11¾	1431	13	9¾							i. 17–23
	b	1684	4	1¾										
Canterbury c p B		2909	17	4⅜	2423	9	6⅜	2608	0	9⅞	2373	13	9⅞	i. 7–16
Canterbury St. Gregory's p A		166	4	5½	115	8	5							i. 24–6
Canterbury St. Sepulchre's p B n ...		38	19	7½	29	12	5½	33	7	11½	27	7	5½	i. 29–30
Cumbwell p A		89	1	5¾	80	17	7¼	54	8	1¾	47	11	10¾	i. 87–8
Dartford p A n		488	15	2½	355	1	7	471	11	7	403	1	5½	i. 119–20
Dover p B	*a*	232	1	5½	172	14	11½	171	3	9½	139	13	7½	i. 53–5
	b	225	11	11½				166	11	11½				
Dover St. Radegund's a P		142	8	9	98	10	2½	101	16	1	75	17	0½	i. 55–9

[1] I have omitted the corn rent consisting of 25 qrs. of barley.

[2] The bigger number includes normal rents, in the lesser number the actual amount of payments has been summed up.

Faversham a B [1]	362 1 2	286 11 10¾	297 11 2	257 14 9¾	i. 82–5
Folkestone p B	63 0 7	41 15 10	8 0 0	4 9 9	i. 52
Horton p Cl	111 16 7	95 12 2	86 1 7	77 10 6	i. 41–2
Langdon a P	81 3 4	56 6 9½			i. 43
Leeds p A	453 4 2	353 7 5½	107 15 2	76 17 3½	i. 72–5
Malling a B n	258 8 2½	231 2 2½	196 0 10½	172 1 2½	i. 106–7
Muttlinden p Trin	76 19 6	68 2 11½	53 5 10	47 19 3½	i. 81–2
Rochester p B	572 1 1	491 16 5			i. 101–4
Sheppey St. Sexburge a B n	170 2 7	129 7 10½	114 14 11	99 12 4½	i. 77–8
Swinfield co	104 0 2½	87 3 4			i. 36
West Peckham co		63 6 8			i. 113
		LANCASTER.			
Burscough a A	129 1 10	80 7 5	56 1 4	45 6 0	v. 222–3
Cartmell p A	108 13 7	85 0 3	82 10 3	62 10 3	v. 272
Cockersand a C	228 15 4½	158 3 6½	182 18 8½	150 0 0½	v. 261
Conishead p A	124 2 1	97 0 2	51 19 1	43 14 1	v. 271
Furness a C	946 1 10	805 0 5	763 0 10	683 11 6	v. 269–70
Holland p B n	61 3 4	53 3 4	12 10 0	9 16 8	v. 221
Hornby p P	28 8 4½	19 18 4½	28 8 4½	23 18 4½	iv. 151–2
Lytham p B	53 10 10	48 14 6	43 3 7	39 0 3	v. 305
Penwortham p B...	114 16 9	29 18 7	30 2 11	19 15 9	v. 233
Whalley a C	551 4 6	321 9 1½	278 15 10	214 9 3½	v. 227–30
		LEICESTER.			
Bradley p A	20 15 7	20 3 4	20 2 3	19 10 0	iv. 159
Bredon p A	25 8 1	24 10 4	8 8 1	8 1 5	iv. 176–7
Croxton a P	430 11 7¼	365 2 6¼	319 0 7¼	281 15 2¾	iv. 150–2
Dalby Rotheley et Heyther co	274 11 2	231 7 10			iv. 165
Garendon a C	186 15 2½	159 19 10½	172 15 2½	156 5 2½	iv. 173–4
Grace Dieu p A n	101 8 2½	92 3 9½	93 8 2½	86 14 10½	iv. 175
Kirby Beller p A	178 7 10¼	142 10 3¼	122 7 10¼	90 17 8¼	iv. 149
Langley p B n	34 6 2	29 7 4½	17 12 10	15 6 2	iv. 176

[1] I have omitted the corn rent consisting of 1½ qrs. of barley.

		£	s.	d.	£	s.	d.	£	s.	d.	£	s.	d.	
Leicester (*continued*).														
Launde p A		510	16	5½	399	3	3¾	279	4	9½	247	10	11½	iv. 163–5
Leicester St. Mary's a A		1056	18	2¾	946	12	3¾	732	12	0¾	696	1	0¼	iv. 145–8
Olverston a A		174	13	9¼	162	9	2¼	149	0	5¼	138	13	10¼	iv. 158
Ulverscroft p A		101	3	9½	83	10	5½	70	18	9½	66	6	1½	iv. 174–5
Lincoln.														
Ailesham p A		83	17	10	70	0	8	61	5	2	49	12	6	iv. 72
Alvingham p G		141	15	0	128	14	2	100	8	4	93	4	0	iv. 58
Axholme Ch		290	19	7¾	238	0	2¾	173	16	11¼	152	11	10¼	iv. 135–6
Bardney a B		429	7	0	366	6	1	248	13	6	220	8	10	iv. 81–2
Barlings a P		307	16	6	242	5	11½	269	3	2	250	17	6½	iv. 130–1
Belvoir p B	*a*	129	17	6	98	19	5	60	4	10	44	11	6	iv. 116–17
	b				105	0	0							i. 451
Bollington p G		205	15	9	158	7	11	85	9	9	72	16	5	iv. 84
Bourn a A		197	17	5¼	167	14	6½	110	6	9¼	101	18	0½	iv. 103
Cattley p G		38	13	8	33	18	6	29	13	8	27	0	4	iv. 123
Crowland a B		1050	17	9¾	947	3	8	909	5	1¾	844	2	9¾	iv. 85–7
Egle co		129	8	8	124	2	0							iv. 127–8
Fosse p B n		8	5	4	7	3	6	6	5	4	5	13	6	iv. 132
Freston p B		166	8	1½	136	2	0½	84	6	8	79	15	3	iv. 85–7
Goykwell p C n		19	18	6	16	12	10	15	1	10	12	0	2	iv. 140
Greenfield p C n		79	15	1	63	4	1	79	13	1	64	6	5	iv. 53
Grimsby p B n		12	3	7	9	14	7	9	10	3	7	1	3	iv. 68
Hagneby a P		98	8	4	87	11	8	93	15	1	88	8	3	iv. 51
Haverholme p G		75	11	7	57	2	0½	69	1	1½	58	18	11	iv. 118
Hevening p C n		58	13	4	49	5	2	28	0	0	23	12	8	iv. 132–3
Humberston a B		42	11	3	32	1	3	25	11	3	23	4	7	iv. 68
Hyrst p A		7	11	8	5	10	1	7	11	8	5	10	1	iv. 64
Irford p P n		14	13	4	13	19	9	11	6	8	10	19	1	iv. 78
Kirkstead a C		338	16	11¾	286	5	11¾	323	3	3¾	271	14	7¾	iv. 34–6
Kyme p A		138	4	9	101	0	4	85	16	2	80	3	3	iv. 117
Legbourne p C n		57	13	5¼	38	8	4¼	28	0	3¼	24	15	3¼	iv. 52

Lincoln St Catherine's p G		259	18	5	153	9	3½	122	11	9	105	13	10½	iv. 30–4
Lincoln St. Mary Magdalen p B		26	5	2	23	10	2	18	6	10	15	11	10	v. 10
Louth Park a C		169	4	6½	147	13	6¼	146	4	6½	128	11	0¼	iv. 57
Markby p A		163	18	6½	130	14	11½	127	11	10½	116	18	11½	iv. 50–1
Neubo a P		115	10	8	71	3	1½	83	10	8	75	4	9½	iv. 111
Newsome a P		114	1	4½	99	2	10½	73	14	8½	65	10	6½	iv. 74–5
Newstead p A		45	11	8	38	13	5	37	11	8	34	16	1	iv. 71–2
Nocton Park p A		57	19	2½	43	2	8	45	19	2½	40	14	10	iv. 123–4
Nuncotton p C n		53	14	7	46	18	7	41	11	3	36	15	3	iv. 75
Nunormesby p G		98	0	0	80	11	10	74	0	0	63	2	9	iv. 59
Revesby a C		349	8	2	287	5	8½	312	6	6	287	1	0½	iv. 44–5
Sempringham p G		359	12	2	317	3	7	211	2	9	194	8	7	iv. 102–3
Sixhill p G		169	18	8	134	10	8	139	16	8	115	9	4	iv. 83
Spalding p B		878	17	3	765	16	6	740	2	9	684	16	7	iv. 97–8
Stamford St. Leonard's p B	*a*	36	1	5	25	1	2½	33	8	1	22	7	10½	v. 305–6
	b				28	6	1½							iv. 142
Stamford St. Michael's p B n		72	18	10½	65	19	9	37	9	8½	32	3	5	iv. 140–1
Staynesfield p B n.		112	0	5	98	8	1	60	7	1	50	1	1	iv. 88–3
Stixwold a C n		163	1	2½	114	10	2½	129	4	6½	110	17	10½	iv. 37–8
Swineshed a C		175	19	10½	167	15	4	160	14	5	154	16	6½	iv. 96
Thornholm p A		157	0	6¼	106	14	0¾	89	2	2½	78	12	0½	iv. 139
Thornton a A		730	17	2¼	584	9	10¼	591	5	4¾	512	14	6¾	iv. 73–4
Torkesey p A		27	2	8	13	1	4	12	1	4	11	10	0	iv. 131
Tupholm a P		119	2	8	100	14	10	78	9	4	71	11	6	iv. 36–7
Vaudey a C		181	10	7¾	128	1	0½	181	10	7¾	151	16	8¼	iv. 98–9
Wellow a A		152	8	4	95	7	1	79	18	4	50	5	1	iv. 67
Willoughton co		195	3	0½	175	11	1½	158	1	0½	138	9	1½	iv. 137

MIDDLESEX.

Elsing Spital p A		239	13	11½	195	3	7	223	13	11½	194	3	11	i. 389–90
Haliwell p B n		347	1	8	300	19	5	318	11	8	294	10	6	i. 394–5
Hounslow p Trin		80	15	1½	64	8	1½	67	15	1½	61	8	1½	i. 402
Kilburn p B n		86	7	11	74	7	11	77	1	3	72	18	9	i. 432
London St. Bartholomew's p A		773	0	1¾	693	9	10¾	701	10	1¾	627	10	2¼	i. 407–8
London Ch		736	2	7	642	0	4½	613	15	11	562	16	0½	i. 430–1

MIDDLESEX (*continued*).

	£	s.	d.	£	s.	d.	£	s.	d.	£	s.	d.	
London St. Helen's p B n	376	6	0	320	15	8½	365	6	0	346	2	10½	i. 392–3
London St. John of Jerusalem p ...	2286	13	10⅛	2081	0	3⅛	2174	11	0⅛	2035	8	5⅞	i 403–6
London St. Mary Clerkenwell p B n ...	282	16	5	262	19	6	243	13	9	228	4	6	i. 395–6
London St. Mary Graces p C	602	3	8½	545	2	4½	580	4	8½	541	4	10½	j. 398–9
London St. Mary Bishopsgate p Bethl	558	14	9½	500	13	2½	529	14	9½	486	18	2½	i. 400–2
London Minories p Fr n	342	6	10½	318	17	5	304	19	2½	289	0	9	i. 397–8
London St. Thomas of Acres domus	336	11	2	281	8	6	307	17	8	267	11	4	i. 391–2
Stratford at Bow p B n	121	0	6	108	1	11½	108	10	6	97	4	3½	i. 439
Syon a Brig	1943	11	8⅝	1735	4	7⅞	1500	1	1⅞	1366	13	0⅜	i. 424–8
Westminster St. Peter's a B	3912	4	0¾	2409	5	7¼	3164	12	4¾	2974	10	5¾	i. 410–24

NORFOLK.

	£	s.	d.	£	s.	d.	£	s.	d.	£	s.	d.	
Beeston p A	50	7	4⅞	43	3	4⅞	50	7	4⅞	46	3	4⅞	iii. 351
Binham p B				140	5	4							i. 451
Blackborough p B n	76	3	9½	42	6	7½	44	2	1½	36	2	3½	iii. 395–6
Bromholm p Cl	154	19	1¼	100	5	3¼	96	14	9¾	53	5	7¾	iii. 344–5
Buckenham p A	131	11	0¼	108	10	2¼							iii. 316
Carbroke co	76	5	3½	65	2	9½	69	14	5½	63	5	3½	iii. 340
Carrow p B n	84	12	1¾	63	16	6¼	60	0	5¼	53	1	5¾	iii. 305
Castleacre p Cl	334	17	5¾	306	11	4¾	126	16	1¾	113	11	2¼	iii. 390–1
Cokesford p A	151	7	1	121	18	10¼	106	8	1	88	16	5½	iii. 369–70
Crabhouse p A n	31	16	7	25	2	3	26	9	11	25	2	3	iii. 396
Flitcham p A	62	13	6½	55	5	6¾	47	13	10½	43	16	6¼	iii. 396–7
Hempton p A	39	0	9¼	32	14	8	35	14	1¼	29	12	9	iii. 383
Hickling p A	135	2	1¾	100	18	7¾	92	10	1¾	68	0	3¾	iii. 345–6
Horsham p B	193	2	3¼	162	16	11½	109	18	1½	98	3	5½	iii. 365–6
Hulme a B	677	10	0	583	16	4½	557	8	0½	507	14	0	iii. 341–3
Ingham p Trin	74	2	7¾	61	9	7¾	53	5	7¾	44	12	0¾	iii. 346–7
Langley a P	129	0	9½	104	17	5	89	10	1	47	13	9	iii. 304–5
Marham a C n	42	4	7¾	33	13	5¾	39	1	7¾	35	17	1¾	iii. 379
Marmond p G	13	6	1½	10	7	7	10	16	1½	9	15	10½	iii. 379–80
Modney p B				2	3	4							iv. 273

Norwich St. Trinity c p B	1061	12	3½	871	6	11¾	675	6	1½	594	1	0¼	iii. 284–9
Pentney cum Wormgay p A	215	18	8¼	170	5	5¼	151	6	7¼	141	8	3¾	iii. 393–5
Shouldham p G	171	6	8½	138	18	1	127	6	8½	116	16	8½	iii. 378
Thetford p Cl	418	6	3½	312	13	4½							iii. 309–12
Thetford p A	49	18	1	39	6	8	37	10	11	27	12	8	iii. 312–13
Thetford p B n	50	9	8	40	11	2½	31	14	11	27	3	1½	iii. 313–14
Waburn p A	28	7	2	24	19	6½	13	4	6	13	2	8	iii. 362
Walsingham p A	707	7	10⅛	652	4	11⅝	385	5	0⅝	350	10	1⅛	iii. 385–8
Wendling a P	72	5	4¼	55	18	4¾	53	14	11¼	46	4	0¼	iii. 328–9
Westacre p A	308	19	11¾	261	13	7¼	243	9	9¾	231	1	0¾	iii. 392–3
West Dereham a P	252	12	11¾	228	0	0¾	207	19	7¾	189	11	4¾	iii. 376–7
Weybridge p A	9	5	4	7	14	4	4	5	0	3	0	0	iii. 297
Wymondham a B	263	18	2¾	211	16	6¼	188	7	11¾	168	5	8¾	iii. 322–3

NORTHANTS.

Ashby p A	127	18	0	108	19	4¼	86	7	8	75	3	7	iv. 337
Catesby p B n	145	0	6	132	1	11¼	118	0	6	115	5	10	iv. 339
Chacomb p A	93	6	3½	83	18	9½	59	6	3½	57	4	11½	iv. 338
Fineshade p A	62	16	0	56	10	11	58	16	0	53	3	6	iv. 296–7
Luffield p B				45	0	0							i. 412
Northampton St. Andrew's p C ...	335	3	7	263	17	1¼	212	16	1	190	1	9	iv. 313–15
Northampton St. James's a A	213	17	2½	175	8	2½	146	17	2½	141	13	6½	iv. 319
Northampton De la Pré a Cl n	133	15	6½	119	9	7¼	83	15	6½	79	5	7½	iv. 321
Peterborough a B	1979	7	5⅞	1721	14	0⅞	1741	7	6⅞	1591	7	7⅞	iv. 279–84
Pipewell a C	347	0	8½	286	9	11¾	292	15	0½	257	13	4	iv. 294–6
Rothwell p A n	10	10	4	5	19	8½							iv. 302
Sewardesley p C n	18	11	2	12	6	7	11	17	10	11	13	10	iv. 328
Sulby a P	305	8	5½	258	8	5	205	8	5½	180	18	6	iv. 300–1

NORTHUMBERLAND.

Alnwick a P				189	15	0							v. 329
Bamburgh A	124	15	7	116	12	5	16	12	3	14	5	7	v. 64
Blanchland P				40	9	0							v. 328
Brinkburne p A				68	19	1							v. 330
Farn Island B	12	7	8	12	7	8							v. 305

NORTHUMBERLAND (*continued*).

		£ s. d.	£ s. d.	£ s. d.	£ s. d.	
Hexham p A			122 11 1			v. 328
Holiscombe p B n			11 5 6			v. 329
Insula Sacra B		60 5 0	48 18 11	24 2 0	19 9 3	v. 304–5
Neseham p B n		26 9 9	20 17 7	26 9 9	20 17 7	v. 310
Newcastle p B n			36 0 10			v. 327
Newminster a C			100 8 11			v. 329
Tynemouth p B			397 10 5			v. 327

NOTTS.

		£ s. d.	£ s. d.	£ s. d.	£ s. d.	
Beauvale Ch		227 8 0	206 1 4	166 10 6	157 3 10	v. 156
Blyth p B		125 8 2½	112 0 8½	65 14 6½	57 1 2½	v. 176–7
Brodholm p P		18 11 10	16 5 2	16 11 10	14 11 10	v. 185
Felley p A		61 4 8	40 19 0	37 12 0	34 3 6	v. 155
Lenton p Cl		418 7 9	336 2 4½	162 12 1	141 8 7	v. 147–9
Mattersey p G		61 16 7	56 12 5	39 6 7	36 7 5	v. 178
Newstead in Sherwood p A		219 18 8½	167 16 11½	161 18 8½	147 1 0½	v. 153–4
Rufford a C		254 6 8	178 0 4	186 13 4	165 13 0	v. 171–3
Shelford p A		151 14 1	116 14 5½	58 3 5	50 8 4½	v. 162–3
Thurgarton p A		359 16 2	259 2 9¾	210 5 6	186 19 2¾	v. 150–3
Wallingwells p B n		87 8 8	58 7 0	21 8 0	20 1 6	v. 179
Welbeck a P		297 4 8	247 10 3	165 1 0	142 2 10	v. 170–1
Worksop p A		311 7 0	246 8 5	165 7 10	149 18 3	v. 174–6

OXFORD.

		£ s. d.	£ s. d.	£ s. d.	£ s. d.	
Bruerne a C	a	153 16 2	135 10 10	151 16 2	134 1 6	ii. 201–4
	b	171 9 1	141 7 11	169 9 1	148 3 3	ii. 265–7
Burcester p A		178 14 8¾	143 11 4			ii. 187–90
Burford p		16 0 6	13 6 6			ii. 179
Clattercote p A		42 6 3	34 19 11	26 5 2	24 15 10	ii. 197
Dorchester a A	a	219 12 0¾	190 2 4¼	83 5 1½	65 5 1	ii. 170–1
	b	217 5 9½	183 9 5			ii. 167
Eynsham a B		538 9 6½	434 5 10¼	402 14 4½	344 18 7½	ii. 207–12

						Ref.
Godstow a B n	...	320 4 2	26? 14 8	241 11 1	210 13 6½	ii. 191-6
Goring p A n	...{ a	67 9 6	63 19 10	36 14 10	35 10 10	ii. 168
	b	63 8 10½	5? 19 2	32 5 3	31 1 3	ii. 205-7
Oseney a A	...	755 17 6½	65? 13 0	166 15 11	158 12 8	ii. 215-24
Rewley a C	...	189 13 3½	17? 3 9	85 14 8	75 18 5	ii. 254-5
Studley p B n	...{ a	102 16 7	8? 9 4	85 14 8	75 18 5	ii. 186-7
	b	103 16 5	85 14 2			ii. 172
Thame a C	...{ a	293 14 11½	256 13 3	274 15 7½		ii. 213-14
	b	296 1 5½	258 19 0	276 18 9½		ii. 169
Wroxton p A	...	105 3 11½	79 14 ?	86 9 10	72 14 0	ii. 198-200

RUTLAND.

						Ref.
Brooke p A	...		4? 0 0			iv. 343

SALOP.

						Ref.
Bromfield p B	...	78 19 4	67 18 ?	57 11 4	52 4 8	ii. 422
Brewood p C n	...	31 9 4	17 18 ?	17 16 0	11 2 8	iii. 193-4
Buildwas a C	...	129 6 10	110 19 ?	123 6 10	108 3 2	iii. 191-2
Chirbury p A	...	87 1? 4	66 8 ?	16 14 10	8 16 6	iii. 212
Haghmond a A	...	294 12 6	259 13 ?	228 13 11	213 13 2	iii. 192-3
Halesowen a P	...	320 12 6½	263 2 ?	287 7 2	255 10 6½	iii. 206-8
Lilleshall a A	...	324 19 10	230 2 ?	232 16 2½	197 2 7	iii. 197-8
Shrewsbury a B	...	559 4 3½	482 15 ?	415 1 7½	380 17 4	iii. 189-91
Wenlock a Cl	...	448 1 4	4?2 7 ?	346 17 0¾	323 10 3¼	iii. 215-16
Wombridge p A	...	72 15 8	65 7 ?	62 9 0	59 2 0	iii. 194-5

SOMERSET.

						Ref.
Athelney a B	...	290 19 5¼	209 1 ?	271 0 3¼	243 3 6¼	i. 206-7
Barlinch p A	...	167 18 6¼	101 6 ?	117 10 8¾	87 1 9¾	i. 219
Bath a B ...	...	707 13 1	617 12 ?	545 15 7	500 2 8	i. 174-7
Bridgwater p	...	196 13 3	119 4 ?	81 14 10¼	67 11 1½	i. 207-9
St. James's, Bristol p E	...	61 7 10	?5 7 ?	43 7 1	40 8 9	ii. 484-5
Bruton a A	...	528 7 9	456 16 ?	337 15 9	302 4 1	i. 149-50
Byrkley p A	...	6 6 8	6 5 ?	6 2 0	5 18 6	i. 148

SOMERSET (*continued*).

		£	s.	d.	£	s.	d.	£	s.	d.	£	s.	d.	
Cannington p B n		69	17	0	39	15	8	53	1	9	46	9	9	i. 209–10
Cleeve a C		277	3	10¾	155	10	5¼	245	6	10¾	201	19	9¼	i. 217–18
Glastonbury a B		3642	3	0⅜	3311	15	1⅝	3289	13	8⅞	3163	14	7⅝	i. 142–7
Dunster p B		58	15	0	37	4	8	23	16	4	21	14	4	i. 220
Hinton Ch		271	1	4	249	5	6	271	1	4	263	6	2	i. 156–7
Keynsham a A		466	0	6	419	10	4¼	416	13	9	385	3	5	i. 181–2
Minchin Bockland p A n		237	11	2¾	223	7	4¼	122	18	11¾	116	2	1¾	i. 210–11
Montacute a Cl		463	2	6½	391	4	5¾	379	0	0½	360	12	5¼	i. 195–7
Muchelney a B		511	2	0	488	9	8½	393	18	0	371	1	8½	i. 193–4
Mynchen Barwe B n		29	6	9½	23	14	4¾	20	11	10	19	7	0	i. 183
Taunton p A		452	19	1½	282	18	4	264	11	5½	235	6	6½	i. 168–70
Templecombe co		124	0	3½	107	17	3½	122	13	7½	113	17	3½	i. 201–2
Wells St. John's p		69	6	8¾	40	0	2¾	50	4	2¾	38	16	8¾	i. 140
Witham Ch		249	0	3	215	15	0	239	10	5	221	11	10	i. 157–8
Worspring p A		112	15	2	87	3	0	97	11	10	94	8	6	i. 188
STAFFORD.														
Brewood p B n					11	1	6				11	1	6	iii. 103
Burton upon Trent a B	*a*	356	16	3½	267	14	3	271	11	3½	241	9	3½	iii. 144–6
	b	513	19	0½	424	17	0	414	14	0½	384	12	0½	iii. 146–8
Croxden a C		103	6	7	90	6	9	94	11	3	85	0	5	iii. 125
Dieulacres a C		243	3	6	227	5	0	174	13	2	160	15	2	iii. 123
Dudley p Cl		36	8	0	34	1	4	15	11	4	13	4	8	iii. 104
Hulton a C		87	10	1½	76	14	10½	67	0	1½	59	16	7½	iii. 107–8
Ronton p A		102	11	1	90	2	11⅓	56	9	7	50	14	3	iii. 114–16
Roucester a A		111	11	7	100	2	10½	64	17	9	60	14	3½	iii. 124
St. Thomas's, Stafford p A		181	1	9½	141	16	0 7/12	130	19	5½	115	12	5¼	iii. 110–12
Stone p A		130	2	11	110	14	11⅓	54	12	11	50	19	6	iii. 113–14
Trentham p A		121	3	2	106	3	8⅔	83	19	10	77	14	0	iii. 108–9
Tutbury p B		244	16	8	119	14	10	170	18	4	150	4	4	iii. 142–4
SUFFOLK.														
Bliburgh p A		60	13	4	48	8	10	28	13	4	22	14	4	iii. 439

Brusyard a Fr n	74	7	0½	56	2	1	57	16	7½	43	15	0	iii. 442–3
Bungay p B n	73	0	0½	62	2	1	35	16	2½	28	14	0½	iii. 430–1
Bury St. Edmunds a B	2336	3	10¼	1659	4	6¼	2204	1	4¾	1963	2	10¾	iii. 459–65
Butley p A	387	6	4	318	0	2	265	15	9	221	7	2½	iii. 418–22
Campsey p A n	249	11	5¾	182	9	5	215	6	5½	158	19	5½	iii. 415–16
Eye p B	183	9	9⅛	160	2	5⅓	112	19	5⅓	100	13	9⅜	iii. 476–7
Flixton p A n	38	17	11	21	7	0	32	9	7	23	2	0	iii. 446
Heringfleet p A	22	5	8	18	13	6½	15	13	8½	13	10	11	iii. 412
Ipswich, Holy Trinity p A	119	16	8	88	13	11	97	0	0	71	10	8	iii. 447–8
Ixworth p A	204	9	5¼	168	19	7½	152	7	3¾	141	3	7½	iii. 482–3
Leiston a P	210	3	11⅛	182	3	4⅓	168	3	11⅓	145	3	1⅛	iii. 436–8
Letheringham p A	32	13	4	26	18	5	9	13	4	7	16	9	iii. 423–4
Redlingfield p B n	81	2	5½	67	0	1	68	10	11½	63	4	10	iii. 478
Sibton a C	278	0	11¾	250	13	11½	228	8	8¼	212	14	5½	iii. 434–6
Sudbury p B				10	0	0							i. 411
Wangford p Cl	49	3	0	30	9	5	19	9	8	5	5	7	iii. 438
Woodbridge p A	58	13	0	50	3	5½	47	19	8	41	5	3½	iii. 422–3

SURREY.

Bermondsey a B...	548	2	5½	474	14	4¾	412	6	0	356	3	6	ii. 58–60
Chertsey a B	738	0	2¾	653	2	3¾	591	9	8¾	555	10	2¾	ii. 56–7
Merton p A	1036	1	3½	957	14	6½	758	10	3½	714	7	11½	ii. 48–51
Newark near Guildford p A	294	17	4½	258	10	11½	219	2	0½	190	6	9½	ii. 33–4
Reigate p A	78	4	11½	69	10	7	61	4	11½	55	3	11	ii. 66–7
Shene Ch	961	3	6	777	12	0½							ii. 51–4
St. Mary's Overey, Southwark p A ...	556	10	0½	624	6	6	456	8	8½	433	19	1	ii. 62–3
Tandridge p A	86	7	6½	78	16	6¾	61	9	2½	54	15	8¾	ii. 68
Waverley a C	196	13	11½	174	8	3½	196	0	3½	181	19	0½	ii. 34–5

SUSSEX.

Battle a B	909	7	10⅛	803	1	7⅝	773	16	6⅛	719	8	6¼	i. 346–9
Boxgrove p B	186	3	0	145	14	3½	110	19	8	100	6	0	i. 306–7
Dureford a P	108	13	9	98	4	5	102	7	1	93	6	1	i. 321 + vi. App xiii.–xiv

	£	s.	d.	£	s.	d.	£	s.	d.	£	s.	d.	
SUSSEX (*continued*).													
Easeburn p B n	47	3	0	29	16	7	22	14	1	18	19	7	i. 323
Hastings p A	57	18	2	51	8	7½	44	11	6	38	11	9½	i. 354
Lewes p Cl	1091	9	6⅛	921	14	10⅛	577	7	8⅛	508	10	4⅛	i. 326–32
Michelham p A	182	0	3	160	13	6	154	13	7	129	1	8½	i. 352–3
Robertsbridge a C	272	9	6	248	10	2	253	9	2	232	10	10	i. 350–1
Rusper p B n	40	0	0	39	14	7							i. 319
Shulbrede p A	79	15	4	72	18	9½	61	7	10	56	13	11½	i. 322
Tortington p A	101	4	1	75	12	3½	81	6	9	68	14	6½	i. 312–13
WARWICK.													
Alcester p B	101	14	0	66	2	2	28	1	3	26	14	7	iii. 88
Avecote p B	34	9	0	28	6	2	30	17	0	28	3	8	iii. 242 and 7
Balsall co...				200	0	0							i. 405
Combe a C	342	1	7	310	16	5	327	4	11	302	18	5	iii. 54–5
Coventry C p B	753	12	10	543	4	1	653	19	10	515	1	10	iii. 49–52
Coventry Ch	251	5	9	131	6	4	21	10	5	16	10	5	iii. 53–4
Erdbury p A	122	14	7	94	12	2	58	14	7	40	13	2	iii. 56
Henwood p B n	23	8	7½	21	2	0½	23	8	7½	21	6	0½	iii. 79
Kenilworth a A	643	14	8	538	19	4½	375	8	6	348	16	3	iii. 64–6
Maxstoke p A	129	11	8½	87	12	3½	56	14	8½	45	7	5½	iii. 73–4
Merevale a C	303	10	0	252	3	1	228	5	4	211	0	1	iii. 71–2
Nuneaton p B n	290	10	5½	253	9	10½	234	4	5½	214	8	10½	iii. 76–7
Pinley p B n	27	13	7	23	5	11	27	13	7	24	15	3	iii. 90
Pollesworth a B n	109	5	0	87	14	9	60	0	0	52	8	5	iii. 77–8
Stoneleigh a C	178	0	4	150	18	2	178	0	4	168	8	6	iii. 67–8
Studley p A	181	3	6	117	1	5½	92	5	6	83	6	2	iii. 86–7
Thelesford p Trin	25	6	8	23	9	10	20	13	4	18	16	6	iii. 95
Warwick p A	49	13	6	41	10	2	38	2	10	33	12	0	iii. 86
Wroxall p B n	78	10	1½	72	14	10	46	6	9½	42	11	5½	iii. 89
WESTMORELAND.													
Shappe a P	166	10	6½	154	17	7½	103	7	2½	97	12	1½	v. 293–4

WILTS.

Amesbury p B n	595 13 2¾	496 13 4	411 16 7¼	328 17 4½	ii. 93–5
Anstey co	90 1 9½	81 8 5½			ii. 108
Bradenstoke p A	270 11 8	212 0 3	249 7 8	228 19 8	ii. 123–5
Edindon p Bon	521 12 5½	442 9 7¾	393 8 11½	324 4 8½	ii. 140–2
Eston p Trin	55 14 4	42 12 0	22 16 10	18 15 10	ii. 149
Farleigh p Cl	217 0 4½	156 7 6½	161 6 8½	105 3 8½	ii. 143–4
Ivychurch p A	141 9 1	123 8 9½	69 11 3½	59 0 1½	ii. 96–7
Kington p B n	38 3 10	25 9 1½	26 1 2	18 19 10½	ii. 113–14
Lacock a A n	203 14 0½	168 10 11	181 0 8½	166 0 9½	ii. 115–18
Maiden Bradley p A	198 18 8	180 10 4	193 9 5	181 18 9	ii. 98–9
Malmesbury a B	886 16 4¾	798 0 2¼	849 8 2¾	776 12 0¼	ii. 118–22
Marlborough p G	38 19 2	30 9 6	34 19 2	29 2 6	ii. 148
Pulton p G	21 15 2	20 3 10			ii. 129
Stanley a C	222 19 4	177 0 8	206 6 0	182 4 0	ii. 114–15
Wilton a B n	674 6 2⅞	600 14 0⅞	632 16 2⅞	601 15 2⅞	ii. 109–12

WORCESTER.

Bordesley a C	421 17 10¾	389 7 2¾	364 9 4½	348 18 9½	iii. 271–3
Cokehill p C n		35 9 3		16 5 4	iii. 262–3
Dodford		7 0 0		7 0 0	iii. 207
Evesham a B	1313 5 3½	1138 13 6	1067 19 6½	985 19 7½	iii. 248–54
Great Malvern	453 4 0¼	306 4 1¾	301 6 6¼	239 10 6¼	iii. 237–41
Little Malvern p B	121 16 5½	98 10 7½	72 17 2	66 6 2½	iii. 242–4
Pershore p B n	725 16 11	648 2 9	549 13 11	500 7 9	iii. 259–62
Westwood p B n	78 8 0	75 18 11	65 15 2	64 7 11½	iii. 276–7
Whiston p C n	58 7 9	53 3 7	35 2 2	30 9 8	iii. 230
Worcester c and p B	1444 14 3½	1296 11 1¼	1095 16 8¼	1017 14 2¼	iii. 220–7

YORKSHIRE.

St. Agatha's a P	188 16 2	111 17 11½	167 9 2	150 13 4	v. 235–6
Arden p B n	13 7 4	12 0 6	13 7 4	12 12 6	v. 86
Arthington p B n	19 0 0	11 8 4½	9 0 0	8 8 4½	v. 16
Basedale p C n	21 19 4	20 1 4	21 19 4	20 1 4	v. 87

YORKSHIRE (*continued*).

	£	s.	d.	£	s.	d.	£	s.	d.	£	s.	d.	
Beverley co				164	9	10							v. 142
Bolton p A				212	3	4							v. 144
Bridlington p A	682	14	1	547	7	3½	321	12	9	293	13	3½	v. 120–1
Byland a C	295	5	4	238	9	4							v. 93
Coverham a P	208	2	10	166	7	5	117	2	10	107	7	11	v. 243
Drax p A	121	18	3½	91	16	10	62	1	7½	59	11	4	v. 15
Eglestone a P	65	5	6	36	7	2	53	12	10	44	3	0½	v. 236–7
Ellerton p G	78	0	10	62	8	10	58	0	10	53	19	8	v. 128
Elreton p C n	15	14	8	15	10	6	15	14	8	15	10	6	v. 244
Esholt p C n	19	0	8	13	5	4	19	0	8	17	5	4	v. 16
Ferreby p A	97	7	7½	61	17	2½	79	0	11½	72	3	2½	v. 128–9
Fountains a B	1178	19	3½	1004	5	4½	1103	5	11½	1004	8	1½	v. 253–4
Gisburn p A	707	6	6½	623	13	4	413	16	6½	370	10	0	v. 80–1
Grosmont p B	12	2	8	10	2	8	12	2	8	12	2	8	v. 86
Haltemprice p A	178	0	10	100	0	3½	104	14	2	82	10	0½	v. 127
Hampole p C n	85	5	11	63	1	7½	36	10	7	32	0	7½	v. 43–4
Handale p B n	20	7	8	13	19	0	20	7	8	18	18	8	v. 87
Helagh Park p A	91	13	4	72	10	9	71	12	8	69	6	0	v. 3–4
Hull Ch				174	18	4							v. 126
Jervaulx a C	455	10	5	234	18	4½	340	14	11	273	6	2½	v. 241–2
Keldholme p C n				29	6	1							v. 145
Kirkham p A	300	15	5	269	5	9							v. 103–4
Kirklees p C n	20	7	8	19	8	2	15	14	4	15	1	6	v. 67
Knaresborough p Trin	86	15	8	35	10	11	24	11	0	15	6	8	v. 254–5
Marrick p B n	65	1	9	49	1	2½	55	5	9	53	3	2	v. 237
Marton p A	183	2	4	151	5	0	134	7	8	128	15	6	v. 93–4
Meaux a C	445	0	9½	299	16	8¼	291	18	3½	272	3	5¼	v. 108–9
Middleborough p B	21	3	8	17	4	2	18	15	6	15	16	0	v. 83
Molesby p B n	32	6	2	26	2	10	29	6	2	25	16	2	v. 95
Monk-Bretton a Cl	323	8	2	239	9	6½							v. 42–3
Mountgrace Ch	382	5	11½	323	2	10½	277	19	3½	253	16	3½	v. 84–5
Mount St. John co	137	2	0	102	13	10	81	8	8	54	12	0	v. 94–5

Newburgh p A	457	13	5	367	8	3½	200	4	1	170	0	8½	v. 92–3
Newland co	202	3	8	129	7	3½	120	10	4	86	4	11½	v. 68–9
Nostell or St. Oswald p A	606	9	3½	492	18	2½	236	12	7	226	2	9½	v. 62–4
Nun Appleton C n				73	9	10							v. 4
Nunburnholme p B n	10	3	3	6	15	3	10	3	3	10	1	11	v. 129
Nunkeling p C n...	50	17	2	35	15	5	46	11	6	35	5	5	v. 115
Nunmonkton B n	85	14	8	75	12	4½	62	14	8	56	10	4½	v. 255
Old Malton a G				197	10	0							v. 144
Pontefract p Cl	475	3	8½	340	13	0	269	12	3½	233	13	10	v. 65–6
Ribstone co	224	9	7	207	9	7	208	9	7	191	9	7	v. 256
Richmond p B	32	15	5	28	15	1	12	0	5	9	7	1	v. 10–11
Rievaulx a C				278	10	2							v. 144
Roche a C	261	19	4	224	2	5	219	4	8	205	5	10	v. 41–2
Rosedale p B n				37	12	5							v. 144
Sawley a C				147	3	10							v. 144
Selby a B	829	4	4½	739	13	0¼	555	6	5¾	507	11	9¾	v. 12–14
Sempringham G				63	13	4							v. 126
Sinningthwaite p C n	62	6	0	60	15	2	60	6	0	58	15	2	v. 4
Swine p C n	133	6	9½	82	3	9½	79	17	9½	69	11	3½	v. 114
Thickhed p B n	23	12	2	20	18	10	23	12	2	20	18	10	v. 94
Thockwith p A	8	0	0	8	0	0	8	0	0	8	0	0	v. 64
Warter p A	211	3	10	143	7	8							v. 126
Watton a G				360	18	10							v. 126
Whitby a B	483	1	5	419	8	7	310	8	5	287	15	1	v. 82
Wickham p C n				25	17	6							v. 145
Widkirk p A	49	7	2	47	0	4	34	10	2	32	11	4	v. 64
Wilberfoss p B n...				21	16	10							v. 142
Yedingham p B n				21	16	6½							v. 144
York St. Clement's a B n	57	7	9				41	10	1				v. 2–3
York St. Mary's a b ... ... *a*	1053	18	1¼	650	7	9¼	578	15	2¼	391	13	11¾	v. 4–9
York St. Mary's a b ... ... *b*	2091	4	7⅛	1650	7	0⅛							

BERKS.

	£	s.	d.	
Abingdon a B ...	1876	10	9	ii. 155-7
Bisham p A ...	285	11	0½	ii. 154
Donnington p Trin ...	19	13	10	ii. 157
Hurley p B ...	121	18	5	ii. 154
Poughley p B ...	67	10	4	i. 411-15
Reading a B ...	1938	14	3¾	ii. 154

CAMBRIDGE.

	£	s.	d.	
Anglesey p A ...	124	19	0	iii. 505
Barnwell p A ...	256	11	10¼	iii. 506
Cambridge St. Edmund's p G...	14	18	8½	iii. 506
Chatteris p B n ...	97	3	4	iii. 499
Denny a Fr n ...	174	0	0	iii. 499
Ely c p B ...	1084	6	9	iii. 499
Fordham p G ...	40	13	4½	iii. 504
Iklington p B n...	71	9	10½	iii. 505
Shengay co ...	175	4	6	iii. 503
Swaffham Bulbeck p B n ...	40	0	0	iii. 505
Thorney a B ...	411	12	11	iii. 499

ESSEX.

	£	s.	d.	
Barking B n ...	862	12	5½	i. 435
Berden p A ...	29	6	4½	i. 440
Bileigh a P ...	157	16	11¼	i. 446
Coggeshall a C...	251	2	0	i. 444

ESSEX (*continued*).

	£	s.	d.	
Colchester St. Botolph's p A ...	113	12	8	i. 443
Colchester St. John's a B ...	523	16	0¼	i. 443
Colne p B ...	156	12	4½	i. 444
Dunmow p A ...	150	3	4	i. 438
Hatfield Peverell p B ...	60	14	11	i. 451
Hatfield Regis p B ...	122	13	2½	i. 436
Hedingham p B n ...	29	12	2	i. 441
Lees p A ...	114	1	4	i. 449
St. Osyth p A ...	677	1	2	i. 442
Prittlewell p Cl ...	155	11	2½	i. 447
Stratford Langthorn a C ...	511	16	3⅛	i. 435
Thremhall p A ...	60	18	7½	i. 439
Tiltey a C ...	167	2	6	i. 438
Walden a B ...	372	18	1	i. 438
Waltham Holy Cross a A ...	900	4	3	i. 435

HERTFORD.

	£	s.	d.	
St. Albans a B ...	2102	7	1¾	i. 451
Cheshunt p B n ...	13	10	0	i. 452
Flamstead p B n...	30	19	6½	iv. 276
Hertford p B ...	72	14	2½	i. 276
Hitchin p G n ...	13	16	0	iv. 276
Redburn p B ...	9	2	0	i. 451
Royston p A ...	89	16	0	i. 452
Sopwell p B n ...	40	7	10	i. 451
Wymondley p A...	29	19	11½	iv. 276

INDEX LOCORUM

The Index refers to religious houses, rectories, and manors. The names of the religious houses are mostly modern. The names of the rectories and the manors are almost always those of the sixteenth century; but the modern form of each where possible is given after the county. Where no second name is given the old form and the modern are the same. 'm' means *monastery*. Names without 'm' stand either for rectories or for manors. I have had very valuable assistance of Miss Toulmin in ascertaining the modern names and revising the Index for the press. In one or two cases topographical errors in the text have been corrected.

INDEX RERUM

II

DE PATROCINIIS VICORUM

A COMMENTARY ON

CODEX THEODOSIANUS 11, 24

AND

CODEX IUSTINIANUS 11, 54

BY

FRANCIS DE ZULUETA, M.A.

OF LINCOLN'S INN, BARRISTER-AT-LAW, FELLOW OF NEW COLLEGE,
FORMERLY FELLOW OF MERTON COLLEGE, OXFORD

II

DE PATROCINIIS VICORUM

THE notion of patronage is familiar to all students of Definition of the subject. antiquity. Patron and client, patron and freedman, patronus orator, patronus civitatis, patronus and colonus—these are all relations of a legal, and still more of a customary, character, which profoundly affected ancient society. Their importance has not been overlooked by modern writers,[1] and it is not our purpose to deal with the subject in all its aspects. We are concerned only with patronage on its agrarian side, or, to speak more accurately, with the exposition and illustration of two titles in the Codices Theodosianus and Iustinianus, C. T. 11, 24, and C. J. 11, 54. These contain eight constitutions: C. T. 11, 24, 1 of Constantius of the year 360; ibid. 2 of Valentinian Valens and Gratian of 370 (? 368); ibid. 3 of Arcadius and Honorius of 395; ibid. 4 of the same, dated 399; ibid. 5 of the same authors and year; ibid. 6 of Honorius and Theodosius, dated 415; C. J. 11, 54, 1 of Leo and Anthemius dated 468; ibid. 2 unaddressed and undated, which I take to be of Justinian.[2] These eight constitutions, covering the years 360 to 534, are directed against the patronage afforded by powerful folk to the peasantry, primarily with a view to defeating the taxgatherer. This is no isolated phenomenon, for similar practices were adopted by the artisans of the towns to evade collatio lustralis,[3] by navicularii to avoid their transport duties,[4] and

---

[1] e. g. Fustel de Coulanges, Les Origines du Système Féodal, ch. 4, s. 5, and ch. 9. Seeck, Geschichte d. Untergangs d. antiken Welt, I cc. 4 and 5, II 4. 6. 7. Dill, Roman Society in the last century of the Western Empire, bk. 3, ch. 2, especially pp. 222 ff.

[2] 'Ex compositione' it is later than the first constitution; Const. Haec, s. 2. It is an independent enactment, for it adds fresh penalties.

[3] C. T. 13, 1, 15. 21.   [4] C. T. 13, 7, 1. 2.

by pistores and suarii against their special burdens.[1]   All
these, in one form or another, were doing the same thing,
namely, using the loose and equivocal connexion of patron
and client, so thoroughly in accord with the sentiments and
even the law of the age, to secure for themselves favourable
treatment from the administration.

Our case is the most central, because agriculture was
naturally the greatest industry and the land-tax the principal
source of revenue.   This tax was collected through the
civitates, but fell ultimately on the small villagers, the lesser
possessores and the coloni ; we shall therefore not altogether
escape the problems of the colonate, and shall be led into
difficult questions relating to the collection and incidence of
taxes.   Further, since agricultural patronage was of communities as much as of individuals, the subject of village
organization will necessarily arise.

Inquiry
limited to
the East.   The constitutions in C. T. 11, 24 are mainly directed to
Egypt, and consequently involve an examination of the
papyri.   As a set-off to this large field of study we shall
confine ourselves to the Eastern Empire, so that amongst the
literary sources we shall pay less attention to the well-known
passages of Salvianus[2] than to Libanius, whose Oratio de
Patrociniis is contemporary with our earlier constitutions,
and less remote from them in local application than Salvianus'
work.[3]   Finally, in point of time we shall stop short with the
C. J., and so exclude Justinian's Novels and the later Byzantine legislation.[4]

The subject will be divided as follows :—

(1) Analysis of the constitutions, (2) Analysis of Libanius'
Oration, (3) Problems of Egyptian land-tenure and village
organization, arising out of the constitutions.

---

[1] C. T. 14, 3, 3 ; 4, 5. 9.

[2] De Gub. Dei iv, 4. v, 4. 5. 8. 9.   Fustel de Coulanges, op. cit. pp. 95
and 244.

[3] Oratio 47.   Reiske, II 499.   Förster, III 404 (Teubner, 1906), the
edition to which we shall refer.   Gothofredus Opuscula.

[4] Nov. Just. 17, 13–15.   Tib. II, De Divinis Domibus, Coll. I, Nov. 12
(578–582).

I

The Constitutions. About these, two preliminary remarks Fiscal must be made. First, as appears from their tenor and from object of the con- their position in the codices, their preoccupation is exclusively stitutions. fiscal, with the result that they present the facts chiefly from that point of view. What to Libanius seems a grievance of the landlords, to Salvianus an oppression of the peasants, is to the emperors a device for evading taxes. This difference of point of view, if borne in mind, is instructive and involves no contradiction.

Secondly, the constitutions are primarily Eastern in appli- Local cation. Although the evidence of Salvianus proves the exis- applica- tion. tence of agricultural patronage of the obnoxious kind in Gaul, and though the very fact of inclusion of the constitutions in the C. T. and the C. J. is against purely local applicability, they were as a matter of history evoked from Eastern Emperors in view of eastern difficulties. This is proved by the address of six of the eight constitutions to the praefectus praetorio Orientis, C. T. 11, 24, 3 being addressed to the Comes of Egypt, and C. J. 11, 54, 2, which is unaddressed, being in Greek. It would, however, be going too far in this direction to limit the application of the constitutions in the C. T. 11, 24 to Egypt. It is true, as Gothofredus in his commentary on this title points out, that ll. 1, 3, 4 and 6 contain special references to Egypt, while l. 5 is a mere sequel to l. 4. But l. 2 is perfectly general, and the officials enumerated in l. 4 carry us into every part of the East, if not of the Empire ; the addresses to the p. pō. Orientis are prima facie against restriction to one diocese. The contemporary oration of Libanius extends the infected area to Syria, and the later C. J. 11, 54, 1 expressly mentions the dioceses of Thrace, Oriens, Egypt, Pontus and Asia. In fine there is only one constitution which by its use of technical local terms is incapable of general application, viz. C. T. 11, 24, 6 of 415, with its Augustalianum iudicium, arurae, logografi chomatum, and Constantinopolitana atque Alexandrina ecclesiae.[1]

---

[1] Note, with Gothofredus, the significant omission of Antioch.

The special preoccupation of the legislators about Egypt is no reason for assuming that it was the only, nor even an exceptional, field of patronage. From that country came the annona for Constantinople, so that its disorders were of the first importance. Thus C. T. 11, 24, 4 was promulgated by Arcadius on March 10, 399, almost simultaneously with C. T. 13, 7, 1, which threatens with heavy penalties (not so heavy however as those in the first-mentioned law) both those 'qui naves suo nomine vel defensione a transvectionibus publicis excusare temptaverint', and their clients the shipowners, 'qui neglectis necessitatibus publicis potiorum voluerint patrociniis excusari.' Patronage in fact was cutting off the supplies both at their source and on the way.[1]

The contents of the constitutions, to which we now turn, will be dealt with in the following order; we shall treat first of the parties concerned in an agreement of patronage, viz. the patrons and the clients; next of the penalties provided for them by our constitutions, then of their respective motives for continuing to brave these penalties, finally of the relations set up between patron and client and of the various forms under which the penalized agreements appear to have been cloaked.

The patrons.   The offending patrons are described in terms both particular and general: C. T. 11, 24, 1 'Qui variis honoribus fulciuntur, ducum etiam'; ibid. 3 'Quicumque ex officio tuo' (*sc.* comitis Aegypti) 'vel ex quocumque ordine hominis'; ibid. 4 'Cuiuslibet ille fuerit dignitatis, sive magistri utriusque militiae sive comitis sive ex proconsulibus vel vicariis vel Augustalibus vel tribunis sive ex ordine curiali vel cuiuslibet alterius dignitatis'; ibid. 6, 6 'Ecclesiae venerabiles, id est Constantinopolitana atque Alexandrina'; C. J. 11, 54, 1 'nobiliores', and 'mediocris fortunae'. The general result of these descriptions is quite clear : any one is a patron who is strong enough; the mischief goes as low as the curiales, but it is specially rife amongst the official classes, both civil

---

[1] The Edict 13 of Justinian offers the fullest illustration of the chronic anxiety of the government about the annona, felix embola, of Constantinople and Alexandria (c. 4), and its transport (c. 7).

and military, and not only the higher grades of these. The
specific terms must however be examined, as they indicate
particular facilities for patronage.

The most general title is that of Comes, which was applied The
to the holders of certain offices as of course, and was also Comites.
bestowed as a personal honour upon individuals, these also
being chiefly officials or ex-officials. It covers therefore all
the highest military and civil officials, besides many of their
subordinates. The comites rei militaris, who may be taken
as typical, denote 'men who have the rank of the Comitiva,
and at the same time are military commanders, but within
these limits the term can be applied to persons of the very
highest and of quite inferior rank'.[1] The honour was likewise enjoyed as of course by civilians such as the governors of
provinces and their assessors,[2] and even by curiales who had
passed through the whole course of municipal burdens.[3]

The purely military titles are magistri militum, duces and Military
tribuni, among whom the dux or comes Aegypti is prominent. patrons.
The first are the chiefs of the whole army, and the immediate
commanders of the Palatini and Comitatenses; the second
are subordinate to the first, and command the territorial force,
Limitanei, of each frontier province ; lastly the tribuni are the
chiefs of detachments, subordinate to the first two.[4] In the
period with which C. T. 11, 24 deals, the military authority in
Egypt, as in the other provinces, was separated from the
office of the governor, and in the hands of a special comes or
dux.[5] Later, in 469, the principle of separation was abandoned in lower Egypt, the offices of dux and praefectus
Augustalis being united, while in the Thebais we find civil
and military jurisdiction in the hands of the dux Thebaidos.[6]

---

[1] Seeck, article Comes, Pauly-Wissowa, IV 1, 622.
[2] C. T. 6, 15, 1 ; 17, 1.
[3] C. T. 12, 1, 75. 109. 127, &c.   On the comes generally cf. Seeck, l. c.
[4] Marquardt, L'Organisation militaire chez les Romains, translated
from the second German edition with notes by M. Brissaud, pp. 365 ff.,
370 n. 1.   Mommsen, Hermes 24, 195, 260 ff.; and 36, 531 ff.
[5] He has the title 'comes' for the first time in 393, C. T. 16, 10, 11.
His rank was the highest amongst the duces, with precedence over his
equal the Comes Ponticae dioeceseos.   C. T. 6, 14, 3; 13, 1.
[6] C. J. 1, 57, 1. 2, 7, 13. Just. Ed. 13, c. 23.

For us the important point is that the comes Aegypti, Heraclianus, to whom, in 395, C. T. 11, 24, 3 was addressed, was a military commander, and not, like the comes Orientis, a civilian. The special significance of this fact is, that, as constitutions were not usually addressed to the generals, we may infer that Heraclianus' subordinates had been special offenders as patrons, and also that the evil could in some cases only be dealt with manu militari.[1]

It may be asked, in view of the strict separation of civil and military functions, which was the foundation of the system inaugurated by Diocletian, what opportunities the military had of interfering with the collection of taxes, and of patronage generally? Simple violence is an explanation which is not to be minimized,[2] but we shall find that patronage as far as possible clothed itself in legal forms. Again, in these warlike centuries the mere influence of the dux might easily overpower or overawe the civil governor, as we shall see later. But had the system of Diocletian and Constantine been possible in its logical application, patronage of the military would have found it much harder to gain a foothold. The two great branches of civil administration are the judicial and the fiscal, and from neither could the military officers be wholly excluded. Their jurisdiction was no doubt limited in criminal as in civil cases to those in which a soldier was defendant, but usurpation of jurisdiction was a well-known phenomenon.[3]

Opportunities for military patrons.

---

[1] Cf. C. T. 16, 10, 11, a constitution dealing with anti-Jewish riots, addressed to the praefectus Augustalis and comes Aegypti jointly, a. 393.

[2] See the evidence of Libanius below.

[3] Definition of jurisdiction C. T. 2, 1, 2. 1, 15, 7. C. J. 3, 13, 6. Conflict of jurisdiction C. T. 8, 4, 4. 1, 7, 2. 1, 5, 10. Just. Nov. 24, 1 'in quibusdam provinciis . . . et iudex civilis erat et militaris alter, semper quidem adinvicem contendentes, semper vero litigantes'. Usurpation of jurisdiction C. T. 12, 1, 128 of 392 'Militaribus viris nihil sit commune cum curiis; nihil sibi licitum sciant, quod suae non subiectum est potestati; nullum iniuria, nullum verbere, nullum gravi pulsatione, tribunus dux ille an comes sit, curialem principalemve contingat'. See also C. T. 1, 21, 1 of 393 'Numquam omnino negotiis privatorum vel tuitio militis vel executio tribuatur', and C. T. 2, 1, 9 of 397 'Si quis neglectis iudicibus ordinariis sine caelesti oraculo causam civilem ad militare iudicium crediderit deferendam'. C. J. 1, 46, 2 of 416 to the same effect.

An even greater difficulty was felt in maintaining the principle of separation in the collection of taxes, because in this case the civilians were only too ready to rely on the military arm against refractory tax-payers, and because the whole system of payments in kind and of forced services or corvées encouraged direct collection by the greatest spending department, the army. Exclusion and subordination of the military are indeed affirmed in general terms,[1] but the C. T. and the C. J. teem with laws not only against purely illegal extortion by the soldiers, but also regulating their lawful use as tax-gatherers.[2]

Add to the encroachment of the military in the judicial and financial spheres the special difficulties arising from recruiting, which involved the all-important question of status and consequent privileges and burdens,[3] and it will be evident that, without any outrageous abuse of simple force, the military officers had abundant opportunities for both favouritism and extortion under colour of legal process.[4]

[1] Seeck, Gesch. II 82 ff., citing C. T. 7, 4, 3 of 357 'Comes militaris rei per Africam constitutus contra vetitum species annonarias de conditis arbitrio suo dicitur usurpasse'. See also C. T. 7, 4, 30. 11, 25, 1. 8, 4, 6.

[2] C. T. 1, 14, 1 addressed to the civil governor of Egypt in 386. '... officium tuum et officia iudicum competentium omnia tributa exigere suscipere postremo compellere iubemus, ita ut, si qui militares possessores in memoratis provinciis fuerint, hi in tantum per militare officium exigantur. Iam si qui de provincialibus nostris ad inferenda quae debent audaces extiterint, ad nostram clementiam referes, ut, ubi nos iusserimus, per castrenses milites exigatur.' This theoretical division is completely abandoned in Just. Ed. 13 on Alexandria and Egypt. The existing system of collection is fully explained in a law of 401, C. T. 11, 7, 16. See generally Gothofredus Paratitl. to C. T. 7, ed. Ritter 2, 255, and also his notes to C. T. 7, 4, 26 explaining the functions of the various military collectors, particularly of the opinatores, who properly might put direct pressure only on the civil official, the iudices, not on the tax-payers. For their abuses cf. C. T. 7, 4, 26; 5, 1. 8, 8, 6. 11, 7, 16. Nov. Val. 1, 3, 2. Nov. Maj. 2, 2. The last constitution gives a vivid picture of the evils of executio militaris.

[3] The army as a refuge—e. g. C. T. 12, 1, 113. 175. 181, &c. 7, 20, 12. 8, 4, 4. 8, 7, 11. C. J. 12, 33. Escape from the army—C. T. 7, 22 and 18. Army privileges—many references in Schiller, Gesch. d. röm. Kaiserzeit III, pp. 95–6.

[4] It is not altogether irrelevant to call attention to the position of a praefectus castrorum in Egypt in the fourth century, as illustrated by the correspondence of a certain Abinnaeus. A summary is given P. Lond. II, p. 267.

Turning now to the civilians, we find express reference to proconsuls, i. e., confining ourselves to the East, the governor of Asia, and occasionally of Palestine ; also to the praefectus Augustalis, who is the civil governor of Egypt, to the vicarii, and finally to the curiales. Thus all governors of dioceses and provinces, together with their officia, are meant to be included, and in their case there is small need to specify opportunities of patronage. Holding the administration of justice and of finance in their hands, they had obviously the way, if they had the will. The abuses of the civil administration are amply vouched for by the C. T.,[1] and though naturally the officials were responsible for their conduct, the central government was chiefly interested in securing the full contribution of taxes from each province.

It is worth while to observe how the essential principle of the financial system worked in with the manœuvres of the various civilian patrons. The main care of the central government was to get in a predetermined total, and repartition was of comparatively minor importance. The system therefore was to tax a civitas upon the basis of an assessed number of juga and capita, and to hold the curia liable for that total, regardless of whether land had decreased in value, gone out of cultivation, or been exempted by law or fraud. The same principle was applied to the smaller units, the vicus and the pagus. The result was that one tax-payer could only be favoured at the expense of the rest ; the burden could be shifted, it could hardly be annulled.

With the origin of this system we are not for the moment concerned. Declareuil [2] has recently attributed it to the invention by Aurelian of ἐπιβολή of deserted land, the device namely of sharing out amongst the owners of cultivated lands the deserted tracts, and the taxes which fell upon them.[3]

---

[1] See especially C. T. 8, 15, forbidding the acquisition by officials of property within their sphere. Seeck, Gesch. II, 513, n. to 100, 5, gives a number of references illustrating the corruption of the officia. The violence and venality of the Egyptian government are shown by C. T. 12, 1, 80. 126. 190. 192.

[2] Nouvelle Revue Hist. 1902, p. 448 and p. 456.

[3] C. J. 11, 59, 1.

A broader view is taken by Seeck in his brilliant article Decemprimat und Dekaprotie,[1] and in our third section we shall find distinct traces of what is inherently probable, namely the earlier existence of some form of corporate liability.[2]

At any rate there is no doubt of its existence at the end of the fourth century, and the result was that the patronage of some meant the oppression of others.   Thus it was ordered by C. T. 11, 24, 1, of 360, that the clients be made to repay 'debita quaecumque vicani, quorum consortio recesserunt, e propriis facultatibus fisci docebuntur commodis intulisse'. It is very characteristic that those surcharged appear to have no claim against the state.   Equality of repartition was no doubt desirable, but it was not the first consideration.   It is in this spirit that C. T. 11, 1, 26, of 399, ordains 'nullum gratia relevet, nullum iniquae partitionis vexet incommodum, sed pari omnes sorte teneantur', and that in 429 C. T. 12, 1, 186 enacts 'neminem curialem pro alieni territorii debitis adtineri'.[3]   And if Zeno by an undated constitution, C. T. 11, 57, 1, orders in general terms 'ut nullus ex vicanis pro alienis debitis vicanorum teneatur', we should understand a prohibition of arbitrary exaction of one individual's taxes from another, rather an abolition of the system of corporate liability.

We say nothing about the glaring inequalities involved in the principles of census laid down by Diocletian ;[4] what we wish to emphasize is the fact that the delicate duty of repartition lay within the competence of each civitas, not to say vicus, and hence it is that one of our lists of patrons ends with the words 'sive ex ordine curiali'.   In spite of the multiplication of officials, the leading curiales, variously described as primates, principales, decem primi, continued to be employed by the central government in this work,[5] which gave boundless

Patronage involves oppression.

---

[1] Beitr. z. a. Gesch. I, pp. 147, 172.   [2] Post, pp. 54 and 65.
[3] See again C. T. 11, 1, 31 of 412.
[4] As to these see Seeck, Die Schatzungsordnung Diocletians, Zeitschr. f. Soc. u. Wirtschaftsgesch. IV 275.
[5] Seeck, Decemprimat, &c., ubi supr., and see C. T. 8, 15, 5 s. 1 'Praeterea officiales adque municipes, qui exactiones quascumque susceperint, eos etiam, quibus vel discussionis indago vel negotium censuale

opportunities for the easiest and most elusive form of patronage. We cite as typical the words of C. T. 13, 10, 1
'Quoniam tabularii civitatium per conlusionem potentiorum
sarcinam ad inferiores transferebant . . .' &c.[1]

Similarly in the actual collection the curiales played a large
part, though the exact distribution of the work between them
and the officials is not very clear. So it is that C. T. 11, 7,
12, of 383, enacts, as much for the undoing of the mighty as
for the protection of the humble: 'Potentiorum possessorum
domus officium rectoris exigere debet, decurio vero personas
curialium convenire, minores autem possessores defensor
civitatis . . . compellere.'

The
Churches
as patrons

Last on the list of patrons come the churches of Constantinople and Alexandria, the church of Antioch having no connexion with the Egyptian annona. The churches appear as
patrons on at least two grounds : first, as being the only body
which could make any serious stand against the state,[2] so that
the church was the natural protector of the weak. This function appears clearly in the growth of the bishop as a municipal
magistrate, and also in the extended use of the ancient right
of asylum, which had been inherited from the heathen
temples.[3] Secondly, the church enjoyed many privileges,[4]
and it was largely by illicit extension of privilege that
patronage throve. Holy orders and the cloister, like the
army, offered a means of escape from the ordinary burdens,[5]

mandatur, insuper principales, a quibus distributionum omnium forma
procedit, curatores etiam lex ista contineat'. Add. C. T. 10, 4, 2. 12, 1,
117.
[1] See also C. T. 13, 10, 8. 11, 16, 3 and 4. 11, 1, 9 and 11. 12, 1, 173.
Nov. Maj. 7, 8. C. J. 11, 60, 1. Seeck, Gesch. II 271.
[2] Seeck, Gesch. II 175 ff.—full of interesting matter. Note especially
the struggle of Synesios, bishop of Ptolemais, at the beginning of the
fifth century, to protect decurions against the oppression of the governor.
[3] Several constitutions on this subject mention especially the church
in Egypt. C. T. 9, 40, 15. 16 '. . . damnatos nulli clericorum vel
monachorum, eorum etiam quos synoditas vocant, per vim adque usur-
pationem vindicare liceat ac tenere.' 11, 36, 31 '. . . nec ulla episco-
porum vel clericorum vel populi suggeratur intervenire aut intervenisse
persona'. 9, 45 'De his qui ad ecclesias confugiunt'. Just. Ed. 13
limits very severely the granting of λόγον ἀσυλίας against the tax-
gatherer by even the patriarch of Alexandria: chapters 10, 11, 20, 28.
[4] On the privilegium fori see R. Génestal in Nouv. Rev. Hist. 1908,
p. 161.   [5] e. g. C. T. 12, 1, 121.

and church property enjoyed exemptions which it was often sought to usurp.[1] The passage quoted in the note shows how directly the privilege of one man might impose a fresh burden on others.

The churches conclude our list of specifically named patrons, but let us recall the fact that the list is not exhaustive. There are also the general words 'qui variis honoribus fulciuntur', 'ex quocumque hominum ordine', 'cuiuslibet ille fuerit dignitatis', 'nobiliores', 'mediocris fortunae'. There is really no qualification for the position of patron except power, and though we have laid stress on the special opportunities for patronage conferred by office, we must not forget that the class from which the high officials were largely drawn, the great landowners simply as such, had opportunities of its own, which were due to the fact that large estates were, from a variety of historical causes, in many cases 'agri excepti', that is, outside the network of civitates, and in direct dependence on the central government. Often lands were exempt as being the property of Caesar, the divina domus, the church, or senators, but in other cases the privilege rested on express grant.[2] These estates, which might include whole villages, were ruled by the territorial magnates through their procurators,[3] and we find already in the C. T. the beginnings of a distinction between civitates and possessiones, from which was developed later the Byzantine division of χωρία ἐλευθερικὰ and ἰδιόστατα.[4] In theory the agri excepti were not exempt from imperial taxes, though no doubt in practice they enjoyed better treatment than other lands, but they were in any case

Margin notes: Landowners and potentes generally as patrons.

Agri excepti.

----

[1] e. g. C. T. 11, 16, 21. 22. 16, 2, 30. 11, 1, 1; 37; 33. The church of Thessalonica is exempted in the last constitution from an imposition, 'ita tamen, ut aperte sciat, propriae tantummodo capitationis modum beneficio mei numinis sublevandum nec externorum gravamine tributorum rem publicam ecclesiastici nominis abusione laedendam,' a. 424. See further references given by Declareuil, Nouv. Rev. Hist. 1908, p. 557 n. 4, seq.

[2] I refer for brevity simply to Schulten, Die röm. Grundherrschaften, especially pp. 3–9 and 119–122. See also Declareuil, Nouv. Rev. Hist. 1908, pp. 553–9.

[3] Dill, Roman Society, pp. 222 ff.

[4] Schulten, op. cit. pp. 7 and 8; Zachariae von Lingenthal, Gesch. d. griech.-röm. Rechts, pp. 218 ff.

free from the heavy municipal charges. It is not surprising
to find owners of these estates extending them by every means
in their power, and the humbler possessores struggling to be
included within the charmed circle. These operations frequently took the form of a patrocinium.

The
Clients.

The other offenders are the clients, and the following is
a list of their descriptions: C. T. 11, 24, 1 coloni, vicani; ibid.
2 agricolae; ibid. 3 vici; ibid. 4 rustici; ibid. 5 agricolae vel
vicani propria possidentes; ibid. 6, pr. and 3 possessiones,
possessores, homologi coloni; ibid. 6, 1 metrocomiae vel
aliquid in his; ibid. 6, 6 and 8 metrocomiae, publici vici;[1]
C. J. 11, 54, 1 refers to the owners of vici or possessiones;[2]
ibid. 2 to κωμῆται or γεωργοί, both free and servile (δοῦλοι).
Note the rubrics C. T. 11, 24 'De patrociniis vicorum', and
C. J. 11, 54 'Ut nemo ad suum patrocinium suscipiat vicos
vel rusticanos eorum'.

Coloni and
Posses-
sores.

As the above citations raise a slight difficulty, let us first
state our conclusion, which is that the clients included both
coloni adscripticii and possessores of land of their own,
in fact the smaller agriculturists generally, regardless of
status. Moreover, a striking feature of the movement towards
patronage, and the one to which legislation was especially
directed, was that the clients constantly acted by vici, in
organized groups.

The great authority of Gothofredus is, however, in favour of
construing the constitutions of C. T. 11, 24 as referring to
possessores only, not coloni adscripticii. He says, ad l. 1,
n. c., 'Coloni hic sunt rusticani qui proprias terras habebant
... non quo alioquin sensu coloni, qui alienis terris adstricti
erant.' But I think that the commentator must have been
momentarily misled by a desire to guard the reader against
understanding 'coloni' simply in its narrower sense, for he
himself identifies (tentatively) the law which Libanius (Oratio
de Patrociniis, c. 35) begged the emperor to enforce with the
second law of C. T. 11, 24. Now Libanius, as we shall see,

---

[1] The passages in C. T. 11, 24, 6 are very difficult and are only quoted
provisionally. See post, pp. 21 ff., 56 ff., 60 ff., &c.
[2] The text is doubtful; cf. post, p. 19.

is quite conclusive that we are to think of coloni proper amongst the clients ; and besides, C. J. 11, 54, 2 expressly distinguishes free and servile clients. Of course it is even clearer that the legislator had also in mind landowners, and not merely small landowners. The terms 'possessores', 'propria possidentes', 'metrocomiae', &c., speak for themselves, and one may infer that the rustici in C. T. h. t. l. 4 must be pretty substantial persons to be fined 80 pounds gold, while in C. J. 11, 54, 1 we find ' vicis etiam vel possessionibus ad patrocinia confugientium publico vindicandis '.[1]

In sum, although certain clauses, notably those which impose confiscation of the clients' land, can only refer to possessores, the constitutions cover also, under the general words ' agricolae ', ' vicani ', ' rustici ', ' coloni ', the patrocinium of coloni proper. The decisive evidence is C. J. 11, 54, 2 and Libanius, l. c. The explanation of the greater prominence of the patrocinium of possessores is that this involved a more direct fraud on the revenue, consisting in a simple withholding of taxes, or in an unjust transference of the burden to neighbouring possessores. Where, on the other hand, the client (village or individual) was unfree, the direct fraud was on the legal master, who was responsible to the state for taxes,[2] and was deprived of the rents out of which he repaid himself. There was in this second case only an indirect injury to the revenue, in so far as the master became insolvent, and the sources of wealth were transferred into the hands of persons strong enough to resist the tax-gatherer.

We must say a few words on the condition of these tillers of the soil, the smaller possessores and the coloni proper, deferring for later consideration the interpretation of the phrases in C. T. 11, 24, 6 'homologi coloni' and 'metrocomia.'

The colonate[3] is the dominating fact in the agrarian situation during our epoch. The well-known law of Constantine, C. T. 5, 17, 1, of 332, which marks the point at which legisla-

The Colonate.

---

[1] The text however is doubtful. See post, p. 19.
[2] C. T. 11, 1, 14.
[3] See Seeck, Colonatus, Pauly-Wissowa, IV 1.

tion, after a long preparation by custom,[1] converted contract into status, was only the beginning of a series of laws which extends throughout our epoch, and we are therefore commenting on facts which are contemporary with the remoulding of the whole of agricultural life. The colonate was not introduced by one stroke of the pen into all the provinces. The constitutions, C. J. 11, 51, 1, and 11, 53, 1, are witness of a gradual extension to Palestine and Illyria, and it is the opinion of Seeck[2] that the capitatio humana, and with it the colonate proper, was only introduced into Egypt at the end of the fourth century.[3] Again, many important details remained unsettled by the constitution of 332,[4] and so from year to year, and month to month, the status of the peasant was undergoing vital changes. To the accompanying unrest patrocinium vicorum was related both as cause and effect.

The proper object of the colonate as an institution was to keep the men on the land, and so to enable the land-taxes to be paid. No doubt aristocratic influence sometimes got the better of public policy and turned agrarian legislation to its own ends,[5] but the constitutions show many attempts to prevent the colonate from being an instrument of mere oppression,[6] and, in fact, the treatment of desert and emphyteutic land proves that the imperial government did not rely simply on force in order to create a supply of labour.[7]

Certainly, on the whole, the colonate legislation fostered the centrifugal tendencies of which our titles are an illustration, and was a lesson to the small men to look to the local magnates as standing between them and the government.

---

[1] See Seeck, loc. cit., and especially Fustel de Coulanges, Recherches, Le Colonat.

[2] loc. cit. p. 501. His interpretation of C. T. 11, 24, 6 s. 3 must, however, be rejected: post, p. 58.

[3] C. T. 11, 24, 6 s. 3 is in fact the first evidence that we possess of the colonate on private lands in Egypt: post, p. 51.

[4] C. T. 5, 17, 1, above referred to.

[5] Dangerous laws are C. T. 11, 1, 14, circa 366, ordering the domini fundorum to pay the land-tax themselves, and recepta compulsionis sollicitudine to recover it from the coloni, and C. J. 11, 50, 2, of Arcadius and Honorius, limiting the right of a colonus to sue his patron.

[6] cf. C. J. 11, 50, 1. 11, 48, 5; 7. C. T. 13, 10, 3. 11, 1, 26. 2, 25, 1.

[7] This point of view has been insisted on by Professor Vinogradoff, Growth of the Manor, pp. 76 ff.

But the voluntary movement towards dependence with which Patronage and the Colonate. we are dealing, while it puts a better colour on that legislation, outstripped altogether the desires of the government. The coloni preferred a strong to a weak master; the small possessores, who were still free, were showing an inclination for the security of dependence : in both cases the government was losing hold of the best material for taxation, the small and middling landowner.[1] The poor were not degraded without a dangerous strengthening of the great, and here lies the explanation of the apparent discrepancy between our anti-aristocratic constitutions and the creation of the colonate.

There is no sharp distinction either economically or legally between coloni and small possessores. As in our texts so elsewhere, colonus often includes payers of annual sums, such as the small emphyteutae and holders of ager vectigalis.[2] What is the difference between paying a heavy annual tax as possessor or a rent as colonus ? Even the technical distinction was jeopardized when, as might happen, a colonus besides being subject to a patronus owned land of his own. It was decided in 365[3] that he might not alienate his own land without recourse to his patron ; though by a constitution of 366[4] he was, unlike the ordinary colonus, to answer directly for his own land-tax.

There is no difficulty in including such possessores as these Curiales as clients. amongst our clients ; the question is rather how far we are to go in the direction of including superior classes. Of course, possessores not big enough even to be curiales are meant,[5] but we have to remember that the splendidissimus ordo contained many whose position was far from splendid. Patronage of curiales is a certain fact : ' multos animadvertimus, ut debita

---

[1] C. T. 11, 24, 6 s. 1 ' . . . quibus pensitanda pro fortunae condicione negari non possunt '. C. T. 11, 1, 14 ' . . . propriae commissos medio-critati '.

[2] Mitteis, Erbpacht, p. 38.

[3] C. T. 5, 19, 1.

[4] C. T. 11, 1, 14.

[5] ' Minores possessores,' as C. T. 11, 7, 12 calls them, in opposition to ' curiales personas '. C. T. 12, 1, 72 and 133 provide for their promotion to the curia if wealthy enough. A constitution of 342, C. T. 12, 1, 33, not however included in C. J., fixes the qualification at 25 jugera culti-vated, even though some are held as colonus, ex re privata nostra.

praestatione patriam defraudarent, sub umbra potentium latitare';[1] and really the curialis as client is far more conceivable than the curialis as patron. There were however, naturally, distinctions of class amongst curiales, which also account for their appearance in both capacities.[2]

In fact, although a curialis patron might obtain for his clients a more favourable repartition of liturgies and taxes,[3] a greater man might do much more: he might rescue them from the unpopular ordo altogether. Such practices are aimed at by e. g. C. T. 12, 1, 76, of the year 371, which runs: ' Ex omnibus domibus producti qui origine sunt curiali, ad subeundam publicorum munerum functionem protrahantur,' and further provides penalties for the occultatores ' si utilitatem publicam privatis studiis et patrociniis postponant'. We have just quoted C. T. 12, 1, 146, of 395, and referred to several similar constitutions ;[4] and all the evidence goes to show that patronage flourished largely at the expense of the municipal organization. We connect this withdrawal of curiales under the shadow of potentes very directly with the extra-municipal position[5] of the large estates, and call attention to the prominent part played in the 'susceptio' of curiales by the procuratores or actores of the potentes.[6] That this withdrawal meant the ruin of the civitates was obvious to all, including the government.[7]

Villages as clients. This point comes out perhaps even more strongly when we pass from the individual clients to the vici. Vici resist the tax-gatherer ' defensionis potentia aut multitudine freti', we are told by C. T. 11, 24, 3, but the real issue is whether metro-

---

[1] C. T. 12, 1, 146 of 395 ; cf. ibid. ll. 6. 50. 76 of 319, 362, 371. Add. Nov. Maj. 7, 4 ; 9.

[2] See Declareuil, Nouv. Rev. Hist. 1907, pp. 609 ff. on the principales, primates, decem primi. Curialis is not necessarily decurio, ibid. pp. 475 ff. See on this point Preisigke, Städtisches Beamtenwesen im röm. Aegypten, p. 48, where it is shown that the great majority of liturgists in Egypt were not βουλευταί.

[3] C. T. 13, 10, 1 and 8. Supra, pp. 11–12.   [4] Supra, n. 1.

[5] Supra, p. 13.

[6] cf. C. T. 12, 1, 6. 50. Nov. Maj. 7, 4. Dill, op. cit. loc. cit. supra, p. 13, n. 3.

[7] 'Curiales nervos esse rei publicae ac viscera civitatum nullus ignorat.' Nov. Maj. 7, pr.

comiae or publici vici are to remain publici iuris, or become
privati iuris, the appanage of a great man or the church :
C. T. 11, 24, 6. ss. 1. 6. 7. and 8.   We can now appreciate the
significance of the two rubrics, and may well doubt whether
the true reading of the passage in C. J. 11, 54, 1, '. . . vicis
etiam vel possessionibus ad patrocinia confugientium,' should
not be 'confugientibus', which has some manuscript authority,
and is confirmed by Bas. 56, 13, 1.[1]   Here then we are
clearly beyond petty jobbery and favouritism, and are face to
face with the breaking up of the civitas, upon which the
administration of the empire was based.   Patronage of a vicus
might mean to a civitas the loss of a whole slice of its
territory, and not merely of a single decurio ; that is to say,
a loss of a fraction of its revenue without necessarily any
reduction of its liability.   So the matter would appear to the
curiae, whose remaining duties were almost entirely financial,
and to whom every question was a fiscal question.   Naturally
these things were only possible in a state of general anarchy,
and were not accomplished without open violence.   But even
here it was the vicious system of quite legal privilege that first
opened the door to the patron.[2]   The obscurity of the subject
of village organization causes us to defer it for the moment.

The remaining questions arising out of the constitutions are
the nature of the relation set up between patron and client,
the object of the transaction, and the penalties.   These
last begin with mere reparation, C. T. 11, 24, 1.   In the
succeeding laws the patrons are visited with a gradually
increasing fine, and later with confiscation of their property.
The clients by C. T. 11, 24, 2 are subiugandi supplicio, to
be corporally punished at discretion (I can discover no ground
for Gothofredus' comment 'capitali'), while C. J. 11, 54, 2 runs
σωφρονισθέντες . . . τύπτονται μετὰ δέκα τῶν πρωτευόντων τῆς
κώμης καὶ διηνεκῶς ἐξορίζονται.   By C. T. 11, 24, 4 they are
to be fined actually twice as much as their patrons, and finally
by C. T. 11, 24, 5 and C. J. 11, 54, 1 their land is confiscated.

(margin: Effect on the civitas.)

(margin: The penalties.)

---

[1] As Krüger notes, τῆς κώμης τοῦτο ποιούσης.
[2] Just as the benefits of the Land Purchase Acts in Ireland cannot be
applied to one estate without producing anarchical results on its neighbours.

Accomplices, such as tabelliones, who draw up fictitious sales and the like to cover the agreement of patronage, or the headmen of the village are also punished by C. J. 11, 54, 1 and 2. As a set-off to these penalties the government was sometimes obliged to give up the struggle against patronage, and to recognize the position of patrons after a lapse of a certain time, upon terms of their accepting the public charges on the land. We shall shortly have to consider these provisions in detail.[1]

Object of the client. The object of the client in these transactions is steadily represented as the evasion of taxes. The purely fiscal character of the constitutions is however quite consistent with there being other objects, and in fact Libanius will tell us of coloni revolting from their private duty to their masters, it is true under very special circumstances. The possible advantages of having a great patron are obviously incalculable, but we have every right to assume that the constitutions deal with the most characteristic, as well as the most dangerous, abuse.

Object of the patron. The object of the patron is less on the surface. Among the penal clauses occurs one which we have purposely deferred : C. T. 11, 24, 2 has it 'et non quantum patroni suscipere consuerant, sed dimidium eius fiscus adsumat'. The consuetudo of the patron was doubtless to take a revenue, and so he is represented in C. J. 11, 54, 2 as taking for his services ὑπόσχεσιν προσόδων ἢ ἕτερον κέρδος. Similarly Libanius describes how the patron gets a revenue.[2] Gothofredus, quoting the well-known passage of Salvianus,[3] says the practice was for the patron to take the whole fundus, and that our constitution must therefore be interpreted to order the confiscation of half the fundus. This interpretation is adopted

---

[1] Post, p. 25.
[2] Or. 47, c. 4. See post, p. 29.
[3] De Gub. Dei. 5, 8, 9 'Ut vim exactionis evadant, faciunt quod unum valent. Tradunt se ad tuendum protegendumque maioribus, dediticios se divitum faciunt, et quasi in ius eorum ditionemque transcendunt.' This would be well enough 'si patrocinia ista non venderent'. Patronage is another name for spoliation. 'Omnes enim hi, qui defendi videntur, defensoribus suis omnem fere substantiam suam prius quam defenduntur addicunt,' and more to the same effect.

by Paul Roth,[1] but it is clearly wrong. Quite apart from
C. J. 11, 54, 2 and the evidence of Libanius, confiscation
is not a measure to be ordered in ambiguous language, and
when it is ordered thirty years later by C. T. 11, 24, 5, no
room is left for doubt. Again, we have shown, against
Gothofredus, that the clients might be coloni of another man,
and constitutions which are not, like C. T. 11, 24, 5, confined
to vicani propria possidentes must therefore be construed
to apply to coloni clients as well as to possessores. But
in the case of coloni, confiscation would punish not only
them, but their already injured masters.

So much for the interpretation of this particular phrase Territorial
in C. T. 11, 24, 2, but we must not be understood to deny self-ag-
that the object of the patronus was, in general and essentially, grandize-
his own territorial aggrandizement. On the contrary, it is ment.
clear that patronage was of the land as much as of the client,
and C. T. 11, 24, 2 and 4 assess the penalties on the patrons
'pro singulorum fundorum praebito patrocinio'.[2] Similarly we
shall see that C. T. 11, 24, 6 treats the acquisition of the land
by the patron as the principal evil to be combated, and C. J.
11, 54, 1 by its terms annuls the colourable gifts, sales, and
leases, by which agreements of patronage are sought to be
cloaked. And even where the land was not actually transferred, the natural arrangement was for the client to stay
on the land, and pay his patron a kind of rent, which in later
times was itself called πατρωκίνιον.[3]

These conclusions lead us naturally to the consideration Relation
of the nature of the relation set up between patron and client. between
More light is thrown on this subject by the two later con- patron and
stitutions, C. T. 11, 24, 6, of the year 415, and C. J. 11, 54, 1, of client.
the year 468. We must consider these separately and in detail.

The relevant sections of C. T. 11, 24, 6 are the pr. and
sections 1, 6, and 7. Pr. 'Valerii, Theodori et Tharsacii
examinatio conticiscat, illis dumtaxat sub Augustaliano iudicio

---

[1] Feudalität und Untertanverband, p. 284.
[2] Fustel de Coulanges, Les Origines du Système Féodal, p. 243 n. 2.
[3] Coll. I, Nov. 12, c. 4.   Zachariae v. Lingenthal, Gesch. d. griechisch-
römischen Rechts, p. 219.

pulsandis, qui ex Caesarii et Attici consulatu possessiones sub
patrocinio possidere coeperunt.   Quos tamen omnes functionibus publicis obsecundare censemus, ut patronorum nomen
extinctum penitus iudicetur.   Possessiones autem athuc in
suo statu constitutae penes priores possessores residebunt,
si pro antiquitate census functiones publicas et liturgos, quos
homologi coloni praestare noscuntur, pro rata sunt absque
dubio cognituri.'   1. 'Metrocomiae vero in publico iure et
integro perdurabunt, nec quisquam eas vel aliquid in his
possidere temptaverit, nisi qui ante consulatum praefinitum
coeperit procul dubio possidere, exceptis convicanis, quibus
pensitanda pro fortunae condicione negare non possunt.'
6. 'Quidquid autem in tempus usque dispositionis habitae
a viro inlustri decessore sublimitatis tuae ecclesiae venerabiles,
id est Constantinopolitana atque Alexandrina possedisse
deteguntur, id pro intuitu religionis ab his praecipimus firmiter
retineri, sub ea videlicet sorte, ut in futurum functiones omnes,
quas metrocomiae *debent'* (*del.*) 'et publici vici pro antiquae
capitationis professione debent, sciant procul dubio subeundas.'
7. 'Nequaquam cefalaeotis, irenarchis, logografis chomatum
et ceteris liturgis sub quolibet patrocinii nomine publicis
functionibus denegatis, nisi[1] quid ex his quae exigenda sunt
vel neglegentia vel contemptus distulerit.'

The text printed above is Mommsen's, but in translating
I have followed the manuscript in reading at the end of
section 1 'a quibus' for 'quibus', and have adopted in the
same place Gothofredus' emendation 'negari' for 'negare'.
I translate as follows :—

Translation
of C. T.
11, 24, 6.   Pr. and 1. 'Let the inquiry of Valerius, Theodorus, and
Tharsacius cease, and let those only be disturbed under
judgement of the praefectus Augustalis who have begun to
possess estates under their patronage from after the consulship of Caesarius and Atticus' (a. 397).   'Provided nevertheless that all of these make good the public liabilities,
so that the name of patron may be absolutely abolished.
But those estates which have been established in their existing
condition at any time up to the said date shall remain with

---

[1] *Scr.* si : Mommsen.

their possessors as before these presents, if in accordance with
the ancient census these possessors will clearly accept in due
proportion the public burdens and liturgists, according as the
homologi coloni are known to provide them. The metrocomiae shall continue under unimpaired public dominion, and
no one is to attempt to possess them, nor anything in them,
unless his possession clearly began before the aforesaid consulship, excepting fellow villagers, who by reason of their state
of life cannot refuse their dues.' Proceeding with sections
6 and 7 : 'Whatever the venerable churches, that is the
churches of Constantinople and Alexandria, are shown to
have possessed up to the date of the enactment made by the
illustrious predecessor of your highness,[1] we. ordain out of
respect for religion that they retain undisturbed, of course
upon the terms that for the future they clearly recognize that
they must submit to all public burdens, which according
to the ancient assessment are due from the metrocomiae and
public villages. In vain have the cefalaeotae, the irenarchs,
the logografi of the dams and the other liturgists been refused
the public dues under whatever pretext of patronage, *save
so far as*[2] neglect or contumacy has delayed anything which
must be exacted.'

Though a translation is the best commentary, we must Difficulties.
reinforce our interpretation of some of the phrases. We
understand 'sub patrocinio possidere' not in its prima-facie
sense of possession by a client under a patron, but in that
of possession by a patron under his patronage ; and so by the
first section the patrons whose possession dates from before
397 are quieted in their title, while patrons of subsequent
date are to be evicted. A similar usage of 'pulsare' is found
in Paul D. 19, 2, 54, 2, and even if it only bears the general
sense of 'arraigned', eviction is clearly implied as the
result of the proceedings by the subsequent clause quieting
the title of 'priores possessores'.

---

[1] The enactment is not extant, and its date is unknown. But it falls
within the period July 405 to February 415, during which Anthemius,
the predecessor in question, was p. pō. Or.

[2] See p. 22, n. I.

'Sub patrocinio possidere.' That the possession referred to is the possession of patrons, not of clients, is further proved by two considerations, first the connexion which is established by this interpretation with section 1, which prohibits on fiscal grounds the capture of metrocomiae by powerful outsiders, and even their intrusion into these communities, and secondly the parallel afforded by sections 6 and 7, dealing with the encroachments of the churches, which have evidently taken place sub patrocinii nomine. The words ' possessiones autem athuc in suo statu constitutae penes priores possessores residebunt ', express a thought which an English statute might have put otherwise. What is meant is that illegal titles which have been established at any date up to the aforesaid consulship shall remain with their owners as before the present statute. We should probably have said 'before' instead of ' up to the aforesaid consulship', but the meaning here is quite certain from the exactly similar phrase in section 6, ' in tempus usque dispositionis habitae.'

We notice, finally, the curious conjunction of ' functiones publicas et liturgos quos homologi coloni praestare noscuntur', which we shall suggest[1] is due to the fact that not the least public burden was the provision of liturgists. This subject and the explanation of the terms 'homologi coloni' and ' metrocomiae ' had best be deferred to our third section.

Result of patronage in practice. It is from these passages that we see that it makes very little difference in the long run what form the original agreement of patronage took. A man comes with his land, or with land which he holds as colonus of a third party, under patronage, and henceforth, as regards the state and third parties, the patron claims to represent the lands. He may be said 'sub patrocinio possidere ', for he is the de facto possessor. A client might hope to retain the beneficial possession by agreement with the patron, but he was shortsighted if he believed the patron would always be content with a reasonable rent for his services. The client's position was precarious[2] and would tend, even if he were originally a possessor, to degenerate into that of a colonus.

[1] Post, pp. 60 ff.   [2] Post, p. 47.

A colourable transfer of the land was considered in many cases a convenient cloak, and this would give the loose relation of patron and client a more definite aspect ; but even without a legal transfer the land was virtually the patron's, and we have just seen that the state was prepared to legitimatize such titles after a certain time, simply because a legitimate possessor offered a better guarantee for the taxes. We notice that the date before which the lay titles are valid, 397, is nearly contemporaneous with the third, fourth, and fifth constitutions of C. T. 11, 24, which break a silence of nearly twenty years. A similar quieting of titles is implied by section 2 of the law of 468, C. J. 11, 54, 1.

On the other hand the state was ready, where it was able, to annul formal titles which were in reality based upon patronage. This policy does not appear in our enactments until the middle of the fifth century, the year 450, if we take the earliest possible date of Marcian's lost constitution, referred to in C. J. 11, 54, 1 ; but it is of course impossible to say when so obvious a device was first resorted to in practice.[1] *Nullification of colourable transfers.*

We come now to C. J. 11, 54, 1, which must be read with C. J. 10, 19, 8, and 11, 56, 1, of the same address, and of even date (Sept. 1, 468). The first named runs : 'Si quis . . . in fraudem circumscriptionemque publicae functionis ad patrocinium cuiuscumque confugerit, id, quod huius rei gratia geritur, sub praetextu donationis vel venditionis seu conductionis aut cuiuslibet alterius contractus, nullam habeat firmitatem.' The law is to take effect from the dates fixed by Marcian's constitution, namely, from 437 and 441 in different dioceses. *C. J. 11, 54, 1.*

Next to be quoted is C. J. 10, 19, 8, which makes even a genuine transfer, 'non patrocinii gratia, sed emptionis iure vel quolibet alio titulo legitimo,' to the divina domus or to any person of any rank whatsoever, of land extra metrocomias, dependent for its effect on the transferee acknowledging the public burdens which had previously attached to the land. In *C. J. 10, 19, 8.*

---

[1] cf. C. T. 12, 1, 6, of 319, 'Igitur si legis latae die repperietur quisquam' (decurio) 'patrimonium suum alienasse atque in dominum servulae contulisse' &c. See also C. J. 3, 1, 8. 12, 3, 1 and 2. Nov. Maj. 7, 9. On the general law of colourable transactions see the third century constitutions of C. J. 4, 22.

the contrary event, the lands are to be assigned 'curiae eiusdem civitatis sub qua vici siti sint'.

C. J. 11, 56, 1, and C. T. 11, 24, 6 s. 1. Finally, C. J. 11, 56, 1 altogether forbids the alienation of land in places commonly called metrocomiae to any one except 'ad habitatorem adscriptum eidem metrocomiae'. We recall the similar provision of section 1 of C. T. 11, 24, 6 'nec quisquam eas' (sc. metrocomias) 'vel aliquid in his possidere temptaverit exceptis convicanis a quibus pensitanda pro fortunae condicione negari non possunt'.[1] We have thus four classes of prohibited titles : (a) sub patrocinio possidere, which is purely illegal, apart from statutes of limitation, C. T. 11, 24, 6, pr. and 6 ; (b) possession under colour of legal transfer, but patrocinii gratia, C. J. 11, 54, 1 ; (c) possession extra metrocomias under legal transfer, not patrocinii gratia, but without accepting the public duties attaching to the land, C. J. 10, 19, 8 ; and (d) possession, under legal transfer or otherwise, within metrocomiae, which is absolutely forbidden except to a convicanus or habitator adscriptus eidem metrocomiae, C. T. 11, 24, 6, 1, and C. J. 11, 56, 1. The motive of all these laws is the difficulty of exacting the taxes from the rich and powerful.

It was precisely this difficulty which caused a natural gravitation, by means fair and foul, of land into the hands of the potentes. Whatever may be thought of the legality of the exemption of their lands, it is evident that in fact they did escape a great many burdens, particularly the purely municipal liturgies and the responsibility of collecting the taxes. Hence the agri excepti must be regarded as one of the most important factors in the decay of the municipal institutions, upon which the fiscal system depended.[2] We have already dealt with the injustice resulting from the combination of exemptions with a system of corporate liability.[3]

Evils of the fiscal system. In a word, assessment and repartition were vicious and unequal, the collecting authority was weak, and patronage was, in the main, part of the revolt against these conditions. The legislation we have just been considering does not confine itself to penalizing patronage, but attempts to block at all points

---

[1] An illustration of the same phenomena in a later period is Nov. Just. 17, 13, of 535.   [2] Supra, pp. 13 and 18.   [3] Supra, pp. 10 ff.

the economically inevitable drain of curial land. If we went The caste deeper into the legislation of the period we should find a system. general tendency to stereotype the lands of the members of a given curia as subject to the curial burdens, even if the curialis becomes a senator, soldier, or takes holy orders, and even if the land is alienated to outsiders. Restrictions are placed upon the alienation of curial land, and the curia develops a kind of eminent domain in the lands of its numbers. But the continued legislation is a sure sign of its partial failure, and nothing could really have stopped the process of squeezing out the middling possessor, or of turning him into a colonus, except an abolition of class privilege, and a general enactment that taxes constituted a real charge on all lands.[1]

Exactly similar legislation recurs with reference to the property of other corporations, such as the pistores, suarii and navicularii.[2] With this we are not concerned, but we would Special emphasize the fact that the government felt the necessity of of the extending special protection, not merely, as by the institution village of an official patron, the defensor plebis, to the humbler rustic body. population, but to the smaller agrarian communities, the vici and metrocomiae as such. These were a particularly easy and willing prey for the potens, and the result was that the government strengthened by all means in its power the corporate life of these natural unions, even to the extent of excluding outsiders altogether. Hence it becomes an interesting question, in considering their constitution, what elements are the creation of the government for its own purposes, and to what extent we are confronted with the results of a legal definition and sharpening of what was already in existence, the product of immemorial custom.

It must be admitted that the emperors were not always Imperial consistent in policy. C. T. 11, 24, 6 concludes (s. 8) with the grants. words : ' Metrocomias possidere nostro beneficio meruerunt, et publicos vicos committere compellantur,' and one thing at least is clear, that the process of exemption of the metro-

---

[1] We must simply cite C. T. 8, 15. 12, 1, 6; 50; 76; 130; 146; 160; 187. 3, 1, 9. 2, 29, 2. 12, 3, 1 and 2. Nov. Maj. 7, 9.
[2] See above, pp. 3–4.

comiae from the ordinary municipal organization had sometimes been sanctioned by the emperors.   We recall the words
of Hyginus:[1] 'Excepti sunt fundi bene meritorum, ut in
totum privati iuris essent, nec ullam coloniae munificentiam
deberent, et essent in solo populi Romani.' I can neither find
nor think of any satisfactory interpretation of the words 'publicos vicos committere compellantur', and give Gothofredus'
for what it is worth.   Reading 'Qui metrocomias', &c., he
explains committere as denoting a kind of ἐπιβολή, 'caeterorum
vicorum, quorum metrocomia mater est, onera agnoscere.'
I can discover no parallel for this usage of 'committere', and
believe the passage to be too corrupt to be intelligible.

Further examination of C.T. 11, 24, 6 is deferred to our
third section.

II.

General
plan of
Libanius'
Oratio De
Patrociniis.

Libanius' Oration Περὶ τῶν Προστασιῶν.[2]   This speech, which
was addressed by Libanius to an unnamed emperor in the
second half of the fourth century,[3] contains, besides an introduction (cc. 1–3) and a peroration (cc. 35–38), two main parts :
(a) description of various forms of patronage, and (b) refutation
of supposed objections to the suppression of patronage.

(a) This section has four subdivisions : (1) cc. 4–10, patronage by the military of κῶμαι μεγάλαι πολλῶν ἑκάστη δεσποτῶν
(c. 4), ἕκαστον μέρος οὐ πολὺ κεκτημένον (c. 11) ; (2) cc. 11–12,
patronage of ἀγροὶ οἷς εἷς ὁ δεσπότης ; (3) cc. 13–16, interference by a military patron between Libanius and his coloni,
and (4) c. 17, frequency of patronage ; deserter coloni.

Patronage
of large
villages.

(1) We start, then, with the patronage of large villages with
many small landowners, in contrast with patronage of a large
estate.   The distinction, we shall see, is not merely rhetorical.
The villages buy the alliance of the local soldiery, ἰδρυμένοι
στρατιῶται, with gifts of kind or money, and then take to a life

---

[1] Lachmann, p. 197, l. 10.
[2] Oratio 47. Reiske, II 499. Förster (Teubner, 1906), III 404, to whose
edition we refer. The editio princeps is in Gothofredus' Opuscula, with
valuable translation and notes. The Oration was dealt with analytically
by Paul Roth, Feudalität u. Untertanverband, pp. 283-4. See also
Fustel de Coulanges, Origines du Système Féodal, pp. 241-3.
[3] We discuss the exact date later.

of brigandage at the expense of their neighbours, in which they are joined by the soldiers. These are represented as quartering themselves on the villages, indulging in debauchery of all kinds, and insulting civilians, who do not dare to retaliate.[1] The police, φύλακες τῆς χώρας, shut their eyes to the proceedings διὰ τὸν προστάτην (cc. 4-6).

The προστάτης is to the civilian Libanius always a military officer, tribunus, or dux, and is later described as στρατηγός, the writer as a purist avoiding the more usual δούξ. The small owners[2] get patronage through their village, which de facto at any rate acts as a body. The patron, as we have noted, gets a revenue, and the first result of his work is brigandage. Brigandage is mentioned in connexion with patronage, not indeed by our special constitutions, but by C. T. 1, 29, 8, addressed to the p. pō. Or. in 392. It runs : 'Per omnes regiones, in quibus fera et periculi sui nescia latronum fervet insania, probatissimi quique atque districtissimi defensores adsint disciplinae et cotidianis actibus praesint, qui non sinant crimina impunitate coalescere. Removeantur patrocinia, quae favorem reis et auxilium scelerosis impertiendo maturari scelera fecerunt.'[3]

Brigand-
age and
patronage.

Libanius proceeds in cc. 7-10 to describe what the constitutions treat as the characteristic evil of patronage, the evasion of taxes.

Evasion
of taxes.

In performance of their λειτουργία, the tax-gatherers go down to the villages, ἐπὶ τὰς κώμας ταύτας τὰς διὰ τῶν στρατηγῶν τετειχισμένας. The suggestion of this expression, as also of πυργούς in c. 17, is of a castellum or fortified post, but neither need be taken literally. Especially in the present passage Libanius, whose civilian bias is obvious throughout the speech, is seeking

---

[1] Gothofredus, Paratitl. C. T. 7, ed. Ritter 2, p. 261.

[2] 'quibus pensitanda pro fortunae condicione negari non possunt' C. T. 11, 24, 6, 'propriae commissos mediocritati' C. T. 11, 1, 14.

[3] cf. the retinue of the potens Nov. Theod. 15, 2, of 444, and on brigandage generally see Seeck, Gesch. II 554, n. to 295, 14. He cites a Fayum papyrus, B. G. U. 909, of 359, complaining of the brigandage of a father and son, and particularly of their violent interference with τοὺς γινομένους μερισμοὺς ἐν τῇ κώμῃ τῶν δημοσίων πραγμάτων. See also now P. Leips. 37 of 389 ; and two third-century inscriptions, Dittenberger, O. G. I. S. 519 and 609.

to heighten the impression of military licence. Arrived on the scene, the liturgists find their requests and threats met with equal contempt, and on their proceeding to arrest the headmen (ἄρχοντες) of the village, they are resisted by the population, and return to the city with wounds instead of φόρος. There they find no one to take their part, ἡ γὰρ τοῦ τὸν μισθὸν εἰληφότος δύναμις οὐκ ἐᾷ; all are afraid of the hired patron. Faced with the alternative of paying the taxes which they have failed to collect, or of being flogged and declared bankrupt, they sell their property, their dearest slaves, their ancestral land, and thus are reduced to beggary. The public evil, which is the loss to the city of decuriones, upon whom its whole life, aye, and that of the empire, depends, is described in striking terms : 'ταῦτ᾿ ἐλάττους ποιεῖ τὰς βουλὰς ἀντὶ μειζόνων, ταῦτ᾿ ὀλίγους τοὺς καθ᾿ ἑκάστην ἀντὶ πλειόνων. ταυτὶ δὲ ζημία πόλεως ὅλης.'[1]

The above is simply the tale of the constitutions from the point of view of the decuriones. It is noticeable that, though Libanius puts a military colour on the affair, the resistance comes from the villagers themselves, armed only with stones. The patron preserves the exterior decencies.

Administrative position of large villages.

We observe also that these large villages, which are legally represented by ἄρχοντες who are secondarily responsible for the taxes, fall within the fiscal competence of a civitas, whose decuriones have the liturgy of collecting their taxes. The term ' metrocomìa', be it technical or popular, general or local, is not applied to them, but they are κῶμαι μεγάλαι πολλῶν ἑκάστη δεσποτῶν, with their own magistrates. In other words they are, to quote C. T. 11, 24, 6, publici iuris, and, pursuant to the description of C. T. 11, 24, 3, 'defensionis potentia aut multitudine freti,' they refuse their taxes. We have already pointed out that the last-named constitution, which is of the year 395, and therefore probably about contemporary with our oration, by its address to the comes of Egypt indicates the necessity of using armed force against the recalcitrants.

[1] c. 10, Förster, III 408, 23, and more to the same effect. See Nov. Maj. 7, pr. cited above : ' Curiales nervos esse rei publicae ac viscera civitatum nullus ignorat.' On the depletion of the curiae cf. Or. 49, Pro Curiis, c. 8, and further references Seeck, Gesch. II 556, n. to 298, 25.

(2) Patronage of ἀγροί (also κῶμαι) οἷς εἶς ὁ δεσπότης is the Patronage
subject of cc. 11–12. This is a very different matter, for here of lands
belonging
the master pays the taxes, and the peasants, his coloni, do not to one
come into direct contact with the collector.[1] Encouraged by owner.
the patronage of a general, τὸν μισθωτόν, as Libanius con-
temptuously calls him, whom they pay at the expense of
their lord, the coloni of the estate claim the right not to work
unless they choose, and of course the evil is contagious.[2] The
master seeks legal redress, and is defeated by the corrupt
influence of the patron. All this in spite of the fact that the
master is a man of position, who would be a sufficient patron
for any lawful purpose.[3]

We have previously insisted that coloni as well as
possessores had recourse to patronage, and we need only
observe that Libanius is quite conclusive on this point.

(3) We pass at once to Libanius' troubles with his Jewish The
coloni, cc. 13–16. They are described as Ἰουδαῖοι τῶν πάνυ, Jewish
coloni of
Jews by race and religion, who, having been four generations Libanius.
on the land, now claimed to cast off the yoke, and to be
judges, τοῦ πῶς ἡμῖν αὐτοῖς χρηστέον. Libanius, finding them
recalcitrant, went to law, but the account of the proceedings
is obscure, perhaps owing to corruption of the text. The
judge, on learning the state of the case, and particularly who
was the patron of the defendants, ordered some persons to be
imprisoned, and others to be brought (ἄγεσθαι), or perhaps led
away.[4] It is quite uncertain who these various parties are.
P. Roth [5] understands that on the first impulse the judge
imprisoned the defendants, and then, on Libanius' representa-

---

[1] C. T. 11, 1, 14=C. J. 11, 48, 4 of 366 (?). An earlier trace of the
same system, C. T. 5, 17, 1 of 332, with which cf. C. T. 11, 24, 6 s. 3, of
415.

[2] We have not here a vestige of forced labour on the demesne. Simply
the coloni are reacting against their more or less recent servitude. The
difficult phrase 410, I, τοῦτο τῆς γῆς βουλομένης, is explained by the expression in C. J. 11, 53, 1, s. 1 'in redhibitione operarum et damni, quod
locis quae deseruerant factum est'; and cf. C. T. 11, 16, 4. These constitutions show how public policy coincided with the interests of the
masters.

[3] See the remarks on great landowners supra, pp. 13, 18, 26.

[4] The passage is in Förster, III 410 ad fin. Reiske, II 509.

[5] Op. cit. p. 284.

tion, set them free. But Libanius would be more likely to demand the liberation of his own witnesses. At any rate, after this demand the judge gets angry, and goes the other way: χαλεπήνας πρὸς ἐμὲ μνησθέντα λύσεως ᾤχετο ἀπιὼν ἑτέρωσε. Thereupon the defendants bribe the general, and after that the case is as good as over. With indecent haste, and manifestations of bias, the judge gives judgement against Libanius, though his guilty conscience drives him to volunteer oaths to his visitors that justice had been done. If these things are done to a famous orator like Libanius, what is likely to be the fate of others?

Patronage of coloni.

This concrete example of patronage of coloni is extremely instructive. The patron interferes between master and colonus to protect the latter against impositions which are alleged to be illegal. Except indirectly, the whole matter is one of private rights and interests, and not a direct refusal of public liabilities. All that Libanius has to rely on is a consuetudo of four generations; he does not attribute to his peasants any definite status, he appeals to no imperial constitution. If we may read between the lines, the peasants were in a state of customary servitude, but the colonate legislation had not yet been applied to them. This was exactly the position of the Palestinian colonus before the constitution, C. J. 11, 51, 1, which belongs to the years 384–389, as may be inferred from its address to Cynegius, p. pō. Or.[1]

C. J. De Colonis Palaestinis.

The constitution runs as follows : 'Cum per alias provincias, quae subiacent nostrae serenitatis imperio, lex a maioribus constituta colonos quodam aeternitatis iure detineat, ita ut illis non liceat ex his locis quorum fructu relevantur abscedere neque ea deserere quae semel colenda susceperunt, neque id Palaestinae provinciae possessoribus suffragetur, sancimus, ut etiam per Palaestinas nullus omnino colonorum suo iure velut vagus ac liber exsultet, sed exemplo aliarum provinciarum ita domino fundi teneatur, ut sine poena suscipientis non possit abscedere : addito eo, ut possessionis domino revocandi eius plena tribuatur auctoritas.' Now the claim of Libanius'

---

[1] See on this point Krüger ad C. J. 5, 20, 1, and Mommsen ad C. T. 8, 84, 17.

tenants was precisely 'velut vagi ac liberi exsultare', and
there seems to have been nothing very definite against them,
except the analogy of what had been settled in other provinces, and possibly some length of custom. The description
of his coloni as 'Ιουδαῖοι τῶν πάνυ makes it very probable that
his estate was in Palestine, and the general identity of conditions described by him with that referred to in the constitution
confirms such an inference. Accepting that view, it is clear
that the constitution was later than the lawsuit, and indeed
than the present speech : otherwise the rhetorician must have
referred to it, as making good his pretensions against the
peasants. The probability is that his and similar troubles led
to the enactment of the constitution.

Before the law was thus definitely settled, the status of the Patronage
peasantry was really uncertain, and we shall therefore be as the
natural
taking a one-sided view of patronage, at any rate in the fourth refuge
of the
century, if we forget that in some cases it represents simply peasant.
a natural reaction of the peasantry against the steady depression of their status. It is noticeable that the constitution just
referred to assumes that a runaway colonus will certainly have
a suscipiens, a term which is almost technical in this connexion.[1]

(4) Patronage is everywhere, c. 17. Another illustration is Deserter
coloni.
the protection of deserter coloni.[2] A retainer of a general is
safe from further prosecution, for the general has only to say
that he is interested in the accused, and the suit is lost.
The first half of the speech closes at this point with a prayer
to the emperor for redress.

Before passing on we must draw attention to the feature
which all the four cases discussed have in common, namely,
that the patron really relies on his influence over the judge,
and not on armed force. Consequently Libanius, in incrimi-
nating only the military officers, is less impartial than the
constitutions. What happens in each case is that, encouraged
by the promises of an influential friend, the humble tillers of

---

[1] Fustel de Coulanges, Origines du Système Féodal, p. 238.
[2] So common a phenomenon that we need scarcely refer to e. g. C. T.
5, 17, 1. 2. 3. 11, 24, 6, s. 3. C. J. 11, 51. 52. 53, &c.

the soil resist a claim which they might otherwise not have ventured to contest. They have force on their side, and the claimant, be he decurion or owner of an estate, is put to his remedy at law, nor need we assume that the peasants have nothing to say for themselves. At this point the patron steps in.

The patron and the law-courts. The very name patronus, προστάτης, has an association with the law-courts which cannot be overlooked. The class of advocati was only in the fourth century becoming strictly professional: gradually it became a militia, the local bars were formed into corporations, with numbers, education, orthodoxy, and privileges regulated by statute.[1] The times were therefore passing away when a litigant was represented by an unprofessional patronus, his most influential friend. But the vicious idea of personal influence which had so long been associated with judicial patronage [2] was never entirely dropped, though the more professional character of the actual causidici was so much to the good.[3]

Other speeches of Libanius. Libanius' account of the corruption of the tribunal might have been more lucid if the evil had been less familiar to his hearers. He deals, however, more fully with judicial scandals in two contemporary orations, viz. Adversus Assidentes Magistratibus and Adversus Ingredientes Domos Magistratuum.[4] These represent as the chief offenders not the professional advocates, nor even the soldiers, but physicians, professors, and other hangers-on. The characteristic evil is that the judges are unable to draw the line between their official and social relations. Suitors and their supporters invade the judge's privacy, robbing him and themselves of their siesta, and pester or flatter him into making the decrees they want. The parable of the importunate widow was well understood.

[1] C. J. 2, 6 and 7. See Lécrivain's article 'patronus' in Daremberg-Saglio, vol. vii, p. 355, and cf. Mitteis, Reichsrecht u. Volksrecht, 189 sq.
[2] Asconius, Verr. 104 Orelli, 'qui defendit alterum in iudicio patronus dicitur si orator est : aut advocatus si aut ius suggerit aut praesentiam commodat amico.'
[3] Amm. Marc. 30, 4, however, gives a very unfavourable picture of the bar at the end of the fourth century.
[4] Gothofredus, Opuscula, with translations and valuable notes. Or. 51 and 52. Reiske, II 590, III 72. Förster, 4, 6 and 25.

Under these conditions arose a class of professional inter-
mediaries, who having the ear of the judge were resorted to by
litigants as a matter of course. Naturally, they did not work Power.
for nothing; on the contrary, some of them amassed riches,
and exercised tyrannical power in their cities and the surrounding country. There is a passage in the speech Adversus
Ingredientes,[1] which describes their operations in terms which
recall the accusations of brigandage with which our Oratio De
Patrociniis begins. It runs : 'Οἳ καὶ κώμην πολλάκις ἀνέστησαν
ἀδικουμένην ὑπὸ μείζονος διὰ τὸ μείζω τὸν μίσθον εἶναι τὸν παρὰ
τῆς μείζονος.' The bolder miscreants sit in court, and drown
the pleadings with their partisan interruptions,[2] but in general
the methods are more insidious.

The remedy suggested by Libanius in these two speeches, Legislation
namely that judges should be forbidden to receive visits from against symptoms.
any one, except a doctor when they are ill, and that they
should neither entertain to meals, nor be entertained, would
seem chimerical, were there not extant contemporary constitutions in that sense.[3] The futility of such legislation
is apparent, and even Libanius sees that nothing can prevent
influence from being exercised by letter, as is indeed the
practice of persons whose rank does not allow them to dance
attendance on the judge.[4]

Influence and jobbery in litigation are the object of another Champerty
group of constitutions, the earliest of which, C. J. 2, 13, 1, and maintenance.
of 293, punishes with loss of their case litigants 'qui sibi
potentiorum patrocinium advocassent', apparently by getting
a potentior to act as procurator or actor. A later constitution inflicts a similar penalty on a creditor who resorts to
a formal transfer of a debt to a potens.[5] Another trick was
to inscribe the name and arms of a potens upon buildings, to

---

[1] Or. 52. Förster, 4, 34, 4.
[2] Or. 52. Förster, 4, 27–8. These may be the advocates proper, but
see the conduct of a powerful curialis described Nov. Theod. 15, 2, s. 1.
In any case these παρακαθήμενοι or προσεδρεύοντες are not the official
assessors, πάρεδροι. Distinguish also προσεδρεύειν, an Egyptian liturgy
involving compulsory attendance, apparently as scribe, at the praefect's
court : P. Amh. II 82 ; P. Oxy. I 59.
[3] C. T. 1, 16, especially 9, 10, and 13.   Also C. T. 1, 20.
[4] Or. 51. Förster, 4, 11–12.   [5] C. T. 2, 13, 1, of 422.

deter claimants, or after judgement to prevent execution [1]. The imperial name and arms were similarly abused,[2] and the fiscus was not guiltless of lending its influence as procurator in private suits,[3] sometimes under the pretext, which recalls the writ of 'quominus', that the plaintiff was debtor to the crown.

These persistent attempts of litigants to get influence on their side betray a deep-seated judicial disorder, which was more responsible for the abuse of patronage than even the anarchy and weakness of the executive. Judicial patronage was in its origin legal, and certainly in thorough accord with public opinion: it was therefore specially unamenable to legislative reform.

(*b*) It is time to return to the Oratio De Patrociniis, which we quitted just before the orator had begun to deal with the two imaginary objections which are the subject of cc. 19–34. The first, cc. 19–24, asserts the natural right of every man to have a patron, and the answer is extremely significant, for it does not consist in a denial of the legality of patronage, but rather in an attempt to distinguish licit and illicit patronage. The master is the natural protector of his peasants and servants, and it is no more right for them to seek a second and more powerful patron, than it is for a woman to claim the advantages of having a rich paramour. Such perversions of natural relations would undermine the whole structure of society. A man cannot serve two masters, and if in a given emergency the master is an insufficient protection, he, not his subordinates, is the proper person to appeal for more powerful assistance. There is no valid reason why a general should refuse to the master the patronage which he would accord to the poor peasants (cc. 21–22), unless indeed there be a sinister motive (c. 23).

The right to a patron. Libanius' admissions.

---

[1] C. T. 2, 14, 1, of 400. It appears that the consent of the potens was sometimes dispensed with. We have spoken above of formal transfers of land.

[2] C. J. 2, 15, 1 and 2. The latter constitution is in the strongest terms. Cf. also Nov. Just. 17, 15 of 535, and Nov. Tib. Col. I. 12, 4 of 578–582.

[3] C. J. 2, 17, 1-4. 11, 72, 1, 'Conductores hominesve augustissimae domus nostrae . . . nec aliorum litigatorum negotio intercedant nec sententiam iudicantium aut illicito patrocinii sui fomite iura conturbent, nullive exsecutionis suae turbulentum ministerium audeant commodare,' &c.

It is quite evident that Libanius, so far from challenging The ideal
the principle of patronage as a whole, sees in the great land- patron.
owner an ideal patron. We have already [1] observed in our
first section, that the territorial magnates were evidently
within the scope of the constitutions against patronage, and
we can only attribute Libanius' preference of them to class
prejudice.

Other legitimate sources of help are put forward in an
obscure passage at the beginning of c. 19 : [2] 'πρώτην μὲν τὴν
παρὰ τῶν θεῶν' (sc. βοήθειαν), 'ἢ γένοιτ' ἂν εὐχαῖς τε καὶ θεραπείαις·
ἔπειτα τὴν δι' ὑδάτων βλαπτόντων μὲν ἀπωθουμένων, μελλόντων δὲ
ὠφελεῖν ἐπαγομένων.' Gothofredus translates: ' primum scilicet
illud ' (sc. auxilium) ' quod a Diis votis cultuque impetratur ;
deinde illud quod per aquas praestatur ; quae eos laedunt qui
improbantur, prosunt autem iis qui probantur.' He makes
a far-fetched suggestion : 'aquas auxiliares hic indicat Libanius, quae probis ad eas confugientibus auxilio fuerint,
contra damnosae improbis,' possibly waters ' prope Antiochiam
in Daphne loco aquis celeberrimo '.

It seems clear that the second source of help suggested
is irrigation works, and the only question is, what is the
meaning of referring the peasants to the divine assistance
and improved drainage. If taken quite literally the advice
is so frigid and unsympathetic as to sound like a bad joke.
Professor Vinogradoff has suggested to me that Libanius
has in mind not so much the actual temples and irrigation
works, as the fact that assistance of this kind would be obtain-
able from a well-known class of legitimate patrons, the patroni
civitatis, coloniae, pagi. [3] This suggestion seems, if I may say
so, entirely satisfactory, as besides getting rid of what is prima
facie a simple ineptitude, it helps to explain why it was impossible for Libanius, in the face of such well-known examples
of patronage, simply to condemn the whole institution.

No doubt modern notions would have supplied Libanius
with a short answer : patronage and legality are fundamentally

---

[1] Supra, pp. 13, 18, 19, 26.
[2] Förster, 3, 413, 10.   Reiske, II 513.
[3] See the immense number of inscriptions collected by Lécrivain, Daremberg-Saglio, vol. vii, p. 358. Also Dessau, Inscr. Lat. Sel. Cap. 14, passim.

Patronage and legality.

irreconcilable. But then antiquity in some obscure way managed to reconcile them, and that is why such an answer was not open to Libanius. It is true that in the Or. Adversus Assidentes[1] he presses the obvious dilemma that the so-called favours resulting from patronage are either legal, in which case they are not favours at all, or, if really favours, are illegal. But that argument was directed by Libanius against a particular form of patronage to which he objected, and besides is not treated by him as conclusive. He is obliged to admit the existence of a custom of patronage, and even that his own hands are not quite clean.[2]

The fair conclusion from the first objection and the answer thereto is that in seeking a patron the peasants were only using means of defence which seemed perfectly legitimate to their betters when used by themselves, or when they themselves were the patrons.[3]

Abuses of the generals.

The second objection, cc. 25–34, that patronage is profitable to the generals, is hardly worth answering. In fact it is simply a peg on which to hang a tirade against the generals, who are represented as rich enough already from other corrupt sources. But an attack on the generals is essential to Libanius' position, since he does not really condemn patronage as an institution. We have already observed that to treat, as Libanius in the first part of this speech treats, the military patron as being the sole source of the disturbances following upon agrarian patronage, betrays a bias. He is the spokesman of an extreme irritation of civilians at the arrogance of the military, and at their assumption of jurisdiction.[4] We mention these passages as it was they, presumably, which led Gothofredus to conjecture, not very plausibly, that the oration occasioned the passing in 392 of C. T. 12, 1, 128.

The peroration however, cc. 35–38, begs the emperor to enforce his own existing law, and raises the question to what law Libanius refers. If he was addressing Valens, we should

[1] Or. 51, cc. 26–28. Förster, 4, 18–19.
[2] Or. 51 and 52. Förster, 4, 19 sq.; 34, 11; 44 sq.
[3] cf. S. Aug. Conf. ed Bruder, 6, 10. Dill, Roman Society in the last century, &c., p. 224, citing Symmachus, Ep. iv. 68; ii. 41; ii. 87.
[4] See cc. 5, 17, 23, 33. Förster, 3, 406, 15; 412, fin.; 415; 420.

have no difficulty in identifying it as C. T. 11, 24, 2, of 370 or Valens
or Theo-
dosius?
368. But this involves the assumption that the emperor
addressed is not Theodosius the Great, who might equally
well be described as the conqueror of the Scythians and de-
stroyer of a tyranny.[1] Now the conclusion of Gothofredus,
and of the most recent editor Förster, is that the emperor
in question was Theodosius.

This conclusion seems to rest chiefly on the fact that all
Libanius' orations of this kind were addressed to Theodosius,
but the difficulty has been to find some argument which will
remove the presumption in favour of Valens created by C. T.
11, 24, 2. To my mind such an argument exists in C. T. 5, C. T. 5,
17, 2.
17, 2, a constitution addressed on October 25, 386, to Cynegius,
p. pō. Or.,[2] which has been previously overlooked. It reads:
' Quisquis colonum iuris alieni aut sollicitudine susceperit aut
occultatione celaverit, pro eo, qui privatus erit, sex auri uncias,
pro eo, qui patrimonialis, libram auri cogatur inferre.' We
have already observed [3] that susceptio has almost a technical
meaning in such contexts, and what this constitution deals
with is the patronage, open and secret, of coloni alieni, precisely the form of patronage of which Libanius complains
most bitterly. Here then is a constitution of Theodosius the
Great to which Libanius' oration may refer just as well as to
that of Valens, C. T. 11, 24, 2.

There is, however, an objection to supposing that this is the C. J. 11,
51, 1.
constitution spoken of, if we assume, with Krüger, that it was
originally only part of a larger rescript, composed also of
C. J. 11, 51, 1, De Colonis Palaestinis, and of other constitutions which are not here relevant.[4] The Palestinian constitution,[5] though certainly within the years 384-9, is, as we
concluded from Libanius' silence, posterior to his oration.
And if it and C. T. 5, 17, 2 were promulgated together, Libanius cannot have referred to one more than the other. But
I know of no reason, other than general probabilities, in favour

---

[1] Förster, 3, 421, 15 'τὸν σβέσαντα μὲν τυραννίδα, στήσαντα δὲ Σκυθικὴν
φλόγα.'
[2] = C. J. 11, 64, 2.   [3] Supra, p. 33.
[4] See Krüger ad C. J. 11, 59, 7.
[5] See supra, p. 32, where the text is set out in full.

of Krüger's hypothesis, so that the inference is permissible that the constitution to which Libanus appeals is C. T. 5, 17, 2 of 386, and that the Palestinian constitution was enacted shortly afterwards, possibly in response to his appeal, and in order to settle the really doubtful status of the coloni in question.

Probable conclusion that the speech must be dated 386–389.   On our showing, then, the speech falls within the years 386–389, and the reason for accepting this result with caution is simply that the disorders of the times were chronic, and apt to repeat themselves with dreary monotony.[1] Thus a second constitution of Theodosius, addressed in 392 to another p. pō. Or., has already been cited as containing a remarkable reflection of Libanius' denunciation of brigandage in combination with patronage.[2] The only absolutely certain fact is that these years of Theodosius' reign were a period of disorders very similar to those which Libanius pictures.

Results of Libanius' oration.   Details apart, the oration is chiefly valuable as showing the actual working of these patrocinia. The clients are groups rather than individuals, coloni as well as possessores. The patronus' pay is a revenue, his work is to tamper with justice, and in so doing he is not committing an obvious illegality. Moreover, the revolt of the coloni is to some extent a reaction against the depression of their status, which is only gradually being legalized. The resultant evil is not purely fiscal, the direct sufferers being the decuriones, and the possessores of estates who are not quite strong enough to fill the part of patronus themselves. Roughly then it is the middling possessores who are hit by patronage, partly as tax-gatherers, partly as masters of coloni, or as both. The state suffers through its interest in the prosperity of the curiae.

---

[1] I do not consider the words in the opening phrase of the speech describing the emperor as ἐν πολλῷ χρόνῳ χαίροντά τε τοῖς τῶν ἀρχομένων ἀγαθοῖς as a serious objection. Theodosius after all had reigned from 379.

[2] The text of this constitution, C. T. 1, 29, 8, is given in full, p. 29, supra.

III

We have reserved up to this point two questions which we must now face, though they could only be adequately dealt with by a papyrological expert.[1] They can be put quite specifically: (a) who are the homologi coloni, and (b) what are the metrocomiae, mentioned in C. T. 11, 24, 6, of the year 415 ? And the constitution is so definitely Egyptian in destination, that the answers must certainly be sought in the papyri.

(a) The homologi coloni.

As the economic history of Egypt has yet to be written, a few general remarks on the agrarian conditions are necessary.[2] Wilcken has called attention to the practical absence of slave-labour in both the Ptolemaic and Roman periods.[3] Small owners worked their own farms with the assistance of free servants and journeymen, while even on the larger estates, including the vast public domains, we find no traces of the slave system of the latifundia. The most familiar member of society is the γεωργός, a term which, like colonus in its earlier sense, covers every class of free man who himself works on the land, with a tendency to the special meaning of small lessee of another's land.

Egyptian land-system.

If the γεωργός was not a slave, how far was he free ? Something like the colonate existed on the extra-municipal domains of other Hellenistic monarchs as early as the third century B.C.,[4] and in Egypt free municipalities were a very rare exception, while royal domains were everywhere.[5] But where the

Status of γεωργός on royal domains.

---

[1] Professor Grenfell and Dr. Hunt have very kindly given me information on various points.

[2] Modern studies, like the texts, are very scattered. Besides the notes of the various editors, and comments, chiefly Wilcken's, in the Archiv f. Papyrusforschung, we refer here generally for the sake of brevity to Wilcken, Ostraka ; Rostowzew in Philologus, 57, 564, and in Beitr. z. a. Gesch. 1, 295 ; and to his Staatspacht, Philologus Suppl. 9, 331 ; P. Meyer, Beitr. z. a. Gesch. 1, 424 ; Seeck, Colonatus in Pauly-Wissowa ; Waszyński, Bodenpacht, I.

[3] 1 Ostr. 698.

[4] This was pointed out by Rostowzew, Beitr. z. a. Gesch. 1, 295, commenting on a Seleucid inscription, which can now be referred to easily in Dittenberger, O. G. I. S. 225.

[5] On their uncertain extent see Bouché-Leclercq, Hist. des Lagides, vol. iii, 191 n. 2, and 231 n. 1 ; vol. iv, 336 fin. The Fayum cannot be

livelihood of a dense population depends upon agriculture, a very large landowner is necessarily in a favourable position. Economic pressure will, so long as conditions are at all tolerable, secure him the cultivation of his land at high rents. Hence forced labour on the royal domains was the exception in Ptolemaic and early Roman Egypt, there being usually no scarcity of cultivators.

But in times of crisis administrative pressure (legal is hardly the word) was readily used to reinforce economic motives. The corvée for works of public utility, especially the dams and canals, was indeed part of the regular system.[1] But the government held in reserve a more far-reaching principle, which was asserted whenever political or economic troubles threatened to bring the industry of the country to a standstill.

The principle of ἰδία. This was the principle that every man had an ἰδία, a place of origin in which he had his proper sphere of activity, and to which he could be held in the public interest. We cite in the note below a remarkable catena of texts testifying to the operation of the rule of ἰδία[2] from the Ptolemaic period onwards. We may quote as typical the edict of the praefect, of 154 A.D., B. G. U. 372, which concludes with the following threat: ' ἐάν τις . . . ἐπὶ ξένης πλανώμενος φανῇ, οὗτος οὐκέτι ὡς ὕποπτος, ἀλλὰ ὡς ὁμόλογος κακοῦργος συνλημφθεὶς πρὸς μὲ ἀναπεμφθήσεται.' The general duty is ' ἐν τῇ οἰκείᾳ τῇ γεωργίᾳ προσκαρτερεῖν'.

We might point backwards to the precisely similar terms of the royal ordinance of 118 B.C., P. Tebt. I 5, 7, but it is more to our purpose to point forward to the rescript of 415, C. T. 11, 24, 6, s. 3 : 'Ii sane, qui vicis quibus adscripti sunt derelictis, et qui homologi more gentilicio nuncupantur, ad

---

taken as typical for the reason given by Grenfell and Hunt, P. Tebt. I, App. I, p. 542. See, however, Rostowzew, Archiv III 206.
  [1] Illustrations are hardly necessary, but see e. g. P. Fay. 25, and 77–79.
  [2] Ptolemaic period : O. G. I. S. 90, 19–20.   P. Taur. VIII 13 ff., 19 ff.   P. Tebt. I 5, 7.   Roman period: first century, P. Oxy. II 251–3. O. G. I. S. 669, 34.   P. Lond. II 260, 120.   Second century, B. G. U. 372. 15 I. 475. 902. 903.   P. Fröhner (Wilcken in Festschr. zu O. Hirschfeld). P. Gen. 19.   P. Tebt. II 327. 439.   Third century, B. G. U. 159.   P. Gen. 16.   A new edict of the year 212 is announced by P. Meyer, Z. S. S. 1908, 473, to be published in the Giessen Papyri in the course of 1909.

alios seu vicos seu dominos transierunt, ad sedem desolati
rūris constrictis detentatoribus redire cogantur, qui si exsequenda protraxerint, ad functiones eorum teneantur obnoxii et
dominis restituant, quae pro his exsoluta constiterit.'[1]   These
words are based partly on the principle of ἰδία ('ad alios . . .
vicos '), and so far formulate an accusation which would have
been understood in Egypt centuries before the Roman colonate
legislation ; but they imply also a new idea, which marks the
approach or even the arrival of the colonate. This idea is
the protection of the interest of a dominus in his tenants
or labourers by means of local servitude. The idea is new,
though it rests on the older public duty, ἐν τῇ οἰκείᾳ τῇ γεωργίᾳ
προσκαρτερεῖν. The theory of ἰδία was certainly one of the
roots of the colonate.

Before this constitution traces of the colonate on private
lands in Egypt are still to find.   With the public lands it is Forced
different : the cultivation of γῆ βασιλική or δημοσία, which was leases of
publicland.
ordinarily conducted by means of free lease, was also, when
necessary, imposed by way of liturgy or forced lease, with the
result that the δημόσιος γεωργός was not far removed from the
colonus patrimonialis.   We have again a long series of texts
proving the antiquity and continuity of this practice,[2] but no
study of the series as a whole is known to me, and to attempt
one here would be out of place.   The extreme significance of
P. Tebt. I 5, 231, a royal ordinance of B.C. 118, has been
rather overlooked : it forbids βασιλικοὶ γεωργοί to sell all their
property ; they must keep at least one house containing their
implements, their cattle, and other instruments of agriculture,
and they may not transfer these to temple and other land.
In other words, the little stock of the γεωργός is no better
than the peculium of a colonus.[3]

---

[1] This section is considered in detail post, pp. 57 ff.
[2] Ptolemaic period : P. Paris 63, republished by Mahaffy, P. Petrie III,
p. 15.   P. Tebt. I 26. 41. 61 (b), 29 ff., 197. 5, 231.   Roman Period :
first century, Edict of Lusius Geta in Archiv II 433 ; of Tiberius Julius
Alexander, O. G. I. S. 669, 10.   P. Lond. II 445.   P. Fay. 123 ; second
century, P. Amh. II 65. 95, 4. B. G. U. 372. 648.   P. Oxy. VI 899.   P. Tebt.
II 327 ; third century, P. Lond. II 322.   P. Amh. II 94.   C. P. R. 6, 16.
Also many of the passages cited supra on ἰδία, p. 42.   See D. 49, 14, 3, 6,
and post, p. 78, Note A.   [3] See e. g. C. J. 11, 50, 2, 3.

Com-
pulsory
βασιλικὴ
γεωργία. We cite other general characteristics, without discrimination of epoch : the burden was hereditary, ran sometimes with the ownership of other land, and was remitted to females. But the more servile features mentioned by the Ptolemaic papyrus just cited have not, so far, reappeared in the Roman papyri. The compulsory conductor of public land elsewhere was a capitalist performing a liturgy, not a serf fulfilling the duties of his status. The distinction between the two is obviously fine in the case of small men, and in Egypt the acreage of demised land runs small. It is therefore hard to say in every case under which conception the compulsory lessee of γῆ βασιλική is to be brought.

At any rate, P. Tebt. I 5, 231, shows that centuries before our period βασιλικοὶ γεωργοί had been in a position not far removed from that of a colonus, and their status would serve as a model for the colonate. But this observation does not explain how and when the colonate came into existence on private lands, questions which arise directly out of C. T. 11, 24, 6, s. 3. We turn, therefore, to the history of private tenancies in Egypt.

Waszyński
on the
gradual
depression
of the free
tenant. Waszyński's careful study [1] of this subject has the merit, amongst others, of making the materials more accessible to the beginner.[2] His general thesis, that the Ptolemaic and early Roman periods were characterized by freedom of contract and general prosperity, but that subsequently there was a gradual depression of the status of the tenant corresponding to the decline of the rest of the empire, is, we think, fully justified. At the same time we must not exaggerate the evidence. The gradual predominance of forms of lease emanating from the lessee is really a very equivocal symptom ; because the evidence of a contract is one-sided, there is no reason to assume that the contract binds one side only.[3] The shortening of the normal term to one year is also an important, but not of itself decisive, fact.[4] This phenomenon, which appears at the beginning of the fourth century, cannot be

---

[1] Bodenpacht, I (Teubner, 1905).
[2] See the Table of Leases at the end of his volume.
[3] Op. cit. p. 46, fin.
[4] Op. cit. pp. 91 and 163. The author rightly interprets it as a sign of economic uncertainty and unrest.

interpreted favourably to the tenant, from the economic point of view, but as a matter of law it has an effect just the reverse of the colonate. And even from the economic point of view the position of a tenant for a year would be alleviated by the great cause of the agricultural crisis, the shortage of labour.

The most striking piece of evidence produced by Waszyński Tenancy is the appearance at the end of the fifth century of leases ἐφ' at will. ὅσον βούλει χρόνον, that is, leases terminable at the pleasure of the landlord. It is a pure misapprehension, however, to compare them with the English tenancy at will, as is done by Waszyński[1] following Mitteis.[2] In the first place, it is evidently not understood that our tenancy is as much at the will of the lessee as of the landlord ; and, secondly, what is more to the point, we have no system of tenancy at will ; it occurs occasionally, chiefly by construction of law, and is no part of our agricultural arrangements.

The first lease at the will of the lessor that has been found, according to Waszyński's table, is of the year 486, and the second of 553, after which this kind is common.[3] These fifth and sixth century leases have a general aristocratic flavour which can only be appreciated by comparison with the earlier. There are, however, a good many fourth-century leases of private land for fixed terms, though till recently P. Grenf. I 54 was the only one that could be definitely dated as contemporary with our C. T. constitutions. Now in P. Lips. 20-24 we have some interesting contemporary leases for fixed terms, including three examples of colonia partiaria at a rent of half the gross produce. In colonia partiaria, as in the case of the Colonia shortening of the term to one year, we have a fact of great partiaria. economic importance, which however has no immediate connexion with the colonate. These leases are on the face of them as much contracts as if the rent had been a fixed amount.[4]

---

[1] Op. cit. p. 92.

[2] Hermes, 30, 606. Waszyński makes things worse by confusing our tenancy from year to year. Even the yearly tenancy, which was objectionable on political and social, rather than on economic, grounds, has of course been much modified by recent statutes.

[3] Wessely, Hernals 16, 1. B. G. U. 364. See however post, p. 78, Note B.

[4] Outside the classical locatio conductio, however, cf. Gaius 3, 142. Fustel de Coulanges, Recherches, p. 13, treats colonia partiaria as a factor

The lease
ἐφ' ὅσον
βούλει
χρόνον.

But returning to the lease ἐφ' ὅσον βούλει χρόνον: what is its significance? It indicates relations between landlord and tenant which we may suspect were very often not put in writing, relations which may have been common long before 486, and in which the lessee, even if we make the fullest allowance for the effects of the shortage of agricultural labour, must have occupied a position of comparative dependence. For we must take it that he could be evicted without notice immediately before the harvest. Further, on a literal interpretation he would have no right to determine the lease of his own motion, but we doubt whether that is the meaning of the clause ἐφ' ὅσον βούλει χρόνον. At any rate, it would still be open to him to break his contract, and we shall see that there is a difficulty in allowing the landlord any action on such a contract, except possibly for past use and fruits. Of course, we might be outside contract, in the domain of status, but this possibility is really excluded by the consideration that the only available status is the colonate, which is in flat contradiction with the clause ἐφ' ὅσον βούλει χρόνον. For the patronus was not free to eject his colonus. Hence the intention of the lessor may well have been, by the insertion of this peculiar term, actually to prevent his lessee from acquiring the colonus' fixity of tenure.

The
Roman
precarium.

There is no need, however, to discuss the matter so much in the abstract, for the clause clearly reproduces the essential feature of quite another Roman institution, the precarium.[1] Its importance in the fourth century practice of the Western Empire has been well brought out by Fustel de Coulanges in a highly suggestive chapter. His conclusion[2] may be given in his own words: ' Le colonat d'une part, le précaire de l'autre, devinrent les deux modes de tenure les plus usités, le premier étant le plus rigoureux et plus sûr, le second étant plus honorable et plus libre.' Tenure precario, as he shows, arose

in the development of the colonate. Vinogradoff, Growth of the Manor, p. 80, n. 91.   Waszyński, p. 148 ff.
[1] D. 43, 26 De precario.   Windscheid, 376.   Seeliger, Grundherrschaft im früheren Mittelalter, p. 13. Roth, Feudalität, &c., p. 145.   Fullest and best, Fustel de Coulanges, Origines du Système Féodal, ch. 4.
[2] Op. cit. p. 108.

frequently as the result of a regrant by creditor to debtor of
land which was the security of the debt : 'cottidie . . . precario
rogantur creditores ab his qui pignori dederunt . . .' &c. Ulp.,
D. h. t. 6, 4.[1]　In other cases the ordinary lessee degenerated
into a precario rogans, and then the line between conductor
and precario rogans might be hard to draw.[2]　Most important
of all, for our purpose, were the regrants on precarious tenure,
which according to Salvianus[3] were the normal result of
patronage constituted by surrender of the client's land.

We have shown that Libanius' evidence makes it necessary   Precarium
to take a somewhat more elastic view than would be suggested   and
by Salvianus alone of the modes of constituting agrarian   patronage.
patronage, at any rate in the East.[4]　Similarly, even in those
cases, and they were frequent, in which patronage assumed
this definite form, we would avoid laying down a universal
rule as to the subsequent relations between patron and client.
Evidently the client remained on the land, paying the patron
some sort of rent,[5] and evidently his tenure would be precarious in the broad sense of the word.　But there is no
direct evidence that he always remained as a precario rogans
in the strict sense.

The question depends on *a priori* probabilities, and it
is obvious that the precario rogans and rogatus were in a
relation to each other which reproduced very faithfully the
general relations of patron and client.　The rights of the   Precarium
rogatus against the rogans, which are worked out in con-   in the
siderable detail in the Digest,[6] are simply the logical deduc-   Digest.
tions from his rights as owner.　He has, however, in addition
a special interdict,[7] and an actio praescriptis verbis : 'cum
quid precario rogatum est, non solum interdicto uti possumus,
sed et incerti condictione, id est praescriptis verbis,' Julian D.
h. t. 19, 2.　Though the rogans may take the fruits[8] and has
a possession protected by the interdicts against strangers,[9]

---

[1] Cf. Celsus, h. t. 11.　Gaius, 2, 60.　Isidor. Orig. 5, 25, 17.
[2] Ulp. D. 41, 2, 10.　Julian, D. 41, 3, 33, 6 sub fin.
[3] De Gub. Dei. v, 8.　　　　[4] Supra, pp. 20, 24 ff., 29.
[5] Supra, p. 24.
[6] D. 43, 26, passim, especially l. 8, 3-7.　Also D. 50, 17, 23.　Paul,
Sent. 5, 6, 10-12.　　　[7] Ulp. h. t. 2.　　　[8] Ulp. h. t. 8, 4.
[9] Pomponius, h. t. 17.　Ulp. h. t. 4, 1.　D. 41, 2, 21.

his possession is not strong enough to displace the simultaneous possession of the rogatus, according to Pomponius h. t. 15, 4. He has indeed against the rogatus no rights at all: 'Qui . . . precario possidet ab adversario impune dejicitur,' Paul, Sent. v, 6, 7,[1] or as Ulp. h. t. 1, 2 puts it more explicitly '. . . qui precario concedit, sic dat quasi tunc recepturus, cum sibi libuerit precarium solvere.'

Essential revocability.

This right to revoke the grant at pleasure is of the essence of the transaction, and holds even when, as often happened,[2] the precarium was originally granted for a term: Celsus, h. t. 12 'Cum precario aliquid datur, si convenit, ut in kalendas Iulias precario possideat, numquid exceptione adiuvandus est, ne ante ei possessio auferatur? Sed nulla vis est huius conventionis, ut rem alienam invito domino possidere liceat.' As if to complete the picture of patron and client, the precarium, dependent and servile as it is, is always represented as a benefit, an act of generosity, which the jurists are at some pains to distinguish from a donatio proper: 'Quod genus *liberalitatis* ex iure gentium descendit,' Ulp. h. t. 1, 1, 'Magis . . . ad donationes et beneficii causam, quam ad negotii contracti spectat precarii condicio,' Paul, h. t. 14.

Rent and liberality.

How are we to reconcile the character of a liberality with the fact that in our leases ἐφ' ὅσον βούλει χρόνον the rogans promises a rent? Strictly there is no difficulty; a gift may be made upon conditions, and the element of liberality really depends upon the nature of the conditions. But the insight of Fustel de Coulanges had already led him[3] to deduce from the older evidence the fictitious character of the liberality. This is obvious in the case of creditor and debtor, and apparent also from the passages already cited which deal with the occasional difficulty of distinguishing conductor and precario rogans;[4] we may add the clear inferences to be drawn from Salvianus, and the express words of a constitution of 365, which after denying to precario possidentes the right to acquire ownership by forty years' possession, adds 'eos

---

[1] Cf. Gaius, 4, 154. [2] See h. t. 4, 4 ; 5 ; 8, 7.
[3] Op. cit. pp. 81 and 98 ff.
[4] Ulp. D. 41, 2, 10. Jul. D. 41, 3, 33, 6 sub fin.

autem possessores non convenit appellari, qui ita tenent, ut ob hoc ipsum solitam debeant praestare mercedem '.[1]

There were in fact obligations between rogans and rogatus, but they were extra-legal. Possibly the rogatus could sue by the actio praescriptis verbis for rent accrued due in respect of past occupation and for waste : otherwise one does not see the use of this action in addition to the interdict.[2] But the rogatus' substantial remedy was his power to evict, which rested not on his contract, but on his ownership.

Extra-legal character of precarium.

Fustel de Coulanges [3] seems to me to misunderstand the real distinction, which caused precarium to be classed as a liberalitas rather than as a locatio conductio. He holds that if there had been a fixed rent, the contract would have been locatio conductio. But Gaius, 3, 142, only says: 'Nisi enim merces certa statuta sit, non videtur locatio et conductio contrahi': not that where there is a merces there is necessarily a locatio conductio.[4] The proper ground is that the rogatus bound himself to nothing, and therefore legally the rogans was in possession as a pure bounty. The point is put in technical form by Gaius, 3, 137, where speaking of the consensual contracts he says: 'Item in his contractibus alter alteri obligatur de eo, quod alterum alteri ex bono et aequo praestare oportet; cum alioquin in verborum obligationibus alius stipuletur, alius promittat. . . .' In short, precarium could never be classed as a bilateral contract.

Why precarium at a rent not a species of locatio conductio.

Of course where there is no merces, or only a nominal merces, there is no conductio, and where precarium and conductio are the only possible alternatives, the absence of a real merces proves that there is a precarium. This seems to be the true explanation of the passage, which is used in another sense by Fustel de Coulanges,[5] Ulp. D. 41, 2, 10: ' Si quis et conduxerit et rogaverit precario, uti possideret, si quidem nummo uno conduxit, nulla dubitatio est, quin ei

[1] C. J. 7, 39, 2.
[2] Ulp. D. h. t. 2, 2. Julian, h. t. 19, 2, Supra, p. 47.
[3] Op. cit. pp. 80–81.
[4] cf. Inst. 3, 24, pr. ' ⸳ . locatio et conductio *ita* contrahi intellegitur, si merces constituta sit.' Fustel de Coulanges, op. cit. p. 81, n. 1, follows D. 19, 2, 2, pr., in omitting the word ' ita ', and so obscures the point.
[5] Op. cit. p. 107.

precarium solum teneat, quia conductio nulla est, quae est in
uno nummo: sin vero pretio, tunc distinguendum, quid prius
factum est.'

The papyri and Fustel de Coulanges.

Starting from this faulty premiss, the great scholar whom
we have ventured to criticize came to conclusions which are
obviously at variance with the documents now before us.
There is no shyness about naming the rent to be paid by the
precario rogans, and the rent is quite definite.[1] Of the eleven
leases of this kind which have as yet been published, only
two, B. G. U. 364 of 553 and B. G. U. 312 of 658, have a purely
money rent, four secure to the rogatus a proportion of the
fruits, viz. Hernals 16, 1 of 486,[2] P. Lond. 113, 3 and 4, both
of the end of the sixth century, and B. G. U. 308 of the
Byzantine period. Of the other five, two, Hernals 16, 3 and 5
of the sixth to seventh centuries, have a fixed rent partly in
money, but mainly in kind, while in Wiener Denkschriften
37, 21, pp. 149 and 152–3, of the Byzantine period, the rent is
missing.[3] In spite of the legally precarious character of the
tenure, there is no doubt that these holdings might develop
a customary fixity of great strength. Thus the law of 365
already cited, C. J. 7, 39, 2, speaks of holdings lasting over forty
years and threatening to extinguish the ownership of the domini,
whose rights are however evidenced by the ' solita merces '.

Patronage and precarium.

There is an *a priori* probability that this form of tenure
would spring up between a patron and a client from whom he
had received a formal surrender of the lands, as the earlier
conclusions of Fustel de Coulanges show, and the case is very
much strengthened by the appearance of these documents
from Egypt, one of the great fields of agrarian patronage.

But so far as leading us in the direction of the colonate,
these documents, as we have said, point the other way. Of
course the colonate as a developed institution undoubtedly
existed in Egypt, even on private lands, at a period later than

[1] Contra, op. cit. pp. 80–81.

[2] XVI. Jahresbericht des k. k. Staatsgymnasiums in Hernals, Wien,
1890 ; mit Papyruseditionen von C. Wessely. I have unfortunately not
been able to see this publication, and take the details from Waszyński's
table.

[3] The rent is also missing in P. R. Ist. Veneto 1 of 536 : cf. supra,
p. 45, n. 3.

the C. T., in the time let us say of the C. J. It is enough to cite such documents as P. Oxy. I 135 and VI 996 of 579 and 584 respectively.[1] As the colonate depends ultimately on custom, we can only hope in the future to unearth indirect evidences of its origin in Egypt. The constitution of Anastasius, C. J. 11, 48, 19, allowing the creation of coloni by prescription, must have assisted the tendency to bind free men, such as these precario rogantes, to the soil; and again, it is clear from Justinian's C. J. 11, 48, 22 that leases were often the means of degrading free tenants by their own act. That constitution moreover suggests that, when in B. G. U. 364 the precario rogans described himself as ἀπὸ τοῦ ὑμετέρου ἐποικίου, he had made a very dangerous admission of origo. He is not describing merely his present domicile, for this would be expressed as in P. Grenf. I 54, τὰ νῦν οἰκοῦντος [2] &c.

We return, after this long introduction,[3] to the problem of the homologi coloni, with the conclusion that the reference to private coloni in C. T. 11, 24, 6, s. 3 is earlier than any which has as yet been found in the papyri.

The words ὁμολογεῖν and ὁμολογία in the papyri, as else- 'Ομολογεῖν, where, ordinarily denote agreement, contract. But the word ὁμολογία and ὁμό- ὁμόλογος, at any rate in untechnical contexts, is not found in λογος. this common meaning; in B. G. U. 526, of A.D. 86–7, for instance, we find the phrase οἱ ὁμολογοῦντες applied to two sub-lessors of δημόσια ἐδάφη, as though one preferred to say ' the contracting parties ' rather than ' the contractors '. The word, by a usage which is found elsewhere in Hellenistic speech, is applied as an adjective to πρᾶσις in B. G. U. 917, 21 of the year 348, if the reading be correct, to denote the thing agreed to. The phrase ὁμόλογα σύμβολα, which occurs in P. Tebt. I 105, 49, a lease of 103 B.C., is translated by the editors as ' the equivalents of the amounts in the tax-receipts ', which is clearly the general sense of this defective passage. We have here a trace of the word in its mathematical sense of ' corresponding to ': see Aristotle, Eth. N. 3, 6, 9, where, after

---

[1] See also the contemporary P. Lond. III 775. 778. 774. 777.
[2] Contrast in this respect P. Lips. 20 with P. Lips. 21–23.
[3] Supra, p. 41.

speaking of the highest forms of danger, he adds ' ὁμόλογοι δὲ τούτοις καὶ αἱ τιμαί'. Yet another common meaning occurs in B. G. U. 372, II 21, the praefect's edict of A. D. 154, and in P. Leips. 37, 28, a plaint of A. D. 389, where it is used of admitted or manifest wrongdoers.

These citations give no clue to the meaning of the word where it is found as a technical term in papyri and ostraka of the first three centuries of our era, and are only adduced to show that there is no strong presumption in favour of 'contractor', which has been suggested by Wilcken as the technical sense.[1] It would be excessive to resume here all the theories which have been put forward on the subject, and I propose to mention them only incidentally to our examination of the texts, which are less numerous than is sometimes implied.[2]

Technical usage of ὁμόλογος— as applied to men.

Let us take first the passages in which the mysterious term is applied to men.

(1) B. G. U. 560, I, of the second century, after a list of names proceeds (1. 20 ff.):

γεωργοῦντες ὁμόλογοι ἄνδρες ρμδ̄

.. γεωργοῦντες δημοσίαν καὶ οὐσιακὴν γῆν ἄνδρες ριε̄

after which the papyrus becomes very fragmentary, the word ἔγγραπτοι perhaps occurring in the next line.

(2) P. Lond. II 259, a census list of 94–95, after a list dealing with poll-tax [3] proceeds (ll. 190–1) ἐπὶ τὸ αὐτὸ ἄνδρες χ·... ὧν ὁμόλογοι ἄνδρες χ ...

(3) P. Lond. II 261 of 72–73, similar to the last, proceeds (ll. 142–3) καὶ τῷ α ἔτει Οὐεσπασιανοῦ ἀπὸ ξένων κα ... σὺν τοῖς πατράσι ἐν ὁμολόγοις ἀνειλημμένοι'.[4]

(4) There is also a Vienna papyrus described by Wessely,

---

[1] 1 Ostr., 253–4.
[2] Literature: Wilcken, 1 Ostr. 254, n. 1, followed by P. Meyer, Deutsche Lit.-Zeitung, 1900, p. 2346. A divergent view is supported by Mitteis, Aus d. griech. Papyrusurkunden, n. 57 and ad P. Lips. 105. See particularly Grenfell and Hunt's note to P. Oxy. III 478, 22, and Rostowzew, Staatspacht, Philologus, Suppl. 9, p. 489. Also Wessely, Wien. Denkschr., Sitzungsberichte 142, 9, 24-25, and Stud. z. Pal. &c. I, pp. 9–11. Waszyński, Bodenpacht, I 49.
[3] Grenfell and Hunt l. c. supra.
[4] The abbreviations are resolved as by Grenfell and Hunt, l. c.

Stud. 3. Pal. &c., I, pp. 9–11, containing the words ὄντες ἐν ὁμολόγοις, or ἐν ὁμολόγῳ λαογραφίᾳ.
(5) We must add the ostraka cited by Wilcken, Ostr. 1, 253–4.
It is obvious that these passages raise the question, but by themselves do nothing to solve it.

Secondly the word is applied to the λαογραφία itself, δι᾽ ὁμολόγου λαογραφίας, in P. Oxy. III 478, 22, an application in connexion with ἐπίκρισις of the year 132, and also in B. G. U. 618 I. 13, which is a return of men by a village scribe for χωματικὰ ἔργα of the year 213–4, ἐκ μὲν ὁμολόγου λαογραφίας ἄνδρες δ̄, according to Grenfell and Hunt's probable correction. Here we may conjecture that we have a usage derived from the application to men, and that the lists are lists of ὁμόλογοι. ^{As applied to λαογραφία.}

The decisive passages seem to me to be the two in which ὁμόλογος is applied to land. The recently published first-second century P. Lips. 105 is interpreted by Mitteis as follows: it is a letter, probably from a bailiff, telling the owner of an estate how many ἄρουραι thereof had been reported by the village scribe as entitled to remission of taxes through being ἄβρυχοι, unwatered. He had reported only 127 out of 1,850 claimed. The letter concludes (the subject of the sentence is the village scribe): τὰς γὰρ λοιπὰς εἰς πλήρωσιν τῶν δτ καὶ πρὸς τῶν διὰ τοῦ ἐν κεφαλαίῳ λόγῳ σημανθεισῶν ὑπ᾽ αὐτοῦ βεβρεγμένων παρεῖκεν μὴ μεταδιδοὺς ὡς ὁμολόγους οὔσας. 'The scribe, in order to make up the (total of) about 4,500 ἄρουραι which had been declared in the summary report as watered, omitted the rest (of the 1,850 claimed), and did not report them, on the ground of their being ὁμόλογοι'—to quote Mitteis' words, 'weil sie gleichfalls steuerpflichtig seien.' Recalling that ὑπόλογος has, from its constant usage in P Tebt. I, been ascertained to mean 'deducted', i. e. from a total of taxable units, we infer that ὁμόλογος is the reverse, and is applied to taxable units to denote their liability along with the rest of a group. ^{As applied to land.}

This actual contrast of ὑπόλογος and ὁμόλογος occurs in a passage, P. Amh. II 68, 49, of the end of the first century, ^{Ὑπόλογος and ὁμόλογος.}

which, owing to the fact that the word ὑπόλογος has only been interpreted in the light of P. Tebt. I,[1] has up to the present remained unexplained.[2]   We have here again a question of deduction of land from taxation, of placing it ἐν ὑπολόγῳ.

P. Amh.
II 68.

The prefect Ursus, on receiving a certain report ' ἔκρεινε τὸν στρατηγὸν καὶ βασιλικὸν ἐξετάσαι εἰ ἀπὸ τοῦ καθήκοντος ὑπολόγου ἡ παράδειξις ἐγένετο, καὶ ὁμόλογον ἀναφέρειν.' I translate ' decided that the strategus and royal scribe should inquire whether the (previous) registration had been on the basis of what was properly deducted as not liable, and should report what was properly to be counted in as liable '.

Smyly's
theory.

Smyly [3] has suggested that ὁμόλογος means ' assessed at the same rate', but this does not give the proper opposition to ὑπόλογος. The idea is rather that of liability along with the rest of a group. This conclusion is confirmed by the Byzantine terms ὁμόκηνσος and ὁμόδουλος, which denote groups of property not merely equally, nor even simultaneously, but jointly or solidarily liable, the owners of ὁμόκηνσα being styled consortes, contributarii.[4]

The result is that ὁμόλογοι γεωργοί are a group of cultivators jointly liable for something determined by the context, and ὁμόλογος λαογραφία is a list of the members of such a group. The word in this technical usage is affected by the meaning of the root which is illustrated by λόγος in the sense of account.

Rostow-
zew's
theory.

Rostowzew,[5] writing before the publication of many of the passages I have cited, arrives at a conclusion not far removed from the above. According to him the γεωργοὶ βασιλικοί or δημόσιοι were in Ptolemaic times a distinct portion of the population, and formed themselves into partnerships or unions, in order to deal with the state and to act in other economic relations as a corporate body. The bond of union was the guarantee given by the society for its individual members, who were technically known as ὁμόλογοι or ὁμολογοῦντες ἄνδρες. He cites on this point B. G. U. 526. 560. 512. and C. T. 11,

[1] See P. Tebt. I, p. 540, and App. I, s. 9.
[2] See Mitteis, Z. S. S. 1901, p. 156.
[3] Ad P. Oxy. III 478, 22.
[4] Zachariae von Lingenthal, Gesch. d. griech.-röm. Rechts, p. 228 ff.
[5] Staatspacht, Philol., Suppl. 9, 489.

24, 6. They were represented by special liturgists, πρεσβύτεροι
γεωργῶν or ἀρχιγεωργοί—B. G. U. 85. 471. P. Gen. 16. P. Grenf.
II 37—and the requirements of the administration in respect
of taxes were imposed upon the corporate body—C. P. R. 33.
B. G. U. 84. 471. 589. 659. Edict of Tib. Jul. Alex. l. 32. In
fact, these partnerships, which arose in Ptolemaic times out of
considerations not entirely fiscal, were converted by the
Romans into a system of responsibility for one another's taxes,
and in this capacity lasted throughout the period of Roman
domination.

In a later article[1] the same writer observes that in the
Roman period the πρεσβύτεροι κώμης play the part of the
Ptolemaic πρεσβύτεροι γεωργῶν as representatives of the γεωργοί
in their quality of taxpayers. 'They stand between the
Praktores and the taxpayers in order to facilitate the work of
both parties and to augment the number of persons liable.
They form the bridge to the later Dekaprotoi.' But though
the Ptolemaic evidence has accumulated[2] the writer offers no
fresh information as to the nature of the associations of
ὁμόλογοι.

I think I am not doing this very interesting account an
injustice in supposing, that the suggestion is that the γεωργοί
were called ὁμόλογοι because they were associated by ὁμολογία
agreement. To this there are two objections. First, ὁμολογία
connotes agreement simply ; ὁμολογεῖν as a legal term means
simply to promise, more particularly to promise in answer to
a stipulatory question ;[3] whereas what is wanted is an agreement of guarantee, or at least of partnership. The nearest
approach to the sense of guarantee is found in ecclesiastical
usage, e. g. St. Matthew 10, 32 πᾶς οὖν ὅστις ὁμολογήσει ἐν
ἐμοὶ ἔμπροσθεν ἀνθρώπων, &c.[4] A homologetes, confessor, is
one who answers for Christ. I do not think we can rely
on this usage for our present purpose.[5] My second objection

*Improba-
bility of
union by
ὁμολογία—
agreement.*

---

[1] Archiv III 201, at pp. 214–15.
[2] Archiv III 204, 208.
[3] See e. g. Theoph. Par. Inst. 3, 15 sq.
[4] See Sophocles, Greek Lexicon, s. v.
[5] I have to thank Professor Gilbert Murray for drawing my attention
to it.

is that these supposed associations of γεωργοί must be understood in a rather different sense. I do not doubt that the γεωργοί had a corporate life for other purposes as well as that of fiscal responsibility,[1] but the organization, though all social organizations are in a manner artificial, was not artificially created by ὁμολογία in the sense of agreement, and the occurrence of the term ὁμόλογος must be explained in another way. It is used in fiscal documents to denote the relevant aspect of corporate union, that namely of joint liability.

The village the natural union. During the Ptolemaic, as well as the Roman period, the village was steadily the unit of administration, and indeed in all matters the peasant's natural union in Egypt, as everywhere, was the village. The change from πρεσβύτεροι γεωργῶν to πρεσβύτεροι κώμης is from the present point of view an insignificant variation of phraseology, and it is a mere accident due to particular causes that in 201 A.D. B.G.U. 63 speaks of πρεσβύτεροι οὐσίας Θεωνείνου, or that in the seventh century P. Oxy. VI. 999 records a payment to a great landlord παρὰ τοῦ κοινοῦ τῶν γεωργῶν ὑπὲρ ἰδίας γῆς. Meanwhile we welcome Rostowzew's authority for the antiquity of the system of corporate liability, to which C.T. 11, 24, 6 will almost immediately force our attention.

Mitteis' theory. Mitteis[2] still adheres to a view founded on that of Zachariae von Lingenthal,[3] namely that homologi coloni are peasants inscribed·in the census against a private estate, for whom the estate was liable to pay taxes. To this view Wilcken's objection,[4] that inscription is ἀπογραφή, not ὁμολογία, still seems to me to be fatal. Moreover, the sense will be found not to agree with C.T. 11, 24, 6.

Our conclusion in the light of C.T. 11, 24, 6. Let us consider now the picture of homologi in the year 415 A.D. presented by that constitution. Its general object is the preservation of the metrocomiae as tax-paying bodies. Powerful outsiders are to be excluded, save so far as rights

---

[1] cf. post, p. 67.
[2] Aus den griech. Papyrusurkunden, n. 57, and ad P. Lips. 105.
[3] Gesch. d. griech.-röm. Rechts, p. 227, n. 734, commenting on C. T. 11, 24, 6: 'Homologi heissen sie weil sie in den Professionen beim Census angegeben werden mussten.'
[4] I Ostr. 254, n. 1.

have been acquired by prescription,[1] and even imperial grantees are docked of their privileges.[2] The landholders form a corporate union by the very fact that if one refuses his contribution the rest suffer. For the collatio or ἐπιβολή of land that has gone out of cultivation [3] necessarily involves joint liability, and it is small compensation that by s. 5 desert land is only open to the squatter if the curiales formally renounce their rights, and even then only on terms of coming within the corporate liability. We raise for the moment no question of the possible connexion of the metrocomiae with some civitas. We are dealing at any rate with a group of consortes, whose lands are ὁμόκηνσα in the exact sense of later Byzantine law.[4]

Two passages in the constitution, pr. and s. 3, mention C. T. 11, homologi coloni. The first has already been translated,[5] and 24, 6 pr. we need only add here, that when we read that intruding possessores dating from before 398 are quieted in their titles, provided that they acknowledge 'pro antiquitate census functiones publicas et liturgos quos homologi coloni praestare noscuntur ', the only possible inference is that the homologi are the old possessores for whose liabilities, now that they have been displaced, the new-comers are to answer.[6] The intruders in fact become homologi coloni, unless indeed they have swallowed up the whole metrocomia, and so have to answer for the whole of what was previously the corporate burden.

This passage, which is not so usually quoted as the second, is thus of cardinal importance. Colonus, at this date and later,[7] was not necessarily a colonus adscripticius, and *the colonus homologus is first and foremost a possessor*.

The more usually quoted s. 3 runs as follows :—' Ii sane, C. T. 11, qui vicis quibus adscribti sunt derelictis, et qui homologi more 24, 6, s. 3. gentilicio nuncupantur, ad alios seu vicos seu dominos transierunt, ad sedem desolati ruris constrictis detentatoribus redire cogantur, qui si exsequenda protraxerint, ad functiones eorum teneantur obnoxii et dominis restituant, quae pro his exsoluta

---

[1] Pr. and ss. 1 and 6.   Supra, p. 22 ff.   [2] s. 8.   Supra, pp. 27–8.
[3] s. 2 and see supra, p. 10.   C. T. 11, 24, 1 and C. J. 11, 56 ; 57.
[4] Zachariae, Gesch. p. 228 ff.   [5] Supra, p. 22.
[6] Post, p. 65.   [7] See Zachariae, op. cit. pp. 222–3.

constiterit.' Mommsen notes : ' qui homologi m. g. nuncupantur et vicis quibus adscribti sunt derelictis ad alios ' *scr.*

The phrase 'more gentilicio'. The learned Gothofredus was so struck by the phrase
' more gentilicio ', that he advanced the incredible theory that
homologi were Gentiles, barbarians who had become coloni
adscribti by an agreement of surrender—ὁμολογία, whence
homologi.[1] It is certainly extraordinary to find Theodosius II so qualifying a merely Greek term, when addressing
a country in which the official language was Greek, and
in which the term had long been familiar. ' Gentilicius '
ordinarily denotes ' heathen ' or ' barbarian ', here it must
mean simply ' foreign '. After all it is natural for a Greek
priding himself on his official Latin to apologize for the
intrusion of a Greek word.

Construction of this section. The reading of the earlier part of the sentence is perhaps
corrupt, though Mommsen's emendation is not absolutely
necessary, since we may treat the clause ' et qui homologi
more gentilicio nuncupantur ' as parenthetical. On either
reading it is impossible to treat the words as other than
a further description of those who ' having deserted their
villages have betaken themselves to other villages or masters '.
We are prevented by the mere syntax from following Seeck,[2]
who treats the subject of the main sentence as though it were
composed (1) of those who were adscribti vicis, not dominis,
i. e. of small independent possessores, and (2) of homologi
coloni, who according to his view were, up to the passing
of the present law, the freely contracting servants or tenants
of domini. A second objection to Seeck's interpretation is
that adscribti vicis and adscribti dominis is not a proper
opposition. Though he himself has taught us that adscribtus
means adscribtus censibus rather than adscribtus glebae, it is
universally held that registration would take the form of
entry under a particular estate, with the well-known results
upon the status of those registered.[3] Both the supposed
classes would thus be entered, with the land to which they
belonged, in the census roll of the village area in which the

---

[1] cf. C. T. 5, 6, 3.   [2] Pauly-Wissowa, IV. 1, 500–501.
          [3] Seeck, loc. cit. p. 499.

land fell.   We may confidently conclude that the subject
of the sentence is not expressly subdivided.

Nevertheless we must admit that two classes of persons are
indicated, if not by the words ' ad alios seu vicos seu dominos '
and the purposely indecisive ' ad sedem desolati ruris ', at any
rate by the fact that the second penalty clearly contemplates
that the fugitives may have had domini who have been forced
to pay their capitatio even in their absence.   This only shows
that non-possessores were within the scope of the joint liability,
and might equally be described as homologi, unless indeed,
as is quite probable, the interpolation of the parenthesis
' et qui homologi m. g. nuncupantur ' was an afterthought,
which did not quite square with the rest of the sentence.

Possible inclusion of coloni proper in the homologi coloni.

In sum, the passage is, as we pointed out above,[1] the last
as yet known of the long series of enactments forbidding the
Egyptian γεωργός to leave his ἰδία.

(b) The metrocomia.   Village organization.[2]

The word metrocomia implies a village which, without
being large enough to be a town, is nevertheless a centre of
administration for surrounding villages and hamlets.   Thus
Dittenberger observes:[3] ' caput regionis alicuius si civitatis
ius ac formam habet μητρόπολις, sin minus, metrocomia appel-
latur.'   In later times the synonym κεφαλοχώριον is found.[4]
From the phrase of C. J. 11, 56, 1, ' in illis quae metrocomiae
communi vocabulo nuncupantur,' it may be inferred that the
word, though well understood, was not strictly a technical
term, a fact which may account for its not being found in any
papyrus hitherto published.   But since it is not to be supposed
that this impressive rescript, drawn up after a special commission of inquiry, would make use of terms unfamiliar to the
province to which it was addressed, we must attribute the

The word metro-comia.

---

[1] Supra, p. 42.
[2] The general references will be found in Marquardt, Org. de l'Emp.
Rom. I, p. 1, ff.
[3] O. G. I. S. 609, n. 3.
[4] Zachariae, Gesch. d. griech.-röm. Rechts, p. 218, n. 691.

silence partly also to the poverty of our present material for
the study of Egypt at this period.[1]

General characteristics indicated by C. T. II, 24, 6. But there is a great deal more in our constitution besides the
name. The metrocomia has officers of its own ;[2] its lands are
held together by the strait bonds of ἐπιβολή or collatio glebae
inutilis ;[3] no one except a convicanus may acquire them ;[4]
consequently deserted lands are only open to the occupation
of a squatter after a formal renunciation by the curiales ;[5] it
is, and is to remain, a publicus vicus, in publico iure et integro ;[6]
its members are bound to stay in their ἴδια ;[7] and provision is
made for filling the places of those metrocomiae which have
fallen into decay.[8] These are the general features of the
metrocomia which we desire to illustrate from the papyri.

Logografi chomatum. (1) *The Liturgi.* Of the officers mentioned, the logografi
chomatum explain themselves, but the actual title is not known
from other sources. In B. G. U. 12, 10–11, of A. D. 181–2,
however, we find χωματεπιμεληταί, whose office, according
to Rostowzew's conjectural reading,[9] was combined with
that of κατασπορεύς or overseer of the sowing : this conjecture
is not supported by a subsequently published passage which
speaks of a χωματεπιμελητής, viz. P. Lond. III 1159, 39,
a return by the town-clerk of Hermopolis of the years 145–7.

---

[1] The term, however, occurs in some Syrian inscriptions. To those
cited by Marquardt, op. cit. II, p. 379, add O. G. I. S. 769.

[2] Pr. '. . . liturgos quos homologi coloni praestare noscuntur . . . '
s. 7 'Nequaquam cefaleotis, irenarchis, logografis chomatum, et ceteris
liturgis sub quolibet patrocinii nomine publicis functionibus denegatis '.

[3] s. 2 'Et quicumque terrulas contra morem fertiles possederunt,
pro rata possessionis suae glebam inutilem et conlationem eius et munera
ne recusent '.

[4] s. 1 'Metrocomiae vero in publico iure et integro perdurabunt,
nec quisquam eas vel aliquid in his possidere temptaverit, nisi qui ante
consulatum praefinitum' (A.D. 397) 'coeperit procul dubio possidere,
exceptis convicanis, a quibus pensitanda pro fortunae condicione negari
non possunt'. Cf. supra, p. 23.

[5] s. 5 'Arurae quoque et possessiones, quas curiales quolibet pacto
publicatis aput acta provincialia desideriis suis vel reliquerunt vel possidere alios promiserunt, penes eos qui eas excoluerunt et functiones publicas
recognoscunt, firmiter perdurabunt, nullam habentibus curialibus copiam
repetendi'.

[6] ss. 1, 6, and 8.   [7] s. 3 supra, p. 42.

[8] s. 4 'Et in earum metrocomiarum locum, quas temporis labsus vel
destituit vel viribus evacuavit, ex florentibus aliae subrogentur '.

[9] Archiv III 213, n. 1.

One would expect the actual management of the dams to be highly centralized, but that is no reason for supposing that there may not have been village officers specially concerned with the assessment and collection of expenses of upkeep. For instance, B. G. U. 618 shows us a κωμογραμματεύς active in this department in the year 213. Wilcken makes the interesting suggestion, that in our period the burden had ceased to be assessed by the poll, and was distributed amongst the possessores according to their interest.[1] He cites C. T. 15, 3, 5 of 412 : ' per Bithyniam ceterasque provincias possessores et reparationi publici aggeris et ceteris eiusmodi muneribus pro iugorum numero vel capitum quae possidere noscuntur, adstringi cogantur.' It is not to be supposed that the immemorial corvée was on that account given up, and the unpopularity of that form of tax, as well as the vital importance of the work, sufficiently accounts for the special mention in this rescript of logografi chomatum.

In their functions and in their mode of selection the irenarchs of the papyri correspond to the descriptions and regulations of the legal texts.[2] They are those ' qui disciplinae publicae et corrigendis moribus (motibus ?) praeficiuntur ', D. 50, 4, 18, 7. A rescript of Hadrian, quoted by Marcianus, D. 48, 3, 6, regulated in some detail their duties as subordinate police officers, and it appears from a passage of Aristides [3] that they were chosen by the governor from a list of ten leading men sent up to him from each πόλις. By a constitution of 409 Theodosius II sought to ensure that the person selected should be ex locupletioribus, by entrusting the final nomination to the praefectus praetorio ; [4] and later he required imperial confirmation of the appointment.[5] Justinian reverted to nomination by the praeses provinciae.[6]

This legislation points to a certain previous degradation of the office in the fourth century, and it is interesting to observe that in the papyri the irenarch from the middle of the fourth

(Irenarchae.)

<hr/>

[1] 1 Ostr. 335.
[2] See Cagnat, Daremberg-Saglio ; Hohlwein, Musée Belge, 1907, p. 205. The commentary of Gothofredus, C. T. 12, 14, 1, is quite out of date.
[3] Ἱερῶν λόγος δ, ed. Dindorf, p. 523.
[4] C. T. 12, 14, 1.   [5] C. T. 8, 7, 21.   [6] C. J. 10, 77, 1.

century onwards is a village liturgist, whereas in a papyrus of the third century, P. Oxy. I 80 of 238–244, we find iren-archs of a nome. Hohlwein¹ conjectures that the village irenarch displaced the older archephod, who disappears in the fourth century.

As his name implies, the irenarch stands for the public peace of the metrocomia; he was subordinate to the military authori-ties,² but the mode of nomination to this munus personale was not different from that to other village liturgies.³ It does not seem necessary to consider his functions more closely.⁴

Cefaleotae.   The new texts ⁵ in which the term κεφαλαιωτής occurs, make Gothofredus' interpretation—capitationis exactores—quite im-possible,⁶ but do not themselves solve the problem.

In P. Grenf. II 80–82 we find two κεφαλαιωταὶ τοῦ ἡγεμονικοῦ πολυκώπου τοῦ ὑπὸ 'Απίωνα ἀρχικυβερνήτην, who give receipts of payment for a substitute by a person under an hereditary liturgy to serve as rower in the state galley. A similar receipt is given by Apion himself in P. Grenf. II 81 (a), while in 82 the two κ. claim their lien on the services of the liturgist from two persons who had impressed him for some unnamed liturgy. Wilcken translates ' Hauptleute' or ' Capitaine', but he does not refer to the Leipsig texts, which we shall presently examine, and it seems unreasonable not to connect these two groups of passages, most of which are practically con-temporaneous with each other.

P. Lips. 89 is a receipt for the linen tax given by a κ. ταρσικαρίων, while in B. G. U. 367 we meet a κ. τοῦ ἀναλώ-
Mitteis' ex- μ">ματος. Hence Mitteis infers that κ. can be used as a general
planation. term not by itself denoting any particular office, and the evidence of the now corrected P. Grenf. II 80–83 supports his

---

¹ Musée Belge, loc. cit.   ² P. Gen. 47. P. Amh. II 146.
³ See P. Amh. II 139.
⁴ See P. Gen. 47. 54.   P. Lond. II 242, 12. 240, 9. III 1309, 2.
B. G. U. 151. 899. P. Amh. II 146. P. Reinach 58, 4.
⁵ P. Lips. Index IV β and p. 159. B. G. U. 367, 6 ; 22 ; V⁰. 2 of the Arabian period. P. Grenf. II 80–82, as corrected by Wilcken, Archiv III 125, of about 370. I owe these references to the kindness of Dr. A. S. Hunt.
⁶ He meant, as Mitteis points out, P. Lips. p. 159, n. 3, the capitatio terrena. The poll-tax did not exist in Egypt at this date, and besides would be ἐπικεφάλαιον, not κεφάλαιον : see I Ostr. 241, 3.

view. He thinks it implies a function of repartition of some burden amongst those liable (Köpfe) in a given area. In the new light of P. Grenf. II 80–82 this second conclusion, which is etymologically improbable, seems open to doubt.

On the other hand, in P. Lips. 47–52 passim, occur persons P. Lips. described as ἀπὸ κεφαλαιωτῶν τῆς x ἰνδικτιῶνος or ἐπινεμήσεως ; in 40 III 17 we find κεφαλαιωτής simply, as also in 52, 14 κεφαλαιωτία ; in 48 V° and 50 V° there is the word κεφαλαιωτής with addition of a local designation, Ὑψηλιτῶν and Πτολεμαΐδος respectively. From these passages, if they stood alone, we should infer just the contrary, namely that κεφαλαιωτία was some particular office. But taking all the passages together it is clear that the κεφαλαιωτ αί of a given year are the persons invested with some fiscal function, the work involved by which was divided by distributing the various taxes to one or more individuals amongst them. What exactly was the function of the κεφαλαιωτής in relation to a tax to which he was appointed? Etymology would make of him a person who sums up amounts into a total, but this is a function of every one engaged in collection of taxes. The κεφαλαιωτὴς τοῦ ἀναλώματος of B. G. U. 367, who gives the γραμματεὺς ἀπὸ τῆς Ἀρσινοιτῶν πόλεως an acknowledgement of certain payments, reminds me of the λογογράφος τοῦ εὐτυχῶς ἐπισκευαζομένου θερμῶν δημοσίου βαλανίου of P. Oxy. I 53, 5, though I do not lay much stress on B. G. U. 367, owing to its late date.

The present material is, as we said, indecisive. The only certain function is that of giving receipts, cf. P. Grenf. II 80 and 81, and P. Lips. 89, and this involves control of the collection, though not necessarily personal collection, which was generally in the hands of subordinate ἀπαιτηταί and ἐξάκτορες. We need not go into difficult questions connected with the methods of collection.[1] Returning to our text C. T. 11, 24, 6, s. 7, it is extremely unlikely that the imperial government would have forgotten in its enumeration the liturgists charged with the tax-collection, though no doubt there are the general words 'et ceteris liturgis'. The cefaleotae, then, stand for

---

[1] See on these points Wilcken, I Ostr. 623 ff. Mitteis, P. Lips. p. 160 and ad P. Lips. 64, 9.

the tax-collection, as the irenarchae stand for the peace of the metrocomia.

The metro-comia and its liturgists. We have assumed that the liturgists referred to by the constitution are village liturgists, not liturgists of the βουλή of a superior μητρόπολις, and the assumption is fully justified by the words of the pr. 'liturgos quos homologi coloni praestare noscuntur'. We propose now to illustrate the relation of a village in this period to its liturgists from a papyrus of the year 350, P. Amh. II 139, though we may remark that, except as to the names of the officials, there is no change from the system of earlier centuries, which has been set out by Wilcken.[1]

System of proposal and guarantee-οἱ ἀπὸ τῆς κώμης. The document in question is a return from two komarchs of a village in the Hermopolite nome, to the praepositus of the twelfth pagus, giving lists of persons proposed for the offices of komarch, irenarch, sitologus, and ἀπαιτητὴς ἀννώνης respectively.   It runs '. . . . δίδομεν καὶ εἰσαγγέλλομεν τοὺς ἑξῆς ἐνγεγραμμένους κωμάρχας καὶ εἰρήναρχοι καὶ σιτολόγοι καὶ ἀπαιτη-τὰ{ι}ς ἀννώναις ὄντας εὐπόρους κινδύνῳ ἡμῶν καὶ πάντων τῶν ἀπὸ τῆς ἡμετέρας κώμης'; there follow the several lists, after which ' οὕσπερ ἐγγυώμεθα καὶ παραστησόμεθα ἐξ ἀλληλεγγύης ἀμέμπτως τὴν ἐνχιριστῖσαν αὐτοῖς λιτουργίαν ἐν μηδενὶ μεμφθῆναι, ἐὰν δέ τις αὐτῶν ἀφυστερήσῃ καὶ μὴ παραστησόμεθα ἡμεῖς αὐτοὶ τὸν ὑπὲρ αὐτοῦ λόγον ὑπομενοῦμεν κτλ.' These nominations were sub-ject to appeal and to veto at head quarters,[2] but what we are concerned with is that they were made ' κινδύνῳ ἡμῶν καὶ πάντων τῶν ἀπὸ τῆς κώμης '.   The duty of providing and guaran-teeing liturgists falls on komarchs in the first place, but also upon the whole of the inhabitants of the village as a joint liability, ἐξ ἀλληλεγγύης.[3]   This system protected the govern-ment from any immediate loss occasioned by individual default, the risk being shifted on to the backs of the body of guarantors, οἱ ἀπὸ τῆς κώμης.

Danger of outside influence. Nevertheless the government was naturally interested in the equitable distribution of the joint liability, and hence, as

[1] 1 Ostr. 601–3.
[2] Fresh details P. Fior. I 2 and 3, on which Wilcken, Archiv III 529.
[3] That this is the meaning of οἱ ἀπὸ τῆς κώμης has been disputed by Hohlwein, Musée Belge, 1905, 189 ff.; 1906, 36 ff.   But this contention has now been disposed of: Wilcken, Archiv III 529, 551; IV 223.

we have seen,[1] it objected to the intrusion of over-powerful outsiders into metrocomiae. At this point also we detect the objection of the government to patronage, and therefore C. T. 11, 24, 6 pr., whilst confirming the titles of patrons to acquisitions made before 397, made it an express condition that they should shoulder their proper share (*pro rata*) of the liability for 'functiones publicas et liturgos quos homologi coloni praestare noscuntur'. The word 'praestare' exactly represents this duty of providing and guaranteeing. What we know of the liturgy system makes the conclusion inevitable that we must identify the homologi coloni with the persons described in the papyri as οἱ ἀπὸ τῆς κώμης'. Thus the internal constitution of the metrocomia confirms our previous interpretation of the term ὁμόλογος.

Homologi coloni = οἱ ἀπὸ τῆς κώμης.

(2)[2] *Illustrations of joint liability in Egyptian villages before Diocletian.* In our period joint liability of villages takes the form of ἐπιβολὴ ἀπόρων, collatio glebae inutilis : see for instance our constitution, C. T. 11, 24, 6. It is important to discover how far the system of Diocletian and his successors was a new creation, and in what way it was derived from previous institutions. The very detailed census which the Romans inherited from the Ptolemies no doubt made possible individual adjustments and remissions which were unattainable by the rough and ready methods of the later era. The taxing-lists, particularly the ἀπαιτήσιμα κατ' ἄνδρα, give great prominence to the individual liability, and therefore the traces of joint liability to be found in the earlier documents are all the more precious. We cannot deal with the subject exhaustively, and make no apology for relying largely upon Rostowzew's general conclusion, which we have already cited.[3] One important testimony has already been cited, the liturgy system, which, based as it was upon joint liability, was inherited by the fourth century unaltered in essentials from the previous period. We wish only to add some illustrations of the earlier working of joint liability which may not be familiar to all our readers.

The Ptolemaic system.

---

[1] Supra, p. 26, &c.   [2] See pp. 22 and 57.
[3] Philologus, Suppl. 9, 489, and Archiv III 201. See supra, p. 56.

66 DE PATROCINIIS VICORUM [PT. II

Illustrations from the Roman period:— B. G. U. 85.

Perhaps the clearest expression is that of B. G. U. 85, a very fragmentary Fayum papyrus of the time of Antoninus Pius, which records (Col. I) a payment by two named persons, τῶν β̄ καὶ τῶν λοιπῶν πρεσβυτέρων, and by two other named persons καὶ τῶν λοιπῶν γεωργῶν τῶν ἀπὸ τῆς κώμης πάντων ἐξ ἀλληλεγγύης. The nature of the payment is, however, only indicated by a mutilated passage in which occur the letters . . . ς προσοδ(ου?), from which it has been inferred that the payment was for rent of γῆ προσόδου.

The burden of mutual guarantee was not so much felt in times of prosperity. But in the later half of the second century things began to go badly with the Roman Empire, nor did Egypt escape the general depression.[1] Chance has preserved to us three remarkable documents dealing with the difficulties of the village of Soknopaei Nesus at the close of the second century and the beginning of the third. These are P. Lond. III 924 of 186-7, and P. Gen. 16 and P. Cattaoui II,[2] both of October 207. We should add, but for its obscurity, B. G. U. 23 of about the same period.[3]

P. Lond. III 924.

In the first papyrus the πράκτορες σιτικῶν of the village complain that, whereas they pay in full the rent (ἐκφόρια) on τὴν ἐπιμερισθεῖσαν τῇ προκειμένῃ κώμῃ ἀπὸ πεδίων κώμης Βακχιάδος γῆν, and whereas there is near their own village of S. Nesus αἰγιαλῖτις γῆ, upon which in the bad years they have made up ἐκ τῶν ἰδίων τὴν ὑπὲρ αὐτῆς παραγραφήν, in the present good year, after the said αἰγιαλός had been flooded by the Nile and sown, the men of Theogenes, a neighbouring village, had forcibly taken possession of it. Therefore the petitioners pray that the aggressors be made to pay the παραγραφή (of past years?), and for further somewhat unintelligible relief, in order that they may not be driven into flight from their ἰδία and from their duties.

We shall return to the highly suggestive phrase τὴν ἐπιμερισθεῖσαν τῇ προκειμένῃ κώμῃ ἀπὸ πεδίων κώμης Βακχιάδος

[1] See the very interesting contribution of Wilcken to Festschr. zu O. Hirschfeld.
[2] Bull. de l'Inst. Fr. d'Archéol. Or. III 187, corrected and explained by Wilcken, Archiv III 548, IV 548.
[3] See however thereon Rostowzew in Archiv III 215, 1.

γῆν later. The struggle between the two villages for the αἰγιαλός might be put down as nothing but an illustration of their natural solidarity, but there is more to follow. From the two other papyri it appears that this αἰγιαλός, and also certain pastures, were not only paid for, but also enjoyed, by the men of S. Nesus in common. The communal system was of course not the rule in Egypt, but, as Professor Vinogradoff has pointed out,[1] it is a system which may be found wherever certain conditions are satisfied. Pastures are more easily and naturally enjoyed in common than any other land, and the peculiar character of this αἰγιαλός would make against individualistic appropriation. When cultivable it was highly productive, but as often as not it was not cultivable at all ; moreover, if the name ' beach ' is apt, it would vary in shape and size from year to year. There is no reason to suppose this village to have been unique in having common interests, besides a joint liability for taxes ; indeed, it would have been impossible to impose joint liability from above upon men who had nothing more in common than mere local contiguity. But neighbours must have common interests, and in particular the Egyptian agriculturist must have been forced into partnership in matters of water-supply and irrigation.

The two later documents, P. Gen. 16 and P. Cattaoui 11, are petitions from the whole body of δημόσιοι γεωργοί of the village about a dispute which had arisen, this time within the village itself, concerning various matters, amongst them this same αἰγιαλός. As both petitions deal with the same trouble we will summarize the story of both together. A certain Orseus and his four brothers, who are apparently rich members of the village, refuse to be συνείσφοροι with the other villagers, terrify the village scribe out of presenting them for liturgies, monopolize certain pastures, part of an οὐσία, to the rent of which they do not contribute, and forcibly eject from the αἰγιαλός their fellows who have sown it, though its produce is absolutely necessary for the payment of taxes by the village, and though without it the villagers will be forced to fly from

Common lands.

P. Gen. 16 and P. Cattaoui II.

---

[1] Growth of the Manor, pp. 83 ff., and p. 113, nn. 102 and 105.

their ἰδία, to which they have only recently been recalled by an imperial edict.

This tale speaks for itself: the villagers enjoy in common certain benefits and burdens, and the complaint against the five brothers is that they monopolize the benefits and shirk the burdens. We have ἀπαιτήσιμα κατ' ἄνδρα referring to this αἰγιαλός,[1] but evidently the failure of one man to pay his share means a greater payment for his fellows, so that the individual liability does not exclude the joint. The village crisis is well summarized by the final prayer of P. Cattaoui II, that the delinquents συνεισφόρους εἶναι τοῖς δημοσίοις τελέσμασι καὶ λιτουργεῖν τὰς ἁρμοζούσας αὐτοῖς λιτουργίαις καὶ ἔχεσθαι ἐξ ἴσου ἡμῖν πᾶσιν τῆς ἀποκαλυφθείσης γῆς ἵν' ὦμεν ἐν τῇ ἰδίᾳ συμμένοντες τῇ τύχῃ σου. Wilcken recalls a similar complaint of βασ. γεωργοί in a Ptolemaic fragment, P. Grenf. I 13, ἐκομίσαντο ἔντευξιν οἱ βασιλικοὶ γεωργοὶ περὶ τοῦ μὴ [a blank] ν γῆν συνεισφέρειν αὐτοῖς. It is even more apposite to recall C. T. 11, 24, 6, s. 1, on the desirability of convicani 'a quibus pensitanda pro fortunae condicione negari non possunt'. To put it shortly, συνείσφοροι γεωργοί are nothing more than homologi coloni.[2]

It need scarcely be said that if corporate liability is proved for the second and third centuries, there is an *a fortiori* argument for its existence in the fourth and fifth. We shall therefore be content simply to cite, by way of example, B. G. U. 21, a village account of the year 340, from which Seeck[3] has most ingeniously deduced a corporate village liability for a round sum.

(3)[4] Ἐπιβολή. We have already observed that the fiscal solidarity of the metrocomia in C. T. 11, 24, 6 rests upon ἐπιβολή, that is upon the liability of the owner of fertile land to be charged with the ownership, and therefore with the taxes, of a proportion of gleba inutilis.[5] We have now seen

Side notes: Συνεισφέρειν. / Ἐπιβολή in the fifth century.

---

[1] C. P. R. 33 of 215.   B. G. U. 659 of 228–9.
[2] See post, p. 78, Note C.
[3] Zeitschr. f. Soc. u. Wirtschaftsgesch. IV, p. 275, s. 6. See also I Ostr. 256, n. 2. P. Oxy. VI 989.
[4] Supra, pp. 10 and 60.   [5] s. 2, quoted supra, p. 60.

that corporate liability existed in the Egyptian village long before Diocletian, and even long before Aurelian, to whom the institution of ἐπιβολή is generally attributed on the strength of the constitution of Constantine, C. J. 11, 59, 1.

It seems, therefore, that we should finally abandon the view [1] that ἐπιβολή was one of the means by which the state created, and enforced, a joint liability for its own purposes; rather we should regard it as a device of which no one would have thought, except as a way of distributing an already recognized joint liability.[2] No doubt the system of making communities liable for a fixed total of taxes was extended as the Roman Empire grew less prosperous, but this was a tendency which had been fostered in many cases by the fact that the communities were the successors of the publicani, who had been essentially guarantors to the state of a predetermined total sum. Now this succession took place also well before the reign of Aurelian.[3] *The result, not the cause, of joint liability.*

It may be taken for granted that ἐπιβολή did not exist as a general institution of the Empire until Constantine's constitution, C. J. 11, 59, 1, adopting the policy of Aurelian, and that it was not developed into a system until the period of the Novels.[4] The very interesting question remains, What were the antecedents of this very peculiar and characteristic contrivance?

A shadow of the coming of ἐπιβολή may be detected as early as the reign of Hadrian, in the fact that the Lex Hadriana de Rudibus Agris appears to have contemplated that the conductores of a saltus would regularly leave part of the land uncultivated.[5] From this Schulten somewhat adventurously infers that the system, quite familiar in the later *Inscription of Ain-Ouassel.*

---

[1] Zachariae, Gesch. 228 ff.
[2] Seeck, 'Επιβολή, Pauly-Wissowa, VI. 1, 30.
[3] See Seeck, Decemprimat u. Dekaprotie, Beitr. z. a. Gesch. I, circa p. 180. Rostowzew, Staatspacht, Philologus, Suppl. 9, p. 415 ff.
[4] Nov. Just. 128, cc. 7 and 8; cf. Zachariae, Gesch. 228 ff. The older laws are in C. T. 13, 11 and C. J. 11, 59. The distribution of sterile land was a delicate operation, and an opportunity for the patron : see e. g. C. T. 13, 11, 5 and 9, of 393 and 398 respectively.
[5] Inscription of Ain-Ouassel, II 6–7 (Schulten's reading) and III 16. Bruns, Fontes 382. Girard, Textes 186. See also the new papyri cited post, p. 78, Note A.

Empire, of forcing the conductores to take and pay for bad land with good, was already in vogue.[1]

Public land a charge on other land. Another very natural application of ἐπιβολή occurs in the treatment of public land, which when leased to an owner of private land became, as it were, a real charge upon that private land even in the hands of an alienee. The lessee's fortune was part of the security of the state, and the state held to it firmly. Seeck has pointed to this application as one of the roots of the later fully developed institution, but his references carry us no further back than the C. T.[2] It has not, I believe, been observed that the papyri offer clear evidence of the existence of this form of ἐπιβολή in Egypt at the beginning of the second century. We find that private ἄρουραι are sometimes conveyed with warranty that they are καθαραὶ ἀπὸ βασιλικῆς γῆς or γεωργίας, and this can only mean that purchasers of land had to guard against the risk of ἐπιβολή of γῆ βασιλική by way of forced lease.[3]

The term ἐπιβολή in the papyri. Again, in certain leases in which, as is the prevailing custom, the taxes are put upon the lessor, amongst the taxes specified are ἐπιβολαί and ἐπιμερισμοί of all kinds. In view of the warranty on sale which we have just discussed, it seems likely that these terms are meant to cover the risk of an ἐπιβολή in the strict post-Aurelian sense, ἐπιβολή at least of γῆ βασιλική, if not of private land, which had ceased to meet its public burdens.[4] It must be admitted, however, that though the word ἐπιβολή occurs elsewhere, in the Ptolemaic period,[5] but chiefly in the Roman period from the second century onwards, its meaning is disputed, and the most that can be said is that the post-Aurelian technical sense is not impossible in some of the passages.[6]

---

[1] Die röm. Grundherrschaften, p. 128.
[2] Pauly-Wissowa, VI. 1, 31. See especially C. T. 11, 1, 4 of 337.
[3] See P. Amh. II 95, 4 of the year 109, and 96, 3 of the year 213. Also C. P. R. 6, 16 of 238 and P. Leips. 6, 6 of 306.
[4] The earliest such lease is P. Lond. III 938 of 225. See also P. Strass. 10 of 268; P. Amh. II 106 of 282 ; C. P. R. 44; B. G. U. 519; P. Lond. III 979 of 346—the last three of the fourth century. The clause in C. P. R. 44, e. g., runs: τῶν δημοσίων πάντων καὶ ἐπιβολῶν καὶ ἀννωνῶν καὶ ἐπιμερισμῶν ὄντων πρός σε τὸν γεοῦχον. See generally Waszyński, op. cit., p. 118 sq.
[5] P. Tebt. I 99, 10 and 51.
[6] See I Ostr. 193-4, and the editors ad P. Tebt. II 346, 7.

The words μερισμός and ἐπιμερισμός have also been much The term
discussed,[1] but besides the general senses of division and ἐπιμερισμός.
repartition,[2] and of amounts resulting due after repartition,[3]
the only special usage that has been proved, when the word
stands without qualification, is in connexion with the συν-
αγοραστικὴ κριθή, a special impost ordered by the praefect for the
army, and divided by ἐπιμερισμός of the pragmatici of the nome
amongst the κῶμαι.[4]   This usage interests us only in so far as
it shows that the word was connected with extraordinary taxes.

But we must notice here two specially significant usages of
ἐπιμερισμός.   The first occurs in an isolated phrase of a
papyrus of the year 186–7, which we have already had
occasion to quote:[5] τὴν ἐπιμερισθεῖσαν τῇ προκειμένῃ κώμῃ ἀπὸ
πεδίων Βακχιάδος γῆν.   This passage has not attracted much 'Επιβολή
attention, yet I do not see what meaning can be attached to from village to
it, except that of a sharing out amongst various villages of village.
land subject to public charges (rent: ἐκφόρια), which appear
to be heavy.   The geography of the district does not permit
of definite conclusions,[6] but there is no doubt that Bacchias
was a neighbouring village, which a little later, in 211, we find
apparently combined with another village, Hephaestias, and
in fiscal relations with the village to which the present passage
refers, Soknopaei Nesus.[7]   I infer that Bacchias having fallen
into partial decay, S. Nesus was subjected to an ἐπιβολή of
some of its unremunerative land, in accordance with a policy
similar to that suggested by s. 4 of our constitution, C. T. 11,
24, 6: ' Et in earum metrocomiarum locum, quas temporis
labsus vel destituit vel viribus vacuavit, ex florentibus aliae
subrogentur.'[8]

The other usage to which we refer[9] occurs in the phrase 'Επιμερισ-
ἐπιμερισμὸς ἀπόρων, which is found in a few documents, all of μὸς ἀπόρων.

---

[1] See Wilcken, 1 Ostr. 161, 256.   Archiv I 177.
[2] B. G. U. 21 I, &c.   [3] e. g. P. Lips. 98.
[4] B. G. U. 807. 842.   P. Grenf. I 48.   P. Amh. II 107–9; 173–7.
Archiv I 177.
[5] P. Lond. III 924.   Supra, p. 66.
[6] See P. Tebt. II, App. II s. 5.   [7] B. G. U. 711.
[8] A translatio of gleba inutilis from one civitas to another was not
unknown, to judge by the prohibitions in C. T. 11, 22.
[9] This point was very kindly suggested to me by Dr. A. S. Hunt.

the first half of the second century or thereabouts,[1] and all of them receipts given by πράκτορες ἀργυρικῶν for quite small charges, commonly in connexion with other small charges, such as συντάξιμον[2] and various guard-taxes.[3] In P. Lond. III 911, of the year 149, we have a γραφὴ ἀπόρων which seems to be a list or certificate of ἄποροι. Wilcken has pointed out that a list of ἄποροι would have a significance as determining disqualifications for liturgies, these falling on εὔποροι. There is, however, no clear connexion between this γραφὴ ἀπόρων and the ἐπιμερισμὸς ἀπόρων.

Pagan philan-thropy ?

The view tentatively put forward by Wilcken, that the ἐπιμερισμός was a poor-rate, levied as a kind of poll-tax, is disputed by Grenfell and Hunt, who regard it as an extra levy to make up deficiencies caused by the inability of ἄποροι to pay taxes. The latter view gives an interesting instance of the system of corporate liability. There is however one more possibility to be considered. The phrase recalls the Byzantine ἐπιβολὴ ἀπόρων, in which ἀπόρων is the genitive of ἄπορα, not ἄποροι.[4] Ἄπορα, by a usage known also in fourth-century Egypt,[5] are simply lands derelict or unequal to their burdens, i. e. those which have to be imposed by ἐπιβολή upon the owners of better land. As the recorded payments for ἐπιμερισμὸς ἀπόρων are all small money payments, instead of being considerable and in kind, I do not think the terminological coincidence, though very striking, is sufficient to satisfy the burden of proving the identity of ἐπιμερισμός and ἐπιβολὴ ἀπόρων ; but as no other interpretation is more satisfactory, the suggestion is worth making.

Byzantine προτίμησις.

(4)[6] *Exclusion of Outsiders.* Section 1 of our constitution[7] deals with this subject, which is really a corollary of village solidarity. In the same way the Byzantine ἐπιβολή welded the holders of ὁμόκηνσα and ὁμόδουλα into solid groups with rights of pre-emption (προτίμησις) over each other's land. Both

[1] The era of pagan philanthropy.
[2] Meaning uncertain.
[3] The documents are : 2 Ostr. 613.   P. Fay. 53 ; 54 ; 256 ; 316. B. G. U. 881.   P. Tebt. II 544 and 545.   Comments : 1 Ostr. 161. Archiv IV 545.
[4] Zachariae, Gesch. 228 ff.   [5] Post, p. 77.
[6] Supra, p. 26, &c.   [7] Quoted supra, p. 22.

the general liability to ἐπιβολή, and the general right of προτίμησις, were the products of post-Diocletian legislation, which
only took a fixed shape after many fluctuations.[1] The duty
of mutual guarantee created mutual interests in each other's
land, that it should not come into the hands of too powerful
a man or too bad a farmer.

But the protection of the convicanus stands outside and Special
exceeds the general right of προτίμησις, which is denied both by protection of con-
the C. T. and the C. J.[2] Our present section 1 is therefore an vicani.
exception to the ordinary law, due to the special circumstances
of the metrocomia, an exception which is reaffirmed in C. J.
11, 56, 1 of 468.[3]

It seems to be agreed that the general right of προτίμησις
had no roots in classical or in local law, but was simply born
of the financial policy of Diocletian and his successors,[4] though
it is perhaps relevant to observe, that in earlier times the
benefits of grants of land on emphyteusis were sometimes
sought to be confined within a restricted circle.[5] Nor, in spite
of the antiquity of the union of Egyptian ὁμόλογοι γεωργοί, can
I find in the papyri any traces of προτίμησις, or of the stricter
right of the metrocomia to exclude outsiders altogether,
existing before the enactment of the present section. The
explanation probably is that the problem hardly arose in
Ptolemaic and early Roman Egypt, the ordinary γεωργός
cultivating the public land near his village, and being held fast
to his ἰδία. Such a person could not be a seller of land; it is
possible that he would own the plot in the village on which
his house stood, and just for that reason the royal ordinance
of 118 B. C., P. Tebt. I 5, 231, which we have already quoted,[6]
limited the right of βασιλικοὶ γεωργοί to dispose of their houses.

[1] See Gothofredus ad C. T. 3, 1, 6. Zachariae, Gesch. 236 ff. The
goal is the Novel of Romanus Lacapenus of 922, Coll. III Nov. 2. I have
not seen Obs. sur le dr. de Πρ. en dr. byz., G. Platon, Paris, 1906.
[2] C. T. 3, 1, 6 of 391 = C. J. 4, 38, 14.
[3] Discussed supra, p. 26.
[4] Gothofredus ad C. T. 3, 1, 6. Mitteis, Reichsrecht u. Volksrecht,
p. 69, n. 6.
[5] Mitteis, Erbpacht, p. 12, and in Z. S. S. 1901, 151–160, commenting
on a second-century inscription from Thisbe in Boeotia, and P. Amh.
II 68, 8, late first century.
[6] Supra, p. 43.

Our conclusion with regard to this section is that its enactment was provoked simply by the special necessity of combating patronage and aristocratic influence generally. It should be observed that the prohibition contemplates the acquisition of the whole metrocomia, as well as of a holding in it.

Agri excepti.

(5) *Ius publicum* and *Ius privatum.* We have already [1] dealt with the absorption of lands subject to the ordinary municipal jurisdiction by great men, with the result in Hyginus' words,[2] ' ut in totum privati iuris essent nec ullam coloniae munificentiam deberent, et essent in solo populi Romani.' This is one of those movements which is best judged by its ultimate outcome; in this case the later Byzantine distinction between χωρία ἐλευθερικά and χωρία ἐξακτωρικὰ ἢ βουλευτικὰ ἢ ἑτέροις ὅλως προσήκοντα.[3] A glimpse of the extent to which the process had gone in Egypt by the middle of the sixth century may be obtained by perusing the documents relating to the affairs of the Oxyrhynchite magnate Flavius Apion and his family.[4] He is addressed as ἡ ὑμετέρα ὑπερφύεια, or ἐνδοξότης ; he has ἐναπόγραφοι and he is acquiring others ; his clients hail from ἐποίκια belonging to his excellency, or more significantly still ἀπὸ κώμης παγαρχουμένης ὑπο τῆς ὑμετέρας ἐνδοξότητος.[5] In one case, P. Oxy. I 133, a loan from his excellency of 200 artabae of seed-corn is acknowledged by τὸ κοινὸν τῶν πρωτοκωμητῶν τῆς κώμης Τάκονα τοῦ 'Οξυρυγχίτου νομοῦ, παγαρχουμένης ὑπὸ τοῦ οἴκου τῆς ὑμῶν ἐνδοξότητος. The exact meaning of παγαρχουμένης is wrapped in darkness, along with the rest of the administration of Egypt at this period,[6] but the phrase suggests to my mind an almost feudal obliteration of the distinction between jurisdiction and property. The house of Flavius Apion was the patron of these villages.[7]

---

[1] Supra, pp. 13 and 26 ff.   [2] Lachmann, p. 197.
[3] Coll. I, Nov. 12, c. 4. Zachariae, Gesch. 218 ff.
[4] P. Oxy. I 133-9. 192-202. P. Lond. III p. 278 ff.
[5] P. Lond. III 776, 6. P. Oxy. I 139.
[6] See Bell, Journ. Hell. Stud. 1908, p. 101 ff. The older view (Milne, Hist. of Egypt under Roman rule, p. 13 ; Wilcken, Hermes 27, p. 287 ff. ; 1 Ostr. 435) treats the pagarch as the head of the pagus, which was undoubtedly a division of the nome in the fourth and fifth centuries. Bell distinguishes the πάγαρχος from the praepositus pagi, and the παγαρχία from the pagus ; he identifies the παγαρχία with the nome.
[7] So Milne, op. cit. p. 14.

(6)¹ *Metropolis and Metrocomia.* From the problems Was the metrocomia subordinate to the metropolis?
which have occupied us up to this point we have excluded, as
far as possible, the question of the position of the metrocomia
in the administrative hierarchy. Dealing with the metrocomia from the inside, it has been safe to assume its general
similarity to the ordinary Egyptian κώμη. But it would be
wrong to conclude this article without at least raising the
question hitherto excluded, though, in the absence of studies
on this period of administration, I am unable to answer it of
my own knowledge. The question is whether the organization
by πόλεις had so far decayed in Egypt by the year 415, that
we are to understand by metrocomiae centres of administration
independent of any πόλις, and comparable to the χωρία ἐλευθερικά of later Byzantine law.²

A contemporary of C. T. 11, 24, 6 writes: Νομὸς δὲ λέγεται
παρὰ τοῖς τὴν Αἰγυπτίων κατοικοῦσι χώραν ἑκάστη πόλις καὶ αἱ
περιοικίδες αὐτῆς καὶ αἱ ὑπ' αὐτῇ κῶμαι.³ This seems decisive as to
the general form of administration, so that the problem really
is, how far the general form was beginning to break down.
The tendency of the age was in the direction of municipal
decentralization, and in other provinces oppida and castella
were beginning to assert their independence of the civitates.⁴
Nor was the subordination of the κώμη to the βουλή of the
πόλις so deeply rooted in Egypt as in many provinces,
seeing that it was only introduced, probably for fiscal
reasons, at a time when municipal life was already on the
wane,⁵ and that, alongside of the βουλή and the δεκάπρωτοι,⁶

---

¹ Supra, pp. 30 and 59.
² The curiae were not formally abolished in the East till Nov. 46 of
Leo the Wise, but the silence of the Basilica on the subject of decuriones
shows that their continued existence was merely formal: Fiebiger,
Decuriones, Pauly-Wissowa, IV. 2, 2351.
³ Cyrillus, Comm. in Esai. c. 19, vol. ii, p. 2849, ed. Lut. 1638. I take
the quotation and reference direct from Wilcken, Obs. ad Aeg., 1885,
p. 11.
⁴ See the short but vivid sketch of Declareuil, N. R. H. 1908,
p. 547 ff.
⁵ In 202: 1 Ostr. 430 ff.; Preisigke, Städtisches Beamtenwesen im röm.
Aegypten, p. 6.
⁶ There were usually two of these for each toparchy: 1 Ostr. 627;
Preisigke, op. cit. pp. 23-4.

the strategus and the other officials were maintained in their old functions.[1]

Presumption against autonomy of metrocomia.   These are general considerations, but in the absence of direct evidence we have no right to assume the autonomy of the metrocomia. The contrary suggestion, which is undoubtedly contained in the term itself, can be disposed of on various hypotheses. In the first place ' metrocomia ' was not a technical term, but ' commune vocabulum ',[2] and therefore is not to be pressed. Its use in our rescript may have been partly dictated by necessity of finding some expression which would emphasize the distinction between ἐποίκια belonging to great landowners, and the κῶμαι of Egyptian public law. We may recall the clumsiness of Libanius in making a similar distinction between villages.[3] Moreover, we must remember the general decline and evacuation of Egyptian villages at this time, to which our constitution[4] bears witness, and of which there is other evidence.[5] Such a decline would enhance the importance of the villages which survived, and would lead to a centralization of local government in them. A κώμη might thus obtain, in popular speech, the style of metrocomia, as having become, though still subordinate to the metropolis of the nome, the primary centre of a considerable agricultural district.

In short, nothing is known which rebuts the presumption that the metrocomia was subject to the metropolis of the nome, nothing which excludes a secondary liability of the decuriones of the metropolis for the dues of the homologi coloni. Hence the curiales, who are mentioned as having the ultimate disposition of the desert lands of the metrocomia,[6] may well be the curiales of the metropolis, the πολιτευόμενοι of

---

[1] 1 Ostr. 628. The strategus, however, disappeared in the course of the fourth century: Wilcken, Hermes 27, 297 ff.   1 Ostr. 435, n. 3.
[2] C. J. 11, 56, 1.   Supra, pp. 26 and 59.   [3] Supra, p. 28.
[4] ss. 3 and 4.
[5] See Appendix II to P. Tebt. II, p. 360.
[6] s. 5 'Arurae quoque et possessiones, quas curiales quolibet pacto publicatis aput acta provincialia desideriis suis vel reliquerunt vel possidere alios permiserunt, penes eos, qui eas excoluerunt et functiones publicas recognoscunt, firmiter perdurabunt, nullam habentibus curialibus copiam repetendi.' = C. J. 11, 59, 14.

the various cities who are so often mentioned in the Leipsig Papyri.[1] Nevertheless Gothofredus came to the opposite conclusion : 'igitur lapsus est interpretum qui de curialibus civitatum hanc legem accipiunt.' But it is to be noticed that he brings no arguments, beyond quoting various texts,[2] which make out a doubtful case for the existence of curiales of vici.[3]

It must be admitted that about this period the papyri reveal the village as the responsible manager of its own ἄπορα. We have four documents of the last quarter of the fourth century, in which the village of Philadelphia (Fayum) deals by way of lease with land ἀπὸ ἀπόρων ὀνομάτων, or ἀπὸ τοῦ ἀπόρου τῆς κώμης.[4] The lessors in P. Gen. 66 are the komarchs, in 69 the πρωτοκωμῆται,[5] in 70 certain names καὶ τὸ κοινὸν τῆς κώμης, while some of the names in 67 appear as those of lessors in the other papyri. On Gothofredus' view, the curiales of s. 5 would be the members of the κοινόν or σύνοδος of the village.[6]

The village ἄπορα in fourth-century Egypt.

In P. Gen. 67 and 69 we find that the public taxes are left upon the lessors, the village : τῶν δημοσίων πάντων ὄντων πρὸς ἡμᾶς τοὺς μεμισθωκότας. Waszyński[7] shows that in P. Gen. 66 and 67 the rent is paid two years, and in P. Gen. 69 one year in advance. The village was obviously in difficulties, needed ready money, and had on its hands ἄπορα for which it had paid taxes.

But isolated pieces of evidence, such as that of these leases, are not decisive of the question of ultimate responsibility and

Ultimate liability.

---

[1] P. Lips. Index 13, s. v.   The word recurs in Nov. Just. 128, and is translated in the Auth. by curiales; they are tax-collectors, Nov. Just. 128, c. 5, and are concerned with ἐπιβολή, ibid. c. 8.   See Zachariae on Ed. Just. XIII, n. 5.   Bell, Journ. Hell. Stud. 1908, p. 103, n. 20.

[2] C. T. 7, 18, 13 'primates urbium, vicorum, castellorum'.   Salvianus, De Gub. Dei, v, 4, who asks what villages there are 'ubi non quot curiales fuerint tot tyranni sunt'.   C. T. 16, 2, 16 and 33.   Paul, Sent. 4, 6, 2. Further references at the beginning of the Paratitlon to C. T. 12, 1.

[3] Denied by Fiebiger, Decuriones, Pauly-Wissowa, IV. 2, 2323.

[4] P. Gen. 66. 67. 69. 70.   My attention was called to these documents by Waszyński, op. cit. pp. 24, 26, 43, 107–8.

[5] Or something similar.   The reading is προτ/ώμης.

[6] See also P. Grenf. II 67.   In P. Gen. 63 II 7–8, and 64, 9 the phrase is τὸ κοινὸν τῶν ἀπὸ κώμης . . . .   See also C. P. R. 41.

[7] Op. cit., pp. 107–8.

control. We cannot at present say whether behind the κοινόν of the village stood the βουλή of a metropolis. The large mass of already discovered but unpublished papyri makes further discussion of a conjectural character more than usually unprofitable and gratuitous.

ADDENDA

NOTE A.—Add to the evidence cited p. 43, n. 2, the papyri of the beginning of Hadrian's reign recently published by Kornemann, Beitr. z. a. Gesch. 8, 398 ff., and by Wilcken, Archiv V 245 ff., with Rostowzew's comments, ibid. 299.

NOTE B.—Since writing p. 45, n. 3, my attention has been drawn to a lease πρὸς ὃν βούλῃ χρόνον, of the year 536, published by G. Ferrari, Atti del Reale Istituto Veneto, 1908, at p. 1186, = P. R. Ist. Veneto 1.

NOTE C.—See supra, p. 68, n. 2.

The term συντελεστὴς ἀπὸ κώμης 'Αφροδίτης is applied to the lessor by the lessee, γεωργὸς ἀπὸ τῆς αὐτῆς κώμης, in P. R. Ist. Veneto 1. P. Oxy. VI 989 is a third-fourth century list of persons and ἐργαστήρια at various villages, concluding 'ἀξιοῦμεν τούτους συντελεῖν σὺν ἡμεῖν'. The usage of συντελεῖν hardly requires illustration, but see e.g. Archiv I 410; B. G. U. 927; P. Lond. II 483; P. Oxy. I 39, 22 and 24; Nov. Just. 17, 9. 128, 5, and especially Nov. Rom. Lac. De pot. Col. III 5, in which συντελεστής appears to be used as equivalent to ὁμοτελής in the same emperor's Nov. 2.